Concerning *Theology for Disciples*

I cannot express in words my excitement over this new material which is not only theologically sound and exceptional but also practical to use with leaders in the church body. His theological thought, his systematic approach to the scriptures and his writings are some of the most exceptional that I have ever read. On a theological basis, his work on the creation account and his systematic approach for making disciples is something I will use as I structure my own disciple making process.

—Robin Wood
Pastor, Mountain Park Community Church, Chandler, Arizona

Written from the perspective of what it means to be a disciple, it brings abstract thought to life and informs Christian living in an exciting way.

—Rev. O. C. Edwards, Jr.
Visiting Professor, Duke University Divinity School

Dr. Gilbert Stafford successfully includes the classroom and the church in the common mission of making disciples, thinking as disciples, and seeking the holiness and unity intrinsic to the company of disciples. *Theology for Disciples* is a church-oriented theology reflecting Stafford's commitment to the Church of God and incorporating insights from other Christian traditions.

— Susie C. Stanley
Professor of Historical Theology, Messiah College

The quality of the writing and the difficult subject matter addressed serve to indicate the discipline of a scholar as well as the skill of a wordsmith. Chapter 20 of *Theology for Disciples* is a bright light in the Church of God.

— Arlo F. Newell
Former Editor in Chief, Warner Press

Scholars, clergy, and students will be refreshed by Stafford's broad learning and commitment to the 'one, holy, catholic, and apostolic church.' Laity and inquirers will be enlightened and enriched by the book's lucid, understandable, and thorough discussion of many aspects of Christian faith, life, and witness."

—Norman A. Hjelm
Director, Commission on Faith and Order

Theology for Disciples is a wonderfully comprehensive guide to Christian discipleship. Drawing upon his unique combination of scholarly and homiletical gifts, Gil Stafford has fashioned an instructive resource for persons seeking fuller illumination of their Christian vocation with respect to the Scriptures and Christian theology. This book is equally useful for introductory or advanced study in church-based discipleship training.

— Cheryl J. Sanders
Associate Professor of Christian Ethics, Howard University

I find the work to be extraordinarily comprehensive, yet accessible to the popular reader. His understanding of the biblical roots of Christian thought, his wide ecumenical reading in the history of Christian thought, his sensitivity to the modern church and his ability to relate all of this to the daily disciple of faith are remarkable. The work is truly that of a seasoned mind and heart

—Robert Webber
Professor of Christian Theology, Wheaton College

I like his writing style. It is clear and straightforward. By and large, the reader will not get bogged down with the unfamiliar theological terms. When such terms are necessary, he offers a brief definition or explanation.

—Marshall K. Christensen
President, Warner Pacific College

It is especially satisfying to have Stafford's example of theology constructed out of traditions of discipleship and sanctification, where the two sides of these core beliefs are explained: disciples also become disciplers; and the indwelling Spirit of faith is Jesus Christ also becomes the Spirit poured out in the Pentecostal experience of effusive faith, for mission in the world.

— Clyde J. Steckel
Emeritus Professor of Theology
United Theological Seminary of the Twin Cities

In *Theology for Disciples* Dr. Gilbert Stafford has ministered to the church once again. His work is not just a systematic theology, it is a systematic theology with an audience in mind and we—disciples—are that audience.

—John Alan Howard
Dean of Faculty, Gardner College

Theology for Disciples

Systematic Considerations
about the Life of Christian Faith

by
Gilbert W. Stafford

To Bill Harris
friend in Christ.

Church Ministries Division
Warner Press
Anderson, Indiana

Blessing in your walk with the Lord.
Gilbert W. Stafford
June 19, 1996
Col 1:15-20

© 1996 by Warner Press
ISBN #0-87162-674-8   Stock #D5602
UPC #7 30817 05602 9

David C. Shultz, Editor in Chief
Dan Harman, Book Editor
Caroline Smith, Copy Editor
Cover by Todd Tufts

to

Darlene

My Companion in Christian Discipleship

and to

Matt, Heather, Anne, and Josh

Journeyers with Us on the Way

Contents

Foreword

In the last book from his pen, the late Hans Frei offered a classification of theologians and their works, explaining that what some theologians produce is best viewed from the standpoint of philosophical disciplines within the academy, while the work of some others is best understood as an activity within and for the Christian community. Although highly respected by those who work within his scholarly discipline, Gilbert Stafford has written this *Theology for Disciples* as an activity within and for the Christian community. The "systematic considerations" he has offered here about the life of Christian faith not only help to make theology intelligible but to make Christian discipleship in particular intelligible, persuasive, and a shared life.

This is a book for which its author can be proudly accountable. There are no places in it where he seems to feel his way, but he rather reports with responsible bearing what he has distilled from his depth study of the Christian Scriptures, the relevant literature within his chosen field of scholarly expertise, his own long and fruitful ministry, and his prolonged observation about the perennial needs of the church and the world. Some of the formulations voiced herein have been reshaped across the years, corrected or confirmed by interaction with other minds and lives, but the accent he places on the imperative for disciples to be informed by their faith is from an unchanging conviction, indeed a wisdom generated by his own serious faith and dedicated learning as a believing, teaching scholar.

This book is multidimensional in its scope, but singular in its focus. It explains Christian discipleship, a discipleship that involves both a life-long learning "at the feet of Jesus" and a life-long involvement in the church, with each believer receiving from and supporting the church's "way of being and manner of doing," always with an eye toward being faithful to the church's Lord. In the way he has sought to identify the major themes of the church's thought life (i.e., the church's message, doctrines, and beliefs), Gilbert Stafford has also sought to show how reflection on these should lead not only to an informed and sustained faith but on to responsible action.

It is important that the reader understand that this writer seeks to remains in constant dialogue with him or her, and with a respectfulness that is utterly open and genuine. This is no narrowly conceived, selfishly motivated, or denominationally oriented study.

Knowing the author as I do, as a forthright, honest, and open person, I take at face value his concern that this book be viewed in the light of his intention for it, namely as "one disciple's contribution to the church's ongoing conversation about its faith." Readers can expect here not only an immense scholarship from Stafford's well-informed mind, but guidance for their serious inquiries, and solid substance for their questing spirits. Here is a solidly biblical but contemporary statement that puts discipleship not only in context but in strict focus. This study is well-conceived and carefully written. One looks up from its thought-stirring pages with the realization that Christianity does not need to be reinvented — as some post-moderns would assert — but thought about with due seriousness and lived out in full trust.

Gilbert Stafford is a practicing theologian whose classes at Anderson University's graduate School of Theology have been lively and stimulating. He is also a well-traveled preacher whose voice and vision are known across the English-speaking world through his long-term ministry as radio speaker on the "Christian Brotherhood Hour." Prior to his tenure as seminary professor, he held pastorates in Massachusetts and Michigan. Across several years our separate offices in the seminary building were adjacent, and we spent quality time with each other. During that same period I was privileged to serve as his dean and was blessed by the wisdom, warmth, and cooperativeness that characterized him as a faculty member.

In this book, "theology" and "discipleship" are inextricably related, as in its writer's life. This book is a call to explore the roots of our faith and to experience the reach of our possibilities as believers. All who take seriously what has been set forth here will find adequate help to understand and deal with the peculiar and pernicious alterations in church life that modern circumstances have occasioned. Gilbert Stafford points us beyond what is peripheral to what is central, to what honors the church's Lord and makes his purpose in coming fulfilled.

James Earl Massey
Dean Emeritus, and
Distinguished Professor-at-Large
Anderson University School of Theology

Preface

Theology for Disciples springs from the conviction that the essence of church life is discipleship. Disciples are learners. The church is a community of learners at the feet of Christ Jesus. Regardless of how long we have been in the church and regardless of what office we may hold, we should continue thinking of ourselves as learners.

As a Christian reared in a parsonage, I have breathed the air of Christian discipleship from infancy. This book, therefore, is, first of all, one disciple conversing with other disciples. I write, also, as an ordained minister, the purpose of which calling I understand to be that of helping the church to be a better community of disciples.

More specifically, though, I write as a systematic theologian, that is, one who identifies the major themes of the church's thought life, weaves them together so that they can be seen as a whole, and highlights each theme so that it can illuminate the others. In the whole process a systematic theologian critically analyzes the church's thinking as to whether it is faithful to its Lord.

In this book, then, we consider in a systematic way the classical topics in theology. God is understood as the One who calls us both to faithful pilgrimage under holy guidance and to divine mission in the world. Christ Jesus is understood as the fulfillment of Old Testament hopes and promises regarding the establishment of the Kingdom. He is our Savior and Lord. The church is understood primarily as a circle of disciples called to be a band of Spirit-empowered emissaries of the gospel. The universal work of the Holy Spirit is understood as providing the divine connection between God and all flesh, and between the church and all peoples. The trinitarian God is understood as being the God of mystery, revelation, and mission. The mode of existence for God's people is understood in light of God's trinitarian life.

Since this book is written from the perspective of Christian discipleship, a strong emphasis is placed on such matters as spiritual formation, prayer, holiness, and service. What we believe as disciples influences how we act as disciples. The church's thought life shapes its practical life—its worship and witness, its caring and serving, its organization and procedures, its hopes and dreams, its internal relatedness and external connectedness, its way of being and manner of doing. What the church thinks is not simply what it says it thinks but how it lives it out—that tells the true story about what it really believes.

I agree with Frederick Herzog's comment:

> The task of all reflection and writing in the Christian community is [perhaps he ought to have said should be] aimed at making disciples again. "Go therefore and make disciples of all nations" (Matt. 28:19) is at the core of what Kierkegaard meant when he said: "Each generation has to be again converted to Christ."[*]

Theology for Disciples is not intended as an official answer book for every question. Instead, it is offered as one disciple's contribution to the church's ongoing conversation about its faith. I hope that it inspires fellow disciples to think with me about what it means to be a discipleship church at this point in history. Since the Bible is our primary source about Christ Jesus, what we say as his disciples should be rooted in biblical thought. Since, as the resurrected and reigning Lord, he has never abandoned his church, what we say should be informed by the church's history. This book is an invitation into my class room where together we can take another look at what Christians believe about God, humans, scripture, the Kingdom, the church, the world, sin and evil, and salvation.

I am a life-long member of a church tradition which

had its inception in the late nineteenth century under the leadership of Daniel Sidney Warner, and is referred to nowadays as the Church of God (Anderson, Indiana). Having emerged out of the holiness movement, it is steeped in sanctification concepts. As a movement concerned with the relational ramifications of holiness for church life, it is steeped also in unity concepts. As one who has been spiritually shaped by this tradition, I bring to this project a strong interest in both the unity of God's people and holiness of life. I believe that the two are not mutually exclusive.

This both/and approach is seen also in the following. I am deeply committed both to the personal piety of the American holiness tradition and to the classical trinitarian theology of historic Christianity. Again, I believe that the two are not mutually exclusive. I am convinced of the importance of both the vigorous pursuit of the missionary enterprise and charitable relations with other major religious traditions. Neither are these mutually exclusive. I am devoted both to being a preacher of the gospel, which I am convinced is the power of God to salvation, and to being a theologian who is critically reflective about the thought life of the church. Nor are these mutually exclusive.

I write to disciples, both in my own tradition and in the wider church, who are serious about Christian thought. The day for narrowly conceived, denominationally oriented systematic theologies is over. While my roots are deep in the Church of God (Anderson), they are not therein root bound; they extend into the rich heritage of the whole church. It used to be that when I appreciated something about another tradition of the Christian faith, I wished it were mine as well. No longer is that the case. I now embrace it as mine. For example, when, in an Anglican service, my soul is blessed by the singing of psalms, I claim that practice as belonging to me, as well. Whenever I recite the Nicene Creed concerning the trinitarian God, I affirm this ancient witness to the faith as belonging to me, too. As I participate in the fervor of evangelicals for the salvation of the world, I am glad to know that such is my heritage, also. These traditions and more are mine! My heart rejoices with all who, as disciples of Christ Jesus, worship with their daily lives the triune God revealed in Scripture. The ancient and ever widening circle of Christian disciples is invigorating, enriching, instructive, and challenging for all members of it who affirm not only a section of the circle but the whole of it.

---

* Frederick Herzog, *God-Walk: Liberation Shaping Dogmatics* (Maryknoll: Orbis, 1988), 20.

I
Theology for Disciples

1

Disciples Making Disciples

Neither Jesus nor any of the Twelve were members of the official "clergy" of their day. Jesus was, in fact, at odds with the official "clergy," and the Twelve were "laypersons" from among the people. The Christian church began as a movement of "lay" believers and not as a movement of professional "clergy." Today's disciples, whether lay or clergy, share a common calling from the Lord. The Twelve give us important information about that calling.

The Twelve

It is theologically significant that Jesus chose twelve, the same as the number of the tribes of Israel. In effect, by choosing twelve, he announced that the new society being gathered around him was the fulfillment of the hopes and dreams of the Old Testament people of God.

Jesus, the pivotal person between the Old Testament and the New, in turn chose the Twelve as a pivotal society between the past, present, and future. They were divinely called benefactors of the ancient heritage to the present generation. They were divinely ordained conveyors of this newly interpreted legacy for future generations. As heirs of the promises, benefactors of the heritage, and conveyors of the legacy, they had a ministry *to* the new community of faith.

The Twelve also *represented* the new community of faith. Though in continuity with the old community of faith, this representative body had been introduced to the newness of life brought by Christ and were commissioned to move beyond their own world with the good news of his salvation. They represented the character of the whole new community of faith — a community in continuity with Israel, a community with newness of life in Christ, and a community on mission with the good news of Christ's salvation.

The number twelve was so significant that when Judas defected, the infant church earnestly sought the will of their resurrected and ascended Lord for a replacement (see Acts 2:12–26). The identity of the number was so readily understood that the Gospel writers often refer just simply to the twelve (e.g., Matt. 26:14, 20, 47; Mark 6:7; 9:35; 10:32; 11:11; 14:20; Luke 8:1; 9:1,

12; 18:31; John 6:67; 20:24; Acts 6:2). The number was of such great theological significance that when Revelation 21:10–14 describes the "holy city Jerusalem coming down out of heaven from God," it is used no less than six times. Three of these are in v. 14 in reference to "the twelve names of the twelve apostles of the Lamb" that are on the city wall's "twelve foundations."

In order to keep the all-important role of the Twelve in proper perspective, however, it is important to remember that the Gospels and Acts call them disciples. The Greek word *mathētēs*, "disciple," is from the word *mathanō*, meaning "to learn." A disciple is a learner, a pupil, a follower of an authoritative one. Disciples accept the teachings of their leader and seek to bring their lives in line with the leader's will and example.

Matthew is particularly explicit about the connection between twelveship and discipleship in that he alone refers specifically to the Twelve as the "twelve disciples" (10:1; 11:1; 20:17). Also, in some twenty other instances in the Gospels at least some of the Twelve are referred to as disciples (e.g., Mark 4:34; 6:45; 8:10; 9:28; 10:10; Luke 9:54; John 6:8; 12:4). Their uniqueness as a specially chosen association—sometimes referred to as a college (from the Latin *collēgium*, meaning an association or a society)—was not, however, simply their status as disciples, for there were other disciples besides the twelve (see Luke 19:37, John 4:1, 6:60–67, 8:31, 19:38); rather, their uniqueness was that they were chosen as a *college* of disciples to be representative of the whole people of God. They represent us.

As Revelation 21:14, referred to above, indicates, however, the Twelve were also a college of *apostles*. Matthew 10:2 refers to "the names of the twelve apostles." (See also Luke 6:13, 22:14; Acts 1:26). Apostles (from the Greek *apostolos,* which is derived from *apo,* from, and *stellō,* to send) are those sent forth on a mission. Being sent forth on a mission, though, was not what made them unique, for Luke 10:1–17 tells about the seventy being sent forth on a mission, and according to Acts 2, on the day of Pentecost, the whole church was empowered for divine mission.

As we have said, the Twelve were special, therefore, not strictly because they were disciples and apostles, but because in God's economy they were selected to be the prototype of the whole community of faith. They are the pattern for the entire company of disciples, which company is also called to apostleship. They are the basic integer (12) resulting eventually in the total integer of the symbolic 144,000 spoken of in Revelation 7:4.

The Twelve represent us, but historically, they also both made the Jesus movement immediately tangible to the people of their day, and ministered to the whole movement in ways unique to their collegial appointment.

In summary, then, the Twelve, as the first fruits of the gospel, were the people of God in embryonic fulfillment of Israel's history. They represented the ongoing, expanding Jesus movement, which at its best is both a circle of learners (disciples) and a band of missionaries (apostles). Not only did they represent it, they were divinely chosen to build it up. They signify:

1) that in God's economy, the whole company of Jesus' disciples—past, present, and future—fulfills the hopes and dreams of the people of God prior to the incarnation of God in Christ Jesus;

2) that all of God's people have the privilege of being in a direct, personal, and transforming relationship with God revealed in Christ even as the Twelve were; and

3) that it is no less than the whole people of God who are to be on mission to the entire world with the good news of the Lord's salvation.

Disciples and Disciplers

That brings us to a consideration of Matthew 28:16–20:

Now the eleven disciples went to Galilee, to the mountain to which Jesus had directed them. When they saw him they worshiped him; but some doubted. And Jesus came and said to them, "All authority in heaven and on earth has been given to me. Go therefore and make disciples of all nations, baptizing them in the name of the Father and of the Son and of the Holy Spirit, teaching them to observe everything that I have commanded you. And remember, I am with you always, to the end of the age.

The disciples were commissioned to become disciplers, but no indication is given that they were to cease being the Lord's disciples when they became disciplers. The basic components of disciple making include the decisional-liturgical and the developmental-didactic. Let us examine these basic components.

"Baptizing them in the name of the Father and of the Son and of the Holy Spirit" implies the decisional-liturgical component. Baptism is the sign that the baptized have declared their allegiance to the Lord. It illustrates their repentant recognition that they need the Savior, their grateful acceptance of his salvation, and their joyous commitment to walk henceforth in the newness of life that he brings. It is thereby decisional. Furthermore, in God's economy of salvation, the decisional component is inextricably bound to the liturgical, i.e., baptism. Baptism is an external act that by its very nature is a communal event since one cannot baptize oneself. Liturgical acts communalize individual decisions, and individual decisions personalize the liturgical. To disciple others, then, involves introducing them to Christ in such a way that they make a decisional response of faith and are led into the liturgical communalization of that decision through water baptism.

The other equally important component of making disciples is the developmental-didactic, for as Jesus in v. 20 instructs his disciples, they are to do their work by "teaching them to obey everything that I have commanded you." In Matthew, the didactic component has to do with what it means to live the new life of the kingdom. The core of our Lord's didactic (or teaching) about kingdom life is set forth in Matthew 5–7, as well as in 13:1–52 where several didactic parables about the nature of the kingdom appear. Chapters 18–25 form yet another major didactic section at the center of which are teachings about the end of time.

Jesus, however, taught not only by what he said but also by what he did. Everything about his life, whether word or deed, was a teaching about what it means to be his disciple.

Since this pivotal passage (Matt 28:16-20) regarding discipleship is found in Matthew, it is appropriate, therefore, to mention a few illustrative emphases in the didactic passages—emphases such as the following:

1) The blessedness of being at the end of one's

resources. This foundational attitude for the coming of the kingdom in the human heart goes far beyond a sense of personal humility. Gene Davenport argues:

> The poor in spirit are all people, at all times, and in all places, who are victims and bondservants of the Darkness in the Old Age. They are those who see no way out, those for whom life has become a dead end, those who have passed over the edge of desperation and no longer have enough energy left even to be desperate.[1]

The beatitudes begin in 5:3 with what to success-oriented people is unthinkable: "Blessed are the poor in spirit, for theirs is the kingdom of heaven."

2) Faithfulness. Jesus' teaching about adultery, lust, and divorce in 5:27–32 has to do with the importance of being faithful in word, thought, and deed to the person with whom one is in the covenant of marriage.

3) Forthright honesty. In 5:37, Jesus says, "Let your word be 'Yes, Yes' or 'No, No'; anything more than this comes from the evil one."

4) Redemptive love. Christ's commandment is this: "Love your enemies and pray for those who persecute you" (5:44).

5) Unpretentious religion. The first half of chapter 6 deals with the unacceptability of any piety, almsgiving, prayer, and fasting that has as its aim the gaining of

public approval. Instead, our religious life is to be characterized by simplicity, genuineness, and the desire to please God rather than seeking public acclaim for ourselves.

6) Daily trust in God. In 6:34, Jesus says, "So do not worry about tomorrow, for tomorrow will bring worries of its own."

7) Bearing fruit. In the parables of the sower (13:3–23), the wheat and the weeds (24–30), the grain of mustard seed (31–32), and the leaven (33), the common theme is that the Lord wants people both to bear fruit and to be a good influence in the world.

8) Being merciful. Two of Jesus' parables in Matthew 18 teach us that followers of the Lord are to show mercy to others. This teaching appears in the one about a single lost sheep out of ninety-nine (10–14) and the one about the servant who was forgiven of a huge debt but who refused to forgive a fellow servant's smaller one (21–35).

9) Compassion for the powerless. To the disciples who tried to keep children away from him, Jesus said, "Let the little children come to me" (19:14).

10) Total surrender to the lordship of Christ. To the rich young man, Jesus says in 19:21, "If you wish to be perfect, go, sell your possessions, and give the money to the poor, and you will have treasure in heaven; then come, follow me."

11) Readiness for the Lord's return. At the end of the parable about the ten virgins (25:13) Jesus said, "Keep awake, therefore, for you know neither the day nor the hour." Five of the virgins had oil for their lamps. Five did not and consequently were not prepared to join the wedding festivities when the bridegroom arrived at midnight.

12) Serving others as the way to serve the Lord. In the final judgment scene, the king announces, "Truly I tell you, just as you did it to one of the least of these who are members of my family, you did it to me" (25:40).

I set forth these examples of Jesus' teachings to indicate their importance in making disciples. Jesus teaches that what one thinks is part and parcel of being his disciple. To be his follower requires both a decisional and a developmental commitment. It involves both the way we feel about God and the way we think about God. It includes both liturgical and didactic involvement in the community of faith. It is a matter of both the heart and the head. It is both new spiritual birth and new spiritual formation. It is a new way of being and a new way of functioning. It is a new way of feeling and a new way of thinking. It is a new way of being in touch with oneself under the reign of God and a new way of being in touch with the whole of reality as God's domain.

The Discipleship Paradigm

A basic paradigm for the church that grows out of this emphasis on discipleship is that of Jesus the discipler at the center of a circle, the circumference of which consists of his disciples. Two kinds of disciples intermingle in this circle—some who are also disciplers and some who are not. The latter are decisionally-liturgically identified with Jesus Christ and are learning the didactic of kingdom life but have not yet assumed personal responsibility for the task of making disciples. They are recipients but not givers. They are respondents but not senders. They think of themselves as church members being discipled but not as the Lord's apostles sent out to make disciples.

So, while some disciples are devotedly doing their part in the work of making disciples (whether it be a supporting role or a leading role such as a proclaimer or instructor), others are still in process of discovering what it means for them to participate in this work. Just as the Twelve were both disciples and apostles, so the whole church is called to be both a church of disciples and a church of apostles.

Offices of Ministry

Ernest Best concludes his study of discipleship in the Book of Mark by contrasting the disciples of Jesus with both disciples of the rabbis and disciples of the philosophers. He writes:

> The disciple of the rabbi, if all goes well, becomes a rabbi; the pupil of the philosopher may equally become a philosopher and have his own pupils; disciples of Christ, however, never become Christs or have their own disciples.[2]

The Book of Mark, usually dated in the eighth decade of the Christian era, was written to a church with thirty to forty years of development since the ascension of its Lord. Who were Mark's readers? What was the church's condition? What were its needs? Were those in offices of ministry forgetful of their own status as disciples? As one has said, "Often they [the church to which Mark wrote] are as ambitious for positions of power and honor as the sons of Zebedee, and family considerations are often involved. Often they are as lacking in vigilance as the disciples in Gethsemane."[3] The message to Mark's original readers was that just as the Twelve were disciples first and foremost, so also should office-holders be in the emerging church. Although Mark restricts discipleship to the Twelve,[4] the point is that holding that office assumed that they were basically disciples of Jesus.[5] Even so, office holders in the ongoing church should think of themselves first and foremost as disciples. If the attitude espoused in Mark is applied to officeholders in general, it means that whatever the office of ministry, it is always to be viewed both as an expression of Christian discipleship and as an assigned responsibility for making disciples.

Ministries in the Life of the Church

If we take discipleship and apostleship as being essential to the nature of the church, it follows that what applies to offices would also apply to all ministries in the church, regardless of whether they are connected to particular offices.

An example of the discipleship attitude can be seen in Paul's instruction to the Corinthian church about tongues. In 1 Corinthians 14:16, he raises the question as to whether the practice of tongues speaking in church has the "outsider" sufficiently in mind. In v. 19, he says, "in church I would rather speak five words with my mind, in order to instruct others also, than ten thousand words in a tongue." The issue, then, is not one's own spiritual enjoyment but the instruction of others.

What Paul says in relation to tongues represents the perspective he has at every point, namely, that there is no priority higher than that of ministering to others "for their upbuilding and encouragement and consolation" — words used in 14:3 when discussing the priority of prophecy over tongues speaking. In v. 5 we again see the priority given to the "discipler" attitude when he says, "One who prophesies is greater than one who speaks in tongues, unless someone interprets, so that the church may be built up." And again, in v. 6, he asks, "If I come to you speaking in tongues, how will I benefit you unless I speak to you in some revelation or knowledge or prophecy or teaching?" Verse 9: "If in a tongue you utter speech that is not intelligible, how will anyone know what is being said?" In each of the above references, his concern is for those who need either to be introduced to the gospel or to be instructed in it. Keeping the basic call to discipleship uppermost in the church's life is prerequisite to a spirituality that is in conformity with the spirituality of the Twelve.

The Discipleship Perspective in the History of the Church

At least three basic perspectives on the nature of church life are identifiable in Christian history. The first is the church as a bureaucracy with a predominant emphasis on hierarchy, institutional life, and ritual. The imperial state church after Emperor Constantine comes quickly to mind, reaching the low point of bureaucratic difficulties in the late fourteenth and early fifteenth centuries. From 1409 to 1415 there were no less than three popes simultaneously contending to be Peter's true successor. Numerous churches, many of which hardly find a place in religious encyclopedias, are bureaucratic in concept and practice. Even congregationalists can be bureaucratic!

The second perspective is the church as an arena of emotionalism with primary emphasis on feelings, passions, and sensations.[6] All one needs to do is to switch on the television to see slayings in the spirit and to hear testimonies about tingles up the spine, private interpretations of Scripture, and new revelations. Independent ministries, however, are not the only examples of emotionalism. Even Anglican churches can be emotionalistic!

The third perspective is the church as a circle of disciples with a predominant emphasis on learning, mission, and mutual edification. In some 29 passages in Acts we find references either to the church as a whole being a fellowship of disciples (e.g., 6:1–2[7]) or to individual believers as disciples (e.g., 9:10[8]).

Acts 11:26 indicates that whereas "Christians" was a later designation for believers, the original designation was that of "disciples." "It was in Antioch that the disciples were first called 'Christians,'" Luke tells us.

Discipleship reformations have taken place throughout church history notably in the monastic movements such as the Benedictines in the sixth century and the Franciscans in the thirteenth, among the Anabaptists of the sixteenth century, and in the Wesleyan revival of the eighteenth (see For Further Consideration for bibliographical references). While church groups with names associated with discipleship traditions may continue functioning in a discipleship mode, no guarantee exists that such is, in fact, always the case. A Wesleyan church may have strayed far from its discipleship tradition whereas a Roman church, even with its bureaucracy, or a Pentecostal church with its emotional expression in worship, may be very much in the discipleship mode! The crucial issue is whether a church actually functions first and foremost as a circle of the Lord's disciples (regardless of its traditional identification), or, first and foremost as a bureaucracy or as an arena of emotionalism.

Foot washing is a liturgical practice found in some discipleship groups (e.g., Anabaptists and monastic orders). The Church of God (Anderson, Indiana) with roots in the nineteenth century holiness movement views "washing of the saints' feet" as one of three divinely commanded ordinances. Charles Ewing Brown, editor of the group's chief journal from 1930 to 1953, wrote in 1947: "Foot washing is an ordinance for young and vigorous churches, for missionary churches, revival churches, martyr churches. It has no place in a cold, dead, worldly, and backslidden congregation."[9] It is understood by many to be the dominically authorized liturgical action of a discipleship church.

A strong interest in the discipleship paradigm for understanding the church has been rekindled in our time especially by Søren Kierkegaard (1813–1855) and by Dietrich Bonhoeffer (1906–1945). Kierkegaard, the Danish philosopher and theologian who was dissatisfied with state religion, emphasized the personal dimension of authentic spirituality. Vernard Eller, in his analysis of the discipleship theme in Kierkegaard's works, writes:

> There never lived a more fervent Protestant than Søren Kierkegaard; yet, precisely because of his fervency, because he was a Protestant's Protestant, he could never be happy in Protestantism; in fact, he felt impelled, in the name of Christianity, to mount an attack upon Christendom. But likewise, as a sectary born after the age of sectarianism, and as a melancholy genius, one of mankind's ugly ducklings, where was he to find the Gemeinde which he described but never knew [a church of radical discipleship to Jesus]? Where, in the nineteenth century, was the sort of church he sought? A church stands in the distance, but it has no door for Søren Kierkegaard.[10]

Bonhoeffer, a Christian minister who stoutly opposed Nazism, was imprisoned in a concentration camp and finally executed. His *Cost of Discipleship*, published originally in German[11] in 1937 and translated into English in 1948, has gone through multiple editions and printings. "Christianity without the living Christ," Bonhoeffer maintains, "is inevitably Christianity without discipleship, and Christianity without discipleship is always Christianity without Christ."[12] In reference to Jesus' call of Levi (Mark 2:14), Bonhoeffer writes:

> The disciple simply burns his boats and goes ahead. He is called out, and has to forsake his old life in order that he may 'exist' in the strictest sense of the word. The old life is left behind, and completely surrendered. The disciple is dragged out of his relative security into a life of absolute insecurity (that is, in truth, into the absolute security and safety of the fellowship of Jesus), from a life which is observable and calculable (it is, in fact, quite incalculable) into a life where everything is unobservable and fortuitous (that is, into one which is necessary and calculable), out of the realm of the finite (which is in truth the infinite) into the realm of infinite possibilities (which is the one liberating reality).[13]

He says that "when we are called to follow Christ, we are summoned to an exclusive attachment to his person."[14] Pressing his point, he declares that "discipleship means adherence to Christ, and, because Christ is the object of the adherence, it must take the form of discipleship."[15] Referring to the church as "the disciple community," he says that it "has been torn from the clutches of the world. Of course, it still has to live in the world, but it is made into one body, with its own sphere of sovereignty and its own claim to living-space."[16]

The contemporary interest in the subject of the church as a society of disciples is seen in the publication of books, some primarily studies in academic theology and others primarily practical (see For Further Consideration at the end of the chapter for examples of both). Robert P. Meye stated it well when at the end of his book, *Jesus and the Twelve*, he says:

> When the Church turns its attention to the canonical Gospels, then it finds the power to reformation and restoration flowing from the gospel of Jesus Christ as it is faithfully affirmed by the evangelists. Even in this study it finds itself called, like the disciples of old, to follow Christ in the company of those about him."[17]

Notes

1. Gene L. Davenport, *Into the Darkness: Discipleship in the Sermon on the Mount* (Nashville: Abingdon, 1988). p. 52.

2. Ernest Best, *Following Jesus: Discipleship in the Gospel of Mark* (Sheffield: JSOT, 1981), p. 249.

3. Augustine Stock, *Call to Discipleship: a Literary Study of Mark's Gospel* (Wilmington: Michael Glazier, 1982) p. 206.

4. See Robert P. Meye, *Jesus and the Twelve: Discipleship and the Revelation in Mark's Gospel* (Grand Rapids: Eerdmans, 1968), pp. 137–172.

5. Besides the works already cited, see also Ernest Best, *Disciples and Discipleship: Studies in the Gospel According to Mark* (Edinburgh: T and T. Clark, 1986).

6. See Ronald A. Knox, *Enthusiasm: A Chapter in the History of Religion* (New York: Oxford University Press, 1961). While Knox identifies as enthusiasts those whom I would call emotionalists (e.g., Corinthianism in the first century, Montanism in the late second century and Shakerism, which emerged in the eighteenth century), he also includes in the same category those whom I place—more accurately, I believe—in a third category, that of discipleship churches.

7. "Now during those days, when the disciples were increasing in number, the Hellenists complained

against the Hebrews because their widows were being neglected in the daily distribution of food. And the twelve called together the whole community of the disciples."

8. "Now there was a disciple in Damascus named Ananias."

9. Charles Ewing Brown, *The Apostolic Church: A Study in Historical Theology* (Anderson: Warner, 1947), p. 212. For Brown's "interpretation of radical Christianity" see his *When Souls Awaken* (Anderson, Gospel Trumpet Company, 1954). Also, see chapter XI in this work, on "The Ordinance of Foot Washing."

10. Vernard Eller, *Kierkegaard and Radical Discipleship: A New Perspective* (Princeton: University Press, 1968), p. 428f.

11. Dietrich Bonhoeffer, *Nachfolge* (München: Chr. Kaiser Verlag), 1937.

12. Dietrich Bonhoeffer, *The Cost of Discipleship*, trans. R. H. Fuller (revised and unabridged edition; New York: Macmillan, 1967), p. 50.

13. Ibid., p. 49.

14. Ibid.

15. Ibid., p. 50.

16. Ibid., p. 245.

17. Meye, op. cit., p. 232.

For Further Consideration

Academic Studies in Discipleship

Marcus J. Borg, *Jesus: A New Vision: Spirit, Culture, and the Life of Discipleship* (San Francisco: Harper and Row, 1987).

Eamonn Bredin, *Rediscovering Jesus: Challenge of Discipleship* (Mystic: Twenty-Third Publications, 1986).

Robert E. Coleman, *The Mind of the Master* (Old Tappan: Fleming H. Revell, 1977).

Stephen Happel and James J. Walter, *Conversion and Discipleship: A Christian Foundation for Ethics and Doctrine* (Philadelphia: Fortress, 1986).

Fernando F. Segovia (ed.), *Discipleship in the New Testament* (Philadelphia: Fortress, 1985).

Practical Studies in Discipleship

Robert E. Coleman, *The Master Plan of Evangelism* (Westwood: Fleming H. Revell, 1964).

————, *They Meet the Master: A Study Manual on the Personal Evangelism of Jesus* (Old Tappan: Fleming H. Revell, 1973).

Tom Sine, *Taking Discipleship Seriously: A Radical Biblical Approach* (Valley Forge: Judson, 1985).

David Watson, *Called and Committed: World-Changing Discipleship* (Wheaton: Harold Shaw, 1982).

Discipleship Traditions

Myron S. Augsburger, *Invitation to Discipleship: The Message of Evangelism* (Scottdale: Herald, 1964).

Harold S. Bender, *These Are My People: The Nature of the Church and Its Discipleship According to the New Testament* (Scottdale: Herald, 1962).

Daniel S. Schipani (ed.), *Freedom and Discipleship: Liberation Theology in an Anabaptist Perspective* (Maryknoll: Orbis, 1989).

David Lowes Watson, *The Early Methodist Class Meeting; Its Origins and Significance* (Nashville: Discipleship Resources, 1985).

2

Disciples Thinking About
Their Faith

The New Testament represents the earliest church's thinking about what it means to be disciples of Christ Jesus. Since the Bible is a literary collection, it is evidence that pilgrims of faith throughout the biblical era thought about their faith. Such reflective thinking is at least as old as the Bible. (See chapter 3 for more about the Bible.)

In the post-biblical development of creeds, confessions, doctrines, and dogmas, the church continued thinking about its faith, though, to be sure, in a more formal and ecclesiastical way.

Creeds are concise statements of Christian belief used primarily in worship to give witness to the historical faith as over against some heresy. The word comes from the Latin *credo* meaning "I believe" and is the first word of the Apostles' Creed (fourth century) and of the Nicene Creed, first formulated at the ecumenical council in Nicea in Asia Minor in A.D. 325 and expanded at Constantinople in 381.

Confessions are formal statements of the beliefs held by a particular group of Christians. An example is the Augsburg Confession (1530), which states the beliefs of Protestants under Martin Luther's leadership as over against Roman Catholicism.

Doctrines are extensively argued positions widely held by the church (e.g., the doctrine of the virgin birth) or by a particular segment of the church (e.g., the doctrine of entire sanctification subsequent to justification and prior to glorification).

Dogmas are truth declarations promulgated by an ecclesiastical body about the way things really are. Such truth, therefore, is understood to have universal applicability regardless of whether all agree with it. Dogmas are declarations not about secondary matters but about foundational issues having to do with the very nature of God and the world. Classical examples of dogmas are the Nicene Creed (325 and 381), which declared that the Son is *homoousios* (of the same substance) with the Father, and the Chalcedonian Formula (451) which declared that Jesus Christ is both fully human and fully divine, yet one.

Creeds, confessions, doctrines, and dogmas, then, are ecclesiastically endorsed declarations of the church's faith. The church also finds its faith discussed analytically by its scholars. This analytical endeavor is called theology.

Theology and the Various Uses of the Word

The word theology comes from two Greek words, *theos*, God, and *logos*, word or reason. The Latin form of this combination is *theologia*, discourse about God. We use the word in a variety of ways, each equally valid.

First, theology refers to a particular thinker's formalized position regarding matters of faith. Usually this formalization takes place through the writing of books thus giving others of both the contemporary generation and later generations the opportunity to critique it. Because of this literary endeavor we, for instance, have the benefit of such seminal thinkers as Irenaeus (ca. 115–ca. 230), Tertullian (ca. 160–ca. 230), Origen (ca. 182–ca. 251), Athanasius (ca. 293–ca. 372), the Cappadocian Fathers [Basil of Caesarea (ca. 330–379) and his younger brother Gregory of Nyssa (d. after 394) as well as Gregory of Nazianzus (ca. 329–ca. 389)], Augustine (354–430), John of Damascus (ca. 700–ca. 753), Thomas Aquinas (1225–1274), John Calvin

(1509–1564), Friedrich Schleiermacher (1768–1834), Paul Tillich (1886–1965), and Karl Barth (1886–1968).

Second, theology refers to a school of thought within the church's intellectual history. Such a school represents an approach taken by a plurality of persons sharing similar assumptions, approaches, and perspectives. Some schools of thought are related to ecclesiastical traditions (e.g., Lutheran theology, Reformed theology, Wesleyan theology, Pentecostal theology, Catholic theology, Orthodox theology). Others are related more directly to theological and philosophical issues that cut across ecclesiastical traditions (e.g., liberal, conservative, neo-orthodox, process, and narrative theologies). Today, we are influenced by feminist theology, liberation theology, black theology, and others that are more directly related to contemporary social issues.[1]

Third, theology refers to a discipline of critical analysis, some classical examples being biblical theology focusing on the content of the church's scriptures; natural or philosophical theology focusing on the process of thinking itself; historical theology focusing on the intellectual traditions in the church; dogmatic theology focusing on the ecclesiastically defined pronouncements about the faith such as are embodied in creeds and confessions; spiritual theology focusing on the nature of the Christian life; practical, applied, or pastoral theology focusing on the practice of ministry; fundamental theology focusing on the process of verifying the truthfulness of theology; and systematic theology focusing on the structure of the church's thought within the context of the contemporary world. Each of these disciplines, though not totally independent of the others, has a history of its own; the concentration of each is sufficiently distinct for them to be separate scholarly disciplines.

Systematic Theology

Since this is a work growing out of the discipline of systematic theology, a further word is appropriate. In short, systematic theology searches for the interconnectedness between the various themes of the church's faith. It does this in conversation with the Christian scriptures, the church's intellectual history, and the contemporary church's questions and concerns. It pursues its work and formulates its findings in a logical, consistent, coherent, and comprehensive way.

A literary work in this discipline does not necessarily reflect the official position either of a particular church tradition, or, to be sure, of the whole church. A systematic theology offers a potential reference point for the thought and life of the church in the contemporary world. Systematics attempt to encourage the church to be intentionally reflective about the implications of its faith, to objectify its belief life so that the church can talk about it more easily, to analyze the conceptual adequacy of what it says, and to propose agenda for continuing thought and action.

Sometimes the church acts as though theological works are a nuisance unrelated to the real task of being the people of God. This is unfortunate because, first of all, whenever the church is not analytical about its faith, it inevitably allows itself either to be conformed to the thought patterns that are most prevalent at the time, or to be little more than transmitters of a tradition perfunctorily passed on in authoritative fashion.

Furthermore, viewing theological work as a nuisance is unfortunate because it fails to recognize that everything we do takes place within some conceptual framework whether good or bad. Therefore, the question is not whether we should have a conceptual framework, but whether we choose to have one informed by Scripture, the intellectual history of the church, and the Christian community's faith experience. The negative consequences of devaluing theological reflection can be seen in worship. Those churches that give little or no theological attention to corporate worship find themselves at the mercy of the latest fads and with no consciously operative conceptual framework for evaluating changes brought about by popular demand.

Is all this to say that systematic theology is the way to reach the world for Christ? No, the gospel is. Is systematic theology what is needed for the renewal of the church? No, the Holy Spirit is. Is it systematic theology that Christians need most to read? No, the Bible is.

Why, then, the discipline of systematic theology? It is so that preachers, teachers, and other officers and leaders in the life of the church may both reflect analytically on the content of what they preach, teach and do, and develop in themselves and others a deeper appreciation for that content as a whole.

J. Gordon Melton and Robert L. Moore in their study of the cult phenomenon in the United States hold that one of the reasons some persons join cult groups is because both the church and university leave them in a conceptual vacuum. Consequently, they find it difficult to make "sense out of the confusion of their existence." And so, needing a conceptual frame for understanding life, they turn to a cult group that claims to have the answers.

Melton and Moore write: "The critic, of course, quickly sees the weaknesses, contradictions, and unanswered questions of a cult's world view. 'How could anyone believe that?' But the group supplies a basic metaphor or model by which an individual may approach life."[2]

Systematic theology is the disciplined way whereby

the church remains on the cutting edge of conceptualizing both a Christian world view in the contemporary setting and an integrated understanding of the Christian faith. The aim, of course, is not that all will become systematic theologians, but that those who are leaders in the church may think clearly, communicate well, and make sense of Christian truth. Having a systematic theology provides us with a conceptual framework within which to minister. It makes it possible for us to give people the gift of a perspective so that they can make "sense out of the confusion of their existence." It provides the conceptual context within which the church can evaluate what it is doing, find direction for the future, and address critical issues of faith and order, life and work, evangelism and mission.

Many church members relate to the Christian faith as though it were a jigsaw puzzle never put together. They have a piece called the Spirit, another called the return of the Lord, another called creation, and other pieces called the virgin birth, baptism, Jesus Christ, prophecy, healing, the Lord's supper, redemption, worship, resurrection, sanctification, as well as many others. All of these, however, are a jumble of pieces in the church's puzzle box. From time to time they pick up a piece for examination but never have the joy of seeing how it fits into a fuller picture. They function with a jigsaw puzzle faith which no one has ever helped them put together. Systematic theology is an attempt to put the pieces together so that people can see the faith more as a whole and discover new dimensions of meaning in it.

Theology and Doctrine

We need to distinguish between a theological work and a doctrinal one. A doctrinal work informs the faithful about the cognitive content of faith whereas a theological work deliberates about it. A doctrinal work is catechetical; a theological work is cathartic.

Catechesis is a form of instruction that uses the method of questions and answers both of which are determined by the instructor. Martin Luther, for instance, prepared two such catechisms in 1529, the best known being the Shorter Catechism. The answers reflect the faith community's convictions as to what is important for belief and practice. *Catechesis* refers to instruction which takes place by word of mouth. In the modern era it also refers to doctrinal guides, books, and statements that are published for the purpose of instructing people about the faith. *Catechesis* assumes that there is a body of knowledge to be transmitted to others and that there are understandings to be grasped, commitments to be made, and assumptions to be accepted. All this knowledge represents the collective

wisdom of the faith community that produces the catechetical materials.

But what about the cathartic function of theological
works—to be distinguished from the catechetical function of doctrinal works? We usually use "cathartic" in
relation to our physical or psychological needs. A
cathartic is a medicine for stimulating the evacuation of
the bowels. In the psychological sphere, we speak of
bringing fears, problems, and complexes out into the
open in hopes of alleviating them, thus purging our
emotional lives.

This word is useful, also, I think, for identifying the
difference between doctrinal and theological works.
Theological catharsis deals with inadequate formulations of the faith, encroachments upon it, inconsisten-
cies in the way we think about different dimensions of
faith (e.g., church, salvation, creation) and discrepancies
between conceptualizations of the faith and the practices of the faithful.

Theological works have a cathartic function in that
they provide the opportunity for the Christian community to consider, on the one hand, whether it is being
true to "the faith that was once for all entrusted to the
saints" (Jude 3) or, on the other, whether it has been
polluted and stands in need of being cleansed. To carry
the cathartic analogy a little further: a theological work

can help relieve the faith community of doctrinal constipation, that is, of being stuffed with doctrinal content
that impacts an otherwise healthy digestive system
with passivity, inactivity, and lethargy.

This is not to say that the church needs one kind of
work without the other (either catechesis or catharsis),
but just the opposite: both are needed. On the one hand,
theological works without foundational doctrinal works
lead to exercises in theological speculation. Theological
works are tied to a tradition. On the other hand, doctrinal works without ongoing theological reflection lead to
religious constipation.

The Church as a Network of "Languages"

As the church converses about its faith, it does so in
five different "languages": personally revelatory language, adopted language, inflicted language, observed
language, and foreign language.

Personally revelatory language is that which is genuinely one's own. It pours forth from the depths of one's self
and gives expression of who one is. The word of God is
this kind of language; it is the personhood of God
expressed linguistically. But personally revelatory language is also the language we humans speak whenever
we express how we feel about a matter, whether of joy
or sorrow, thanksgiving or displeasure, gratitude or
lamentation. It is the way we speak in times of authen-

tic prayer, heartfelt testimony, honest discussion and convictional preaching and teaching.

Personally revelatory language is sometimes informal (e.g., conversations) and sometimes formal, (e.g., books, articles, and sermons). But whether informal or formal, its chief mark is that the authors and speakers say what they want to say, in the way they want to say it, and with the words they want to use. It may inspire or discourage, but whatever its influence it is the language of the person himself or herself speaking out of the depths of his or her being.

The second type is *adopted language* that, though having originated with someone else, is so wholeheartedly embraced that one adopts it as one's own. Hymns, quotations, and scriptures are examples. For instance, although we did not write Psalm 23 many of us adopt it as our very own. Confessions of faith and creeds may be this kind of language, providing we genuinely agree with them. Adopted language is that which, though it originates with others, we recognize as being expressive of our own genuinely held convictions.

Third, *inflicted language* consists of statements or affirmations with which we do not agree but which, for whatever reason, we feel obligated to repeat as though we did believe them. Take, for instance, Barney Warren's song declaring:

> Salvation, O glory! its rapture I feel—
> A current of heavenly bliss;
> My soul is delighted, I cannot conceal,
> The deepseated joy I possess.

Other testimonial words in the song include the following: "My pathway is bright as the cloudless noonday" and "I'm feasting with him from above" and "My Eden on earth has begun."[3]

We assume that this is Warren's personally revelatory language, but for others it is adopted language. For still others, however, it may be an inflicted language, as, for instance, when one yields unhappily to a song leader's pressure to sing "like you really mean it." Unison prayers, creeds, and confessions of faith all fit into this category whenever people are made to say that with which they do not agree.

The fourth type is *observed language*. This is language that is primarily the object of serious study, light-hearted enjoyment, disdain, or neutral awareness. It is the kind of language experience we have when we read something simply for the purpose of finding information. Observed language is that which we treat as object whether it be literary works such as books and articles, scriptures and creeds, or the spoken word such as conversations and monologues, testimonies and sermons. We treat what is said as an object to be handled in detachment from its author instead of as the linguistic expression of the author's self with whom we are personally engaged. For instance, Augustine (354–430 A.D.), who became one of the greatest thinkers in the church, initially went to listen to the preaching of Ambrose, bishop of Milan, for the purpose of analyzing his oratorical skills. What began as observed language, however, became for him personally revelatory language, that is, it became for him the captivating word of God.

The. fifth type is *foreign language.* Whatever is said is not understood either because the hearers do not comprehend the terminology, are disinterested, or are distracted by other concerns.

As language creatures, we function linguistically in different ways not only in the public arena but also in the church. What is personally revelatory language for one person may be adopted by another, inflicted upon another, observed by another, and completely foreign to yet another. The same words are experienced in very different ways. The church is a community of human discourse in which there are multiple language experiences. In the midst of this discourse, theology is an attempt to enter into the conversation in an orderly, analytical way. As Gerald O'Collins has said, "Theologians are not spokespersons for God. It is simply that they watch their language in the presence of God."[4]

Conversation about Truth

Driving the church's historical conversation are at least five different levels of truth. The first is Christ Jesus, the incarnate truth, who says in John 14:6, "I am ... the truth." The second is scriptural truth which is, according to 2 Timothy 3:15 "able to instruct you for salvation through faith in Christ Jesus." The third is personal truth that springs forth from one's own experience of God in Christ. "Were not our hearts burning within us while he was talking to us on the road, while he was opening the scriptures to us?" — so said the Emmaus disciples in Luke 24:32. The fourth is prophetic truth that comes from beyond the immediate understandings of the hearers, for the purpose of attuning them to the divine will and purpose. Preaching is often prophetic. Personal conversation also may be prophetic in the sense of speaking to another in a straightforward manner for the purpose of bringing about correction or challenge in accordance with what is perceived by the "prophet" as being of God. So, in Revelation 1:10-11a, the words of John on Patmos:

> I was in the Spirit on the Lord's day, and I heard behind me a loud voice like a trumpet saying, "Write in a book what you see and send it to the seven churches."

Fifth is doctrinal truth that is formulated by the

church through tradition and its teaching offices, and used as the canon by which all other thinking is measured. The church's creeds, confessions, and dogmas, as well as its more expansive doctrinal works, are in this category. Titus 2:1 says "Teach what is consistent with sound doctrine."

Christian theology is a scholarly attempt to converse with the church about truth—incarnate, biblical, personal, prophetic, and doctrinal—to the end that it, too, will "watch [its] language in the presence of God."

Notes

1. For an introduction to many theological schools of thought see Donald W. Musser and Joseph L. Price (ed.), *A New Handbook of Christian Theology* (Nashville: Abingdon, 1992).

2. J. Gordon Melton and Robert L. Moore, *The Cult Experience: Responding to the New Religious Pluralism* (New York: Pilgrim, 1982), p. 34.

3. Barney E. Warren, "Waves of Devotion," *Worship the Lord: Hymnal of the Church of God* (Anderson: Warner, 1989), No. 574.

4. Gerald O'Collins, *Has Dogma a Future?* (London: Darton, Longman and Todd, Ltd., 1975), p. 100.

For Further Consideration

A. Creeds

See Frances M. Young, *The Making of the Creeds* (London: SCM and Philadelphia: Trinity Press International, 1991). Other major studies are Hans-Georg Link, *The Roots of Our Faith* (Geneva: World Council of Churches, 1984); Alan Richardson, *Creeds in the Making* (Philadelphia: Trinity Press International, 1990); J. Stephenson, ed., *Creeds, Councils and Controversies: Documents Illustrating the History of the Church* A.D. *337-451* (Cambridge: University Press, 1989).

For a contemporary study of the Nicene Creed, see Faith and Order Commission of the National Council of Churches of Christ, *Confessing One Faith: The Origins, Meaning and Use of the Nicene Creed: Grounds for a Common Witness* (Cincinnati: Forward Movement Publications, 1988).

B. Theological Studies

For a concise treatment of the classical disciplines see Gerhard Ebeling, *The Study of Theology* (London: Collins, 1979). Also, F. G. Healey, ed., *Preface to Christian Studies* (London: Lutterworth, 1971).

For a short introduction to theological terms, modern

theologians and methodology, see John Jefferson Davis, *Theology Primer: Resources for the Theological Student* (Grand Rapids: Baker, 1981). More comprehensive introductions are G. R. Evans, *Old Arts and New Theology: The Beginnings of Theology As an Academic Discipline* (Oxford: Clarendon, 1980); and Edward Farley, *Ecclesial Reflection: An Anatomy of Theological Method* (Philadelphia: Fortress, 1982).

For a theological dictionary, see Alan Richardson and John Bowden, *The Westminster Dictionary of Christian Theology* (Philadelphia: Westminster, 1983). A small quick reference is Thayer S. Warshaw, Abingdon *Glossary of Religious Terms* (Nashville: Abingdon, 1978).

II

Revelation for the World

3

The Church's Book of Faith

Throughout Christian history Christ's disciples have been guided by their book of faith. The Bible is the autobiography of the pioneer people of God in their pilgrimage of faith and the ongoing conveyor of God's revelation. It is the standard for establishing norms of faith and the foundational material for treatises of faith. Let's examine these four dimensions of the Bible in turn.

Autobiography of the Pioneer People of God

The Bible provides the autobiography of the pioneer people of God in their pilgrimage of faith. It is a story that covers the pilgrimage all the way from the first signs of faith in the Old Testament to the culmination of faith in Jesus Christ. The verbalization of the faith of God's people was eventually inscribed in documents preserving it for subsequent generations. They circulated these documents, read and listened to them being read, cherished them, transmitted them, collected them, and finally sanctioned them as being the authoritative literary documents of their faith.

For Christians, not only did a new collection of authoritative writings emerge, but a new perspective on the Hebrew scriptures, as well. Believers claimed the Hebrew scriptures as theirs also, for they were convinced that the God of Jesus Christ was none other than the God of the Hebrew scriptures. Hebrews 1:1-2 says:

> Long ago God spoke to our ancestors in many and various ways by the prophets, but in these last days he has spoken to us by a Son, whom he appointed heir of all things, through whom he also created the worlds.

The Hebrew scriptures were seen by the Christian community not as crusty literary antiques from their religious past, but as lively, vibrant literary instruments of the contemporary gospel. In fact, it was to these very scriptures that 2 Timothy 3:15 refers as being "able to instruct you for salvation through faith in Christ Jesus." Brevard Childs concludes his *Introduction to the Old Testament* as Scripture by saying:

> The Christian church confesses to find a witness to Jesus Christ in both the Old Testament and the New. Its Bible does not consist of the Hebrew scriptures plus an

appendix called the New Testament. Rather, the form of the Christian Bible as an Old and New Testament lays claim upon the whole scripture as the authoritative witness to God's purpose in Jesus Christ for the church and the world. By reading the Old Testament along with the New as Christian scripture a new theological context is formed for understanding both parts which differs from hearing each Testament in isolation. The Old Testament is interpreted by the New, and the New is understood through the Old, but the unity of its witness is grounded in the One Lord.[1]

Over the course of some three centuries, the church's foundational body of literary works—which we know as the New Testament—came into existence as an extension of the Hebrew scriptures. The Christian scriptures, including the Old and New Testaments, are the only authoritative record we have of the faith of God's people from the beginning of time to the fullness of time. Though written across many centuries by numerous persons, under all sorts of circumstances and for multiple purposes, the Bible emerged with a story line stretching all the way from creation to the consummation of Israel's history in Jesus Christ and pointing to the consummation of world history at the end of the age.

As the book of a particular people, it is, therefore, a historical document that lends itself to historical, literary, and sociological analysis. It is as open to the search light of critical investigation as is any other kind of literature. Denying it such investigation ignores the historical character of biblical faith. The people of God have nothing to fear from the severest and most critical investigations possible. Taking the view that the church's faith can be maintained only so long as it hides its documents from the light of critical investigation, contradicts the historicity of the faith of those who were the writers, collectors, and transmitters of the literary material that we know as the Bible. They knew themselves to be people of a historical process charged through and through with faith in the God of history. It was not secretive, esoteric, privately held ideas with which they were dealing, but the historical life of the people of faith. Discouraging critical investigation of the Bible as historical literature calls into question the Bible as having to do with the stuff of real life. If the church is to be faithful to itself as a people of historical process, there is no logical option other than to encourage such critical investigation.

Ongoing Conveyor of God's Revelation

Merely being the autobiography of the people of God, however, is not sufficient reason for the Bible to be pertinent to us. It is not its historicity as such that affects us, for many historical works influence us little if any and certainly not in the sense of transforming our lives. What makes the Bible different is that it conveys God's faith-inducing revelation generation after generation.

As such, it is not only the book of God's people but also the Holy Spirit's book. Down to the present, the Bible has been and continues to be the literary instrument by which subsequent generations were and are called to and established in faith. This gives rise to the conviction that these writings, experienced as being divinely inspired by the original hearers and readers, are experienced by us also as being divinely inspired. To say that they are divinely inspired is to say that in them and through them we hear God speaking to us in a definitive way.

For a discussion such as this, the classical text is 2 Timothy 3:14–17:

> But as for you, continue in what you have learned and firmly believed, knowing from whom you learned it, and how from childhood you have known the sacred writings that are able to instruct you for salvation through faith in Christ Jesus. All scripture is inspired by God and is useful for teaching, for reproof, for correction, and for training in righteousness, so that everyone who belongs to God may be proficient, equipped for every good work.

According to v. 16 "all scripture is inspired by God." The word translated as inspired is *theopneustos*, literally, God-breathed. Actually, there are two legitimate ways to translate this passage. It could be translated either "All scripture that is inspired by God is also useful" or "All scripture is inspired by God and is useful."

The first translation might lead one to the conclusion that there are some parts of the Bible that are not inspired, in which case our task would be to decide which are inspired and which are not. If that were the case, the temptation, of course, would be to designate whatever we like as being inspired and whatever we do not like as being uninspired. The second translation might lead one to the conclusion that any writing that any group claims as having scriptural status is thereby necessarily inspired.

Which way, then, should v. 16 be translated? The structure of the Greek sentence in and of itself does not give the answer. The decision has to be made on the basis of the immediate context of the statement. Verse 15 refers to the sacred writings—what we call the Old Testament—which nurtured Timothy from childhood. It is that whole set of sacred writings, therefore, that is in view when v. 16 refers to inspiration.

The objection is sometimes made that since the reference is to the Hebrew scriptures—the New Testament not yet having been formed — the passage does not apply to the New Testament. To arrive at such a conclusion, however, overlooks the implied scripture principle that is set forth in this text — a principle that, while stated in relation to the Old Testament, was also operative in the emergence of the New Testament. This principle will be considered below, but at this point we simply call attention to the fact that according to 2 Timothy the scriptures are God-breathed. The question is: How are we to understand their God-breathed character?

Three major views of inspiration have been developed over the course of time: verbal inspiration, plenary inspiration, and dynamic inspiration.[2] Does inspiration have to do with each word in the Bible? Or, does it have to do with the message of Scripture? Or again, does it have to do with the life transforming faith to which Bible writers give witness?

Major View No. 1. The theory of verbal inspiration (having to do with words) holds that each word of Scripture originated with God so that the writers as instruments of God, though using words, sentences, and concepts that were native to them, were actually giving forth the divine words of God in the original act of speaking and writing.

Those who hold to the theory of verbal inspiration, recognizing that the Bible as we now have it does

59

indeed present some problems (e.g., the contradiction between 2 Kings 24:8, which says that Jehoiachin was eighteen when he became king of Judah, and 2 Chronicles 36:9, which says that he was eight), claim that it was the original autographs of scripture that were verbally inspired and that if we were to find those autographs we would discover no such problems. Errors that have crept into the text in the course of translation and transmission were not in the original autographs. As J. I. Packer puts it, "Since God has nowhere promised an inerrant transmission of Scripture, it is necessary to affirm that only the autographic text of the original documents was inspired."[3]

Major View No. 2. The theory of plenary (full) inspiration holds that while the words and thought forms belong to the writers, the message itself is fully God's. The literary form which that message takes is that of the writers who were indeed sensitive to the direction of the Spirit but were nevertheless functioning as people of their own age and place as they gave expression to the divine message inspired in their hearts and minds. While the word "plenary" is also used by those who hold to the verbal inspiration of the original autographs, those who prefer the term "plenary inspiration" often use it with the intent of avoiding the emphasis on individual words instead of the message as a whole.

Although Howard Marshall does not use the term, his position is an example of what is referred to here as plenary inspiration. He writes:

> On a human level we can describe its composition in terms of the various oral and literary processes that lay behind it.... At the same time, however, on the divine level we can assert that the Spirit ... was active in the whole process so that the Bible can be regarded as both the words of men and the Word of God. This activity of the Spirit can be described as "concursive" with the human activities through which the Bible was written.[4]

He goes on to say that this hypothesis does full justice to the claim in 2 Timothy 3:16 that all Scripture is God-breathed in that it is the product of the inspiration of the Spirit of God. "What is being asserted is the activity of God throughout the whole of the process so that the whole of the product ultimately comes from him."[5]

Major View No. 3. The theory of dynamic inspiration (having to do with change and growth) holds that those who wrote the books of the Bible were in a lively, growing faith relationship with God and that as God worked in, through, and with them they grew in their understanding of God. As people with a developing faith, they wrote in response to the inspiration of the Spirit. Paul Achtemeier says:

> It was ... from the interrelationship of tradition, situa-
> tion, and respondent that the Holy Spirit summoned
> forth the words of Scripture. It is in such a dynamic way
> that inspiration is best understood, and ... which best
> allows us to account for the way in which Scripture was
> in fact produced.[6]

Verbal inspiration places the emphasis on the words of Scripture, plenary inspiration on its message, and dynamic inspiration on the faith relationship that produced it. The difference between the three has to do with whether it is the individual words and sentences that are God-breathed or the central message or the faith of the writers.

In the first instance, the emphasis is primarily on the text of Scripture; in the second, on the message of Scripture; in the third, on the experience of Scripture. (To be sure, those who emphasize the text do not discount the message and experience; those who emphasize the message do not discount the text and experience; and those emphasizing experience do not discount the text and the message.) Regardless of these differing emphases, however, in all three of these views, the same conviction holds, namely, that the Bible is the literary location where God continues to speak to us for the purpose of bringing us to faith and offering us newness of life.

Literary Canon for Establishing Norms of Faith

The Bible is also the literary canon, or "measuring rod," which the people of faith use for establishing the norms of faith. What counts as Christian faith? The touchstone for establishing what counts is the Bible. This does not mean that this is always easily determined; rather, it means that the Bible is the focus for the discussion. The sixteenth century reformers grappled with issues of faith by grappling with biblical texts. Scripture was the primary focus for the discussions, diatribes, and declarations.

What gives a body of writings the authoritative status of being called Scripture? The above mentioned "scripture principle" as set forth in 2 Timothy 3:14–17 is a four-fold one:

1. The first dimension of the scripture principle is that people are internally convinced that they hear the very word of God being spoken to them in the words of others. This is often referred to as the testimonium *internum Spiritus Sancti,* i.e., the internal witness of the Holy Spirit.

John Calvin writes:

The testimony of the Spirit is superior to all reason [for proving that the Scriptures are the word of God]. For as God alone is a sufficient witness of himself in his own word, so also the word will never gain credit in the hearts of men, till it be confirmed by the internal testimony of the Spirit. It is necessary, therefore, that the same Spirit, who spake by the mouths of the prophets, should penetrate into our hearts, to convince us that they faithfully delivered the oracles which were divinely intrusted to them.[7]

In his systematic theology—officially commissioned by the Church of the Nazarene—H. Ray Dunning speaks of this witness as being a special case of prevenient grace that is offered to all equally, and, in this case, to all who have been exposed to the contents of the scriptures.[8] The first dimension of the Scripture principle, then, is the Spirit-initiated conviction that particular writings are *theopneustos*, God-breathed, "inspired of God" (v. 16).

2. The second dimension is that such are providentially preserved so that in the course of time they come to have the special distinction of being the definitive literature of the faith, e.g., "the sacred writings" (v. 15). We see evidence of this process at work during the time when the New Testament books were being written, for in 2 Peter 3:16 Paul's writings were already being referred to as scripture.

3. The third dimension is that they "are able to instruct you for salvation through faith in Christ Jesus." In order to be classified as Christian scriptures, writings must point to salvation in Jesus Christ; they have a salvation function with a Christocentric focus.[9] The primary function of Scripture is neither that of informing us of a multiplicity of historical facts nor of serving as a kind of all-purpose answer book, or giving us esoteric understandings, or providing data for unscrambling a time table for future events. Instead, its purpose, through and through, is to lead people to salvation.

The late Boyce Blackwelder, New Testament scholar at Anderson School of Theology, said it well:

> Here we emphasize the affirmation that Jesus Christ is the main theme of the Scriptures. This truth, which is reflected directly in the New Testament and indirectly in the Old Testament, gives theological meaning and unity to the Bible. In this context, all interpretation serves the purpose of finding Christ or delineating his redemptive work.[10]

4. Fourth, the scriptures are "useful for teaching, for reproof, for correction, and for training in righteousness, so that everyone who belongs to God may be proficient, equipped for every good work." They are useful for (a) instructing people about the content of the Christian faith (i.e., *didaskalia*, teaching); (b) rejecting that which is contrary to Christian teaching and practice (i.e., *elegmos*, reproof); (c) aligning (or realigning, as the case may be) the people of God with Christian teaching and practice (i.e., *epanorthōsis*, correction); and (d) shaping spiritually the children of God (i.e., *paideia*, training, or literally, the rearing of a child; the text reads, "for training in righteousness").

The goal of all of this—whether it is instruction in content, rejection of what is contrary to Christian canons, alignment and realignment, or spiritual formation—is that the people of God might be "proficient, equipped for every good work." The Greek word *artios*, translated here as "proficient," means perfect of its kind, suitable, exactly fitted. The idea is that the people of God are to be instructed, judged, aligned and shaped by the scriptures to the end that they will fulfill the purpose for which God calls them.

In short, the Christian scripture principle is that those writings are scripture that are

1) experienced by the church at large as being inspired of God,

2) accepted by the church at large as being sacred writings,

3) instructive for salvation through faith in Jesus Christ, and

4) useful for the purpose of instructing, judging, aligning, and shaping the people of God so that they will come to be and do what God wants them to be and do.

The sixty-six books of the Bible are the books so accepted by the church as a whole (Catholic, Orthodox, and Protestant) as meeting all four of these criteria. While the fourteen or fifteen books of the Apocrypha [11] are accepted by the Roman Catholic Church as scripture and to some extent by the Orthodox Church and Anglicans, they are not generally accepted by Protestants. This Protestant stance was the result of the sixteenth-century Reformers sanctioning as authoritative the listing of the Jewish Council of Jamnia about 90 A.D., which includes only what we know as the Old Testament.

Foundational Material for Treatises of Faith

The Bible is commonly used as the basic reference in the church's discourse about its faith whether that discourse be testimonial or doctrinal in nature, whether informal or formal, whether devotional or analytical. The fact that there are so many traditions in the church, all claiming to be rooted in the Bible, points to the fact that the Bible was written in a wide variety of contexts, reflecting multiple perspectives and emphases.

Those who find this multiplicity intolerable have several options:

1) to reject the Bible on the assumption that if it were God's word, there would be no such multiplicity;

2) to theorize that if we could find the original autographs, such problems would be solved;

3) to harmonize the multiple perspectives and emphases in an effort to make them all say the same thing;

4) to choose that in scripture that one finds acceptable, disregarding the rest;

5) to accept the Bible with all of its multiplicity as God's gift to the church.

Vern S. Poythress, in his book entitled *Symphonic Theology*, discusses the diversity of perspectives within the Bible and sets forth the thesis that "differences between biblical writings by different human authors are also *divine differences*" (emphasis his). Continuing, he writes:

> God uses a multiplicity of perspectives in communicating to us. We may thus view the differences between the emphases in the four Gospels as divinely ordained. Hence we do not need to postulate some underlying single harmonistic account as more appropriate. Harmonization is possible in principle, but it needs to be balanced by an appreciation of divinely ordained diversity.[12]

To this divine variety I would add divinely ordained ambiguity and divinely ordained problems. To try to do away with all diversity, ambiguity, and textual problems is to say no to what God has given to us in the here and now. The Bible as authoritative scripture must be allowed to stand as it is, with Christ at its center integrating all the parts and shedding light on the whole. With all of its diversity, ambiguity, and textual conundrums, the Bible must be translated and transmitted in the public arena so that its multiplicity — a multiplicity which God evidently approves — is preserved for the church's edification. In fact, the unity of the church depends on its willingness to embrace the multiplicity found in Scripture and to profit from it.

The church has a priceless gift in its scriptures. They are the gift of the living God who has spoken truthfully (we can count on God), dynamically (God speaks in the dynamism of the human community and not apart from it), historically (the word of God has to do with time and space) and literarily (the divine word is in the form of written material that can be referred to repeatedly by all sorts of people in all sorts of circumstances and eras of time). By giving the scriptures to us, God has become vulnerable both to our understandings and misunderstandings, both to our proper and improper uses of them, both to our willingness to listen, change, and grow and to our rigid sectarian argumentativeness. God has given us a book that raises questions but that also answers questions about the ways of God and about God's creation, providential care, salvation, and consummation of history. God has given us a book that not only puzzles us so that we are stretched intellectually, but that also clarifies the divine will so that we are given confidence that we, though mere creatures, are nevertheless party to the Creator's plan for us.

In Scripture we have the eternal word in the literary word so that we can experience the transforming word leading to newness of life. I agree with Daniel Migliore when he says:

> Scripture is indispensable in bringing us into a new relationship with the living God through Christ by the power of the Holy Spirit, and thus into new relationship with others and with the entire creation. To speak of the authority of the Bible rightly is to speak of its power by God's Spirit to help create and nourish this new life in relationship with God and with others.[13]

Notes

1. Brevard S. Childs, *Introduction to the Old Testament as Scripture* (Philadelphia: Fortress, 1979) p. 671. See For Further Consideration regarding Childs's work in canonical studies.

2. For a study of various views of inspiration in one church tradition, see Steven Wayne Stall, *The Inspiration and Authority of Scripture: The Views of Eight Historical and Twenty-One Current Doctrinal Teachers in the Church of God* (Anderson, Ind) (unpublished Master's thesis, Robert A. Nicholson University Library, Anderson University, 1980).

3. J. I. Packer, *God Has Spoken* (Downers Grove: Inter-Varsity, 1979), p. 151f.

4. I. Howard Marshall, *Biblical Inspiration* (Grand Rapids: Eerdmans, 1982), p. 42.

5. Ibid.

6. Paul J. Achtemeier, *The Inspiration of Scripture: Problems and Proposals* (Philadelphia: Westminster, 1980), p. 136.

7. Hugh T. Kerr, *A Compend of the Institutes of the Christian Religion by John Calvin* (Philadelphia: Westminster, 1939), p. 16 (I. vii 4 in *The Institutes*).

8. H. Ray Dunning, *Grace, Faith and Holiness* (Kansas City: Beacon Hill of Kansas City, 1988), p. 63. Chap. 2,

"Sources of Theology: The Bible," is an excellent statement of a Wesleyan position on Scripture.

9. George Lyons has written: "Jesus and his followers found no occasion to debate the divine authority of the Scriptures with their Jewish opponents. What distinguished Christianity from Judaism in their attitudes toward Scripture was the former's unwavering conviction that the inspired Scripture found its fulfillment and authoritative hermeneutic in Jesus. Christology, not theories about the inspiration of Scripture, was decisive." "The Spirit in the Gospels," *The Spirit and the New Age,* ed. R. Larry Shelton and R. G. Deasley, Vol. 5 in Wesleyan Theological Perspectives (Anderson: Warner, 1986), p. 60.

10. Boyce W. Blackwelder, "Perspectives on Biblical Studies and Seminary Education," *Listening to the Word of God: A Tribute to Dr. Boyce W. Blackwelder,* ed. Barry L. Callen (Anderson: Anderson University and Warner Press, 1990), p. 24.

11. See "Apocrypha" in *The Interpreter's Dictionary of the Bible* (New York: Abingdon, 1962) for a treatment of its content and history.

12. Vern S. Poythress, *Symphonic Theology: The Validity of Multiple Perspectives in Theology* (Grand Rapids: Zondervan, Academie, 1987), p. 86.

Also, see Paul D. Hanson, *The Diversity of Scripture: A Theological Perspective* (Philadelphia: Fortress, 1982):

"Even in the Bible, tradition is received by the community of faith not as a homogeneous system of thought, but as a tension-filled stream characterized by divergent perspectives," p. 12. And again: "I believe that thoughtful believers will be receptive to an understanding of the meaning of Scripture which incorporates rather than obscures the rich diversity found at the heart of the Bible itself. For such believers do not regard reality (and certainly not the Author of all reality) as a simple object to be interrogated and described. Reality, on its most basic level, is ineffable, and descriptions must strive for honesty through statements that correct each other," p. 13.

13. Daniel L. Migliore, *Faith Seeking Understanding: An Introduction to Christian Theology* (Grand Rapids: Eerdmans, 1991), p. 46.

For Further Consideration

Recent studies regarding the canon have been dominated by the differing approaches taken by Brevard S. Childs and James A. Sanders. See Childs, *Biblical Theology of the Old and New Testaments: Theological Reflection on the Christian Bible* (Minneapolis: Fortress, 1993); *Introduction to the Old Testament as Scripture* (Philadelphia: Fortress, 1979); *The New Testament as*

Canon: An Introduction (Philadelphia: Fortress, 1985); *Old Testament Theology in a Canonical Context* (Philadelphia: Fortress, 1986). See Sanders, *Canon and Community: A Guide to Canonical Criticism* (Philadelphia: Fortress, 1984); *From Sacred Story to Sacred Text* (Philadelphia: Fortress, 1987); *Torah and Canon* (Philadelphia: Fortress, 1972).

For a comparative study of the two views, see Frank W. Spina, "Canonical Criticism: Childs Versus Sanders," *God's Word for Today,* ed. Wayne McCown and James Earl Massey, Vol. 2 in *Wesleyan Theological Perspectives,* (Anderson: Warner, 1982), pp. 165–94. Spina's observations are that Childs believes that the canonical product should be the object of exegesis, whereas Sanders opts for the process (p. 185); Childs argues that God's Word is present in the full canonical witness whereas Sanders, while accepting the significance of the total context, holds that some parts have been accorded higher status by the community of faith (p. 185); for Childs each separate part of the whole yields a unified Word that can be translated into basic theological affirmations; for Sanders the checks and balances within the text prevent any single part from being made absolute—for him, the canon is an indicator of divine activity as much as of the divine Word (p. 186); Childs understands the canon mainly as a vehicle for revelation; Sanders sees it as a vehicle for salvation (p. 186).

For an introduction to the canonical process, see Lee Martin McDonald, *The Formation of the Christian Biblical Canon* (Nashville: Abingdon, 1988).

For other studies, see James Barr, *Holy Scripture: Canon, Authority, Criticism* (Oxford: Clarendon, 1983); Hans von Campenhausen, *The Formation of the Christian Bible*, trans. J. A. Baker (Philadelphia: Fortress, 1972); Paul R. House (ed.), *Beyond Form Criticism: Essays in Old Testament Literary Criticism* (Winona Lake: Eisenbrauns, 1992).

For a theological treatise on the scripture principle, see Clark H. Pinnock, *The Scripture Principle* (San Francisco: Harper and Row, 1984).

4

The Biblical God

Questions and Answers

How do I know there is a God? Where is God when I need help? What is God like?

The *first* of these questions calls for proving the existence of God and brings to mind the four classical arguments:

1) The ontological argument, as set forth by Anselm of Canterbury (1033–1109), argues from the nature of being itself. God is that beyond which nothing greater can be conceived. Since to exist is greater than nonexistence, God must exist; otherwise, God would not be that beyond which nothing greater can be conceived.

2) The cosmological approach, an argument made by Thomas Aquinas (c. 1225–1274), argues on the basis of causation. Since everything must have a sufficient cause in order to exist and since the world does not possess within itself any causation sufficient to explain the existence of the whole, there must be, then, a sufficient cause beyond the world that brought it into existence, namely God.

3) The teleological approach argues that nature has design and purpose, and therefore must have a designer, i.e., God. This view is found in Thomas Aquinas's fifth demonstration of the existence of God. However, it was William Paley (1743–1805) who gave it its classical form. Peter Bertocci, my professor at Boston University, developed what he called the wider teleological argument having to do with the purposeful interrelatedness of matter, life, and thought, and of the good life and nature.[1]

4) The moral approach, the classical proponent being Immanuel Kant (1724–1804), argues on the basis of an apparent universality of a sense of obligation to others, which points to a source of ought common to all. This universal awareness of that which stands over against us as judge, thus driving us to feel obligated to treat others rightly, suggests the existence of God. (For discussions of these issues see For Further Consideration at the end of this chapter.)

The *second* question, Where is God when I need help? is the cry of existential abandonment. It is a lamentation growing out of the experience of God's absence and implies a view that God should always be there to help whenever we need it.

The *third* question, What is God like? brings to mind discussions both about God's omnipotence (all power-fulness), omnipresence (being everywhere), and omni-science (knowledge of everything) and about God's holiness and love, justice and mercy, veracity and faith-fulness, righteousness and goodness. This question also raises issues having to do with both the mystery as well as with the revelation of God.

The God of Scripture

The Bible begins with none of these questions. It does not seek to prove God's existence; instead it takes it for granted.

The Bible does record instances of the cry of desola-tion such as by Job (e.g., chap. 23), some of the psalms (e.g., 13 and 69), and by our Lord himself when on the cross he cried out "My God, my God, why have you forsaken me?" (Matt. 27:46). However, the major emphasis in Scripture is on the living God who calls, superintends, and challenges us to newness of life. The God of Scripture is God with us bringing us to life, rather than God absent from us abandoning us to deso-lation. (These issues will be addressed in chapter 15 on

"God's Will in the Face of Evil and Suffering" and in chapter 22 on "Praying People.") Furthermore, while the scriptures certainly do speak about the nature of God, they do so not in any abstractly philosophical way but concretely in the history of Israel and, as we shall see in chapters 5 and 6, incarnationally in Christ Jesus.

The God of the Bible calls us to faithful participation in the divine mission in the world. In Scripture, this theme predominates over questions about God's existence, lamentations about God's absence, and abstract discussions about God's nature.

People may reject completely the God of the Bible, but to do so is to reject at least something, even if it is nothing more than the claims made by a people on the basis of their history. To go to the trouble of denying the substance of these claims is thereby to value them at least enough to invest one's intellectual and emotional resources in the denial. Does such an investment exhibit an implicit admission that a theistic reality does present itself to human experience—what Brian Hebblethwaite calls "objective theism"[2] —the denial of which could be tied to one's vested interests, e.g., the exercise of human autonomy unrestrained by a God who stands over against us in judgment?

The God spoken of in Scripture is indeed a substantive ontological reality from whom none of us can extract ourselves. The God who not only stands over against us in judgment also pervades our very being as the one who holds us together. Furthermore, this God is graciously at a distance from us giving us freedom to love God, but also on the horizons calling us onward, and underneath us giving us support. This is the God who is over us superintending our lives, alongside us as a friend, and surrounding us like a loving mother enfolding her child. If we are willing, this God indwells us, empowering us to be and do what we are called to be and do. The biblical God is not a static object but the eternally dynamic subject.

Three Ways to Speak of the Biblical God

1. God Initiates Conversation and Calls Us to Communion.

The biblical God initiated all human speaking. In Genesis 1, God was the first to speak: "Then God said, 'Let there be light' " (v. 3). Later, the human pair were initially addressed by God (1:28, also 2:16ff.), not God by them. When Adam gave names to the animal kingdom, it was in response to the divine directive to do so (2:19-20). The ultimate tragedy, however, is that the first conversation involving the human pair was not with God, but with the serpent. Being addressed by the serpent, Eve was drawn into the discourse (3:1-5).

To enter into conversation about ultimate matters with other than the originator of all conversation was not only to reshape the goodness of the created order into the demonic, but, even more tragically, was to hurl ourselves against the creator of that good order. Having the kind of conversation with the serpent which should have been reserved for God was to reject the eternal one without whom conversation itself would be nonexistent. The primal sin was the rejection of God as a conversation partner and the decision to substitute the serpent for God.

According to Genesis, we were created to be respondents to God. God initiates; we respond. God acts; we react. God speaks; we decide either to listen, obey, and worship God; or to ignore, disobey, and dishonor God.

2. God Comes to Where We Are and Calls Us to Faith.

In Genesis 12:1 Yahweh says to Abram, "Go," and v. 4 says that he went. The subsequent chapters tell of Abram's journey as a respondent to the God who called him to new ventures on the horizons of the unknown.

In chapter 17 God tells Abram to walk before him blamelessly (v. 1), and promises to make a covenant with him and to multiply him exceedingly (v. 2). Abram, having fallen on his face, hears the divine promise that he will be the father of a multitude of nations. Along with this divine word comes a change of name from Abram (exalted father) to Abraham (father of a multitude).

Genesis 22 recounts Abraham's supreme test when he is confronted with the divine command to take his son Isaac to the land of Moriah, there to offer him as a burnt offering (v. 2). Abraham, portrayed here as the faithful one who is willing to make any sacrifice in response to the call of God, goes, Isaac with him, to face the ultimate test. It is only as he lifts the knife to slay the boy that the angel of Yahweh forbids him to slay the lad, calling his attention instead to the substitutionary ram caught in a thicket, by its horns (v. 13).

Throughout the Bible, God is referred to as the God of Abraham and his progeny. In the story of Moses at the burning bush, for example, God makes a self-introduction by saying "I am the God of your father, the God of Abraham, the God of Isaac, and the God of Jacob" (Exod. 3:6). (Also, see Exod. 3:15–16; 4:5; 1 Kings 18:36; 1 Chron. 29:18; 2 Chron. 30:6; Neh. 9:7; Ps. 47:9; Matt. 22:32; Mark 12:26; Luke 20:37; Acts 3:13; 7:32).

Furthermore, in Matthew 1:1 Jesus is introduced as "the son of Abraham." He is understood to be not only the fulfillment of David's royal line, i.e., "the son of David," but also the fulfillment of Abrahamic faith.

People of biblical faith are those who, upon hearing the call of God, respond, like Abraham, in trust and obedience (see Rom. 4 and 9, Gal. 3, Heb. 11, and James 2). The true descendants of the ancient patriarch are those who in Christ are of Abrahamic faith (see especially Gal. 3:16, 29).

3. God Takes Us By Surprise and Calls Us to Mission.
In Exodus 3, when Moses is encountered by Yahweh at the burning bush, Moses hides his face in awe following which Yahweh recounts the plight of the people of Israel in Egyptian bondage. In v. 10 Yahweh calls to Moses: "So come, I will send you to Pharaoh to bring my people, the Israelites, out of Egypt."

Moses, however, wants more information — perhaps it is a stalling tactic? Verse 13: "But Moses said to God, 'If I come to the Israelites and say to them, "The God of your ancestors has sent me to you," and they ask me, "What is his name?" what shall I say to them?' "

Moses resisted the divine call by initiating questions about God's nature. The God of Abraham wanted action but Moses wanted discussion. God had a social agenda whereas Moses had a cerebral and philosophical one. Therefore, instead of replying to Moses' conceptual questions, God said: I AM WHO I AM [also translated, I AM WHAT I AM or I WILL BE WHAT I WILL BE] . Moses was told to say to the people of Israel: "I AM has sent me to you" (v. 14). The relationship between God and Moses includes the following dynamics:

• An extraordinary occurrence took place that was not explainable on the basis of ordinary knowledge. It filled Moses with awe and pointed him to a reality beyond the commonly known categories of human experience; such was the bush that was burning without being consumed. In v. 3, Moses says "I must turn aside and look at this great sight, and see why the bush is not burned up";

• God called to Moses from within the context of the extraordinary occurrence. Verse 4 says that "God called to him out of the bush, 'Moses, Moses!' ";

• Moses responded, saying "Here I am" (v. 4);

• God warned Moses about the holiness of the place of revelation. In v. 5, God says "Come no closer! Remove the sandals from your feet, for the place on which you are standing is holy ground";

• Yahweh gave a statement of self-identification: "I am the God of your father, the God of Abraham, the God of Isaac, and the God of Jacob" (v. 6a);

• Moses experienced awe in the presence of God: "And Moses hid his face, for he was afraid to look at God" (v. 6b);

• The divine call was issued to fulfill God's purposes in the present set of circumstances (vv. 7–10). In v. 10, Yahweh says: "I will send you to Pharaoh to bring my people, the Israelites, out of Egypt";

• A divine-human conversation took place regarding both the call and the nature of God (vv. 11–15), during which Yahweh told Moses that he was to tell the people that I AM, the God of Abraham, the God of Isaac and the God of Jacob sent him to them;

• The sovereignty of God was reiterated, namely, that God is the one who calls people to the divine mission, clarifies it and gives specific instructions about carrying it out (vv. 16–22). In v. 17, the divine promise is as follows: "I declare that I will bring you up out of the misery of Egypt, to ... a land flowing with milk and honey."

Extraordinary occurrence, divine address, human response, the experience of divine holiness, divine self-identification, human awe, divine call, divine-human conversation, and divine clarification about the mission—these were the components of the interchange between God and Moses at the burning bush in which context Moses heard the call and commission to fulfill the divine mission.

These same components appear in the divine-human interchange between God and Isaiah in the temple (see Isa. 6). Isaiah, too, had an extraordinary experience and was divinely addressed; he, too, experienced awe in the presence of the holy God, recognized who was speaking to him, responded in faith to the divine call, and received clarification for the mission to which he had been called.

It was in the incarnation of God in Christ Jesus, however, that the ultimate divine surprise occurred and that the supreme divine mission was launched. Jesus Christ was both the uniquely extraordinary occurrence of all history and the unique emissary for God's once and for all mission to the world.

The divine call and commission did not stop with the incarnation. The day of Pentecost witnessed the extraordinary outpouring of the Holy Spirit on the church — confirming them as the people of God, cleansing and empowering them for participation in God's mission through Christ to the world (see Acts 1 and 2).

Some Implications of This View of God

The God of the Bible is the eternal missionary who comes to earth to establish the kingdom of heaven and to incorporate us into the missionary venture. This is a radically different kind of deity than typically is found in either religious or philosophical history where the gods are thought of either as humans blown large or as stupendous mysteries disconnected from the daily circumstances of life. The God of the Bible is neither. Instead, God, though categorically different from us, has nevertheless become one with us and, though mysterious, has nevertheless been revealed definitively in Jesus Christ.

The implications of this kind of God will, it is hoped, become obvious as we proceed in our consideration of other themes. However, *three preliminary comments* will set the tone for all that is to come.

First, biblical salvation is a matter of hearing the call of God and responding to it in faith. It is an active response to what God wants to accomplish through our lives. Instead of salvation being a static mode of existence, it is an ongoing pilgrimage during which we grow and develop, listen and respond, work and accomplish, progress spiritually and participate vocationally in the mission of God. Biblical salvation means accepting God's claims on our lives and living in accordance with them. It is a matter of living in everyday responsiveness to that call.

Second, the church is called to be faithfully involved in the ongoing mission of God in Christ. Luke 24:47–48 says that the risen Christ instructed his disciples "that repentance and forgiveness of sins is to be proclaimed in his name to all nations, beginning from Jerusalem. You are witnesses of these things." And then, at the beginning of Acts—the second volume of Luke's two-part work—Jesus says to his followers, "But you will receive power when the Holy Spirit has come upon you; and you will be my witnesses in Jerusalem, in all Judea and Samaria, and to the ends of the earth" (1:8). It is a significant indicator of the nature of the church that the earliest account of the church's life is called Acts, which from beginning to end is the story of the church fulfilling its mission to preach the gospel.

Third, the biblical God is neither subject alone nor predicate alone. God is a sentence. We cannot know the subject apart from the predicate, nor understand the predicate apart from the subject. The subject God and the predicate of God's mission in the world are inextricably tied together in the Bible.

Theological reflection on the biblical God is distorted whenever God is treated merely as an object for study. Theology that is faithful to the biblical God is a response to the call of God in Christ; it seeks, in the power of the Spirit, to bring about change in the world so that it will conform more perfectly to God's will. The only way to understand God is to respond to the divine subject by participating in the divine predicate.

The missional God calls us forth into fields of service both charted and uncharted. God as subject of the predicate is always calling us away from demonic oldness into divine newness. The God who, as the subject, said "Let us make humankind in our image, according to our likeness" (Gen. 1:26) is the same God who said to

Abram "Go from your country and your kindred and your father's house to the land that I will show you" (Gen. 12:1), and declared to Moses, I AM WHO I AM; this is the same God revealed in Jesus Christ, and the same one who at the end of the Bible says "See, I am making all things new" (Rev. 21:5).

Ours is the holy God who issues a holy call for us to participate in a holy mission to create holy newness. We come to know God as we respond in faith to God's call, move out in God's power on God's mission and open ourselves continually to God's eternal newness. God is the dynamic one who shatters all rigidities. God is the moving one who defies all narrow, conceptual confinements.[3] God is the living one who abandons all dead religion. God is the personal subject who supersedes all philosophical, theological, and dogmatic objectifications. In reply to all questions about God, the eternal I AM WHO I AM still bids us to tell them that "I AM has sent me to you."

Notes

1. Peter Bertocci, *Introduction to the Philosophy of Religion* (Englewood Cliffs: Prentice-Hall, 1960), pp. 329–387.

2. For a discussion of "objective theism" see Brian Hebblethwaite, *The Ocean of Truth: A Defense of Objective Theism* (Cambridge: University Press, 1988).

3. J. B. Phillips's popular book titled *Your God Is Too Small* (New York: MacMillan, 1968) speaks to our attempts to "put God in a box."

For Further Consideration

Part I: Proving the Existence of God

A. Contemporary Arguments

Contemporary examples of the academic attempt to prove the existence of God include Hans Küng, *Does God Exist? An Answer for Today*, trans. Edward Quinn (Garden City: Doubleday, 1980); Wolfhart Pannenberg, *Metaphysics and the Idea of God*, trans. Philip Clayton (Grand Rapids: Eerdmans, 1988); and Richard Swinburne, *The Existence of God* (Oxford: Clarendon, 1979). Selected related works: John Baillie, *Our Knowledge of God* (New York: Charles Scribner's, 1959); John Hick, *Arguments for the Existence of God* (New York:

Herder and Herder, 1971); Gordon D. Kaufman, *The Theological Imagination: Constructing the Concept of God* (Philadelphia: Westminster, 1981); and Bernard J. F. Lonergan, *Philosophy of God, and Theology* (Philadelphia: Westminster, 1973).

B. Critiques of the Ontological Argument

Jonathan Barnes, *The Ontological Argument* (London: MacMillan, 1972); G. R. Evans, *Anselm and Talking About God* (Oxford: Clarendon, 1978); and Alvin Plantinga (ed.), *The Ontological Argument: From St. Anselm to Contemporary Philosophers* (Garden City: Doubleday, 1965).

C. Critiques of the Cosmological Argument

Donald R. Burrill (ed.), *The Cosmological Arguments: A Spectrum of Opinion* (Garden City: Doubleday, 1967) and Anthony Kenny, *The Five Ways: St. Thomas Aquinas' Proofs of God's Existence* (New York: Schocken, 1969).

D. Critiques of the Teleological Argument

Peter Bertocci, *Introduction to the Philosophy of Religion* (Englewood Cliffs: Prentice-Hall, 1960), pp. 329–387. For a critique of the classical teleological argument, see Thomas McPherson, *The Argument From Design* (London: MacMillan, 1972).

E. Critique of the Moral Argument

H. P. Owen, *The Moral Argument for Christian Theism* (London: George Allen and Unwin, 1965).

Part II: The God of Biblical Faith

For Old Testament studies, see J. Stanley Chestnut, *The Old Testament Understanding of God* (Philadelphia: Westminster, 1968); and Robert W. Gleason, *Yahweh: The God of the Old Testament* (Englewood Cliffs: Prentice-Hall, 1964).

For Christological studies, see Ray S. Anderson, *Historical Transcendence and the Reality of God: A Christological Critique* (Grand Rapids: Eerdmans, 1975). Also, Nels F. S. Ferré, *The Christian Understanding of God* (New York: Harper, 1951) and Roger Hazelton, *Knowing the Living God* (Valley Forge: Judson, 1969).

For classical studies in the doctrine of God, see Herman Bavinck *The Doctrine of God,* trans. William Hendriksen (Grand Rapids: Baker, 1951), written from a Reformed perspective; and Thomas C. Oden, *The Living God — Systematic Theology: Volume One* (San Francisco: Harper and Row, 1987), written from a Wesleyan perspective.

5

Christ Jesus, the Kingdom, and Eschatology

In Revelation 22:13, Jesus says, "I am the Alpha and the Omega [the first and last letters of the Greek alphabet], the first [*prōtos*] and the last [*eschatos*], the beginning [*archē*] and the end [*telos*]."

Christ Jesus: The Beginning and the End

Jesus as the *Alpha, Prōtos,* and *Archē* is set forth in a variety of ways in other parts of the New Testament, as in John 1:3a: "All things came into being through him, and without him not one thing came into being." In 8:58 Jesus says, "Very truly, I tell you, before Abraham was, I am." And, Hebrews 1:2 says, "But in these last days he [God] has spoken to us by a Son, whom he appointed heir of all things, through whom he also created the worlds." Revelation 3:14b refers to Jesus as "the Amen, the faithful and true witness, the origin of God's creation." The most expansive passage on this theme is Colossians 1:15–17:

> [Jesus Christ] is the image of the invisible God, the first-born of all creation; for in him all things in heaven and on earth were created, things visible and invisible, whether thrones or dominions or rulers or powers — all things have been created through him and for him. He himself is before all things, and in him all things hold together.

Not only does the New Testament teach that Jesus Christ is the beginning of all things, he is also the *Omega, Eschatos,* and *Telos.*

The creation, history, and consummation of the world is Christocentric in that he is central to the source of all things, the goal of all things and the cohesion of all things. This one who holds all things together is spoken of in the New Testament as Lord (e.g., John 13:13; Acts 2:36; 10:36; Rom. 10:9; 14:9; 1 Cor. 12:3; Rev. 19:16). He is Lord of creation, Lord of history, Lord of the church, Lord of individual lives and Lord of the consummation of this world order. His lordship is for the purpose of establishing the kingdom of God, a theme given special prominence in Matthew.[1]

Creation is the arena of the kingdom, history is the drama of the kingdom, Christ is the essence of the kingdom, the church is the community of the kingdom. Individual believers are agents of the kingdom and the return of Christ will usher in the consummation of the kingdom.

Creation as the Arena of the Kingdom

Colossians 1:16 says that all things were created for Jesus Christ. Some Christians have reduced their concept of the kingdom simply to historical happenings or to individual experiences. Such views lead to making inadequate connections between personal salvation and ecological matters. According to the Colossians passage, the savior of humankind is also the agent of creation.

The connection between the human order and the rest of the created order is set forth in Genesis 1:26 where Adam and Eve are given "dominion over the fish of the sea, and over the birds of the air, and over the cattle, and over all the wild animals of the earth, and over every creeping thing that creeps upon the earth."

This connection between the two realms is also characteristic of many psalms in which Israel's salvation is seen as being interrelated with the whole created order (e.g., 18, 24, 29, 33, 65, 69, 89, 96, 97, 98, 104, 114, 136, and 148). The human order and the rest of creation are viewed not as two independent realms but as mutually interpenetrating ones. Likewise, this interrelatedness is reflected in Romans 8:19–22, which assumes that what happens in the human realm affects the rest of the created order:

> For the creation waits with eager longing for the revealing of the children of God; for the creation was subjected to futility, not of its own will but by the will of the one who subjected it, in hope that the creation itself will be set free from its bondage to decay and will obtain the freedom of the glory of the children of God. We know that the whole creation has been groaning in labor pains until now.

When sinners are converted, believers are sanctified and the people of God live in the power of the Spirit, the whole created order joins in songs of praise. According to Revelation 4 and 5 heavenly worship includes the whole created order joining in triumphant hymns of adoration.

Commenting on the Revelation 4—5 passage, Philip Hughes says that the "four living creatures" taking part in the vision of praise to God "represent the whole of animate creation."

Thus the one like a lion represents the wild beasts, of which the lion is king; the one like a calf or bull represents the domesticated beasts, of which the ox is king; the one like a flying eagle represents the birds of the air, of which the eagle is king; and the one with the face of a man stands for the king of all animate nature, to whom dominion over the earth was entrusted (Gen. 1:28).[2]

Hughes adds that the statement that the living creatures were full of eyes in front and behind "may be taken to signify the conscious awareness and constant vigilance of the diverse members of the animated creation, particularly in relation to the service in their respective orders of the Creator and his will."[3]

Colossians 1:15–20 sets forth the Christological basis for the essential unity (or, what might be called the ontological interconnectedness) of the whole created order with the human order in that it refers to the one who redeems the people of God as being the same one who holds the created order together. Consequently, there is no dissonance between what Christ does on the historical plane and what he does in relation to the whole created order. The one Lord is creator, redeemer, and sustainer both of his people and of the whole of creation. He is both particularly and uniquely present among his people and universally and pervasively present in creation. The God, then, who works among God's people is none other than the God who is also the cohesive substructure of creation.

History as the Drama of the Kingdom

Israel's choice of David to serve as king is the theme of 2 Samuel 5—7. The three chapters tell about leaders approaching David with the request that he agree to become their king, his ordination as monarch, the conquest of Jerusalem, the building of a palace, David's victory over the Philistines, the bringing of the ark of God to Jerusalem, the prophet Nathan's oracles about God's will for the future of the royal reign, and David's prayer.

This passage has to do with historical events, personal decisions, people movements, conflicts and victories, prophecies and prayers. It speaks of the past, the present, and the future; of people, places, and things; of the intersection of time and space, God and human beings, the eternal and the temporal.

Nathan's divine oracle to David was: "Your house and your kingdom shall be made sure forever before me; your throne shall be established forever" (7:16). After David's death, his son Solomon built a magnificent temple and in many respects had an illustrious reign, but following his death the kingdom fell apart, with Rehoboam, Solomon's son, ruling Judah in the south, and Jeroboam, the populist leader, leading breakaway Israel in the north. Eventually the northern kingdom fell to Assyria in 722–21 B.C. The southern kingdom was taken into exile by the Babylonians in 586 B.C. It was during this time of Israel's dissipation and Judah's exile that the literary prophets emerged both as interpreters of the national predicament and as heralds of divine promise.

Why all the turmoil? The prophets answered that it was the result of national disobedience (e.g., Dan. 9:4–19). The only hope was a new kind of citizen, one with a new heart. Jeremiah, the seventh-century prophet, proclaimed God's promise, namely, that "I will put my law within them, and I will write it on their hearts" (31:33). In the sixth century, the exilic prophet Ezekiel declared a similar divine promise: "A new heart I will give you, and a new spirit I will put within you; and I will remove from your body the heart of stone and give you a heart of flesh" (36:26).

Isaiah 53 speaks of a new kind of citizen leader who would be a suffering servant. The approach of this servant, both to wrongdoing and to the establishment of righteousness, is understood as reflecting God's will for all the people. As Gerhard Von Rad says, "the figure of the Servant embodies all that is good in Israel's existence before Jahweh."[4]

Along with the promise of a new kind of citizen was the more predominant one of a new kind of king. The prophets promised a messiah who would make all things right. In the eighth century, Micah of Moresheth in Judah proclaimed,

> "But you, O Bethlehem of Ephrathah, who are one of
> the little clans of Judah,
> From you shall come forth for me one who is to rule in
> Israel, whose origin is from of old, from ancient
> days." (5:2)

Isaiah, the prophet of Jerusalem whose work stretched across perhaps more than forty years during the latter part of the eighth century and into the seventh, prophesied, saying in 11:1–3:

> A shoot shall come out from the stump of Jesse,
> and a branch shall grow out of his roots.
> The spirit of the LORD shall rest on him, the spirit of
> wisdom and understanding,
> The spirit of counsel and might,
> the spirit of knowledge and the fear of the LORD.
> His delight shall be in the fear of the LORD.

Later, in the seventh and sixth centuries (626–586), Jeremiah of Judah says in 23:5–6:

> The days are surely coming, says the LORD, when I will
> raise up for David a righteous Branch, and he shall
> reign as king and deal wisely, and shall execute justice
> and righteousness in the land. In his days Judah will be
> saved and Israel will live in safety. And this is the name
> by which he will be called: "The LORD is our righteousness."

Daniel, the apocalyptic prophet of a subsequent period, says in 7:13–14:

> As I watched in the night visions, I saw one like a human being coming with the clouds of heaven. And he came to the Ancient One and was presented before him. To him was given dominion and glory and kingship, that all peoples, nations, and languages should serve him. His dominion is an everlasting dominion that shall not pass away, and his kingship is one that shall never be destroyed.

Not only, however, do the Old Testament prophetic themes consist of promises regarding a citizenry with new hearts and a God-ordained messiah, but also a new environment. Isaiah 35 starts off by declaring: "The wilderness and the dry land shall be glad, the desert shall rejoice and blossom; like the crocus it shall blossom abundantly, and rejoice with joy and singing." Verses 5 and 6 promise that the eyes of the blind will be opened, the ears of the deaf unstopped, the lame made to leap like deer, the tongues of the speechless loosed to sing for joy, and waters will break forth in the wilderness and streams in the desert. Verse 9 speaks of the absence of ravenous beasts along the road leading to Zion, and, according to v. 10, "everlasting joy shall be upon their heads; they shall obtain joy and gladness, and sorrow and sighing shall flee away." (See 11:6–9.)

The postexilic prophet, Zechariah, in the late sixth century, spoke in 8:4–5 of a Jerusalem at peace, a place where "old men and old women shall again sit in the streets ... each with staff in hand because of their great age. And the streets of the city shall be full of boys and girls playing in its streets."

A noble citizenry, a perfect messiah, a peaceful environment — these are the historical components of a divine kingdom. Whereas all of these are expressions of God's grace, there is, however, another side to the Old Testament witness, and that has to do with the execution of divine wrath — another form of grace for those suffering from the powers of evil — against all that is in opposition to God's plans and purposes.

This wrath comes clearly into focus in the pronouncements about the coming day of the Lord when God will defeat the powers of evil — a day which is to be not only a historical but a cosmic event.[5] Joel 2:1 and 2: "Let all the inhabitants of the land tremble, for the day of the LORD is coming, it is near — a day of darkness and gloom, a day of clouds and thick darkness." Verse 11: "The LORD utters his voice at the head of his army; how vast is his host! Numberless are those who obey his command. Truly the day of the LORD is great; terrible indeed — who can endure it?"

The kingdom of God is not merely an idea in the

head; it has to do with such historical realities as a citizenry, a king, an environment, and warfare.

Christ as the Essence of the Kingdom

The church came into existence with the conviction that in Jesus of Nazareth what had been prophetically promised was now a reality. He was the perfect citizen, the promised messiah, the new environment, and the victor over all that opposes God.

A. Perfect Citizen

Regarding citizenship Jesus was the perfectly compassionate citizen both during the days of his incarnational ministry and in his sacrificial death. "And being found in human form, he humbled himself and became obedient to the point of death—even death on a cross" (Phil. 2:7c–8). On the cross he gave himself to defeat evil, forgive sin, give life in abundance, and to reveal the love of God. In the most profound way possible, the cross reveals the divinity of Jesus, the new human being. The church recognized Jesus as the fulfillment of the suffering servant promises of Isaiah 53. In fact, it is the suffering servant about whom the Ethiopian eunuch was reading when Philip came alongside him on the Road to Gaza (See Acts 8:32–33). Philip taught him that Jesus is the fulfillment of the passage; Jesus is, as Isaiah 53:7 says, "like a lamb silent before its shearer."

In 1 Peter 2:24 reference is made to the same section of Isaiah: "He himself bore our sins in his body on the cross, so that free from sins, we might live for righteousness; by his wounds you have been healed" (cf., Isa. 53:5).

The Gospel of John speaks not only of the lamb of God who takes away the sin of the world (1:29), but also about the servant who stooped to wash the feet of his disciples (13:1-17). According to John 10:30, Jesus—this perfect citizen—was at one with God: "The Father and I are one." Hebrews 4:15b summarizes that in Jesus "we have one who in every respect has been tested as we are, yet without sin."

The composite picture of Jesus given in the New Testament is that he is indeed the new kind of citizen whose heart is tender toward God. His is the heart of flesh which Ezekiel promised as a replacement for the heart of stone; Jesus is the fulfillment of 36:27, which promised the coming of one who would be "careful to observe my ordinances."

Christ Jesus, perfect citizen of the kingdom that he was, teaches us to be citizens of the same kingdom. Matthew 5—7, the so-called Sermon on the Mount, sets forth the standards of citizenship in the kingdom. Furthermore, it is of no little significance that in the final judgment scene portrayed in Matthew 25:31-46, it is the standard of a perfectly compassionate citizen which determines who belongs on the right hand of divine acceptance and who belongs on the left hand of divine retribution. It is by giving food to the hungry, drink to the thirsty, clothes to the naked, and by visiting the imprisoned that we serve the Lord himself. On the other hand, failure to do such is failure to serve the Lord.

B. Promised Messiah

Besides being the perfect citizen, Jesus is also the promised messiah. Matthew 1 sets the stage for all that follows in the New Testament. The word "christ" is the English form of the Greek *christos*, the translation of the Hebrew word that we transliterate as messiah. Both "messiah" and "christ" mean the anointed one. Matthew begins: "The book of the genealogy of Jesus Christ, the son of David, the son of Abraham."[6] Verses 18-25 tell about his conception in Mary's womb by the Holy Spirit's miraculous work, about his being named Jesus[7]—from the Hebrew Joshua meaning "Yahweh is salvation," "for he will save his people from their sins" (v. 21), and about his being called Immanuel—God with us, a word used in Isaiah 7:14 in connection with a nationalistic hope for a new king.

In the conversation between Simon Peter and Jesus regarding Jesus' identification, Peter in Matthew 16:16

confesses, "You are the Christ, the Son of the living God" (RSV). This messianic reference to Jesus as the Christ is found throughout the New Testament in twenty-six of the twenty-seven books, the third epistle of John being the only exception. The witness of the New Testament as a whole can be summed up in the words that Andrew spoke to his brother Simon Peter in John 1:41, "We have found the Messiah." Indeed the New Testament community of faith came into existence because they were convinced that they had found the promised messiah.

Besides the explicit messianic references to Jesus as the Christ, two other evidences of his being messiah are found in the New Testament. The first evidence has to do with Jesus' relationship to David, a relationship emphasized in the synoptics. For instance, the two blind men cried out to him in Jericho, "Have mercy on us, Lord, Son of David" (see Matt. 20:29–31). Also, when Jesus rode into Jerusalem on the "donkey and the colt" (Matt. 21:7), the crowds shouted "Hosanna to the Son of David" (v. 9).

Jesus endeavored to make it clear, however, that he was more than a descendant of David. (See the confusion among the people regarding this matter in John 7:4–43.) To do so he uses Psalm 110:1, "The LORD says to my lord, 'Sit at my right hand until I make your enemies your footstool.' " In the three synoptic references to this psalm (Matt. 22:41–46, Mark 12:35–37, and Luke 20:41–44), Jesus teaches that he is more than simply a descendant of David. He does so by interpreting the psalm as follows: the first reference to the Lord, as is obviously the case, is to God, but the second, not so obvious, is to the messiah. The implied logic of Jesus' interpretive use of the psalm is as follows: How is it that David refers to the Lord God addressing the messiah whom David himself in the psalm refers to as his own lord, i.e., "my lord," if, in fact, the messiah were nothing more than David's descendant and not his lord? Jesus reasons that since even David refers to the messiah as his lord, the messiah must be more than simply David's descendant; he is David's lord. The point is that Jesus is the eternal messianic lord even of David, not merely his descendant.

The importance of the use of this psalm for messianic interpretation is found elsewhere in the New Testament. According to Acts 2:34–36, Peter declares in his Pentecost sermon that Jesus is not only a Davidic messiah but a divine messiah before whom even David bows in adoration:

> For David did not ascend into the heavens, but he himself says, The Lord said to my Lord, 'Sit at my right hand, until I make your enemies your footstool.' "
> Therefore let the entire house of Israel know with cer-

tainty that God has made him both Lord and Messiah, this Jesus whom you crucified [See also, Heb. 1:13. Cf. 1 Cor. 15:25, Heb. 10:13 and 1 Peter 3:22].

Revelation 22:16 says, "It is I, Jesus, who sent my angel to you with this testimony for the churches. I am the root and the descendant of David." In his commentary on the the Book of Revelation, Philip Hughes observes that as the root he is David's God and Creator, and as the shoot he is, in the incarnation, the promised royal deliverer, "descended from David according to the flesh" (Rom. 1:3; cf., Heb. 7:14). As both root and descendant, the incarnate Son is a theanthropic person, both truly God and truly human.[8]

Besides the explicitly Christological references found throughout the New Testament and the use of the Davidic psalm discussed above, the messianic role of Jesus is also expressed in the "son of man" phraseology picked up from Daniel 7:13, which says that "there came one like a son of man, and he came to the Ancient of Days."[9]

The son of man is a divine personage in human form who accomplishes the divine will on the earth. While traditionally the Daniel passage has been understood as referring to an individual, there are those who argue that he is "a societal person" representing "the saints of the Most High."[10] In fact, James Dunn argues that the term is "simply the appropriate symbol for Israel in contrast to Israel's savage enemies. Of this figure's individual existence or preexistence there is no suggestion."[11] Dunn discusses 1 Enoch 37–71 (known also as the Similitudes or Parables of Enoch), and 4 Ezra, two Jewish writings both of that use the son of man terminology in relation to an individual. His contention is that both are post-A.D. 70 writings that seek to generate hope among the Jewish community after the Roman destruction of Jerusalem. Given the lack of evidence that New Testament writers were aware of these Jewish documents, Dunn concludes that the individualization of the Danielic son of man in relation to Jesus is wholly new for the Christian community: "The earliest datable interpretation of Daniel's "son of man" as a particular individual is the Christian identification of "the son of man" with Jesus."[12]

Son of man references in the New Testament fall into three categories:

1) apocalyptic sayings, referring to the future coming of the son of man (e.g., Luke 12:8–10 and 17:29–30, Matt. 24:27 and 37–39);

2) references to the earthly activity of Jesus as that of the son of man (e.g., Mark 2:10–11, Matt. 8:20, 11:18f.);

3) the suffering son of man sayings (e.g., Mark 8:31, 9:31, 10:32–34, 14:21 and 41).[13]

C. New Environment for the People of God

As we have seen, then, Jesus, is held by the New Testament to be the perfect citizen of Israel as well as the promised messiah. It teaches also that he is the promised new environment for the people of God.

The Gospel of John is especially rich in imagery regarding the environment provided by Christ. According to John 6:35, he provides spiritual nourishment: "I am the bread of life. Whoever comes to me will never be hungry, and whoever believes in me will never be thirsty."

According to chapter 7, he provides us with spiritual resources spoken of as rivers of living water flowing out of the believer's heart. The setting for the events of this chapter is the festival of booths,[14] which was one of Israel's most important annual celebrations, observed in the autumn at the end of the agricultural year. Its name derived from the fact that during the Israelites' wilderness sojourn they had stayed in temporary shelters. Booths was a time for renewing the covenant relationship with the Lord and rejoicing in God's divine provisions. One of the celebrative rituals that had developed in the course of time was the bringing of water from the Pool of Siloam to the center of the city. Each day a procession of priests carried libations from the pool to the temple while the people gave praise and thanksgiving for the Lord's salvation and sustaining grace. God had taken them through the sea, had brought forth water in the desert, had led them across the Jordan River, and had provided them with water in Zion. The libation ritual reminded them of God's grace in relation to both the waters that destroy and the waters that give life. This is the context for understanding vv. 37–38:

> On the last day of the festival, the great day, while Jesus was standing there, he cried out, "Let anyone who is thirsty come to me, and let the one who believes in me drink. As the scripture has said, 'Out of the believer's heart shall flow rivers of living water.'"

Jesus is also spiritual illumination. In 8:12, he says "I am the light of the world. Whoever follows me will never walk in darkness but will have the light of life."

According to 10:9, he also provides divine salvation, for he says "I am the gate. Whoever enters by me will be saved, and will come in and go out and find pasture."

Furthermore, according to 10:28, he provides security, for he says, "I give them eternal life, and they shall never perish. No one shall snatch them out of my hand." As long as we are in Christ by faith, we are secure from the enemy. To abandon Christ is to abandon our security.

Other books of the New Testament refer to this new

spiritual environment in other ways. According to Luke 4:16–17, Jesus brings in the "jubilee"[15] when wrongs are made right, suffering is alleviated, and abnormality is rectified. After reading promises from Isaiah regarding the messianic jubilee, Jesus says "Today this scripture has been fulfilled in your hearing" (v. 21). Our Lord provides in his person the new jubilee environment.

Paul's treatment of the new environment is our being in Christ. Second Corinthians 5:17: "So if anyone is in Christ, there is a new creation: everything old has passed away; see, everything has become new!" In fact, the whole book of Ephesians is a treatise on the newness that belongs to those who are in Christ. This new environment includes "every spiritual blessing in the heavenly places" (1:3), adoption as God's children (vv. 4–5), redemption, and forgiveness (v. 7). It includes the knowledge of the mystery of the divine will (v. 9), the joy of a divine inheritance (v. 11) and the assurance of being "marked with the seal of the promised Holy Spirit" (v. 13). It includes the knowledge of hope and of "the immeasurable greatness of his power" (vv. 18–19), the blessedness of a reconciled humanity (2:14–16) and ready access to the Father (v. 18). It includes membership in the household of God (v. 19), participation in the holy temple (vv. 21–22), living both as heirs of God (3:6) and as beneficiaries of "the power at work within us" which "is able to accomplish abundantly far more than all we can ask or imagine" (v. 20). It includes personalized grace (4:7–13), the privilege of being children of light (5:8), and the confidence that comes from having the whole armor of God available to us (6:11–17). All of this is the new environment that we have by virtue of being in Christ by faith.

The Book of Hebrews has yet another way of viewing this new environment. It is one of a wholly new religious reality. As 9:11–12 indicates, in Christ we have a perfect temple, a perfect high priest, and a perfect sacrifice:

> But when Christ came as a high priest of the good things that have come, then through the greater and perfect tent (not made with hands, that is, not of this creation), he entered once for all into the Holy Place, not with the blood of goats and calves, but with his own blood, thus obtaining eternal redemption.

Concerning this new religious environment, 12:22–24 declares:

> But you have come to Mount Zion and to the city of the living God, the heavenly Jerusalem, and to innumerable angels in festal gathering, and to the assembly of the firstborn who are enrolled in heaven, and to God the judge of all, and to the spirits of the righteous made per-

fect, and to Jesus, the mediator of a new covenant, and to the sprinkled blood that speaks a better word than the blood of Abel.

D. Victor Over Evil

In addition to being the perfect citizen, the promised messiah and the new environment, Jesus is also the victor over all that opposes God (see the section headed "Christ's Universalized Work" in chap. 6). During his incarnational ministry, he healed the sick, opened blinded eyes, made the lame to walk, and raised the dead. He cast out demons and pronounced judgment on evil both by word (e.g., the woes on the scribes and Pharisees in Matt. 23) and by action (e.g., the cleansing of the temple in Matt. 21:12–14, Mark 11:15–19, Luke 19:45–46 and John 2:13–17). His victory over the powers of evil was finalized on the cross, for his enemies could not defeat his mission to redeem us from sin. As John 1:29 puts it, he is the lamb of God who takes away the sin of the world.

In the resurrection, his victory was historically sealed, for as the risen Lord, his earthly destiny could no longer in any way whatsoever be touched by human schemes and plots. Being alive on the other side of death, he was present in ways that defied earthly, historical categories.

In an extensive discussion of the importance of the

incarnational life of Jesus in the divine work of atonement, Thomas Finger concludes:

> The life of Jesus Christ cannot be separated from his
> death. Jesus did not die from accident, illness, or old
> age. He died because of the way he lived. Because Jesus,
> guided by the Spirit, lived in uncompromising fidelity
> to God his Father and to his kingdom and because the
> dawning of that kingdom aroused fierce opposition
> from the beginning, Jesus' ministry was characterized
> by conflict throughout. It was this escalating opposi-
> tion—religious, political, and, at bottom, demonic—
> which eventually put him to death. Systematic theolo-
> gy, therefore cannot separate the reasons why Jesus
> died from the reasons why he lived, or the meaning of
> his death from the meaning of his life.[16]

Paul rejoiced in this divine victory accomplished not
only in Christ's incarnational life and sacrificial death,
but also in his resurrection. Ephesians 1:20–23 says that

> God put this power to work in Christ when he raised
> him from the dead and seated him at his right hand in
> the heavenly places, far above all rule and authority and
> power and dominion, and above every name that is
> named, not only in this age but also in the age to come.
> And he has put all things under his feet and has made
> him the head over all things for the church, which is his
> body, the fullness of him who fills all in all.[17]

The Church as the Community of the Kingdom

In that the church is the community of Jesus Christ, it is thereby the community of the kingdom. Even though the church, while being the body of Christ, is not Christ, likewise, though it is the community of the kingdom, it is not synonymous with the kingdom.

Whereas the kingdom comes from God (e.g., "Your kingdom come," Matt. 6:10; Luke 11:2), the church is built by Jesus (e.g., "I will build my church," Matt. 16:18). Whereas the kingdom is a qualitative reality (e.g., "righteousness and peace and joy in the Holy Spirit," Rom. 14:17), the church is a quantitative reality (e.g., "Go therefore and make disciples of all nations," Matt. 28:19). Whereas the kingdom is the reign and rule of God alone, free of all human frailties (e.g., "My kingdom is not from this world," John 18:36), the church is called to submit to his reign and rule but is not free of the frailties of human participation (e.g., "built upon the foundation of the [very human!] apostles and prophets," Eph. 2:20). Whereas the kingdom grows only by grace and not at all by human strategy (e.g., "No one can see the kingdom of God without being born from above," John 3:3), the church grows by grace together with human strategy (e.g., "You will be my witnesses in Jerusalem, in all Judea and Samaria, and to the ends of the earth," Acts 1:8). Whereas the kingdom will be brought to consummation at the end of the age (e.g., "Then comes the end, when he hands over the kingdom to God the Father, after he has destroyed every ruler and every authority and power," 1 Cor. 15:24), the church will be gathered for the consummation of the kingdom (e.g., "We who are alive, who are left, will be caught up in the clouds together with them to meet the Lord in the air; and so we will be with the Lord forever," 1 Thess. 4:17).

The church as the community of the kingdom prays for the coming of the kingdom, grows in the qualities of the kingdom, trusts in the Lord of the kingdom, rejoices in the spread of the kingdom and looks forward to the consummation of the kingdom.[18]

As the community of the kingdom, the church is both herald and sign of the kingdom. According to Luke 9:1–2,

> Jesus called the twelve together and gave them power and authority over all demons and to cure diseases, and he sent them out to proclaim the kingdom of God and to heal.

Just as its Lord proclaimed the good news of the kingdom (Matt. 4:23; 9:35; Mark 1:14; Luke 4:43), so the church is called to do the same. In Matthew 24:14, Jesus says, "And this good news of the kingdom will be proclaimed throughout the world, as a testimony to all the nations; and then the end will come." (See also Luke 9:60; Acts 8:12; 20:25; 28:31.)

Just as their Lord was a sign of the reign of God, even so his church is such a sign. According to Acts, the church is empowered by the Spirit to be not only heralds of the kingdom (1:8), but also signs of it as they live in a worthy manner (2:47), bring healing to the sick, minister to the distressed (e.g., 3:1–10), and experience divine guidance and counsel as people who are committed to the reign of God (e.g., 6:1–6).

Individual Believers as Agents of the Kingdom

The Bible is about persons both as a people and as individuals. Peoplehood enhances individuality and individuality is the means by which peoplehood is expressed. The basis for saying this is Christological. Jesus Christ was who he was, not only by virtue of his eternal nature but also by his identification with the Hebrew people. The significance of the genealogies in Matthew 1 and Luke 3 is that they show that Jesus had a peoplehood identity. The fact that the church continued using the Hebrew scriptures as its own is witness to the importance of Jesus' identity as a Jew. Marcion (a shipbuilder from Asia Minor who went to Rome about 139) developed a canon of scripture consisting only of Luke and ten Pauline epistles (omitting the pastoral letters to Timothy and Titus). While his theological concern had to do primarily with the nature of God (he held that the God of Jesus Christ was not the same as the God of law and wrath whom he found in the Old Testament), the practical result was that he tried to interpret Christ apart from the peoplehood of which he was a member. The church rejected Marcion's ideas and affirmed more directly than ever before that the Hebrew scriptures are a necessary part of the story of Christian faith.

While Jesus is unique in God's economy, he is not rightly understood apart from the people of God. His peoplehood enhanced his individuality, and his individuality was the means by which the peoplehood of Israel was uniquely expressed.

Taking Jesus as the paradigm, it follows in our case also that kingdom individuals exist in relation to the communal kingdom of which they are a part, but also that the expression of the kingdom is always personal. The story of the New Testament is of individuals such as Mary the mother of Jesus, Peter the fisherman, Mary Magdalene, John the beloved, Mary and Martha of Bethany, Stephen the martyr, Lydia of Thyatira, Paul the apostle, and Priscilla and Aquila the clarifiers of the gospel to Apollos. It is the story of individualized expressions of the communal kingdom. Writing to the

Corinthian church in its struggle over the relationship between individuality and corporateness, Paul says: "To each is given the manifestation of the Spirit for the common good" (1 Cor. 12:7). To the Romans, he wrote in 12:5–6: "So we, who are many, are one body in Christ, and individually we are members one of another. We have gifts that differ according to the grace given to us."

In the account of Pentecost, we see the same emphasis on both corporateness and individuality. Whereas the wind filled the entire house where the believers were gathered as a corporate body, the tongues as of fire rested on each of them individually (Acts 2:1–4).

Acts 3 tells about Peter and John going up to the temple at the hour of prayer. When a lame man asked for alms, Peter, instead of giving alms, spoke the word of divine healing, "and immediately his feet and ankles were made strong" (v. 7). Verse 8: "Jumping up, he stood and began to walk, and he entered the temple with them, walking and leaping and praising God." The reign and rule of God manifested that day had taken place through the ministry of individual believers. Our conclusion is that each believer is to become in human history a personalized expression of the presence of the kingdom.

The Return of Christ as the Ushering in of the Consumation of the Kingdom

The synoptics speak of the consummation of the kingdom in parallel passages: Matthew 24,[19] Mark 13,[20] and Luke 21.[21] At the center of the consummation is the public *parousia* of the son of man. Matthew 24:27 says: "For as the lightning comes from the east and flashes as far as the west, so will be the coming [*parousia*] of the Son of Man." The point is not that he will come from the east but that his coming will be in the public realm of experience, as lightning is. This is in contrast with the secretiveness that is rejected in the verse just preceding (i.e., he will not come in the desolation of the wilderness nor in the privacy of an inner room).

The publicness of the Lord's *parousia* is spoken of also in vv. 30–31:

> Then the sign of the Son of Man will appear in heaven, and then all the tribes of the earth will mourn, and they will see 'the Son of Man coming on the clouds of heaven' with power and great glory. And he will send out his angels with a loud trumpet call, and they will gather his elect from the four winds, from one end of heaven to the other [See also 1 Cor. 15:52, 1 Thess. 4:16 and Rev. 1:7].

His *parousia* is not restricted to the spiritually fortunate but is in public view for all to see regardless of their spiritual status. The New Testament knows nothing whatsoever about a secret *parousia* for the elect; it knows nothing about two comings of the Lord, one for the spiritually ready and the other at the cataclysmic end of the age. At the one and only *parousia* of the Lord, all people on the face of the earth, as well as all people who have ever lived, will recognize what is happening, and the faithful, both those who have already died and those who are still alive, will be caught up into the glorified presence of their Lord (1 Thess. 4:13–17).

Associated with this one and only public *parousia* is the cataclysmic end of the world order as we know it. Using language reminiscent of day of the Lord passages in Isaiah 13:10, 34:4, Ezekiel 32:7, Joel 2:10–11 and Zephaniah 1:15–16, Jesus says in Matthew 24:29: "Immediately after the suffering of those days the sun will be darkened, and the moon will not give its light; the stars will fall from heaven, and the powers of heaven will be shaken."[22] (See also 1 Thess. 5:1–3; 2 Thess. 2:8; 2 Peter 3:7, 10, 12; Rev. 6:12–17; 9:1-6; and 16.)

Matthew is the only one of the synoptics that has *eutheōs*, i.e., immediately, v. 29. (Mark 13:24 has "But in those days, after that suffering." Cf., Luke 21:25–28.) Rather than the suffering referring to the coming of the Son of Man mentioned in the preceding verse, it is better to see it as a reference to the great suffering spoken of in v. 21 ("such as has not been from the beginning of the world until now, no, and never will be"). In other words, immediately after that suffering the cataclysmic end will come. What is that unique suffering?

Given the story line of Matthew's account, it is logical to hold that it is the anguish of those committed to the temple-centered religious system. Chapter 23 is a scathing pronouncement of divine judgment on Jewish religiosity, ending with Jesus saying in v. 37, "Jerusalem, Jerusalem, the city that kills the prophets and stones those who are sent to it!" and again in v. 38, "See, your house is left to you, desolate."

Indeed, not only did Jesus himself depart from the temple for the last time (which Burnett argues was the departure of the Shekinah[23]), but his crucifixion was accompanied by the curtain of the temple, separating the Holy Place from the inner sanctum of the Holy of Holies, being torn in two, from top to bottom (Matt. 17:51). The final departure of Jesus from the temple was God's judgment in the person of our Lord; the rending of the temple curtain was God's judgment in the realm of religious life; the destruction of the temple in A.D. 70 was God's judgment in the public sphere.

Temple religion has not been reinstituted since A.D. 70. From Matthew's perspective, the end of temple-centered religion is the unique suffering spoken of in v. 21.

It is the political anguish of those who have lost their spiritual, religious, and cultural center. In fact, the emotional attachment to the remains of the temple—the so-called Wailing Wall, Jewish control of which was gained in the 1967 War—is a matter of public record. Its designation as the Wailing Wall grows out of the fact that for centuries those committed to the reestablishment of temple religion have flocked to it on the anniversary of the destruction of the temple to bemoan their national and religious plight.

If the unique suffering spoken of in v. 21 is indeed the ongoing absence of temple-centered religion, then the "immediately," *eutheōs* of v. 29 can be understood chronologically in relation to this ongoing period of spiritual and religious anguish experienced by those who long for the reestablishment of temple religion. This anguish will continue until Christ returns. Therefore, "immediately after the suffering of those days," the cataclysmic end will come when the Lord returns.

The *parousia* will establish in the public arena that which the people of faith already know, namely, that Jesus is Lord. Philippians 2:9–11 sets forth the divine purpose when it says:

> Therefore God also highly exalted him [Christ] and
> gave him the name that is above every name, so that at

the name of Jesus every knee should bend, in heaven and on earth and under the earth, and every tongue confess that Jesus Christ is Lord, to the glory of God the Father.

The consummation of this world order at the time of the *parousia* will manifest to the whole world not only the lordship of Jesus Christ but also the fact that Satan is a defeated foe. This is the theme of the Book of Revelation. Written for a church under persecution, the natural question, of course, would be something like this: Is Jesus really Lord, and is Satan really a defeated foe? The Apocalypse answers both questions with a confident yes. In 20:4–6 the answer to the first question is: Yes, Jesus is Lord during this prolonged time (symbolically spoken of as a thousand years) before the *parousia*. Verses 7–10 answer the second question: Yes, even though the evidence seems to point in the opposite direction, Satan and his cohorts are defeated foes, a fact to be demonstrated in the public domain at the end of the age:

> When the thousand years are ended, Satan will be released from his prison and will come out to deceive the nations at the four corners of the earth, Gog and Magog,[24] in order to gather them for battle; they are as numerous as the sands of the sea. They marched up over the breadth of the earth and surrounded the camp of the saints and the beloved city. And fire came down

from heaven and consumed them. And the devil who had deceived them was thrown into the lake of fire and sulfur, where the beast and the false prophet were, and they will be tormented day and night forever and ever.

We know what the binding of Satan spoken of in v. 7 is by contrasting it with what he does at the time of his short release: he gathers together all the enemies of the people of God for the purpose of surrounding and destroying God's people. During this short time, Satan finally gets his act together. The whole antagonistic army of evil is united in its supreme purpose, namely, to obliterate the people of God. Just as they surround the "camp of the saints and the beloved city" divine judgment is visited on them: "fire came down from heaven and consumed them."

The binding of Satan during the present period, then, is God's restriction that keeps him from being able to unite all the forces of evil for the purpose of obliterating the church, as perhaps the persecuted saints of the Apocalypse thought he would. The defeat of Satan that was secured in the incarnation, finalized in the crucifixion, vivified for believers in the resurrection, experientialized in the church by the power of the Holy Spirit, will be publicized for the whole human family at the *parousia*. Referring to the resurrection of the dead that will take place at that time, 1 Corinthians 15:24 says,

"Then comes the end, when he hands over the kingdom to God the Father, after he has destroyed every ruler and every authority and power."

Jesus, as the Lord of the consummation of this world order, makes cosmic display of the kingdom of God, which is grandly described in Revelation 21 – 22:7 as

• "a new heaven and a new earth" (21:1),

• "the holy city, the new Jerusalem, coming down out of heaven from God, prepared as a bride adorned for her husband" (v. 2),

• existence where "mourning and crying and pain will be no more" (v. 4),

• a place where "the Lord God the Almighty and the Lamb" will be the temple and where the glory of God will be its light and its lamp the Lamb (vv. 22–23),

• a reality so resplendent that "the nations will walk by its light" (v. 24),

• a habitation with perpetually open gates (v. 25),

• a holy environment for the saints of the Most High (v. 27), and

• a garden with "the river of the water of life" flowing through the middle of the city's street, and on either side of the river "the tree of life with its twelve kinds of fruit, producing its fruit each month; and the leaves of the tree are for the healing of the nations" (22:1–2).

The kingdom in consummation will be an eternal

sanctuary where the people of the Lamb will worship their Lord face to face and reign with him forever and ever (vv. 3–5).

Notes

1. See Frederick Dale Bruner, *The Christbook: A Historical/TheologicalCommentary, Matthew 1 – 12* (Waco: Word, 1987) and *The Churchbook, Matthew 13 – 28* (Dallas: Word, 1990).

2. Philip Edgcumbe Hughes, *The Book of the Revelation: A Commentary* (Leicester, England: InterVarsity; Grand Rapids: Eerdmans, 1990), p. 73f.

3. Ibid., p. 74.

4. Gerhard Von Rad, *Old Testament Theology, Vol. II: The Theology of Israel's Prophetic Traditions,* trans. D. M. G. Stalker (New York: Harper and Row, 1965), p. 260.

5. See Ibid., pp. 119–125. In his treatment of "The Day of Jahweh," the following passages are discussed: Amos 5:18–20; Isa. 2:9ff.; 13; 34; Ezek. 7; 30:1ff.; Jer. 46:3–12; Joel 2:1–11; Zeph. 1:7–18.

6. Revised Standard Version. The New Revised Standard Version renders *Christos* as Messiah.

7. The English word "Jesus" goes back to the Latin *Iesus* which is a transliteration of the Greek word used to translate the Hebrew "Joshua."

8. Hughes, op. cit., p. 239.

9. Revised Standard Version. The New Revised Standard Version translates v. 13: "I saw one *like a human being* coming with the clouds of heaven. And he came to the Ancient One and was presented before him" (emphasis mine). I use the RSV rendering in order to maintain consistency with the son of man usage in the New Testament.

10. Archibald M. Hunter, *The Work and Words of Jesus* (Philadelphia: Westminster, 1950), p. 86.

11. James D. G. Dunn, *Christology in the Making* (Philadelphia: Westminster,1980), p. 75.

12. Ibid., p. 96.

13. This is Heinz Eduard Todt's classification used in an article by Hendrikus Boers, "Where Christology Is Real: A Survey of Recent Research on New Testament Christology," *Interpretation*, XXVI, 3 (July 1972), 300.

14. Also called tabernacles; referred to as "the festival of harvest" in Exod. 23:16, "the festival of the LORD" in Lev. 23:39 and simply as "the festival" in 1 Kings 8:2.

15. See Lev. 25. The jubilee was the final year in a cycle of fifty years, i.e., seven "weeks" of seven years each plus the fiftieth, which was the jubilee, a word deriving from the Hebrew word for the ram's horn used to announce great celebrations.

16. Thomas N. Finger, *Christian Theology: An Eschatological Approach*, Vol. I. (Nashville: Thomas Nelson, 1985), p. 303. See especially chaps. 15–17 for

Finger's focus on the life and death of Jesus.

17. See Herman Ridderbos, *Paul: An Outline of His Theology,* trans. John Richard De Witt (Grand Rapids: Eerdmans, 1975), pp. 387–392. In reference to Ephesians and Colossians, he writes: "On the one hand the victory of Christ over the powers is nowhere proclaimed more plainly and more triumphantly than here. God has disarmed them in Christ, made a public example of them, and harnessed them to his triumphal chariot (Col. 2:15; cf. Eph. 1:20ff.; 4:8ff.). Through him God has reconciled, pacified, subjected all things to himself ... (Col. 1:20). On the other hand it continues to hold for the church as well that it has to wage war not against flesh and blood, but against the principalities, the powers, the world rulers of this darkness, the evil spirits in the heavenly places (Eph. 6:12). The powers, however much already vanquished in Christ, have not yet become harmless. But in order to be able to contend against them suitably, the church has received an armor from God, so richly furnished that it is able to continue to stand (Eph. 6:13ff.)" p. 392.

18. See Howard A. Snider, *A Kingdom Manifesto: Calling the Church to Live under God's Reign* (Downers Grove: InterVarsity, 1985). "Biblically, the church is by definition a community, not an institution. In fact, it is a countercultural community, the embryonic community of the kingdom, distinct from surrounding society at every point where that society is in bondage to the

'basic principles of this world' (Col. 2:8, 20)" p. 115.

19. See Bruner, *Churchbook*, pp. 838–885; Fred W. Burnett, *The Testament of Jesus-Sophia: A Redaction-Critical Study of the Eschatological Discourse in Matthew* (Washington: University Press of America, 1979); William Hendriksen, *New Testament Commentary: Exposition of the Gospel According to Matthew* (Grand Rapids: Baker, 1973), pp. 843–874; R. C. H. Lenski, *The Interpretation of St. Matthew's Gospel* (Columbus: Wartburg, 1951), pp. 927–960.

20. See Ralph Earle, *The Gospel According to Mark* (Grand Rapids: Zondervan,1957), pp. 153–161; Hendriksen, *Mark* (1975), pp. 511–546; Lenski, *St. Mark's Gospel* (1956), pp. 560–595.

21. See Hendriksen, *Luke* (1978), pp.919–950; Lenski, *St. Luke's Gospel* (Minneapolis: Augsburg, 1964), pp. 1005–1032; Ray Summers, *Commentary on Luke* (Waco: Word, 1974), pp. 251–267.

22. For a discussion of cosmic shaking, see Hughes, op. cit., pp. 90-92.

23. Burnett, op. cit, pp. 63–81, 166f.

24. Ezekiel 38 and 39 speaks of Gog of Magog, Gog being a demonic prince of a cruel northern nation called Magog. The prince and his armies threaten the Lord's people. John speaks of Gog and Magog. In keeping with the symbolic nature of the book, he no doubt uses Gog to refer to demonic rulers and Magog to refer to non-believers who actively oppose the church.

6

The Person and Work of Christ Jesus

In the previous chapter, Jesus was discussed as the essence of the kingdom of God. Christology is inadequate apart from studies in the kingdom, and studies in the kingdom are distorted apart from the kingdom's Christological center. With that agenda already addressed, we now turn to a summary of Jesus' incarnational ministry and to additional Christological and soteriological considerations. Mark 1:39 says, "And he [Jesus] went throughout Galilee, proclaiming the message in their synagogues and *casting out demons*" (emphasis mine here and following). The parallel passage in Matthew 4:23 reads: "Jesus went throughout Galilee, *teaching* in their synagogues and *proclaiming the good news of the kingdom* and *curing every disease and every sickness* among the people." (See also Luke 4:44.)

Mark 6:6b says, "Then he went about the villages teaching." The parallel in Matthew reads: "Then Jesus went about all the cities and villages, teaching in their synagogues, and proclaiming the good news of the kingdom, and curing every disease and every sickness" (9:35). Jesus' ministry was that of teacher, preacher, exorcist and healer. He taught a way of life, preached the good news of the kingdom, cast out demons, and healed the sick and diseased.

Christ's Universalized Work

While the descriptive statements quoted above are important summaries of our Lord's ministry while he walked this earth, they do not tell the whole story. The summit of the Gospels is his crucifixion, resurrection, ascension, and session (where he sits, intercedes, and reigns) "at the right hand of Power" (Matt. 26:64), without which we would know nothing about the Palestinian ministry of Jesus of Nazareth. It was this final drama during the incarnation that catapulted Jesus' Palestinian disciples into becoming the first fruits of the universal church of Christ. This decisive, historical, multidimensional occurrence (i.e., crucifixion, resurrection, ascension, and session) precipitated the church's later confessions about the universal significance of the person and work of Jesus.

The church confessed that Jesus is the eternal Word, not merely a teacher with a word: "The Word became flesh and lived among us" (John 1:14). Jesus, the teacher of the word, is the Word.

The church confessed that Jesus is the promised messiah of the kingdom, not simply one who preached about it. They remembered that he had said, "If it is by the Spirit of God that I cast out demons, then the kingdom of God has come to you" (Matt. 12:28). Jesus, the preacher about the kingdom life, is the very essence of this new life.

Furthermore, the church confessed that Jesus is himself the once and for all victor over the prince of darkness, and not simply another exorcist of demons. When according to Luke 10:17, the seventy who had been sent forth by Jesus both to cure the sick and to tell them that "the kingdom of God has come near to you" (v. 9), they returned with joy, saying, "Lord, in your name even the demons submit to us!" Verse 18 gives our Lord's reply: "I watched Satan fall from heaven like a flash of lightning." The life of Jesus meant the demise of Satan. Jesus, the exorcist of demons, is the victor over no less than the prince of the demons.

Finally, the church confessed that Jesus is the eternal Savior. He is the one who heals what is wrong at the center both of our being and of world history. He is not merely another healer of physical infirmities, but the

Savior who takes away the sin of the world.

It is this saving work of the eternal Word, the promised messiah, the once and for all victor to which we now turn. The Greek word *sōtēria* means deliverance, salvation, preservation, and safety, and it is used in five interconnected ways in relation to God's work in Christ:

1) It refers to that which is central to the whole course of God's work in history. We see this in Matthew 1:21 where the angel of the Lord says to Joseph: "She [Mary] will bear a son, and you are to name him Jesus [in Hebrew it was *Yehoshuah* (i.e., Joshua) meaning "Yahweh is salvation"], for he will *save* his people from their sins" [my emphasis here and following indicates that a form of *sōtēria* is used in the Greek text]. Also, in Revelation 7:10 the great multitude of the redeemed cry out, "*Salvation* belongs to our God who is seated on the throne, and to the Lamb [Jesus Christ]!"

2) It refers to the whole life of Christ, as, for example, in Hebrews 5:9, which refers to Jesus Christ as "the source of eternal *salvation* for all who obey him." (See also Luke 19:9.)

3) The word is used in reference to the immediate result of believing in Jesus Christ. Romans 10:10 says that "one confesses with the mouth and so is *saved*."

4) *Sōtēria* also refers to our working out the ramifications of God's grace in our lives as believers. Paul in Philippians 2:12 says to "work out your own *salvation* with fear and trembling," and 1 Peter 1:9 refers to believers as "receiving the outcome of your faith, the *salvation* of your souls."

5) It refers to the future deliverance and safekeeping of believers at the end of the age when the Lord returns. We see this is 1 Peter 1:5 in its reference to those "who are being protected by the power of God through faith for a *salvation* ready to be revealed in the last time."

Three Scriptural Themes Regarding Christ's Atoning Work

The New Testament has *three major themes* regarding the atoning work of Christ.

Theme 1. The first theme is the death of Christ as the objective, sacrificial offering that God has made on our behalf. Whereas transgression against human life requires the sacrifice of human life (e.g.,"life for life, eye for eye, tooth for tooth, hand for hand, foot for foot, burn for burn, wound for wound, stripe for stripe," as in Lev. 21:24–25), sin against God, being transgression against the Creator of life, requires something more than human life.

The premise of the New Testament is that only divine life can make sufficient atonement for transgression against God. Since, however, it is we who need to make the sacrifice, but only God whose life is sufficient as a sacrifice, we find ourselves in a hopeless predicament.

The gospel, however, is that God through Christ addressed this human dilemma in the incarnational work of Jesus. According to Hebrews, Jesus was the great high priest who offered not the sacrifice of animals, but the sacrifice of himself. "Therefore, he [Christ] had to become like his brothers and sisters in every respect, so that he might be a merciful and faithful high priest in the service of God, and make a sacrifice of atonement for the sins of the people" (2:17). That Jesus himself is the sacrifice is made clear in 9:26: "He [Christ] has appeared once for all at the end of the age to remove sin by the sacrifice of himself." And again in 10:10: "And it is by God's will that we have been sanctified through the offering of the body of Jesus Christ once for all." Therefore, the one making the offering was a fully human person but what he sacrificed was a fully divine life. The theandric Jesus (he was both God and man) did for us what we need to do for ourselves, but cannot. This one and only God-man was our substitute — he, the fully human man offered a fully divine life for our salvation.

First Peter 2:24 says that Christ himself "bore our sins in his body on the cross, so that, from sins, we might live for righteousness; by his wounds you have been healed." Paul in Romans 7:24–25 asks, "Who will rescue me from this body of death?" and answers, "Thanks be to God through Jesus Christ our Lord." (See also Rom. 3:21-26, esp. 24-25.) This substitutionary theme was developed most notably by Anselm (1033-1109), author of *Cur Deus Homo?* ("Why the God-Man?").

Theme 2. The second great theme in the New Testament regarding Christ's atoning work is that of Jesus' sacrificial love that wins us to God. He is the perfect exemplar of the way we are to live, and indeed, his life and death inspire us to faith, love, and service. In Philippians 2:5, Paul says: "Let this same mind be in you that was in Christ Jesus." The mind of Christ is that of one who, according to v. 8, "humbled himself and became obedient to the point of death—even death on a cross."

The example of Jesus is, of course, the salvation theme of the four Gospels. In each, major attention is given to Jesus' sacrificial death for our salvation. He wins us to God through his love both for God and for us. According to the synoptics, to be saved is to take up the cross and follow him (Matt. 10:38; 16:24; Mark 8:34-38; Luke 9:23-26; 14:27), or, as John puts it, it is to be drawn to the crucified Lord ("And I, when I am lifted up from the earth, will draw all people to myself" 12:32).

Hebrews 12:1–3 sets forth the same theme of Christ as exemplar:

> Therefore, since we are surrounded by so great a cloud of witnesses, let us also lay aside every weight and the sin that clings so closely, and let us run with perseverance the race that is set before us looking to Jesus the pioneer and perfecter of our faith, who for the sake of the joy that was set before him endured the cross, disregarding its shame, and has taken his seat at the right hand of the throne of God. Consider him who endured such hostility against himself from sinners, so that you may not grow weary or lose heart.

The name most commonly associated with this subjective, moral influence emphasis is that of Abelard (1079–1142). His atonement theory, set forth primarily in his commentary on Romans, particularly in relation to 3:22ff., is that the demonstration of Christ's love on the cross is the power that reconcilingly wins us to God.

Theme 3. The third great theme regarding Christ's saving work is that of Jesus as the victor over Satan. Because of our Lord's incarnational work, we are set free from the powers of spiritual darkness.

The defeat of Satan is spoken of in John 12:31 where Jesus says, "Now is the judgment of this world; now the ruler of this world will be driven out." The same theme is blown large in Revelation, which from beginning to end is an apocalyptic festival of Christ's victory over Satan. Revelation 12:9: "The great dragon was thrown down, that ancient serpent, who is called the Devil and Satan, the deceiver of the whole world—he was thrown down to the earth, and his angels were thrown down with him." Another graphic passage is 20:2–3:

> He seized the dragon, that ancient serpent, who is the Devil and Satan, and bound him for a thousand years, and threw him into the pit, and locked and sealed it over him, so that he would deceive the nations no more, until the thousand years were ended.

Then, according to v. 10, after his short period of release, "the devil was thrown into the lake of fire and sulphur" and "will be tormented day and night forever and ever."

One sees this theme not only in the Gospels and in the Apocalypse, as indicated above, but also in Paul's theological discourses. Colossians 2:15 says that God through Christ "disarmed the rulers and authorities and made a public example of them, triumphing over them in it [the cross]."

The writer of Hebrews in 2:14 refers to Christ who "through death ... might destroy the one who has the power of death, that is, the devil, and free those who all their lives were held in slavery by the fear of death."

Earlier this century, Bishop Gustaf Aulén of Sweden wrote a landmark treatise on the saving work of Christ titled *Christus Victor* (1931) in which he argued that the classical view of the atonement is Christ's victory over the powers of Satan.[1]

These three atonement themes find expression in the hymnody of the church. For instance, in the gospel song tradition, "Jesus Paid It All" expresses the objective, substitutionary atonement theme:

> Jesus paid it all,
> All to Him I owe;
> Sin had left a crimson stain–
> He washed it white as snow.[2]

"The Old Rugged Cross" expresses the subjective, moral influence theme:

O that old rugged cross, so despised by the world,
Has a wondrous attraction for me;
For the dear Lamb of God left His glory above
To bear it to dark Calvary.

So I'll cherish the old rugged cross,
'Til my trophies at last I lay down;
I will cling to the old rugged cross,
And exchange it some day for a crown.[3]

"There's Power in the Blood" expresses the *christus victor* theme:

Would you be free from your burden of sin?
There's pow'r in the blood, pow'r in the blood;
Would you o'er evil a victory win?
There's wonderful pow'r in the blood....
There is ... wonder-working pow'r
In the precious blood of the Lamb.[4]

The Church's Ongoing Conversation about Jesus

The church did not quit thinking about Jesus' person and work at the end of the first century. It is important for us at this juncture in history to be informed by that ongoing conversation, much of which was and is stimulated by philosophical encroachments from outside and aberrational interpretations from within. Since proponents of each of the differing Christological positions quote the New Testament, such conversations (or arguments as the case may be) require more than mere repetition of New Testament passages. Fruitful conversation requires extended discussions. Consequently, over the centuries, an enormous mass of literature has emerged (see For Further Consideration at the end of this chapter).[5] Studying this literature makes us less likely to make the mistake of thinking that contemporary issues have never before been considered.

The fact of the matter is that most contemporary aberrations about Christ are not new at all. From the beginning of the church's history, it has been called on to defend and explain its understanding of the apostolic view of Christ.

Let's consider three modern examples of aberrations that are also ancient: (1) the Unitarian aberrational view that Jesus Christ was nothing more than a good man endued with divine power;[6] (2) the Mormon aberrational view that Jesus Christ is one of three Gods; and (3) the Jehovah's Witnesses' aberrational view that Jesus Christ is a second level divinity created by the eternal God through whom the eternal God worked for our salvation (for the last two see further discussion and references in chapter 8, "The Trinitarian God"). All three of these aberrational views are also found in the church's early history.

Unitarian Christology is somewhat akin to the Ebionite approach (late first century), which held that God chose a very good man named Jesus for a special mission in the world. Mormon Christology is a polytheistic view rejected both by the monotheism of the Bible and by the church's trinitarian explication of this monotheism. Jehovah's Witnesses Christology is ancient Arianism revisited. Arius (ca. 256–336) argued that Christ was not coeternal with the Father. To be sure, he, having been created prior to the creation of the world, was the one through whom the eternal God created the world and redeemed it; even so Christ was still merely the first creature of God and therefore Arius concluded that there was a point in God's eternity when Christ was not.

The first two ancient aberrations were primarily threats from outside the mainstream of Christianity; the third, however, was a threat from within. Consequently, Arianism was the focus of the church's intellectual energies for the greater part of the fourth century. It was denounced at the ecumenical council of Nicea (325) and again, in expanded form, at Constantinople (381). This aberration was addressed in the second article of the Niceno-Constantinopolitan (Nicene, for short) Creed:

> [I believe] in one Lord Jesus Christ, the only begotten Son of God, begotten of His Father before all worlds, God of God, Light of Light, very God of very God, begotten, not made, *being of one substance [homoousios] with the Father*, by Whom all things were made. (Emphasis added.)[7]

The words that I have emphasized above were central in the controversy between the Arians and those influenced by Athanasius (ca. 297–373). The Arians, like modern Jehovah's Witnesses, maintained that the Son of God is not very God of very God. Nicea, to the contrary, asserted that he is. The key Greek word in the ancient controversy was *homoousios,* meaning same substance. This is the word that followers of Athanasius used in their arguments against Arius who held that Christ is merely of similar substance, that is, *homoeousios,* with the Father.

The problem that Athanasius saw with the Arian position was that if they were right, the incarnation would not be the incarnation of eternal Godhead but of secondary divinity; consequently, our salvation would not have been accomplished by the eternal God but by secondary divinity. The church, in the course of time, said *no* to Arianism and affirmed its faith that Christ is deity of the first order.

We need to be informed by the church's long conversation regarding the person and work of Christ for the sake of avoiding aberrations that have been already addressed. We need also to pay attention to the whole New Testament as we seek to clarify our Christology. We have the whole New Testament available to us, something the New Testament writers did not have since it was still in process of coming into existence. Allowing the whole New Testament to speak to us helps us to see the variety of ways the person and work of Christ Jesus is presented. For instance, John's *Logos* Christology, the synoptic's Christology of prophetic fulfillment, and Paul's *Imago Dei* (image of God) Christology differ very much from each other. John's primary focus is on the incarnational Christ, the synoptics' (Matthew, Mark and Luke) focus is on the historical Christ, and Paul's is on the eternal Christ. This is not to say that one precludes or excludes the other, but that the central focus is different in each case.

Consequently, it is left up to us to sort out how all this hangs together conceptually. Church conversations in the early centuries, such as the ecumenical councils of Nicea and Constantinople, made a unified conceptual statement about Jesus Christ in relation to the Father. The fourth council at Chalcedon in 451 dealt with the two natures of Christ himself, declaring that he was both fully human and fully divine, yet one person. The confession reads:

1 In agreement, therefore, with the holy
2 fathers, we all unanimously teach that we
3 should confess that our Lord Jesus Christ is
4 one and the same Son, the same perfect in
5 Godhead and the same perfect in manhood, truly
6 God and truly man, the same of a rational soul
7 and body, consubstantial with the Father in
8 Godhead, and the same consubstantial with us
9 in manhood, like us in all things except sin,

10 begotten from the Father before the ages as
11 regards His Godhead and in the last days, the
12 same, because of us and because of our
13 salvation begotten from the Virgin Mary, the
14 *Theotokos*, as regards His manhood; one and the
15 same Christ, Son, Lord, only-begotten, made
16 known in two natures without confusion,
17 without change, without division, without
18 separation, the difference of the natures
19 being by no means removed because of the
20 union, but the property of each nature being
21 preserved and coalescing in one *prosopon* and
22 one *hupostasis* — not parted or divided into two
23 *prosopa*, but one and the same Son, only —
24 begotten, divine Word, the Lord Jesus Christ,
25 as the prophets of old and Jesus Christ
26 Himself have taught us about Him and the creed
27 of our fathers has handed down.[8]

Chalcedon addressed several matters in succinct fashion:

1. Nicea Reaffirmed

Chalcedon reaffirmed the position taken at Nicea and again at Constantinople that the second person of the Trinity is of the same eternal Godhead as the first person. In reference to Christ, the creed uses such phrases as "the same perfect in Godhead" (line 4f.), "truly God" (5f.), "consubstantial with the Father in Godhead" (7f.).

2. Against Nestorianism

The Chalcedonian formula took issue with Nestorianism (the position reputedly held by Nestorius who became the patriarch of Constantinople in 428) which maintained that the divine and the human were two separate persons in the historical Jesus of Nazareth so that at times he gave expression to the human person within him (e.g., when he wept at Lazarus' tomb), while at other times he gave expression to the divine person (e.g., when he raised Lazarus from the dead). Chalcedon rejected this idea by referring to Christ's two natures as being "without division, without separation" (17f.).

3. Against Apollinarianism

Chalcedon also rejected Apollinarianism (taking its name from Apollinarius, late fourth century bishop of Laodicea in Syria), which so intensified the Nicene faith's confession of the divinity of Christ that it ended up making him so divine that his humanity, while not denied, was severely compromised. And so, against Apollinarianism, Chalcedon declared that Jesus was "like us in all things except sin" (9). Furthermore, the two natures are "without confusion, without change" (16f.), and again, "the difference of the natures being by no means removed because of the union" (18ff.).

4. Duality and Unity Maintained

Chalcedon rejected both the exaggerated duality of Nestorianism and the exaggerated unity of Apollinarianism. It maintained a creative tension between the two following emphases. The first was that of the so-called Antiochean theologians (related to the Syrian city of Antioch and epitomized by Nestorius) on the separateness of the human and the divine in Christ. The second was the emphasis of the so-called Alexandrian theologians (related to the Egyptian city of Alexandria and epitomized by Apollinarius) on the oneness of the human and the divine in Jesus Christ.

The Antiochean overemphasis on duality tended to sacrifice the conviction that Jesus was a singularly inte-grated person functioning in all instances as the God-man person, and the Alexandrian overemphasis on unity tended to sacrifice the complete humanity of Jesus, the humanity being swallowed up in the divinity. Chalcedon, however, affirmed both the Alexandrian emphasis on unity and the Antiochean emphasis on duality without sacrificing either.

We see the Chalcedonian emphasis on unity in the use of the following phrases: "our Lord Jesus Christ is one and the same Son" (3f.), "the property of each nature being preserved and coalescing in one *prosopon* [i.e., a personal countenance] and one *hupostasis* [i.e., an identifiable essence] — not parted or divided into two *prosopa* [i.e, countenances], but one and the same Son" (20ff.).[9]

But we also see in Chalcedon an emphasis on duality as in the following phrases: "the same perfect in Godhead and the same perfect in manhood, truly God and truly man" (5ff.), "consubstantial with the Father in Godhead, and the same consubstantial with us in manhood" (7ff), "made known in two natures" (15f.), "the property of each nature being preserved" (20f.). Both unity and duality were affirmed, neither without the other.[10]

These two unified conceptual statements (Nicaea and Chalcedon) have played an important role in the history of the church even for those branches of Christianity which consider themselves noncreedal or even anti-creedal. They represent the broadly accepted understanding in the church regarding both the relationship of Christ to the Father and the two natures of Christ. They are significant literary reference points for the church's ongoing conversation about its Lord.

Prophet, Priest, and King

Jesus Christ is often referred to in relation to the threefold offices of prophet, priest, and king. In continuity with Old Testament prophets, Jesus as a prophet spoke the word of God, but, as more than a prophet, he is the Word. In continuity with Old Testament priests, he made an offering to God for the salvation of his people, but as a priest with a difference, he sacrificed himself as "the Lamb of God who takes away the sin of the world" (John 1:29; see also Heb. 10:1-14.) In continuity with Old Testament kings, he too was lord of a particular people (his disciples) but beyond that, he is the universal "King of kings, and Lord of lords" (Rev. 19:16).[11]

The twentieth century German theologian, Jürgen Moltmann, argues that at the heart of Christ's threefold offices is divine friendship. He writes:

> The joy which Christ communicates and the freedom which he brings as prophet, priest and king find better expression in the concept of friendship than in those ancient titles. For in his divine function as prophet, priest and king, Christ lives and acts as a friend and creates friendship.[12]

Moltmann, however, was not the first to consider the concept of friendship as being of the essence of Christ's offices. J. Wilbur Chapman (1859–1918) wrote hymn lyrics celebrating Christ's friendship:

1. Jesus! what a friend for sinners!
   Jesus! lover of my soul!
   Friends may fail me, foes assail me,
   He, my Savior, makes me whole.

2. Jesus! what a strength in weakness!
   Let me hide myself in Him;
   Tempted, tried, and sometimes failing,
   He my strength, my victory wins.

3. Jesus! what a help in sorrow!
   While the billows o'er me roll;
   Even when my heart is breaking,
   He, my comfort, helps my soul.

4. Jesus! what a guide and keeper!
   While the tempest still is high;
   Storms about me, night o'ertakes me,
   He, my pilot, hears my cry.

5. Jesus! I do now receive Him,
   More than all in Him I find;
   He hath granted me forgiveness,
   I am His, and He is mine.

Refrain
   Hallelujah! what a Savior!
   Hallelujah! what a friend!
   Saving, helping, keeping, loving,
   He is with me to the end.[13]

The Man of Galilee in his incarnational ministry as teacher, preacher, exorcist, and healer was also the divine friend, sometimes confronting, at other times comforting, but always loving.

The crucified, resurrected, ascended, and reigning Lord who is also the eternal word, the promised messiah, christus victor, and sacrificing savior is always friend whether it is a matter of his divine *No* to sin or his divine *Yes* to righteousness. His *No* is always motivated by loving holiness and his *Yes* by holy love.

Jesus in his threefold offices is the Word-made-flesh prophet at whose feet we sit as humble disciples, the great high priest who saves to the uttermost, the King of kings and Lord of lords whose reign will never cease. He is the prophet who invites us into the eternal circle of friendship. He is the priest whose work actually makes us friends of God and of each other. He is the king, the goal of whose rule is that we may dwell in his everlasting city of divine friendship, the gates of which "will never be shut by day—and there will be no night there" (Rev. 21:25).

Hallelujah! what a Savior! Hallelujah! what a friend!"

Notes

1. Gustaf Aulén, *Christus Victor,* trans. A. G. Hebert (New York: Macmillan, 1960).

2. Elvina M. Hall, *Worship the Lord: Hymnal of the Church of God* (Anderson, Ind: Warner, 1989), No. 410.

3. George Bennard, op. cit., No. 195.

4. Lewis E. Jones, op. cit., No. 423.

5. When I began writing this chapter, I found that we had 1,893 volumes on Christology in our seminary library, many of them sizeable works, as for instance, Edward Schillebeeck, *Christ: The Experience of Jesus as Lord,* trans. John Bowden (New York: Seabury, 1980), 925 pp. Even non-Christians write, as for instance, Milan Machovec, one time professor of philosophy at the Charles University in Prague, and an atheist, wrote *Jesus Für Atheisten* (Stuttgart, Germany: Kreuz Verlag, 1972), translated in English as *A Marxist Looks at Jesus* (Philadelphia: Fortress, 1976).

6. See Prescott Browning Wintersteen, *Christology in American Unitarianism* (Boston: The Unitarian Universalist Christian Fellowship, 1977).

7. As the text appears in *Worship the Lord,* No. 327. For a contemporary translation of the whole creed, see chapter 7 below, "The Trinitarian God."

8. As the text appears in J. N. D. Kelly, *Early Christian Doctrines* (New York: Harper and Row, 1960), p. 339f.

9. The Greek *prosopon* translates into the Latin *persona* and the latter into the English "person."

The Greek *hupostasis* translates into the Latin *substantia* which in turn translates into the English "substance." *Hupostasis* is also translated into the Latin *ousia* which is translated into the English "essence" or "substance." For a further discussion, see "persona" in Richard A. Muller, *Dictionary of Latin and Greek Theological Terms* (Grand Rapids: Baker, 1985), p. 223ff . Also, see *subsistentia* and *substantia*, p. 290f.

10. For a further discussion of these issues see Kelly, op. cit., chaps. VI, IX, XI, and XII.

11. Regarding the threefold offices of Christ, see Helmut Thielicke, *The Evangelical Faith, Vol. 2: The Doctrine of God and of Christ,* trans. and ed. Geoffrey W. Bromiley (Grand Rapids: Eerdmans, 1977), chaps. XXIV–XXVIII and XXX. For a historical and theological critique of "the threefold office," see Wolfhart Pannenberg, *Jesus – God and Man*, trans. Lewis L. Wilkins and Duane A. Priebe (2nd ed.; Philadelphia: Westminster, 1977), pp. 212–225. For a doctrinal treatise on the person and work of Christ, organized around the threefold offices, see Charles E. Brown, *We Preach Christ* (Anderson, Ind: Gospel Trumpet, 1957).

12. Jürgen Moltmann, *The Church in the Power of the Spirit,* trans. Margaret Kohl (New York: Harper and

Row, 1975), p. 119. Moltmann writes in the paragraph immediately preceding the one quoted in the text: "The concept of Jesus' friendship sums up everything that can be said about fellowship by the titles of office we have used up to now: As the messianic harbinger of joy, Jesus brings the gospel of the kingdom to the poor and becomes the friend of tax-collectors and sinners. As the high priest he offers himself 'for many,' and consummates his love by dying as a friend for a friend. As the exalted Lord he liberates women and men from their bondage and makes them friends for others. As the one who is glorified he intercedes with the Father for the world. In his name friendship with God through prayer and the hearing of prayer comes into being."

13. J. Wilbur Chapman, "Jesus! What a Friend for Sinners," *Worship the Lord*, No. 68.

For Further Consideration

See James D. G. Dunn, *Christology in the Making* (Philadelphia: Westminster, 1980); Walter Kasper, *Jesus the Christ*, trans. V. Green (London: Burns and Oates, and New York: Paulist, 1976); I. Howard Marshall, *Jesus the Saviour* (Downers Grove: InterVarsity, 1990); Wolfhart Pannenberg, *Jesus – God and Man*, trans. Lewis L. Wilkins and Duane A. Priebe (Philadelphia: Westminster, 1977); Jaroslav Pelikan, *Jesus through the Centuries* (New Haven and London: Yale University Press, 1985); and Edward Schillebeeck, *Christ: The Experience of Jesus as Lord*, trans. John Bowden (New York: Seabury, 1980).

Two other works of special interest are John Deschner, *Wesley's Christology: An Interpretation* (Dallas: Southern Methodist University Press, 1985), and Jacquelyn Grant, *White Women's Christ and Black Women's Jesus: Feminist Christology and Womanist Response* (Atlanta: Scholars, 1989).

For a systematic approach to Christology with rich historical resources, see Thomas C. Oden, *The Word of Life – Systematic Theology: Volume Two* (San Francisco: Harper and Row, 1989).

7

The Universal Work of the Holy Spirit

What is God's relationship to those who have lived, are living or will live without ever being introduced to Christ? What is God's relation to all people—past, present, and future?

The Universality of God's Relatedness to All Flesh

In order to address this question, I lift up some themes in the Bible that can help us to think systematically about the issue. The first is the universality of God's relatedness to all flesh. Genesis makes it abundantly clear that God is no tribal God but the God who is related to the whole human race. The creation stories are about the origin not of a particular race of human beings but of generic human beings.

Furthermore, when God brought judgment on the sinfulness of the human family, it was humanity as a whole that suffered the flood (7:17–24). Only those in the ark survived.

When finally the waters subsided, God made a covenant with Noah that never again would judgment be brought in this way, which covenant was not limited to a particular segment of humanity but was made with "every living creature that is with you, for all future generations" (9:12).

The universal nature of this covenant is indicated by the fact that the rainbow was designated as the sign of the covenant. Rainbows, being natural phenomena related to all flesh, are obviously neither restricted to national boundaries nor are they the property of selected ethnic groups. God said, "When the bow is in the clouds, I will see it and remember the everlasting covenant between God and every living creature of all flesh that is on the earth" (v. 16). The covenant with Noah is an indication of God's universal relatedness to all flesh. No member of the human race lies outside that relatedness.

We see the universality of God's relatedness also in the New Testament, particularly in Romans 1 and 2 where Paul addresses the question as to whether those without the law of Moses are thereby not responsible to God.

In 1:19–20, he writes:

For what can be known about God is plain to them, because God has shown it to them. Ever since the creation of the world his eternal power and divine nature, invisible though they are, have been understood and seen through the things he has made. So they are without excuse.

In Romans 2:11 Paul again declares that God shows no partiality. Verse 12: "All who have sinned apart from the law will also perish apart from the law, and all who have sinned under the law will be judged by the law."

The summary of Paul's teaching on this matter is in vv. 14–16:

When Gentiles, who do not possess the law, do instinctively what the law requires, these, though not having the law, are a law to themselves. They show that what the law requires is written on their hearts, to which their own conscience also bears witness; and their conflicting thoughts will accuse or perhaps excuse them on the day when, according to my gospel, God, through Jesus Christ, will judge the secret thoughts of all.

The conclusion we derive from these two major passages—one from the Old Testament and the other from the New, each of which deals explicitly with the issue under consideration—is that God is directly related to all flesh.

This also is the assumption made by Paul at the Areopagus when in Acts 17:27–28 he says that God "is not far from each one of us. For 'In him we live and move and have our being.'" (Note our additional comments in chapter 14 about this Athenian speech.)

The Christ-Centered Work of the Everywhere Presence of God

The way God is related to all that exists is through the Spirit who is the everywhere presence of God. Psalm 139:7, stressing the universal presence of the Spirit, asks rhetorically, "Where can I go from your spirit? Or where can I flee from your presence?" The answer given in the subsequent verses is that there is no place at all that is outside the realm of God's presence. As John Shea in his *An Experience Named Spirit* puts it:

> This relationship to God is alive and functioning even though we are not aware of it. We may be able to blot out other relationships by banishing them from our minds; but this is an ontological constant.... Divine influence is as subtle and as influential as inhalation and exhalation of air and the rush of blood. The words on the wall at Delphi are eternally true: "Invoked or not, God is present."[1]

Revelation 5:6 stresses the universal work of the everywhere Spirit when it refers to "the seven spirits of

God sent out into all the earth." Seven being the number for divine wholeness, the meaning of this symbol is that it is none other than the divine Spirit, i.e., the seven-fold Spirit, who ministers throughout the entire earth.

It is of no little importance that in Revelation 5 the sevenfold Spirit is inextricably linked with Jesus the Lamb. The everywhere Spirit is not out doing the Spirit's independent work; rather, the Spirit is the Christ-centered Spirit, a position corroborated throughout the New Testament and particularly in Luke-Acts[2] and in John 14—16.[3]

In Luke-Acts, the Holy Spirit is the agent at work from the time of Jesus' conception (see Luke 1:35) to the time of the church's ongoing witness to the resurrected Lord (see Acts 2). As George Montague in *The Holy Spirit: Growth of a Biblical Tradition* points out:

> Luke's two-volume work, his gospel and the Acts of the Apostles, is the longest attributed to any one author in the New Testament, including Paul. And surely if we had to single out any one evangelist as the "Theologian of the Holy Spirit," it would be Luke. While the word "spirit" occurs four times in Mark and five times in Matthew, the expression "Holy Spirit" occurs thirteen times in Luke's gospel and forty-one times in Acts.[4]

In John 16:14, Jesus, in reference to the special work of the Spirit in the lives of believers, says , "He will glorify me, because he will take what is mine and declare it to you." As Shea says, "The Spirit is notoriously silent; the Memory of Jesus becomes its voice."[5]

We conclude that the everywhere Spirit is God's way of being actively related to everybody for the purpose either of leading persons to Christ or of building up believers into the fullness of Christ. The Spirit, then, from whom we cannot escape, is, according to the teaching of the New Testament, the Christocentric Spirit. The Spirit precedes the coming of Christ, accompanies his coming, and continues his coming. The Spirit prepares the way for Christ, introduces Christ, and teaches Christ to us. The Spirit inspires the human anticipation of Christ, reveals Christ, and empowers believers to be the emissaries of Christ.

The Supraincarnational Work of the Spirit

The work of the Spirit is not restricted to the time and place of the incarnation. The Spirit was at work prior to the incarnation and has continued working since the incarnation. The Spirit was at work not only in Palestine during the time of Jesus, but outside of Palestine, as well. The Holy Spirit is the everywhere and all-time Spirit.

First Peter 1:10–12 speaks of this Christocentric Spirit being at work in the Old Testament prophets:

> Concerning this salvation, the prophets who prophesied of the grace that was to be yours made careful search and inquiry, inquiring about the person or time that the Spirit of Christ within them indicated when it testified in advance to the sufferings destined for Christ and the subsequent glory. It was revealed to them that they were serving not themselves but you, in regard to the things that have now been announced to you through those who brought you good news by the Holy Spirit sent from heaven — things into which angels long to look!

Later, in 3:19–20 reference is made to those in the days of Noah who were confronted with the work of this Christocentric Spirit, most of whom, however, rejected the Spirit's wooing.[6]

The conclusion of these considerations is that we have a biblical basis for saying that the Christocentric Spirit was at work in the world prior to the time of the incarnation, and that those who were receptive to the Spirit's wooing work, thereby, were not eternally lost. Noah and his family escaped the waters of judgment not because they knew Jesus of Nazareth but because they were receptive to the Christocentric Spirit who directed them to do what they could do at that particular time in the history of God's relationship with the human family.

Anticipatory Faith

The same is true of Abraham, who throughout Scripture is considered our ancestor in faith (see the section "God Comes to Where We Are and Calls Us to Faith" in chapter 4). The New Testament views Abraham as not being eternally lost—for instance, in the story of Lazarus and the rich man. When the beggar Lazarus dies, he is "carried away by the angels to be with Abraham," instead of finding himself in torment where the rich man later found himself (Luke 16:22–24). For Lazarus to be with Abraham meant that he was not lost in torment.

In the Hebrews 11 roster of the faithful, the predominant figure is none other than Abraham (vv. 8-19). It is important to note the anticipatory nature of his faith: he "looked forward to the city that has foundations, whose architect and builder is God" (v. 10). In reference to the company of Old Testament people of faith, v. 16 says that "they desire a better country, that is, a heavenly one. Therefore God is not ashamed to be called their God; indeed, he has prepared a city for them."

Abraham who lived and died prior to the time of the incarnation in Christ Jesus was a man of anticipatory faith in that he was willing to be receptive to the call of God, i.e., the Spirit. As Genesis at many points makes clear, he fell far short of New Testament standards (e.g., he lied, saying that his wife was his sister, 12:10–20; he had more than one wife, 16:1–4; he abandoned Hagar when Sarai grew jealous, 16:6). Nevertheless, Abraham was amenable to the Spirit within the context of his era and location; consequently, in the New Testament his name is prominent in relation to the fellowship of the faithful. He was a man of anticipatory faith in that prior to the incarnation he was as sensitive to the Christocentric Spirit as his circumstances allowed.

If we take seriously the implications of the themes mentioned above—the covenant with Noah, the every-where presence of the Spirit, and the universal ministry of the sevenfold Spirit of the Lamb—then there is no necessity to question that the Spirit who wooed Abraham also wooed every person who has ever lived, and woos every person who now lives .

Just as Abraham lived prior to the incarnation chronologically, many others live "prior to the incarna-tion" in their physical location (i.e., they are not in a geographical location where they can hear the story of Jesus). Others live "prior to the incarnation" in commu-nication (i.e., while they are exposed to people who talk a great deal about the gospel, the talk is so cluttered with extraneous religious and cultural issues that the gospel itself is concealed, or perhaps it is not even yet translated and proclaimed in their own language). Still others live "prior to the incarnation" in terms of their own developmental immaturity or lack of comprehension (i.e., they are either not old enough to respond to the gospel, or, due to brain damage or other mental difficulties, are unable to confess it).

Living "prior to the incarnation" is not only a chronological matter; it can also be a geographical matter, a communications matter, or a developmental matter. We can, therefore, speak of the distance of time, the distance of location, the distance of communication, and the distance of development. The Holy Spirit, however, bridges all such distances in the same sense that the distance of time was bridged for Abraham. All persons within the context of their own particular circumstances, — regardless of who they are or where they are — have the opportunity to respond to the quiet work of the Spirit. The Spirit knows no barriers called wrong time, dislocation, faulty communications, or lack of development. The Spirit has had access to every person since the beginning of history; the Spirit continues having access to every person in every corner of the world now. The Spirit has access to every person regardless of how badly gospel talk is cluttered with confusion, cultural baggage, private interpretations, misunderstandings, pride, and vanity; the Spirit has access to every person regardless of age, level of maturity, brain capacity or emotional state. The Holy Spirit is not constrained by matters which constrain us.

We conclude, therefore, that as persons respond receptively and according to their respective abilities to do so, God thereby brings them to anticipatory faith in the same way that he brought Abraham to this kind of faith. Their lives, their ways, their cultural patterns may be far below the standards set forth in the New Testament, even as Abraham's were, but their responsiveness to the working of the Spirit is, nevertheless, the birth of anticipatory faith.

Responsive Faith as the Culmination of Anticipatory Faith

Anticipatory faith is faith that longs for what can be fulfilled only by Jesus Christ. Many, along with Abraham, in one way or another, live and die "prior to the incarnation." They can, however, live and die with the same Christ-longing faith Abraham had (even though they do not know enough about it to call it such). While they have the benefit of anticipatory faith, they do not experience the joy of responsive faith in Jesus Christ. They experience with great vagueness what they cannot even name. Believers, on the other hand, experience explicitly that which those of anticipatory faith experience only implicitly.

As Thomas Oden observes:

It is said that the saints and prophets of the Old Testament experienced an implicit faith (Calvin, Inst. 3.2.3), while Christian believers are invited to experience a clearer, more well-defined basis for belief, or explicit faith. Explicit faith knows the ground upon which it believes because the salvation event has been revealed. Those who lived before Christ or who have not explicitly heard the good news may share in an implicit faith in the promise of God's coming without grasping particulars of historical revelation. Such faith is efficacious, or "counted for righteousness," as in the case of Abraham.[7]

(Rom. 4:5; Heb. 11:8–19)

Those of anticipatory faith move into the future drawn to one whom they have not yet come to know; those of responsive faith move into the future knowing the Lord of the future, Christ Jesus. Those of anticipatory faith merely feel after the one on whom their faith can one day be fixed; those of responsive faith know conceptually "on whom their faith is fixed" and sing with Charles Naylor:

I know on Whom my faith is fixed,
I know in Whom I trust;
I know that Christ abides in me,

And all His ways are just.
I know on Whom my faith is fixed,
His mercy has set me free;
I know that He will safely keep,
And His love is sweet to me.[8]

The Church's Mission

Three reasons for the church to be on mission with the gospel to all peoples are as follows:

First, we go because our Lord told us to go. In obedience to him, we go knowing that his ways are altogether perfect and that his instructions are for the purpose of accomplishing his mission. He has the total picture; we do not. He knows what our going can accomplish, whereas we see "through a glass, darkly" (a phrase from 1 Cor. 13:12 in the King James Version).

Second, we go because we have found the joy of the Lord so sweet that we want others, also, to experience that same joy. We desire that they, too, will taste and see that the Lord is good. We yearn for them to join us in the blessed circle of Christian discipleship.

Third, we go because all persons of anticipatory faith deserve to have their Christ-longing hearts satisfied. They deserve to be introduced to the one who is at the center of the unknown Spirit to whom they have been tenderly responsive; they deserve to know the Lamb whose seven-fold Spirit woos them (Rev. 5:6).

The Predisposition of Those Hearing the Gospel

Paul in 2 Corinthians 2:15–16 says

> For we [Christians] are the aroma of Christ to God among those who are being saved and among those who are perishing; to the one a fragrance from death to death, to the other a fragrance from life to life.

This passage is of interest in this discussion because it assumes that those who hear the gospel have some kind of predisposition to it, so that even prior to hearing it, people can be spoken of either as "those who are being saved" or as "those who are perishing." Paul appears to be assuming that something of a spiritual nature is going on in the lives of people prior to the hearing of the gospel. When "those who are being saved" hear the gospel (i.e., smell it) they experience it as a fragrance from life to life. However, when "those who are perishing" hear it (i.e., smell it) they experience it as a fragrance from death to death.

Paul does not tell us more about the nature of these predispositions either for or against the gospel. Exegetically, we cannot extract the meaning. However, as we think theologically about the passage, it raises a significant question, namely, how it is that some are in the category of being saved while others are in the category of perishing so that when persons in each category smell the fragrance of the same gospel, to those in the first category it is the fragrance of life while to those in the second category, it is the fragrance of death. One could, of course, answer that those in each of the two categories are there because God had previously decreed that one group should be saved by grace and that others should perish because of lack of grace. Or, one could answer, as I do, on the basis of what has already been said, that the two categories are the result of two different human responses to the universal work of the Holy Spirit. Some resist the preliminary work of the Holy Spirit—even as the majority in Noah's day did—and are therefore those whom Paul refers to as "those who are perishing." Others, however, are receptive to the Spirit's work—as in the case of Noah and his family who entered the ark of safety, and, as in the case of Abraham and others about whom it is written that they "desire a better country, that is, a heavenly one" (Heb. 11:16)—and are, therefore, those whom Paul refers to as "those who are being saved."

The church's mission is to proclaim the gospel to all people so that those whose hearts are tender to the Spirit (i.e., "those who are being saved") may move from the frustrating dimness of anticipatory faith to the joyous clarity of responsive faith. We proclaim the gospel to them so that they may cease being hungry souls longing to partake of the Christ whom they have not yet met, and become nourished souls longing for more of the Christ whom they have met.

Notes

1. John Shea, *An Experience Named Spirit* (Chicago: Thomas More, 1983), p. 97.

2. See George T. Montague, *The Holy Spirit: Growth of a Biblical Tradition* (New York: Paulist, 1976), chaps. 21–23.

3. Ibid., chap. 27.

4. Ibid., p. 253.

5. Shea, op. cit., p. 96.

6. For a fuller discussion of these passages, see my treatment of 1 Peter in "Salvation in the General Epistles," *An Inquiry into Soteriology from a Biblical Theological Perspective,* ed. John E. Hartley and R. Larry Shelton, Vol.1 in *Wesleyan Theological Perspectives,* (Anderson, Ind: Warner, 1981), pp. 202–208.

7. Thomas C. Oden, *Life in the Spirit: Systematic Theology:* Volume Three (San Francisco: Harper, 1992), p. 134.

8. Charles W. Naylor, "I Know," *Worship the Lord: Hymnal of the Church of God* (Anderson, Ind: Warner, 1989), No. 429.

The Trinitarian God

The "Three-Personed God"[1]

The biblical God is the God whom Jesus called Father (Matt. 6:9), and whom the Father called beloved Son (3:17), and whom the Father sent in the name of the Son as the other *Paraclete* (John 14:15–26; v. 26 identifies the *Paraclete* or Helper as the Holy Spirit). The question that the church has wrestled with throughout its history is how best to think of this "three-personed God." How can we be faithful both to the oneness of God taught in Scripture (e.g., Deut. 6:4) as well as to Scripture's thrice personal revelation?

What to do with the Thrice Personal Revelation

Some, such as the Mormons, depart from the Christian faith in their rejection of biblical monotheism, and treat the three as separate divinities.[2] Others, such as Jehovah's Witnesses, follow ancient Arianism by attributing eternal Godhood only to the Father and by subordinating ontologically (that is, in terms of the very being of God) the Son and Spirit to the Father. According to this view, the Son and the Spirit possess divinity but are not coeternal persons with the Father. In this view, Christ is first-order *creation* through whom all other creation takes place, but not first-order *God*.[3] Not only is the Son demoted from the ontological status of eternal being, but the Spirit also is demoted to that of a divinely "controlled force."[4]

In the Mormon approach, plurality displaces the oneness of God. In the Jehovah's Witnesses, oneness displaces eternal plurality.

The third approach is the one taken by Christians, both East and West — Orthodox, Catholic, and Protestant. It is set forth in the Niceno-Constantinopolitan Creed which affirms both the oneness of God and the plurality revealed in Scripture:

We believe in one God, the Father, the Almighty, maker of heaven and earth, of all that is, seen and unseen.

We believe in one Lord, Jesus Christ, the only Son of God, eternally begotten of the Father, Light from Light, true God from true God, begotten, not made, of one Being with the Father. Through him all things were

175

made. For us and for our salvation he came down from heaven: by the power of the Holy Spirit became incarnate from the Virgin Mary and became human. For our sake he was crucified under Pontius Pilate; suffered death and was buried. On the third day he rose again in accordance with the scriptures; ascended into heaven and is seated at the right hand of the Father. Christ will come again to judge the living and the dead, and his kingdom will have no end.

We believe in the Holy Spirit, the Lord, the giver of life, who proceeds from the Father.[5] With the Father and the Son he is worshiped and glorified. He has spoken through the Prophets. We believe in one holy catholic and apostolic Church. We acknowledge one baptism for the forgiveness of sins. We look for the resurrection of the dead, and the life of the world to come. Amen.[6]

The Nicene Creed maintains oneness in plurality and plurality in oneness, and it resists reducing God either to a simple oneness or to a simple threeness. Nicaea expresses faith in the unity of the three-personed God: Father, Son, and Holy Spirit. It reflects the church's faith in the eternal God who was revealed in Jesus Christ and who continues working among and through them in the person of the Holy Spirit. Believers experience God's three-foldness in creation and sustenance, in incarnation and redemption, and in empowerment and ministry.

The Economic Trinity and the Immanent Trinity

The church came to know about this three-foldness by virtue of the biblical teaching concerning *creation* and *salvation,* the so-called divine economy. The word "economy" comes from the Greek word, *oikonomia,* meaning dispensation, activity, administration, or management of a household.[7] Therefore, the God known to us by virtue of the biblical account of creation and salvation (i.e., God's work in establishing God's "household") is referred to as the economic Trinity.

In the course of the church's reflective thought, however, the question emerged as to whether the "economic" God is trinitarian as far as God's eternal life prior to creation is concerned. Has God always been thrice personal in regards to God's very selfhood apart from all considerations regarding creation and salvation? The conclusion was that if the God revealed in Scripture is the eternal God, then the very being of God has always been Father, Son, and Spirit. In other words, God did not become trinitarian in the process of creation and salvation; rather, God's eternal, internal life—even when considered apart from the biblical economy of creation and salvation—is trinitarian.

The Trinity is thus referred to by using a variety of modifiers:
- the ontological Trinity (from the Greek *ontos,* 'being').

• the immanent Trinity (meaning God's internal life, and not to be confused with "imminent" — it is just about to happen, or with "eminent" — a high and prominent place or position). The immanent Trinity, then, refers to the internal relations existing within God as God.

• the essential Trinity (having to do with the very nature of God); or

• the eternal Trinity (the way God has always been).

A Contemporary Paradigm

The challenge for the contemporary church is how we are to be faithful to the biblical and historical faith regarding the trinitarian God while at the same time expressing it in terms that make sense to us. How do we speak about the biblical God who is the God of mysterious depth, the God imaged in Jesus Christ, and the God in contact with all reality outside Godself.

According to Exodus 3, God — self-named *Yahweh* — is the eternal, holy I AM. The eternal I AM is the mysterious person who is always more than we can comprehend; the I AM is the God of surprises. This means that we can never have *exhaustive* knowledge of God's mysterious depth of being.

The eternal God, however, is also the imaged person revealed in Jesus Christ who said of himself, "Whoever has seen me has seen the Father" (John 14:9). Colossians

1:15 calls Christ "the image of the invisible God." Verse 19 says that "in him all the fullness of God was pleased to dwell." The incarnation laid bare God's selfhood. This does not mean that in the incarnation, the reality of God was fully exhausted, but, rather, that in Christ the very essence of the mysterious God was fully revealed. Knowing Christ does not give us comprehensive knowledge of God but it does give us knowledge of God's very nature, which knowledge assures us that all that the mysterious God accomplishes in the world will be consistent with what we know in Christ. The fact that Jesus prayed to the Father during his incarnational life reveals that there is more to God than Jesus of Nazareth. Indeed, in John 14:28, Jesus says, "the Father is greater than I," a recognition that Godhead is more than the incarnation.[8]

Furthermore, God is also the dynamic Spirit spoken of from Genesis to Revelation: moving over the primeval waters at the time of creation (Gen. 1:2); inspiring the prophets to act and speak (e.g., Isa. 59:21, Ezek. 37:1, Micah 3:8); ministering in an all-encompassing way from the birthing of the messiah to the birthing of the church (see Luke-Acts, particularly Luke 1:35 and Acts 1:8); and being "sent out into all the earth" as the sevenfold Spirit (Rev. 5:6).[9]

The historic conclusion of the church is that the scriptures teach that the God revealed incarnationally in Christ (i.e., the Son) is also the mysterious personal ground, source, and fountain of divine life (i.e., Father) as well as the everywhere-present divine minister (i.e., Spirit). The mysterious Father and the ministering Spirit are manifested in the Son–"the image of the invisible God" (Col. 1:15)–who was "destined before the foundation of the world, but was revealed at the end of the ages for your sake" (1 Peter 1:20); in him even we were chosen before the foundation of the world (see Eph. 1:4). The mysterious Father, manifested Son, and ministering Spirit are the three-personed God. God is the mysterious Father who ministers everywhere through the Spirit according to the incarnational manifestation in Christ.

Scriptural passages that give portents of later doctrinal understandings of this thrice-personal God are

• the baptismal formula of Matthew 28:19, "baptizing them in the name of the Father and of the Son and of the Holy Spirit";

• the blessing in 2 Corinthians 13:13, "The grace of the Lord Jesus Christ, the love of God, and the communion of the Holy Spirit be with all of you";

• the doxology in 2 Thessalonians 2:13–14:

But we must always give thanks to God for you, brothers and sisters beloved by the Lord, because God chose you as the first fruits for salvation through sanctification by the Spirit.... For this purpose he called you ... so that you may obtain the glory of our Lord Jesus Christ.

• the commentary on worship in 1 Corinthians 12:4–6, "Now there are varieties of gifts, but the same Spirit; and there are varieties of services, but the same Lord; and there are varieties of activities, but it is the same God who activates all of them in everyone."

Other passages with trinitarian implications are Ephesians 4:4–6 which speaks of one Spirit, one Lord, One God and Father of all; and 1 Peter 1:2, which refers to those "who have been chosen and destined by God the Father and sanctified by the Spirit to be obedient to Jesus Christ and to be sprinkled with his blood."[10]

The Issue of Spatial Demarcation

Our difficulty with conceptualizing the three-personed God is rooted in our tendency to think of God in the same spatial categories we use for thinking about individuals, rather than in the relational categories we use for thinking about persons. Whereas individuals are known by the space they take up, persons are known by the non-spatial relationships they have.

British theologian Colin Gunton argues that "the personal is both that from which other realities take their meaning and that which is irreducible to other ... entities." He goes on to say that "a person is different from an individual, in the sense that the latter is defined in terms of *separation from* other individuals, the person in terms of *relations with* other persons."[11]

When we speak of the three persons of the Trinity, therefore, we are speaking not of three spatially demarcated individuals, but of three persons in holy relationship with each other, devoid of spatial demarcations. This description can be illustrated by what we experience in trinitarian worship: when a believer in the trinitarian God reports to another believer the experience of God in a service of worship, it is highly unlikely that the second believer will ask about the location of the Holy Spirit as over against the location of the Father and the Son. To report the presence of the trinitarian God in a service of worship is to assume that we are talking about a reality that has nothing to do with spatial demarcation. We do not think in terms of where a particular person of the Trinity is located as over against the other two; to do so would be to think in terms of individuals who cannot take up the same space.

As an individual I am here but not there, and if I am here, another individual cannot take up the same space I occupy. God, however, is not like that. Even though God is everywhere, that does not rule out our being someplace, also. God is everywhere, not in the sense that God consumes all space, leaving none for us, but in the sense that God has an all-pervasive presence. To put it the other way round, even though we as individuals take up space, that does not preclude God being in that space as well.

When we think of God, therefore, we need to train ourselves to think of the holy presence who is not limited to occupying an amount of space. This understanding is important for conceptualizing the trinitarian life of God: the three persons of the Trinity are not to be thought of as occupying three different spaces; rather, they mutually inhere each other without any spatial displacement or loss of distinctive particularity.[12]

We can get a sense of what this means in terms of our own social nature. In a very real sense each of us is three persons: the mysterious person of private depth, the imaged person of one's own perception, and the interactive person in contact with reality other than one's self-image. These persons do not take up different spaces inside us; rather they are non-spatial communicants in dynamic relationship with each other. Just as we cannot point to three different spaces in ourselves, taken up by the three persons each of us is, even so we should not impose such spatial categories on God.

A Theological Statement about the Trinitarian God

Having before us this distinction between individuals who are spatially demarcated and persons who are non-spatially related, we are now ready to propose the following theological statement about the trinitarian God of the Bible: God is the eternal, holy, and loving I Am-This-Relating To the other. This way of speaking about God is an attempt to affirm both the oneness of God as well as the thrice personal nature of God. God is the mysterious I AM who encountered Moses at the burning bush. God is the one who was revealed in Jesus of Nazareth. God is the one who relates to all which is not God. God is Father (i.e., I AM), Son (i.e., This), and Spirit (i.e., Relating To the other).

In the above way of putting it, "the other" is not capitalized in order to emphasize that "the other" is not God. However, "Relating To" is capitalized to indicate that the person of the Spirit is always relating to that which is not God.

The trinitarian God is the eternal God who was as truly trinitarian in the Old Testament as in the incarnation and at Pentecost. Israel's pilgrimage of faith prior to the incarnation is the history of the revelation of the eternal *I* AM-This-Relating To the other. The incarnation is the revelation of the eternal I AM-*This*-Relating To the other. Pentecost is the revelation of the eternal I AM-This-*Relating To* the other.

This manner of speaking stresses the truth that the eternal God of the scriptures is not a God in the making. It is inaccurate to think of God as the I AM without being at the same time both the God revealed in Jesus Christ and the God relating to the other. The God revealed in Christ is the same God who spoke to Moses out of the burning bush and the one who was poured out upon the church at Pentecost. The God of the pentecostal effusion is also the God of the burning bush and of the Bethlehem manger.

There has been, however, in the history of revelation, a difference of focus — the focus of the burning bush being on God's isness, the focus of the incarnation being on God's thisness, and the focus of Pentecost being on God's relatedness. We need to keep in mind that one revelatory emphasis does not exclude the other two. The progression that we see in the scriptures is a progression of revelation, not a progression of God's becoming.

The Importance of Trinitarian Thinking

At least five reasons emerge as to why trinitarian thinking is important:

1) Trinitarian thought is faithful to the witness of the Bible, which presents us with one God in three persons: Father, Son, Spirit. The biblical God "is no lonely God, but a communion within Himself."[13]

In reference to the development of trinitarian thought in the New Testament, Arthur Wainwright concludes:

> The problem of the Trinity was being raised and answered in the New Testament. It arose because of the development of Christian experience, worship, and thought. It was rooted in experience, for men were conscious of the power of the Spirit and the presence and Lordship of the risen Christ. It was rooted in worship, because men worshipped in the Spirit, offered their prayers to God the Father through Christ, and sometimes worshipped Christ himself. It was rooted in thought, because the writers tackled first the Christological problem, and then, at any rate in the Fourth Gospel, the threefold problem. The whole matter was based on the life and resurrection of Jesus himself, who received the Spirit during his earthly life and imparted the Spirit to others after his resurrection.[14]

2) Trinitarian thought upholds the glory of the incarnation. In Jesus of Nazareth, nothing less than very God of very God dwelt among us. Catherine Mowry LaCugna in *God for Us: The Trinity and Christian Life* has put it this way: "At the heart of the Christian doctrine of God were two affirmations: God has given Godself to us in Jesus Christ and the Spirit, and this self-revelation or self-communication is nothing less than what God is as God."[15]

3) Trinitarian thought opens up the truth that the eternal God is capable of suffering. God is at one with us in our suffering, instead of being one step removed from us. The sacrificial death of Jesus is nothing less than the experience of the trinitarian God.

Jürgen Moltmann, speaking about the passion of God, says that love makes a person capable of suffering. Summarizing what he calls "one of the most remarkable books about God's capacity for suffering," (C. E. Rolt's *The World's Redemption*),[16] he says that the author develops his doctrine of the Trinity from the axiom that God was self-sacrificing in eternity.[17] This sacrifice is related to the fact that any creation is by virtue of its very createdness something other than God, and therefore, in that sense, over against God. For the Creator to love the creation, divine self-sacrifice is necessary, for love, by its very nature, gives of itself for the sake of the other.

4) Trinitarian thought confesses the church's experience that the God of the Old Testament both revealed God in Jesus of Nazareth and continues to abide with us in the person of the Holy Spirit. This experience is found particularly in the practice of praying to the eternal one in the name of Christ Jesus and in the power of the Holy Spirit.

5) Trinitarian thought maintains unity with the church's long intellectual history of reflecting on the faith, analyzing it and defending it against ideas about

God which are contrary to the biblical revelation (see For Further Consideration, Part II, A, for historical studies). As Gunton observes: "A church that changes its conception of God as radically as the abandonment of trinitarianism would entail could scarcely find it possible to claim to be the same church."[18]

What difference does trinitarian thinking make in the life of the people of faith? Just this:

• it reflects the belief that our salvation is the work of the incarnate God;

• it reflects the church's experience of the presence and ministry of the Spirit being the presence and ministry of the eternal God;

• it reflects our historical connectedness to the ancient church's doctrine of God;

• it reflects the view that instead of God being a self-enclosed singularity, God is an outgoing, relational, creative, redemptive, energizing, superintending lover;

• it reflects the experience of God as being dynamic, communal, and missional rather than static, withdrawn, and satisfied;

• it reflects the understanding of God as being the incarnate, crucified, risen, ascended, reigning, and coming Lord who superintends the human pilgrimage as participant in it, instead of being a detached dispenser of divine decisions;

• it reflects the practice of praying to God the Father in the name of God the Son in the power of God the Spirit;

• it reflects the conviction that we worship the one God who not only created us but who also saves us and continues to walk and talk with us.

The trinitarian God is the God of creation and redemption. The trinitarian God in Christ brought reconciliation to the world. The trinitarian God is the poured-out Spirit of Pentecost. The trinitarian God has never abandoned either the created order or the people of God through their long pilgrimage of faith.

The trinitarian God is the eternal lover. The trinitarian God is the ongoing, outgoing God of history. The trinitarian God is the pilgrim God. The trinitarian God is the here, there, and everywhere God. The trinitarian God is the God of the whole Bible — the God of the Old Testament, the God revealed in Jesus Christ, the God poured out at Pentecost. The trinitarian God is the eternal God — this is the church's faith.

Notes

1. This phrase is borrowed from William J. Hill, *The Three-Personed God: The Trinity as a Mystery of Salvation* (Washington: Catholic University of AmericaPress, 1982).

2. See *History of the Church of Jesus Christ of Latter-Day Saints: Period I., History of Joseph Smith, the Prophet,* by Himself, Vol. VI. (Salt Lake City: Deseret, 1978), pp. 473-479. "I have always declared God to be a distinct-personage, Jesus Christ a separate and distinct personage from God the Father, and that the Holy Ghost was a distinct personage and a Spirit: and these three constitute three distinct personages and three Gods," p. 474.

3. See, for instance, "Should You Believe in the Trinity?" (Brooklyn: *Watchtower*, 1989), pp. 12–20. "Jesus had a beginning and could never be coequal with God in power or eternity," p. 16.

4. See Ibid., p. 20: "It ['holy spirit'] can be likened to electricity, a force that can be adapted to perform a great variety of operations."

5. Under the influence of Augustine (354–430), the Latin West added *filioque,* "and the Son." "After about 800, Western Christians generally recited the creed adopted at Constantinople with the addition of the word." William C. Placher, *A History of Christian Theology: An Introduction* (Philadelphia: Westminster, 1983), p. 101.

6. An updated translation from *Grounds for a Common*

Witness: Confessing One Faith: A Guide for Ecumenical Study (Cincinnati: Forward Movement Publications, 1988), p. opposite 1. Published by the Faith and Order Commission of the National Council of Churches of Christ in the USA, this short introduction to the historical need for and function of the Nicene Creed also includes a contemporary interpretation.

7. "The economy of redemption is the arena of the divine-human relationship. God moves toward us through Christ and the Sprit [*sic*], so that we may come into communion with God and with one another.... God and all of God's creatures dwell together in a common household referred to in the New Testament as the reign of God, the place where God's life rules." Catherine Mowry LaCugna, "The Practical Trinity," *The Christian Century* (July 1992), 682.

8. See Thomas A. Smail, *The Forgotten Father* (Grand Rapids: Eerdman's, 1980), 86–112. Also, for a polemical treatment of the so-called "Jesus only" doctrine espoused by the anti-Trinity branch of Pentecostalism, see Carl Brumback, *God in Three Persons* (Cleveland, Tennessee: Pathway, 1959).

9. For comprehensive studies, see Alasdair I. C. Heron, *The Holy Spirit: The Holy Spirit in the Bible, the History of Christian Thought, and Recent Theology* (Philadelphia: Westminster, 1983); George T. Montague,

The Holy Spirit: Growth of a Biblical Tradition, A Commentary on the Principal Texts of the Old and New Testaments (New York: Paulist, 1976); and John V. Taylor, *The Go-Between God: The Holy Spirit and the Christian Mission* (Philadelphia: Fortress, 1973). Also, see chapter 7 on "The Universal Work of the Holy Spirit."

10. I am indebted to Timothy Ware for this classification of texts, given in "The Doctrine of the Trinity after Nicaea," Oxford University, Hilary Term, 1992.

11. Colin E. Gunton, *The Promise of Trinitarian Theology* (Edinburgh: T. & T. Clark, 1991), p. 10f.

12. The ancient concept of *perichōrēsis*, used by the Greek theologian John Damascene in the eighth century is related to this discussion. See Catherine Mowry LaCugna, *God for Us: The Trinity and Christian Life* (San Francisco: Harper, 1991), pp. 270–278. "*Perichōrēsis* means being-in-one-another, permeation without confusion," p. 271.

13. G. A. F. Knight, *A Biblical Approach to the Doctrine of the Trinity,* Scottish Journal of Theology Occasional Papers No. 1 (Edinburgh: Oliver and Boyd, 1953), p. 78.

14. Arthur W. Wainwright, *The Trinity in the New Testament* (London: SPCK, 1980), pp. 266f.

15. LaCugna, op. cit. p. 209. See chap. 7, "The Self-Communication of God in Christ and the Spirit." "The central theme of trinitarian theology is the relationship

between the pattern of salvation history (*oikonomia*) and the eternal being of God (*theologia*). The idea that God is self-communicating is the essential premise ... of a revitalized theology of God. God by nature is self-expressive.... This is consistent with the biblical images of a God who is alive,who is ineluctably oriented 'other-ward,' who is plenitude of love, grace, and mercy overflowing," p. 230.

Also, Claude Welch, *In His Name: The Doctrine of the Trinity in Contemporary Theology* (New York: Charles Scribner's Sons, 1952), chap. 7 "The Foundation of an Adequate Trinitarianism." "Where ... the conception of God's self-revelation ... in Christ is taken seriously, the doctrine of the Trinity comes inevitably into a central place in the Christian understanding of God," p. 218. And again: "The doctrine of the Trinity is ... not an answer to the question, what is the relation of the deity of Christ to monotheism or a prior conception of the Fatherhood of God?—it is an answer to the question, what is the nature of God as God as he reveals himself in Christ?" p. 233.

16. London, 1913.

17. Jürgen Moltmann, *The Trinity and the Kingdom: the Doctrine of God,* trans. Margaret Kohl (San Francisco: Harper and Row, 1981), 32f. See chap. 2, "The Passion of God."

18. Gunton, op. cit., p. 19.

For Further Consideration

Part I: Trinitarian Experience and Trinitarian Theology

A. First-Century Historical Experience

Norman Pittenger, *The Divine Triunity* (Philadelphia: United Church, 1977), in a chapter titled "The Palestinian Experience": "The first Christians, and after them the first who engaged in the theological task, were convinced of the unity of God. Being faithful to the Jewish tradition ... their problem was to discover how it might be possible ... to incorporate into that abiding unity the patent fact that for them the God of Israel was also the God who had sent, and who was 'in,' the Jesus whom they worshiped and served; and that the Holy Spirit — the new, engracing, and empowering reality they knew in their fellowship — was also ... equally divine ... in the only sense they could conceivably accept: namely, that he too was incorporated in the abiding unity of the God of Israel," p. 21.

B. Ongoing Christian Experience

Karl Rahner, *The Trinity*, trans. Joseph Donceel (New York: Herder and Herder, 1970) in a section titled, "The Trinity as a Salvific Experience and an Experience of Grace": "It is ... from this most existential concern for our salvation, that it [the treatise on the Trinity] lives....

For him who rejects our basic thesis the Trinity can only be something which ... can be told about in purely conceptual statement ... as opposed to God's salvific activity in us.... Then the proof from Scripture will unavoidably begin to look like a method which ... tries to draw conclusions from a few scattered statements.... But if it is true that we can really grasp the content of the doctrine of the Trinity only by going back to the history of salvation and of grace, to our experience of Jesus and of the Spirit of God ... because in them we really already possess the Trinity itself as such, then there never should be a treatise on the Trinity in which the doctrine of the 'missions' [of the Son and of the Spirit] is at best only appended as ... relatively unimportant and additional," p. 39f.

Part II: Selected Bibliography on the Trinity
A. Historical

For the major documents of the early trinitarian debate, see William G. Rusch (trans. and ed.), *The Trinitarian Controversy* (Philadelphia: Fortress, 1980). For a technical introduction to both the debate and the formal resolution, see Bernard Lonergan, *The Way to Nicea: The Dialectical Development of Trinitarian Theology*, trans. Conn O'Donovan (Philadelphia: Westminster, 1976). Also, Edmund J. Fortman, *The Triune God: A*

Historical Study of the Doctrine of the Trinity (Philadelphia: Westminster, 1972); J. N. D. Kelly, *Early Christian Doctrines* (New York: Harper and Row, 1960), pp. 83–279; and Bertrand de Margerie, *The Christian Trinity in History,* trans. Edmund J. Fortman (Still River, Massachusetts: St. Bede's Publications, 1982).

For a defense of classical trinitarian terminology, see Donald G. Bloesch, *The Battle for the Trinity: The Debate over Inclusive God-Language* (Ann Arbor: Servant, 1985).

B. Theological

See Eberhard Jüngel, *The Doctrine of the Trinity,* trans. Horton Harris (Edinburgh: Scottish Academic Press, 1976); T. F. Torrance, *The Trinitarian Faith* (Edinburgh: T and T Clark, 1988). For a nontechnical discussion of the Trinity, written for Christians in general, see Alister E. McGrath, *Understanding the Trinity* (Grand Rapids: Zondervan, 1988). Also, Alasdair I. C. Heron (ed.), *The Forgotten Trinity. A Selection of Papers presented to the British Council of Churches Study Commission on Trinitarian Doctrine Today* (London: BCC/CCBI Inter-Church House).

C. The Economic Trinity and the Immanent Trinity

See Jürgen Moltmann, *The Trinity and the Kingdom: The Doctrine of God,* trans. Margaret Kohl (San Francisco: Harper and Row, 1981), pp. 151–178; Karl Rahner, *The Trinity,* trans. Joseph Donceel (New York: Herder and

Herder, 1970), pp. 101–103; and Claude Welch, *In His Name: The Doctrine of the Trinity in Contemporary Theology* (New York: Charles Scribner's Sons, 1952), pp. 293–294. A related discussion, having to do with the same issues, is Thomas A. Smail, *The Forgotten Father* (Grand Rapids: Eerdmans, 1980), pp. 86–112.

III

People for God

9

The Circle of Disciples as Church

High Ideals for the Church

The expanding circle of Christ's disciples came to be called the *ekklēsia*, usually translated as church. *Ekklēsia* is from *ek*, meaning out of, and *kaleō*, meaning to call or summon. An *ekklēsia*, then, is an assembly called out of the general population for a particular purpose or cause. For instance, the word was used among the Greeks to refer to those who were called together to discuss public affairs, as in Acts 19:39. In the same chapter it is used to refer to the gathering of Ephesians who were incensed about the Christian witness in their city (vv. 32, 41). In the Greek translation of the Hebrew scriptures, it is used to translate references to Israel's gatherings. Even in the New Testament itself, it is used to refer to Israel in the wilderness (Acts 7:38). The circle of Christ's disciples is a new kind of gathering called out from the general population — it is a new kind of *ekklēsia*. They are called out by Jesus to be his disciples and are commissioned to make more disciples for him.

I maintain that the placement of the Gospels at the beginning of the New Testament points to the priority which the early church assigned to discipleship as the basic category for understanding the fundamental nature of the church.[1] It is significant that the use of the word *ekklēsia* occurs in the New Testament for the first time within the discipleship context of Matthew where it is used three times. The most important one for our consideration is in chapter 16. Verse 13 says that "when Jesus came into the district of Caesarea Philippi, he asked his disciples, 'Who do people say that the Son of Man is?'" Verses 16–18:

> Simon Peter answered, "You are the Messiah, the Son of the living God." And Jesus answered him, "Blessed are you, Simon son of Jonah! For flesh and blood has not revealed this to you, but my Father in heaven. And I tell you, you are Peter, and on this rock I will build my church, and the gates of Hades will not prevail against it."

Ekklesia is used twice more in 18:17, "If the member [i.e., the offender] refuses to listen to them [two or three other church members who go with the aggrieved to the offender], tell it to the church; and if the offender refuses to listen even to the church, let such a one be to you as a Gentile and a tax collector." In Matthew, therefore, the discipleship motif is developed with the church in mind; to put it another way, church life is understood distinctively from a discipleship perspective.

Though discipleship is basic to understanding the essential nature of the church, the New Testament describes Christ's *ekklesia* in other ways, as well. References to the church include many descriptive words and phrases, salutations at the beginning of New Testament letters, and pastoral instructions to the churches, as well as more definitive statements.

Bible Images of the Church

In Paul Minear's comprehensive *Images of the Church in the New Testament*,[2] he identifies no less than ninety-six "analogies"[3] of the church which he groups into as many as thirty-one minor images[4] and four major ones: the people of God, the new creation, the fellowship in faith, and the body of Christ. (See For Further Consideration, Part II, at the end of this chapter.)

Of the four major images, what Minear calls "the fellowship in faith" comes closest to the discipleship motif, although the category of discipleship is not the organizing principle for his discussion. He describes this image "as a fellowship of saints and slaves whose life together is characterized by a unique kind of mutuality in gift and in vocation."[5] Included within this galaxy are such references as the sanctified, the faithful, the justified, followers, disciples, the witnessing community, confessors, slaves, and friends.[6] The fellowship characterized by these and similar terms is called into existence by Jesus Christ and finds its identity in his saving work.

Minear's three additional images stand out in the New Testament by virtue of their overt teaching as to who Christians as a corporate body are. Each is related to a declaration that "you are" such and such.

In 1 Corinthians 12:27–28 the church is called *the body of Christ:*

Now you are the body of Christ and individually members of it. And God has appointed in the church first apostles, second prophets, third teachers; then deeds of power, then gifts of healing, forms of assistance, forms of leadership, various kinds of tongues.

In Ephesians 2:11–22 the church is called in v. 15 the *one new humanity,* and in this connection also "citizens with the saints" (19), "the household of God" (19), "a holy temple in the Lord" (21), and "a dwelling place for God" (22). Verse 19 says: "So then you are no longer strangers and aliens, but you are citizens with the saints and also members of the household of God"; and v. 22: "you also are built together spiritually into a dwelling place for God."

And, 1 Peter 2:9-10 calls the church *the people of God:*

> But you are a chosen race, a royal priesthood, a holy nation, God's own people, in order that you may proclaim the mighty acts of him who called you out of darkness into his marvelous light. Once you were not a people, but now you are God's people; once you had not received mercy, but now you have received mercy.

The first definition of the church, as the body of Christ, places the accent on the church as the ongoing means by which the risen, ascended, reigning, and coming Lord makes himself known in history between his first and second advent. The church is here defined Christologically and is seen as having an ongoing role to play in Christ's redemptive work in the world.

The second definition, the one found in the Ephesians passage, places the accent on the church as a reconciled humanity—a humanity at peace both with God and with all of God's people. As such it is the locus of the divine presence on the earth. The church is here defined in human terms and is seen as having a new kind of relationship both with God and others.

The third definition of the church, as the people of God, places the accent on its vocation. As God's chosen they are called to participate in God's work through nationhood and priesthood. The church is here defined in terms of its mission and is seen as having an ancient history, a new experience of God, and a divine destiny.[7]

A survey of church life in the New Testament leads to the conclusion that believers were both blessed by an idealism as to who they were by grace, and plagued by the realism of who they were because of sin. Six dimensions of New Testament church life at its idealistic best include the following.

1) It was a fellowship of those who trusted in Christ as Savior and Lord. The church was a spiritual network of persons whose hearts and minds had been captivated by Jesus of Nazareth, the risen Christ (e.g., Luke 24). During the New Testament era, membership in the church was Christ centered in that it was assumed that church members loved Jesus and were serious about being his followers (e.g., Acts 2:37–47).

2) As people of the new covenant, they were inextricably bound together historically with the Old Testament people of God. This extended family included both those in previous times who had been stewards of the mysteries of God prior to the incarnation, and those in the present era who by faith in Christ were heirs of the promises fulfilled in him. Believers took their place in humbleness of spirit in Abraham's spiritual family, and with confidence they interpreted the family history in light of Christ. With gratitude to God they shared the inheritance with all who were willing to come to Christ (e.g., Gal. 3:15 – 4:7; Eph. 2:11 – 3:13).

3) They were a society of believers devoted to growing in Christ's life. The canon for measuring their life together was nothing less than Christ himself (e.g., Phil. 2:1-8). They were also disciplined by the church's wisdom as to how best to reflect his way of life (e.g., Acts 15:1-29). The church in the New Testament concerned itself with matters of practical piety (e.g., Titus 2:1 – 3:11; James), doctrinal soundness (e.g., Col. 1:15 – 2:23), spiritual wholeness (e.g., 1 Thess. 3:13; 5:23; 1 John 4:17-18), and relational health (e.g., 1 Cor. 11:17 – 13:13), all of which were attempts to reflect the new life revealed in Jesus Christ.

4) The church was an organism of divine grace for the edification of believers and for blessing all. Disciples were a sacramental presence in the world, thereby making God's grace personally real as they ministered to each other within the church as well as to those beyond (e.g., 1 Cor. 14:1-33).[8]

5) It was the sociological expression of God's mission to the world. As such, it was a movement reaching beyond itself to the wider world for the purpose of making disciples. It was a missionary church in that it

had been brought into existence by God's mission in Christ and was thereby inspired to rejoice in that mission, to participate in it, and to trust in God's power to bring it to consummation (e.g., Matt. 28:16–20; Acts).

6) It was a community waiting expectantly for Christ's consummation of world history. Believers lived in the joyous assurance that "though the wrong seems oft' so strong, God is the ruler yet." They were not to fret about where history was going because they already knew the answer—it was moving toward the return of Jesus Christ. They had met the *Eschatos* who already had been revealed in the midst of history (Acts 1:6–11; 1 Cor. 15:20–28; 1 Thess. 4:13–5:11).

Realism in the Church

The New Testament's realistic picture of the life of the church indicates, however, that it did not always live up to the idealism of its ecclesiological definitions and understandings. The New Testament is about the church's struggles, deficiencies, and corruptions, as well as about its idealism.

• Whereas theologically, and for the most part experientially, they were a fellowship trusting in Christ as Savior and Lord, it was also true that some fell short of this experience. The problem that Paul addresses in his letter to the Galatians is that instead of trusting Christ for their salvation, some were trusting in their obedience to the law of Moses. "I am astonished," he writes in 1:6, "that you are so quickly deserting the one who called you in the grace of Christ and are turning to a different gospel." (Also, see 3:1–5 which ends with the question, "Well then, does God supply you with the Spirit and work miracles among you by your doing the works of the law, or by your believing what you heard?")

• Whereas they were the people of the new covenant who were inextricably bound together historically with the Old Testament people of God, the fact was that Paul found it necessary to address the casual attitude on the part of the Roman Christians toward Israel. It appears that they had forgotten the importance of their historical connectedness with Israel and thought of themselves as its replacement—religious and national Israel, therefore, having no further place in the economy of God.[9] Paul, seeking to correct this attitude, says in 11:17–18,

> But if some of the branches were broken off, and you, a wild olive shoot, were grafted in their place to share the rich root of the olive tree, do not boast over the branches. If you do boast, remember that it is not you that support the root, but the root that supports you.

• Whereas the church in the New Testament was the

209

society of believers devoted to growth in Christ's life, it is obvious that some in the church were not so devoted. For example, in 1 Corinthians 5:1–2, the apostle laments, saying:

It is actually reported that there is sexual immorality among you, and of a kind that is not found even among pagans; for a man is living with his father's wife. And you are arrogant! Should you not rather have mourned, so that he who has done this would have been removed from among you?

• Whereas the New Testament church was the organism of divine grace for the edification of believers and for blessing all, it is obvious that at times it was very much of a stumbling block to believers and a detriment to others. For instance, the communal meals in the church at Corinth were selfish and rude. Paul held up a mirror to that congregation when he wrote what he had heard about them: "For when the time comes to eat, each of you goes ahead with your own supper, and one goes hungry and another becomes drunk" (1 Cor. 11:21). Furthermore, the private devotional praise to God taking place through tongues speaking in public worship showed an insensitivity to outsiders, evoking the question: "If you say a blessing with the spirit, how can anyone in the position of an outsider say the 'Amen' to your thanksgiving, since the outsider does not know what you are saying?" (1 Cor. 14:16). A few verses later, another question is asked: "If, therefore, the whole church comes together and all speak in tongues, and outsiders or unbelievers enter, will they not say that you are out of your mind?" (23).

• Whereas the church in the New Testament was the sociological expression of God's mission to the world, the composite picture of the seven churches of Asia, to which John wrote, was that of a church devoid of missionary zeal. They had either turned in upon themselves, become weak in faith and tolerant of major aberrations, or were simply in a survival mode. The Ephesian church had abandoned its first love (Rev. 2:4); the church at Smyrna was struggling to survive (10); the church at Pergamum was tolerating false teachers (14–15), as was the church at Thyatira (20–23); the church at Sardis was asleep spiritually (3:2–3); the Philadelphian church, although faithful, was, nevertheless, in a survival mode (8); and the Laodicean church was lukewarm (15–16). None is described so as to lead us to think of it as a missionary church.

• Whereas the New Testament church was a community waiting expectantly for Christ's consummation of world history, the evidence points toward the fact that some had lost the glow of that anticipation. The church addressed by Matthew appears to have lost the edge of this expectancy, as is indicated by the evident necessity for the strong emphasis on being ready for the anytime return of the Lord. We see this especially in the parable of the ten virgins (25:1–13), five of whom miss the bridegroom's arrival due to their unpreparedness and lackadaisical attitude toward it. Verse 13 concludes with the injunction: "Keep awake therefore, for you know neither the day nor the hour."

One of the important lessons which the New Testament teaches is that the church in the first century was not always perfect. It was a church in process of becoming what God wanted it to become. To be sure, it was not in and of itself identical with the kingdom. Rather, it was the corporate body of those called out of the general population to become the community of the kingdom, the herald of the kingdom, the sign of the kingdom. It was a church in process of growing in the life of the kingdom, and it was on the way to the final consummation of the kingdom.

The New Testament Message Regarding the Church

I am indebted to Hans Küng for distinguishing between what he called the idealist view of the church and the realist. On the one hand, the idealist sees the church as "pure, spotless, blameless, holy," concerned only with the salvation of people and the glory of God.

On the other hand, the realist sees it as being "all too human, both in head and members; a harsh, intolerant machine ... full of every kind of failing." He argues that both are "fundamentally uninterested" in church renewal. "The idealist, seeing only the light side of the Church, thinks it unnecessary; the realist, limited to the dark side, thinks it impossible."[10]

Although writing in a Roman Catholic context, Küng's observations are appropriate for all of us. Some of us strain hard to match the New Testament's idealism about the church, even though we never actually reach it. Consequently, some among us end up with such great dissatisfaction with the historical church that they withdraw from it either actually or emotionally. Others of us focus only on the New Testament's realism about the church—fraught as it was with struggles, dissensions, misunderstandings, and divisions—and end up making easy peace with our own problems. By doing this we marginalize our high calling as the people of God and allow the social and historical forces which influence us to have unhampered reign. Neither approach is good. We need both New Testament idealism and New Testament realism.

If the New Testament is permitted to convey its full message to us about the church, we will learn that although it has a high calling in the economy of God, it is made up of people who have not yet reached eternal glorification. The church is the body of Christ, but it is also in the process of growing up into Christ (Eph. 4:15). The church is the new humanity, but also it has to be reminded not to "gratify the desires of the flesh" (Gal. 5:16). The church is the people of God, but it is required also to persevere in order to be saved (Heb. 6:1–8 and 10:26–39).

The church is a society of people with a new identity given to it by the grace of God, but it is also a band of pilgrims traversing the deserts and rivers of life, climbing mountains, walking through valleys, sometimes falling by the wayside, sometimes failing to follow the signposts, sometimes becoming discouraged and tired and weary, and sometimes forgetting the goal. It is because the church is a band of pilgrims—perhaps we should even say, a ragtag band—that it needs to be schooled well in its new, divine identity given to it in Christ. If it is not so schooled, it will, no doubt, lose heart along the way. In order for the church to keep on keeping on, it needs to hear again and again the message of who it is by grace, namely, the body of Christ, the one new humanity, "a chosen race, a royal priesthood, a holy nation, God's own people, in order that you may proclaim the mighty acts of him who called you out of darkness into his marvelous light."

It is as this new identity is preached and taught patiently, lovingly and neverendingly that the church will be kindled and rekindled in its desire to be continuously re-formed by the Word and re-newed by the Spirit to be Christ's new kind of *ekklēsia*. Only then will it be strengthened as the interpersonal network of those whose hearts and minds are captivated by the Lord Jesus. Only then will it take fuller advantage of its inheritance as heirs of the ancient promises fulfilled in Christ. Only then will it be in earnest about growing up into the fullness of Christ. Only then will it be the sacramental community of God's grace and the missionary task force which makes disciples of "whosoever will." Only then will the church truly be ready for the coming of the bridegroom.

Notes

1. For a study of this priority see Fernando F. Segovia (ed.), *Discipleship in the New Testament* (Philadelphia: Fortress, 1985).

2. Paul S. Minear, *Images of the Church in the New Testament* (Philadelphia: Westminster, 1960).

3. Ibid., p. 268f.

4. Ibid. pp. 28–65.

5. Ibid., p. 67.

6. Ibid., p. 269.

7. See Roger E. Hedlund, *The Mission of the Church in the World: A Biblical Theology* (Grand Rapids: Baker, 1991).

8. See Edward Schillebeeckx, *The Church With a Human Face*, trans. John Bowden (New York: Crossroad, 1985), Parts I and II.

9. See J. Christiaan Beker, *Paul the Apostle: The Triumph of God in Life and Thought* (Philadelphia: Fortress, 1980), pp. 94–108.

10. Hans Küng, *The Council, Reform and Reunion*, trans. Cecily Hastings (New York: Sheed and Ward, 1961), p. 12. Also, see his *The Church*, trans. Ray and Rosaleen Ockenden (New York: Sheed and Ward, 1967).

For Further Consideration

Part I: An Introductory Reading List on "Church"

See Willi Marxsen, *Jesus and the Church: The Beginnings of Christianity*, trans. Philip E. Devenish (Philadelphia: Trinity Press International, 1992). For an extended study beyond the New Testament era, see Stuart G. Hall, *Doctrine and Practice in the Early Church* (Grand Rapids: Eerdmans, 1992); for an anthology of ecclesiological understandings through Augustine, see

E. Glenn Hinson (ed.), *Understandings of the Church* (Philadelphia: Fortress, 1986); for an historical overview which includes special emphasis on the Wesleyan tradition, see Melvin E. Dieter and Daniel N. Berg (eds.), *The Church* (Anderson, Ind: Warner, 1984). Also, Anton Houtepen, *People of God: A Plea for the Church* (Maryknoll: Orbis, 1984).

Part II: Minear's Images

Paul S. Minear, *Images of the Church in the New Testament* (Philadelphia: Westminster, 1960) is the result of work assigned to him by a theological study commission in 1954. He writes: "This commission, under the title Theological Commission on Christ and the Church, was established by the Faith and Order Department of the World Council of Churches as an outgrowth of the Third World Conference on Faith and Order, which met in Lund, Sweden, in 1952. At that conference a vigorous demand was voiced for studies that would explore not so much the formal doctrines of the church, concerning which the several Christian communions are deeply divided, as the inner relationships that link the church to Jesus Christ and to the Holy Spirit and which therefore bind the various communions together even in spite of themselves," p. 11f.

In my "Experiential Salvation and Christian Unity in

the Thought of Seven Theologians of the Church of God (Anderson, Indiana)" (unpublished Th.D. dissertation, Boston University School of Theology, 1973), pp. 284–317, I discuss the ecclesiology of seven seminal thinkers of the Church of God in relation to Minear's four major images. F. G. Smith's ecclesiology has basic affinities with the image of the church as the people of God, H. M. Riggle's and Earl L. Martin's with the image of the new creation, Russell R. Byrum's, Charles Ewing Brown's and Albert F. Gray's with the image of the fellowship in faith, and D. S. Warner's ecclesiology has basic affinities with the image of the church as the body of Christ. (Available in Robert A. Nicholson University Library, Anderson University, Anderson, Indiana.)

10

The Church Preaching the Good News

Christ Jesus was a preacher of the good news of the kingdom (see Matt. 4:23 and 9:35), and his emerging church was a community of response to his preaching. After Jesus' ascension, the church was built up by preaching that was faithful to him, faithful to the whole of Scripture, and faithful to the Spirit's directives. This has been the case throughout the church's history.

Preaching: A Ministry of the Church

The church as a whole is responsible for the ongoing preaching ministry of Jesus. Since disciples in general support and listen to this ongoing preaching, they deserve to participate in the theological conversation about its nature and role. The subject of preaching, then, is not just for seminary classes, but for congregations where it takes place week after week. That which follows is intended both for disciples who are ordained as preachers and for those who support and listen to them.

Christian preaching makes the eternal Word alive in contemporary words. It is a labor of love by those who are chosen and empowered by the Holy Spirit to proclaim in orderly fashion Christ's gospel to others. Ideally, it is the church in action through the public proclamation of its faith by those ordained to speak on its behalf. It is Christ at work through those who interpret the message of the Bible in faithfulness both to the literary text and to the Lord revealed therein.

New Testament Words for Preaching

Several words are used in the New Testament for what we call preaching: *dianggellō,* to publish abroad, e.g., Luke 9:60; *euanggelidzō,* to proclaim glad tidings, e.g., Luke 9:6; *katanggellō,* to proclaim or declare, e.g., Colossians 1:28; and *kērussō,* to herald, e.g., Matthew 4:23.

New Testament preaching was the public declaration of what God had done in Jesus Christ for the redemption of the world. The church was brought into existence by preaching, sustained by it, and extended by it.

The Role of Preaching

Christian preaching grows out of the fact that the gospel has conceptual content that, if the gospel is to have its full effect, has to be told, explained, and applied. Preaching is the explanation of the scriptures in such a way that the gospel comes alive to the hearers, calling them to respond in faith. Consequently, it is both informational and invitational. Whenever it attains its goal, the gift of divine grace is revealed to the hearts and minds of hearers, drawing them to the eternal gospel that has come alive in a word event in their own time and place.

Since the gospel is for the whole person, Christian preaching, at its best, appeals to the heart and mind alike. As James Stalker says of Paul, "Christ was enthroned in ... [his] intellect no less than in his heart."[1] When this is the case, most likely such preachers, in turn, will appeal to the whole person when preaching to others.

In light of contemporary understandings, instead of talking about the mind and heart, we speak of left brain and right, the left being for abstract ideas and the right for pictures and stories. The left is more intellectual, the right more emotional. One contemporary theologian, James I. Packer, has observed that good communication involves both sides of the brain. He points to C. S.

Lewis, John Bunyan, and, above all, to Jesus Christ as powerful communicators because, in terms of contemporary terminology, they were whole-brained people, "who linked affirmations (teaching, exposition, argument) with images (pictures, analogies, stories) in such a way that each gave vividness, credibility, and depth to the view of reality projected by the other."[2]

The Preacher as Interpreter of the Bible's Story Line

Preachers have a multifaceted responsibility within the Christian community. First, he or she is an interpreter of the Bible's story line. Unless the integrity of that story line is maintained, isolated passages from the Bible are easily misunderstood and often misused. The first responsibility of the Christian preacher is to keep the shape of the biblical story before his or her people so that they can develop appreciation for the whole biblical story instead of simply latching on to bits and pieces which they find floating about in a sea of chaotic disconnectedness. P. T. Forsyth, in his *Yale Lectures on Preaching* earlier this century, called the Bible itself the greatest sermon in the world.[3]

The adequate Christian preacher knows the Bible's story sermon so well that he or she is able to develop accurate summaries of it for the benefit of God's people. An example of this sort of preaching is Stephen's sermon in Acts 7 in which he reviews the history of Israel leading up to the advent of Christ. It was a condensed version of the Bible's much more extensive story sermon.

The Preacher as Textual Exegete

Second, he or she is a textual exegete, one who "leads out" the meanings of a given Bible passage. This work calls for careful scholarship. Since the Bible comes to us from another age, we are thereby separated by differences of language, culture, history, and knowledge of the world. A great chasm exists between the ancient world of the Bible and our own.[4] Texts, therefore, are not necessarily immediately understandable. In fact, if the preacher does not know the Bible in terms of its ancient context, she may find herself preaching texts that, while being the actual words of the Bible, are not the ideas of the texts themselves. Therefore, what on the surface appears to be a biblical sermon may not be in actuality a biblical message. Whenever a preacher extricates a passage from its literary/cultural context, the conceptual fabric of the biblical message is in that instance torn apart; in such a case, the passage is mutilated rather than exegeted. Preachers, necessarily, therefore, need to be students of the Bible, a responsibility that calls for both disciplined preparation and continuing study.[5]

The Preacher as Gospel Herald

Third, a Christian preacher is a gospel herald. Paul in Romans 10:14-15 writes:

> But how are they to call on one in whom they have not believed? And how are they to believe in one of whom they have never heard? And how are they to hear without someone to proclaim [*kērussontos*, i.e., the one heralding] him? And how are they to proclaim [*kērux*, i.e., herald] him unless they are sent? As it is written, "How beautiful are the feet of those who bring good news [*euanggelidzō*, i.e., to proclaim glad tidings]!"

In the final phrase above, the emphasis on the good news is doubly stressed by the addition, in the Greek text, of the word *agatha*, meaning good things. The verse translated more literally would be: "How beautiful are the feet of those who proclaim glad tidings about good things!"

By definition, prophets of doom are not Christian preachers, for to be a truly Christian preacher is to be a herald of the good news of God's salvation in Jesus Christ. In Christ there is always hope. Even in the preacher's severest sermon of judgment, the message of the triumph of Christ over sin, Satan, and the grave must be set forth with clarity, if he is, in fact, being faithful to his calling as a Christian preacher. A message that does not offer the Christian hope is no Christian message.[6]

The Preacher as Prophetic Exhorter

Fourth, she is a prophetic exhorter. She looks at present circumstances in light of the revelation of Christ and peers into the future in that same light. It was by gazing at the glory of Christ that John on Patmos was able to discern demonic powers at work in the world. It was not a matter of his seeing Christ in light of the events of his day, but of seeing the events of his day in the light of Christ.

To be a prophetic exhorter does not require more intense study of the world, but more loving worship of Christ. As the preacher fixes her eyes on Jesus, the evidences of antagonistic and destructive powers — whether in the world, in the church, or in oneself — become ever more easily discernable. Having discerned these alien powers, she becomes a mouthpiece on behalf of the living Christ who is victor over them.

The Preacher as Parabolic Storyteller

Fifth, the Christian preacher is a storyteller of parables. He is instructed by the parables of Jesus. Thus, he tells stories to illustrate moral or spiritual lessons. He does not tell stories from the pulpit for the sake of merely entertaining the people of God. Instead, he seeks to unfold the truth of Christ and the secrets of the kingdom so that hearers may be brought face to face with the claims of the gospel. Jesus' parables of the kingdom were not devotional pleasantries with minimal conceptual content; rather, they were means of communicating profound truths about God's kingdom.

As the Christian preacher perfects his skills of parabolic storytelling, he also needs to be growing in his conceptual understanding of the kingdom; otherwise, the stories may be extremely thin doctrinally, and possibly even heretical or at best sub-Christian. It is crucial for us to keep in mind that our Lord, storyteller of parables that he was, was nothing less than the eternal Word made flesh. In his incarnational life — exciting story that it was! — he was, nevertheless, the eternal meaning, concept, idea, and message of God. His life was not just an interesting story; it was a story with eternal conceptual content. Furthermore, the parables he gave during his ministry were nothing less than the wisdom of eternity, the doctrine of the kingdom, and the teaching of the new life.

It follows, therefore, that, in conformity with our Lord, preachers as storytellers of parables should be avid students of the truth of the ages. It is truth content we are about, not entertainment.

Since this form of preaching is so attractive to hearers, those who excel in it have an even greater obligation to be serious students of the Word and devoted to the study of Christian doctrine. No less a parabolic master than Phillips Brooks held that historically those preachers who "have moved and held men have always preached doctrine. No exhortation to a good life that does not put behind it some truth as deep as eternity can seize and hold the conscience."[7] Storytelling, then, should never be seen as an alternative to the intellectual life, but as an expression of it.

The Preacher as Wise Reflector on the Human Condition

Sixth, the Christian preacher is a wise reflector on the human condition. As one who stands in the midst of the community of faith, she has a special opportunity to be in touch with the multidimensional life of the people under her care. As she, in light of the gospel, reflects on their needs and challenges, values and perspectives, strengths and weaknesses, she is in position to address them on the basis of the rich resources of biblical faith and, in so doing, speak a word that may be particularly relevant to their circumstances. She preaches in such a way that people are introduced to resources of the faith that, while there all along, were waiting for the sensitive pastoral preacher to make them understandable and applicable. She presents eternal truth in a manner that not only comforts the people of God but also confronts them. Her message both nurtures those who are mature in the faith and stretches those who are immature.

It is the latter, of course, that often engenders difficulty in the life of the church and requires great maturity, wisdom, and sensitivity on the part of the preacher. What she says may very well call into question understandings generally held in the congregation. Being willing to reflect on the faith in a manner that challenges people to change inadequate ideas and wrong practices may call for courage on her part. Indeed, such challenges may lead to resistance from the people of God, but, as Charles Jefferson once advised students, "It is not courage, but lack of sense, which usually gets preachers into trouble."[8] He goes on to say:

> Laymen are as a rule not unwilling to listen to new conceptions which have a show of reasonableness; but the man who tears to pieces their old truth with a chuckle and stamps upon it with a whoop is sure to be resisted. It is not in human nature to relish reiterated and gloating declarations that nearly all one's old beliefs are both false and silly. If a man has really worked his way into broader and nobler conceptions, let him give his new vision in such a way that the church shall be lifted up and strengthened.[9]

As a wise reflector on the human condition, the

Christian preacher wins the hearts of the people by making it transparently clear that he speaks both as one of them in a common humanity and as one with them in the common faith. Forsyth speaks about the importance of the "directness and spontaneity of the common life. The preacher is not there to astonish people with the unheard of; he is there to revive in them what they have long heard."[10]

The Multidimentional Nature of Christian Preaching

Christian preaching, then, is understood here as interpretation of the Bible's story line, textual exegesis, gospel proclamation, prophetic exhortation, parabolic storytelling, and wise reflection. The purpose of setting forth these categories is not to say that Christian preachers have a menu of possibilities from which they may pick and choose what has particular appeal to them, but to say that Christian preaching at its best is multidimensional. To the extent that preachers are both engaged seriously in the study of the scriptures and involved deeply in the life of the people of God, to that extent their preaching will reflect all six dimensions set forth here. The absence of any one of the first three (interpretation of the Bible's story line, textual exegesis, and gospel proclamation) betrays a major deficiency in their engagement with Scripture, and the absence of any one of the last three (prophetic exhortation, parabolic storytelling, and wise reflection) betrays a major deficiency in their involvement in the life of the people of God.[11]

Christian Preaching as a Charismatic Manifestation

Christian preaching is, first of all, a charismatic manifestation that transforms some of Christ's disciples into divinely designated heralds of Jesus Christ. First Timothy 2:5–7 says: "For there is one God; there is also one mediator between God and humankind, Christ Jesus, himself human, who gave himself a ransom for all—this was attested at the right time. For this I was appointed a herald."

And, 2 Timothy 1:9–11 says:

> [God] saved us and called us with a holy calling, not according to our works but according to his own purpose and grace. This grace was given to us in Christ Jesus before the ages began, but it has now been revealed through the appearing of our Savior Christ Jesus, who abolished death and brought life and immortality to light through the gospel. For this gospel I was appointed a herald [kērux, translated as preacher in the Revised Standard Version] and an apostle and a teacher.

Romans 12:6–8 begins by declaring that "we have gifts [charismata] that differ according to the grace [*charis*] given` to us," and then enumerates several, among which are prophecy, teaching, and exhortation. Also, 1 Corinthians 12:1–11 speaks of various kinds of ministry in the church as being manifestations of the Spirit. Verse 4 refers to the varieties of gifts [*charismata*], some of which have to do with speaking publicly for the benefit of the whole church, i.e., the utterance of wisdom and the utterance of knowledge (v. 8), prophecy and the interpretation of tongues (v. 10). According to v. 7, "To each is given the manifestation of the Spirit for the common good."

As a charismatic manifestation, preaching is not dependent on the church's ordination of the preacher to a particular office of responsibility. Being a charismatic manifestation, it is strictly a vertical gift directly from God; the church can neither give it nor take it away. The church may, to be sure, reject it, but if, in the course of time, the preaching proves to be of God, the church, then, will have suffered great loss to its own detriment. On the other hand, it should be said that the church is to exercise the gift of discernment as to whether someone's claim to be endowed charismatically is of God; the mere claim does not prove the reality. The Bible recognizes the existence of false prophets whom it must be on the alert to oppose.[12]

Furthermore, 1 Corinthians 14:29 sets forth the principle of prophets being subject to prophets: "Let two or three prophets speak, and let the others weigh what is said." Again, in v. 32, Paul says to the church that "the spirits of prophets are subject to the prophets."

Christian Preaching as an Ecclesiological Function

Not only is Christian preaching a charismatic manifestation; ideally, it is also an ecclesiological function. It is the normative way for the church to speak in orderly fashion both to itself and to the world. Forsyth puts it well when he says that the one great preacher in history is the church, and the first business of the individual preacher is to enable the church to preach. "He is to preach to the Church from the Gospel so that with the Church he may preach the Gospel to the world. He is so to preach to the Church that he shall also preach from the Church."[13] He goes on to say,

> The preacher, therefore, starts with a Church of brethren that agree with him and that believe with him; and in its power he goes to a world that does neither. What he has to do is not to exhibit himself to the Church, nor to force himself on it. He offers himself to it in the like faith, as a part of their common offering by the Eternal Spirit to God.[14]

In a particularly promising phrase, Forsyth says that preaching "is the organized Hallelujah of an ordered community."[15] Jefferson, a later Yale lecturer, highlighted the same theme when he said that the preacher "is

232

an organ functioning in an organism, finding his life in the vital relations by which he is bound to other lives."[16] He goes on to point out that the preacher's endowments are only one factor in the work of preaching, the other, of no less importance, being the endowments of the church itself. "The sermon," he writes, "is not the voice of an isolated individual, but the utterance of a body of men baptized into the name of Jesus." Speaking of the nourishing role of the church, he points out that the preacher cannot shape oneself; instead, "he is moulded by the body of believers. He cannot grow in isolation. He is a plant dependent on the atmosphere and the weather, both of which are largely the creation of the Christian people."[17]

To the degree that preaching is truly an ecclesiological function it should be done by those who have been ordained by the church for both the edification of the church and its orderly testimony to the world. Preaching, in this sense, is communal work. We find a metaphor of this in Acts 2:14 where it is reported that on the day of Pentecost, Peter "standing with the eleven, raised his voice and addressed them" i.e., the crowds in Jerusalem's streets. The Twelve, representative of the whole people of God, stood, as it were, to preach, although it was Peter who did the actual speaking.

What he said presumably had their backing, was in essence their word also, and was under the immediate supervision of the whole. In the sermon of Acts 2, therefore, while not all spoke individually, all did speak corporately through Peter.

Following the sermon, the hearers, according to v. 37, "said to Peter *and to the other apostles, 'Brothers,* what should we do?" (emphasis added). The inquiry was addressed to the whole apostleship. Furthermore, in v. 42, we are told that the converts "devoted themselves to the *apostles'* teaching and fellowship" (emphasis added). It was not to Peter's sermon nor to Peter as a person to whom they were devoted, but to the community of faith and to the collegial message. Preaching was communal; conversion was communal; discipleship was communal; their new identity was communal; their ongoing life of faith was communal.

A modern misconception both about the church and preaching is that the church is a gathering around charismatically endowed individuals and that preaching is an activity of one individual addressing others who happen to like his or her style and content. Consequently, the corporate nature of apostolic preaching is lost and the communal nature of Christian discipleship is distorted.

In God's economy, the Christian community is to

give birth to its preachers, nurture them, and hold them accountable both to the Christ of Scripture and to the Spirit's wisdom as it is manifested in the history of the church. The church's role is to discern God's call to particular individuals by issuing its own call to those it believes have received the divine call, and to train, ordain, and support them. The church is built up in the faith by studying the scriptures with its preachers, by praying with and for them, and then by listening to them under the ultimate teaching authority of the Christ of Scripture.

When the church's preachers preach the truth, it is God's will for the whole people of God to stand with them. When, upon hearing the preaching of the gospel, persons are converted, it is only the people of God who can actually receive them into church fellowship. When converts commit themselves to the ongoing life of Christian discipleship, it is the people of God who are responsible for them, and it is the fellowship of the whole church to which they should be devoted.

Christian Preaching as a Christological Sacrament

Preaching is a charismatic gift to the church, an ecclesiological function of the church, and a Christological sacrament within the church. We turn now to examine how preaching may bring the grace of God close to us.

A sacrament is a means whereby the grace of God is

made available to people. In the New Testament, Jesus Christ is the once for all sacrament, for it is in and through him, and him alone, that the grace of God is made available for our salvation: "There is salvation in no one else, for there is no other name under heaven given among mortals by which we must be saved" (Acts 4:12). No one and no thing, then, should in any way whatsoever be allowed to compete with the person of Christ.

There are, however, various means by which this one sacrament of grace is communicated to humans, of which preaching is chief. In that it communicates Christ, preaching, in that sense, is sacramental. The danger, of course, is that a means for experiencing Christ ends up being disconnected from Christ and comes to be viewed as having a power of its own; this is the sin of sacramentalism. In sacramentalism, one concentrates so much on the external form that the person of Christ who always stands beyond the form is treated as though he were bound to it. We are transformed by Christ himself, not by external forms. For example, one may be religiously devoted to a certain tradition, practice, and doctrine of the Lord's Supper and yet never experience the converting power of Christ himself. Or, one may like good preaching and, in fact, be a connoisseur of it, concentrating so intensely on the art and science of it that the converting power of the living Christ declared therein is missed. Sacramentalism is the sin not only of some Roman Catholics, Anglicans, and Lutherans at the table of the Lord; it is also the sin of some Presbyterians, Evangelicals, and Fundamentalists in front of the pulpit of the Lord's servants.

Having issued this caution, we are at greater liberty to say that preaching is a primary means by which the grace of Jesus Christ is communicated both to convert the unconverted and to edify believers. Paul spoke in Romans 1:15 of his great desire to preach the gospel in Rome and added in verse 16 that the gospel is "the power of God for salvation to everyone who has faith."

Preaching is a Christological sacrament in that the redemptive work of Christ is manifested in spoken words. Through the power of the Holy Spirit, Christ himself is present in gospel preaching to forgive, restore, sanctify, teach, and guide. Preaching is Christ at work in the message of his emissaries. It is the historical work of Christ being extended in time and space. It is the ongoing presence of Christ blessing us with salvation. It is the exalted Christ at work in the words of humans of low estate. As Paul says: "We have this treasure in clay jars, so that it may be made clear that this extraordinary power belongs to God and does not come from us." (2 Cor. 4:7)[18]

Notes

1. James Stalker, *The Preacher and His Models* (New York: A. C. Armstrong and Son, 1903), p. 194.

2. James I. Packer, *Christianity Today*, November 11, 1991, p. 15.

3. P.T. Forsyth, *Positive Preaching and Modern Mind* (London: Hodder and Stoughton, 1907), p. 10.

4. See John R. W. Stott, *Between Two Worlds: The Art of Preaching in the Twentieth Century* (Grand Rapids: Eerdmans, 1982).

5. See James Earl Massey, *The Responsible Pulpit* (Anderson, Ind: Warner, 1974).

6. See W. Norman Pittenger, *Proclaiming Christ Today* (Greenwich: Seabury,1962).

7. Phillips Brooks, *Lectures on Preaching* (New York: E. P. Dutton and Company, 1877), p. 129.

8. Charles E. Jefferson, *The Building of the Church* (New York: Macmillan, 1911), p. 31.

9. Ibid.

10. Forsyth, op. cit., p. 91.

11. Phillips Brooks touches on this balanced approach to effective preaching when he says: "If a preacher is not a man of his age, in sympathy with its spirit, his preaching fails. He wonders that the truth has grown so powerless. But it is not the truth that has failed. It is the other element, the person.... People would rather see

old men than young men in their pulpits, if only the old men bring them both elements of preaching, a faith that is eternally true, and a person that is in quick and ready sympathy with their present life" op. cit., p. 29f.

12. In Stalker, op. cit., Lecture 5 is on "The Preacher As a False Prophet," at the beginning of which a collection of Old Testament texts about false prophets is given in a footnote: Isa. 2:6; 28:7; 30:10–11; 47:13; 56:10–12; Jer. 2:8, 26; 4:9; 5:31; 6:14; 14:13–16; 18:18; 23:9–40 (a *locus classicus*); 26:8; 27:9, 16; 28; 29:8; Ezek. 12:24; 13 (a *locus classicus*); 14:9; 20:25; 21:23; 22:25, 28; Mic. 2:11; 3:5, 11; Zeph. 3:4; and Zech. 10:2 and 13:2–4.

13. Forsyth, op. cit., p. 79.

14. Ibid., p. 93.

15. Ibid., p. 95.

16. Jefferson, op. cit., p. 4.

17. Ibid. p. 5.

18. For a comprehensive treatment of preaching as what may be called a "clay jars" endeavor, see David Buttrick, *Homiletic: Moves and Structures* (Philadelphia: Fortress, 1987).

For Further Consideration

Part I: *Yale Lectures on Preaching*

A virtual library on Christian preaching—including the theology of preaching, preparation for it, methodology, and its place in the life of the church—is to be found in the *Yale Lectures on Preaching* dating from 1871.

Part II: Histories of Preaching

See Edwin Charles Dargan, *A History of Preaching*, Vols. I and II; Ralph G. Turnbull, Vol. III (Grand Rapids, Baker, 1974); Paul Scott Wilson, *A Concise History of Preaching* (Nashville: Abingdon, 1992). For both a history and theology, see Bernard Cooke, *Ministry to Word and Sacraments* (Philadelphia: Fortress, 1976).

A virtual library on Christian preaching—including the theology of preaching, preparation for it, methodology, and its place in the life of the church—is to be found in the *Yale Lectures on Preaching* dating from 1871. Examples of lecturers are Henry Ward Beecher (1871–72, 1872–73, and 1873–74) [of special interest is the story of his formative ministry in Lawrenceburg and Indianapolis, Indiana, referred to in the First Series (Boston: Pilgrim, 1872), pp. 10–12]; Phillips Brooks

(1876–77); Washington Gladden (1886–87, 1901–02); Henry Van Dyke (1895–96); P. T. Forsyth (1906–07); J. H. Jowett (1911–12); Henry Sloan Coffin (1917–18); Harry Emerson Fosdick (1923–24); George A. Buttrick (1930–31); Albert E. Day (1933–34); Charles Clayton Morrison (1938–39); Ralph W. Sockman (1940–41); Paul Scherer (1942–43); G. Bromley Oxnam (1943–44); Reinhold Niebuhr (1944–45); Leslie Weatherhead (1948–49); Halford E. Luccock (1952–53); Gerald Kennedy (1953–54); D. T. Niles (1956–57); Lesslie Newbigin (1965–66); Fred B. Craddock (1977–78); Krister Stendahl (1983–84); James Forbes (1985–86); Walter Bruggemann (1988–89).

11

Ministry in the Church

To be a minister is to serve the needs of others for their benefit. In that sense Christ Jesus is our eternal minister, and the Holy Spirit both prepares the way for Christ's ministry and extends it. It is with this Christ-centered focus that we refer to the ministry of the Holy Spirit.

The church as a whole is both ministered to by God through Christ in the power of the Holy Spirit, and, in turn, ministers to God, to each other, and to the world. The church, then, is a fellowship of ministers. It is a ministry and it has ministries. The church at its best has a spirit of ministry that characterizes the whole fellowship, and it includes various offices of ministry within the fellowship.

Four Basic Forms of Church Ministry

The New Testament reflects four basic forms of church ministry. The first is that of the original Twelve—a ministry growing out of the response of discipleship to the incarnate Lord for the purpose of establishing the church. The second is the ministry resulting from the work of the Holy Spirit in and through the lives of believers as believers—a ministry for the general edification of the church. The third is the ministry that takes place through persons specifically chosen not only by God but also by others to function for the benefit of the people of God as a whole—a ministry for the good ordering, stability, and historic continuity of the church. The fourth is that of persons with long-term charismatic vocations who, though not initially appointed by others, come, in the course of time, to be honored by the church as having a special role in the building up of the church.

The Ministry of the Twelve

The twelve apostles—the *dōdeka apostoloi* (Matt. 10; also see Acts 1:21–26; 2:14, 37, 42; 5:2; 6:1–6; 8:14; 11:1; 15)—were chosen by Jesus himself. Their basic qualification was that they were selected and trained by the incarnate Lord. Following his ascension, however, a different set of qualifications came into place for choosing a replacement for Judas. In Acts 1:21–22, Peter specifies that the successor must have accompanied them during the whole period from the time of "the baptism of John until the day when he was taken up from us." After proposing two names, the eleven prayed and then cast lots, no doubt with the understanding that the casting of the lots was the way by which the divine will would be revealed. The lot fell to Matthias.

The Twelve were the historic link between the incarnational Christ and the emerging church of resurrection faith. Their ministry is viewed in Revelation 21:14 as being foundational for Christian faith: "And the wall of the city has twelve foundations, and on them are the twelve names of the twelve apostles of the Lamb." Furthermore, in Luke 22:30, they are spoken of as having an eschatological role when as servants of Jesus they "sit on thrones judging the twelve tribes of Israel."

While the office of the twelve apostles is unique in that no individual successors were appointed to it (except for Matthias), its function is presently performed by the Bible, by the church as a whole, and by individuals with a missionary spirit. The Bible now serves as the basic literary link between Christ — i.e., his religious history as a Jew (the Old Testament), his incarnational ministry (particularly the Gospels), and his ongoing presence with the earliest church (the New Testament) — and us. In addition, the church, being endowed with the Spirit poured out on the day of Pentecost, now assumes the role of the Twelve as it goes to all peoples with the gospel.

This apostolic role of the Spirit-endowed church is personalized in particular individuals who exemplify in their own vocational passion the church's sent-forthness in the power of the Spirit (i.e., missionaries such as Paul and so many others throughout church history).[1] They are what the church as a whole is empowered to be, those sent on mission to "make disciples of all nations" (Matt. 28:19) and to be witnesses "to the ends of the earth" (Acts 1:8). They are apostles both in the way they function vocationally and in the way the church thinks of them, but not in the sense of being elected to the college of the Twelve.

That there were others in the New Testament church who vocationally filled the role of apostle is indicated by Acts 14:14 where both Barnabas and Paul are referred to as apostles. Also, Romans 16:7 may indicate the same: "Greet Andronicus and Junia, my relatives who were in prison with me; they are prominent among the apostles." The question is whether Andronicus and Junia themselves were known as apostles, or whether this is a reference to others known as apostles with whom the two mentioned are associated. In either case, an ongoing apostolic role in the life of the church is indicated, unless, of course, one understands this to be a reference to the Twelve alone, which seems unlikely given Paul's understanding of his own apostleship.

The Ministry of All Christians [2]

The second basic form of church ministry found in the New Testament is that of all believers as believers. By virtue of being recipients of God's converting grace, all are beneficiaries of God's continuing grace working itself out in them individually as they participate in the life of the church. It is believers in general—and not a special group within the church—to whom Paul speaks in Romans 12:4-6a:

> For as in one body we have many members, and not all the members have the same function, so we, who are many, are one body in Christ, and individually we are members one of another. We have gifts [*charismata*] that differ according to the grace given to us.

Likewise, 1 Corinthians 12:4-7 is addressed to the whole body of believers:

> Now there are varieties of gifts [*charismata*], but the same Spirit; and there are varieties of service [*diakonia*], but the same Lord; and there are varieties of activities [*energēmata*], but it is the same God who activates all of them in everyone. To each is given the manifestation of the Spirit for the common good.

After listing several manifestations in particular, Paul says in v. 11: "All these are activated by one and the same Spirit, who allots to each one individually just as the Spirit chooses." In v. 27 he concludes: "Now you are the body of Christ and individually members of it."

The emphasis in both of these passages is on the individual member fitting into the life of the church in such a way that he or she builds it up. The priority is on corporate wholeness, not individual gratification. The *charismata* are manifestations of the grace of God in individual believers for the good of the whole.

Or, as Paul Fiddes, Principal of Regents Park College, Oxford, and a British Baptist systematic theologian, calls them, "act[s] of God's gracious Spirit, creating a gift for service."[3] They have to do first and foremost with what God wills to do in the life of the church. That which God does in the lives of particular individuals is understood as being directly related to the edification of the church.

The question of highest priority is, What are the needs of the church? and not, What is my gift? The attitude consistent with the first question is the willingness to do one's part in fulfilling those needs. The attitude associated with the second may be that of fretting as to whether the church will allow one to use one's gift.

We begin at the wrong point when we first of all seek

to discover "gifts" within ourselves apart from the life of the church of which we are members. The scriptural focus is to consider the needs of the church and then to prayerfully consider how God wants to use us for meeting those needs. One of the problems in the Corinthian church was that some were taking the What is my gift? approach. Paul condemned this approach and urged them to take the second approach, namely, to begin with the needs of the church and to proceed from there. His message is that the *charismata* are never for individualistic pleasure but always for corporate edification.

Paul's argument in 1 Corinthians 12—14 is that it is not "gifts" as such that are crucial but the edification of the church. By translating *charismata* and *pneumatika* as "gifts," one may think that Paul is talking about something inside us that we are to discover and use. We would be much nearer to Paul's meaning if *charismata* were translated as manifestations of grace and *pneumatika* as manifestations of the Spirit. Such translations would read as follows:

12:1, "Now concerning manifestations of the Spirit [*pneumatika*], brothers and sisters, I do not want you to be uninformed."

v. 4, "Now there are varieties of manifestations of grace [*charismata*], but the same Spirit."

v. 9, "To another, grace manifestations [*charismata*] of healing by the one Spirit." (Also in v. 28.)

v. 30, "Do all possess grace manifestations [*charismata*] of healing?"

v. 31, "But strive for the greater manifestations of grace [*charismata*]."

14:1, "Pursue love and strive for manifestations of the Spirit [*pneumatika*], and especially that you may prophesy."

v. 12, "So with yourselves; since you are eager about spiritual matters [*pneumatōn*], strive to excel in building up the church."

Translating the key words in this way helps us to avoid an individualistic view of "gifts" as though they were something in us that we possess, and it reflects Paul's emphasis on the spiritual well being of the community of faith. This emphasis is found especially in chapter 13 where the priority of love is stressed, as well as in 14:1–5 where prophecy and interpretation are given primacy over tongues because the former edify the church whereas the latter in and of themselves do not. In v. 12 of the same chapter, he gives explicit instructions about excelling in building up the church, followed in vv. 13–19 with a personal testimony about his own desire to speak clearly in public so that others may say the Amen and be built up, rather than speaking so as to merely feel good about his private relation-ship with God. Verse 26 reemphasizes the point: "Let all things be done for building up."

But now let us give further consideration to chapter 12, which speaks of a three-fold manifestation that approximates the three-foldness of God. He associates the *charismata* with the Spirit; the *diakonia* with the Lord (Jesus? as in 2 Cor. 13:13?) and the *energēmata* with God (the Father? as in Eph. 4:6?). The emphasis, however, is not on the separate function of each of the three, but on the unitary working of God. It is the one God — God the Father, God the Incarnate One, God the Spirit — who is at work in the lives of believers for the sake of the whole church. We are not free, therefore, to speak of the Spirit's endowment for the edification of the church as though it were the work of only one third of the triune God. Instead, it is the triune God in all of God's fullness who is at work in the life of the church for its edification.

In Ephesians 4:4–7, we see this same emphasis on the one God at work for the well being of the one church:

> There is one body and one Spirit, just as you were called to the one hope of your calling, one Lord, one faith, one baptism, one God and Father of all, who is above all and through all and in all. But each of us was given grace according to the measure of Christ's gift.

It is in and through each Christian that God in all of God's fullness is at work in the church for the purpose of accomplishing the divine mission revealed in Christ. The *charismata* are the evidences that this divine work is taking place in the life of the church.[4]

The Ministry of the Church's Offices

The third basic form of ministry found in the New Testament requires human appointment and is related to particular offices of responsibility. Thomas Oden defines an office as "a position of trust, an assigned service of function, with specified duties and authority."[5] The New Testament presents us with at least two such offices.

The first are the presbyters or elders (*presbuteroi*). At the Jerusalem Council, they played an important role alongside the twelve apostles (see Acts 15:2, 4, 6, 22, 23). They, along with the apostles, had oversight of the church.

First Timothy 3:1–7 and Titus 1:5–9 set forth qualifications for presbyters, called *episcopoi* in both of these passages but in Titus also called *presbuteroi*. Fiddes comments: "This [*episcopoi*] is a Greek title for leadership borrowed from the Graeco-Roman society ... and by now these leaders are identical with the '*presbuteroi*' (elders) which is a Jewish title derived from leadership in the synagogue (1 Tim. 3:1, 5:17, Titus 1:5–7)."[6] The listing of additional qualifications for the *episcopoi/presbuteroi* means that charismatic endowment was not sufficient for holding such a ministerial office.

The wider importance of this office is indicated by the fact that it was not only the Jerusalem church that had *presbuteroi* but others as well: the Ephesian church (see Acts 20:17 and 21:18) and the Philippian church (see Phil. 1:1). Additionally, Acts 14:23 speaks of Paul and Barnabas appointing presbyters (i.e., elders) "in each church," and in Titus 1:5, Titus is instructed to "appoint elders in every town."

On the basis of New Testament references, we conclude that

1) the *presbuteroi* and the *episcopoi* are one and the same (i.e., Titus 1:5 and 7 use the two words interchangeably);

2) their role is that of spiritual oversight of the church as well as pastoral care, (see James 5:14);

3) some, though not all, "labor in preaching and teaching" (1 Tim. 5:17);

4) it is an office of leadership toward which one might move in an intentional manner (1 Tim. 3:1) and receive financial remuneration (5:18);

5) it is a shepherding office under Jesus Christ, the chief shepherd of the church (1 Peter 5:1–5);

6) the church in the New Testament era recognized the need for *episcopoi/presbuteroi* for the purpose of building up the church in the apostolic faith (See Titus 1:9).[7]

As the word *episcopos*, meaning overseer, indicates, the primary role of the presbyters was that of oversight. First Timothy 3:5 speaks of them as having the responsibility to take care of the church of God.

In the subsequent history of the church, the *presbuteroi* and the *episcopoi* were separated into two different offices, the former being responsible for one local congregation and the latter for multiple congregations. However, in the New Testament itself there is no indication of such a separation, the two referring to one and the same office of responsibility, a position returned to by the Reformed/Presbyterian line of the sixteenth century reformation.

Having said that, however, it is true that even in the New Testament there are both those who provide oversight primarily to a local congregation and those who provide oversight for multiple congregations. For example, while Paul is never referred to as an *episcopos*, he does oversee the spiritual well being of multiple congregations. The New Testament also provides evidence, as in the case of the Pastoral Epistles, that there is oversight for persons such as Timothy and Titus, who themselves are charged with the responsibility of spiritual oversight.

As far as Paul is concerned, his ministry of oversight is strictly a charismatic ministry in that no body of Christians actually appointed him to such an office. It is another instance of the Spirit's work in the church for the purpose of meeting its needs. Evidently, the church needed persons who could and would provide spiritual oversight not only to multiple congregations but also to "Timothies and Tituses." Such oversight helped to keep the scattered congregations and their leaders from being disconnected from each other. In the history of the church, even those churches that are most fiercely independent, do, in the course of time, discover the importance of having some spiritual leader from outside the local congregation who cares about them and is able to minister to them. The New Testament knows nothing about radical independence and absolute local autonomy. Its emphasis is very much in the opposite direction, emphasizing the bonds of unity among the faithful.

The second category of ministries requiring appointment to a particular office of responsibility is that of deacons, *diakonoi* (i.e., servants, ministers, attendants). Qualifications for holding this office are set forth in 1 Timothy 3:8-13.

Paul in the salutation of Philippians 1:1 includes the *diakonoi* along with the *episcopoi*. Special instructions are given about a deacon in Romans 16:1-2 where Paul says:

> I commend to you our sister Phoebe, a deacon of the church at Cenchreae, so that you may welcome her in the Lord as is fitting for the saints, and help her in whatever she may require from you, for she has been a benefactor of many and of myself as well.

Also, although they are not called deacons in the text, the seven who were appointed to take care of the daily distribution of food in the Jerusalem church (see Acts 6:1-6) certainly functioned as such in the service of the local church.

On the basis of the etymology of the word itself, meaning service or ministry, and on the basis of the reference to deacon Phoebe, as well as to the Jerusalem seven, we conclude that the office of deacon was one of helping church life to be conducted "decently and in order." As with Phoebe, deacons are "benefactor[s] of many."

While all members of the church are called to be ministering servants, some responsibilities need to be assumed by those who are specifically designated for particular tasks. The appointment of deacons, then, is the way the church has of guaranteeing that ministries that ought to take place in the life of the church do, in fact, take place.[8]

While the apostolic office was primarily foundational and constitutive, the episcopal/presbyterial office is primarily pastoral, interpretive, superintending, and concerned with spiritual oversight; and the diaconal office is primarily for the good of the ordered life of the local congregation.

The ministries of the church's offices, by their very nature, require that special attention be given both to preparation for them and to the church's ordination procedures regarding them. While the New Testament gives no outline for the preparation of its ministerial officers, it is clear that charismatic endowment is not enough. According to 1 Timothy 3 and Titus 1, office holders need to be spiritually sound, ethically pure, emotionally stable, committed to family responsibilities, worthy of confidence, capable of both domestic and church leadership, matured by experience, level headed, knowledgeable of the historic faith, and able to teach it. While preparation for the church's offices, therefore, is biblically mandated, the shape that such preparation takes differs from place to place and from time to time. The mode of preparation and its specific requirements should grow out of the church's collective experience and wisdom.

In the United States, for instance, the church's collective wisdom generally calls for the master of divinity degree, which typically represents three years of study following college. While there is nothing sacrosanct about this mode of preparation, it does provide a formal structure of preparation for the ordained ministry. It gives opportunity for persons to mature emotionally, to be under intensive supervision, to gain historical perspective, to become more fully informed about the scriptures, to critique, revise, and formulate their conceptions of the faith, to develop colleague support systems, to acquire additional ministerial skills, to test their sense of calling, and to expand their knowledge of the cultural setting(s) in which they may be ministering.

The *Baptism, Eucharist, and Ministry* document says it well:

> Candidates for the ordained ministry need appropriate preparation through study of scripture and theology, prayer and spirituality, and through acquaintance with the social and human realities of the contemporary world. In some situations, this preparation may take a form other than that of prolonged academic study. The period of training will be one in which the candidate's call is tested, fostered and confirmed, or its understanding modified.[9]

Adequate preparation for the ordained ministry requires charismatic endowment, emotional and spiri-

tual maturity, a divine call and comprehensive studies—all four. It is not a matter of one or of two or of
three, but of all four. Whenever the church lays hands[10]
of ordination on a person whose preparation is lacking
in *any one* of these four components, it does so at its
own great peril.[11]

The Ministry of Long-term Charismatic Vocations

The New Testament presents us with a fourth form of
ministry, which is that of long-term charismatic vocations. Such persons work for the spread of the gospel
and for the edification of the church but do so without
having been initially appointed by the church to particular offices of responsibility. The ministries that such
persons have are much more vocationally specific than
are the general charismatic expressions manifested in
the daily life of the church.

Paul is an example of this form of ministry. Clearly,
he was not appointed to his work by the church; in fact,
the evidence points in the other direction, namely, that
the established church found it difficult to accept the
manifestation of grace in his life (see Acts 9:26 and Gal.
1:11–17). In his struggle to be accepted, we see the tension that often exists between ministries charismatically
endowed but without ecclesial appointment, and ministries requiring ecclesial appointment. Not only do we

see it between Paul as a charismatic leader and the apostolic Twelve who held special offices of responsibility in the Jerusalem church, but also between Paul and the charismatics in the Corinthian church. The tables had turned: whereas in the first instance, Paul was the somewhat defensive charismatic, in the latter, he was very much on the offensive for the purpose of correcting charismatics.

Furthermore, it is none other than Paul who advances the thought that the church needs the stability of office holders who are more than charismatics, for in 1 Thessalonians 5:12–13a, he encourages respect for those who are in offices of spiritual oversight:

> But we appeal to you, brothers and sisters, to respect those who labor among you, and have charge of you in the Lord and admonish you; esteem them very highly in love because of their work.

Paul's experience of charismatic endowments is instructive for us as we continue to deal with this reality from age to age. His endowments came not from human beings but directly from God; they were used for both the extension of the church and for its edification; they took shape as a divine vocation. In the course of time his vocationally oriented charismatic ministry was recognized both by officers of ministry and by the church in general as being truly of God.

His sense of divine call and his struggle to be recognized by the church's officers of ministry are set forth in Galatians 1:1 – 2:10. In 1:1, he begins with the words: "Paul an apostle – sent neither by human commission nor from human authority, but through Jesus Christ and God the Father." In vv. 15-16 he expresses his claims even more strongly when he says, "But when God, who had set me apart before I was born and called me through his grace, was pleased to reveal his Son to me, so that I might proclaim him among the Gentiles, I did not confer with any human being." In 2:9, however, he does testify to his eventual recognition by the officers of ministry: "And when James and Cephas and John, who were acknowledged pillars, recognized the grace that had been given to me, they gave to Barnabas and me the right hand of fellowship, agreeing that we should go to the Gentiles and they to the circumcised."

In the course of time, not only was Paul's calling recognized by the officers of ministry, but, more importantly, by the church at large. Acts 13 tells about the church at Antioch commissioning Barnabas and Paul for missionary service. Verses 2 and 3:

> While they were worshiping the Lord and fasting, the Holy Spirit said, "Set apart for me Barnabas and Saul for the work to which I have called them." Then after fasting and praying they laid their hands on them and sent them off.

The recognition by the church at large was, of course, wider than Antioch's laying on of hands. In 2 Peter 3 not only is he referred to as "our beloved brother" (v. 15), but also his writings are already referred to as scripture (v. 16).[12] The eventual inclusion of his writings in the church's scriptures was the supreme form of recognition.

Two Necessary Dimensions in the Life of the Church

The different forms of ministry in the life of the New Testament church point to two necessary dimensions in ecclesial life, one being the dynamic dimension with its emphasis on the immediacy of God at work, and the other being the stabilizing dimension with its emphasis on continuity in the life of the church. As George Montague observes, the distinction between the two, as though they were two different types of churches each separate from the other "is a modern invention not founded in the New Testament."[13]

Reality in general is characterized by the same dimensions. The world as we know it is both dynamic and stable. It is dynamic in that the unexpected happens; it is stable in that we can count on it being constant enough to make plans for the future and carry them out.

Indeed, the God whom we meet in the Bible is both

dynamic and stable. As the mysterious one, God surprises us. As the faithful one, God can be counted on.

The stable God of the ancient Hebrews is also the dynamic One who makes all things new (Rev. 21:5). The faithful God of Abraham is also the God who surprised Abraham and Sarah with the news that they were to have a son, surprised Moses at the burning bush, and surprised the world in the unexpected incarnation having to do with a baby in a Bethlehem manger and a dying man on a Jerusalem cross. God's sure promises were fulfilled by the unsettling outpouring of the wind-like and fire-like Spirit on the day of Pentecost.

The Church's Need for All Four Forms of New Testament Ministries

In order for the church to be in health, both stable continuity and dynamic immediacy are necessary. Study of the basic forms of church ministry in the New Testament introduces us in a graphic way to the interplay between the immediacy of experience and the continuity of history that was so much a part of the early church's existence, and of ours, as well.

The church needs both stable continuity and dynamic immediacy in order to be consistent with the kind of God whose church we are, and in harmony with the kind of world God created. Stable continuity is represented by the ministry of the Twelve, of the Bible, of the historic church, and of the church's officers. Dynamic immediacy is often seen in the charismatic endowments in the life of the church in general as well as in charismatic vocations that grow out of such endowments.

The tension that we witness in the New Testament between charismatic endowment and regulated offices is one that has always been with the church and no doubt always will be until the consummation at the end of world history. In God's economy, however, each serves the other, both as a check on the other as well as its complement. While the charismatic ministry focuses on God's sovereign prerogative, regulated offices of ministry focus on the church's responsibility under God.

The relationship between the *charismata* and the regulated offices is somewhat analogous to the relationship between the Holy Spirit and the Word of God. The Spirit prepares for the Word, is the breath of the Word, and brings the Word to our remembrance. The Spirit is the power of the Word, and the Word is the form of the Spirit's power. Likewise, charismatic ministry is the divine power of the regulated offices of ministry, and the offices are the institutional forms of the *charismata*. One without the other is a distortion of the divine economy.

Holding offices of ministry, but without charismatic

power, leads to clericalism. On the other hand, a charismatic ministry that does not have the benefit of the regulated offices of ministry may be devoid of biblical, apostolic, historical, institutional, and intellectual continuity.

The regulated offices of responsibility are designed neither to be over against God's people, between God and God's people, a substitute for God, nor the proxy for doing the work of God's people. Rather, in God's economy, they are designed to function in a specialized way for the purpose of preparing the whole charismatically endowed people of God for works of service, so that the body of Christ may be built up. They are the church's appointed transmitters of the faith, its chosen instructors in the faith, and its representative spokespersons for the faith. They are God's way of

[equipping] the saints for the work of ministry, for building up the body of Christ, until all of us come to the unity of the faith and of the knowledge of the Son of God, to maturity, to the measure of the full stature of Christ.

(Eph. 4:12–13)

Notes

1. See John Howard Schütz, *Paul and the Anatomy of Apostolic Authority* (Cambridge: Cambridge University Press, 1975). "The legitimacy of an apostle lies in the combination of his calling to preach the gospel and his being granted a resurrection vision, but for Paul his authority has as its starting point the call to preach. All authority is possible only on the grounds that it is an extension of this original commission," p. 281.

2. An excellent biblical study of this topic is John Koenig, *Charismata: God's Gifts* (Philadelphia: Westminster, 1978).

3. Paul Fiddes, *A Leading Question: The Structure and Authority of Leadership in the Local Church* (London: Baptist Publications, n.d.), p. 19.

4. See Hans Küng, "The Continuing Charismatic Structure," *Theological Foundations for Ministry*, ed. Ray S. Anderson (Grand Rapids: Eerdmans, 1979), pp. 458–489.

5. Thomas C. Oden, *The Word of Life: Systematic Theology: Volume Two* (San Francisco: Harper and Row, 1989), p. 20.

6. Fiddes, op. cit., p. 29.

7. Other references to *presbuteroi* are Acts 11:30; 16:4; 1 Tim. 5:19; 2 John 1; 3 John 1; Rev. 4:4; 4:10; 5:5–14; 7:11–13; 11:16; 14:3; 19:4.

8. See Thomas F. Torrance, "Service in Jesus Christ,"

Theological Foundations for Ministry, ed. Ray S. Anderson (Grand Rapids: Eerdmans, 1979), pp. 714–733.

9. *Baptism, Eucharist and Ministry,* Faith and Order Paper No. 111 (Geneva: World Council of Churches, 1982), p. 31. See comment in For Further Consideration.

10. Whereas Acts 14:23 speaks of Paul and Barnabas appointing (*cheirotonein*) elders in churches, most ordaining references are to the laying on of hands, seen in the basic texts as a service of commission to a specific assignment (Acts 6:6 and 13:3), a service of recognition of God's call to persons (13:2–3), and as a service of charismatic bestowal (1 Tim. 4:14; 2 Tim. 1:6).

11. An example of the church's collective wisdom regarding the full range of preparedness is the *Readiness for Ministry Project* conducted by the Association of Theological Schools in the United States and Canada: Vol. I, "Criteria," 1975; Vol. II, "Assessment," 1976.

12. 2 Peter 3:15b–16: "So also our beloved brother Paul wrote to you according to the wisdom given him, speaking of this as he does in all his letters. There are some things in them hard to understand, which the ignorant and unstable twist to their own destruction, as they do the *other* scriptures" (emphasis mine; the implication being that Paul's writings were viewed as being scripture, too).

13. George T. Montague, *The Holy Spirit: Growth of a Biblical Tradition* (New York: Paulist, 1976), p. 162.

For Further Consideration

See Kevin Giles, *Patterns of Ministry Among the First Christians* (North Blackburn, Victoria, Australia: CollinsDove, 1992).

For an historical study of Christian ministry, see H. Richard Niebuhr and Daniel D. Williams (eds.), *The Ministry in Historical Perspectives* (New York: Harper, 1956).

For a history of women in ministry in one particular tradition — the Church of God (Anderson), see Juanita Evans Leonard (ed), *Called to Minister ... Empowered to Serve* (Anderson, Ind: Warner Press, 1989).

For a landmark ecumenical statement, see the section on "Ministry" in *Baptism, Eucharist and Ministry, Faith and Order Paper No. 111* (Geneva: World Council of Churches, 1982), pp. 20–32. Major headings include (1) "The Calling of the Whole People of God," (2) "The Church and the Ordained Ministry," (3) "The Forms of the Ordained Ministry," and (4) "Succession in the Apostolic Tradition." It reviews biblical materials and historic positions, states contemporary convergence of thought among major traditions, identifies continuing disagreements, and formulates questions needing further study.

12

The Church as the Jesus Movement

Traditional Forms

Church structures are usually classified in three basic categories: episcopal, presbyterian and congregational. To be sure, New Testament support can be found for each. John Davis in his *Handbook of Basic Bible Texts* lists the following references: Under Episcopal, he lists Matthew 16:18–19; Acts 14:21–23; Philippians 1:1; 1 Timothy 3:1; 2 Tim. 1:6; Titus 1:5. Under Presbyterian, Acts 15:1, 6,22–23, 28–29; 20:17, 28; 1 Timothy 4:14; James 5:14. Under Congregational, Matthew 18:17; Acts 6:3,5; 2 Corinthians 2:6–7; 8:19; 2 Thessalonians 3:14–15; Jude 3.[1]

The episcopal form assumes that emerging in the New Testament is a three-fold ministry: bishops (or overseers), elders (or presbyters), and deacons. The distinctive emphasis is on the Lord's delegation of authority to his apostles, which was then handed on to the bishops. Catholicism, Orthodoxy, and Anglicanism are historic examples of this form.

The presbyterian form assumes that the New Testament presents a two-fold ministry: elders (or presbyters) and deacons. The distinctive emphasis is on the intercongregational assembly of church leaders. Presbyterianism and the reformed churches are classic expressions of this tradition.

The congregational form emphasizes the local assembly of believers as the basic structure for decision making. Congregationalism and a wide assortment of independent churches exemplify this mode of church organization.

The essence of all emerging structures in the New Testament is that they were movemental in nature. Sociologically, the New Testament church was a movement first within Judaism and later to the Gentile world. It was a movement within Judaism regarding the fulfillment of Kingdom and messiahship promises. It was a movement in the Gentile world to convince people that in Christ there was salvation for all who believe. It was a movement with an overarching vision to spread the gospel (Matt. 28:18–20, Mark 16:15, Luke 24:47–48, Acts 1:8), with an underlying commitment to the work of being nurtured in the faith (e.g., Acts 2:42,

Eph. 4:14–16), and with the ongoing challenge to be united in spite of their often very great differences (e.g., John 17:20–23, Eph. 4:1–6, 11–13). The young church was not in search of a perfect organization as an end in and of itself; instead, it was devoted to the spread of the gospel, to maturation in the life of Christ, and to the development of a unified witness to the world. Emerging structures found in the New Testament grew out of a commitment to being a Jesus movement for the redemption of the world.

The Sociology of Movements

In his discussion of sociological movements, Robert Lauer notes that "the very definition of ... social movement involves *change*."[2] (Emphasis added here and throughout this section.) He quotes Luther P. Gerlach and Virginia H. Hine who, in their *People, Power, Change: Movements of Social Transformation,* define a movement as

> a group of people who are organized for, ideologically motivated by, and committed to a purpose which implements some form of *personal* or *social change;* who are *actively engaged in the recruitment of others;* and whose influence is spreading *in opposition to the established order* within which it originated (p. xvi).[3]

Lauer himself goes on to say that "all movements must have a *strategy for change....* Leaders of movements must answer such questions as who or what is to be the target of change and how that target is to be attacked.[4] In addition, according to Lauer, "All social movements, whatever else they do, effect some *change in their members.*" He amplifies this idea by saying that "Whatever the goals of the movement ... social psychological change in members form a part of the overall effects."[5]

In *Social Movements of the Sixties and Seventies,* Jo Freeman identifies two characteristics of social movements: "noticeable *spontaneity* and a *describable structure.*"[6] Further on, Freeman writes:

> Of utmost importance is *the consciousness that one is part of a group with whom one shares awareness of a particular concern.* Individuals [and churches?] acting in response to common social forces with no particular identification with one another may be setting a trend, but they are not part of a movement.[7]

And again: "When it [the missionary impulse] is lacking, it usually indicates that the movement has been successfully repressed or is stagnating. It may also mean that what ought to be a movement has never become one."[8] And finally, "What is necessary is identification of a problem, and if the movement is to grow beyond its initiators, *some vision of a better future*. These alone can create a *belief system* of extraordinary powers."[9]

In these definitions, the following characteristics define sociological movements:

• They are organized for, motivated by, and committed to change;

• members share a common vision;

• additional persons are recruited to join their ranks;

• they are influential in the context out of which they emerge;

• they have a strategy for reaching their goal(s);

• they bring about fundamental changes in their own members;

• dynamism and spontaneity characterize their *esprit de corps;*

• they possess a sense of interconnectedness with others for a common cause.[10]

A Challenge Facing the Contemporary Church

One of the many challenges facing the contemporary church is to tap into the dynamism of the first-century Jesus movement. (The way this happens is through the empowerment of the Holy Spirit, discussed in chapter 19.) The temptation of some Christian groups is to be more concerned about maintaining their own separate movement within the church than they are about aligning themselves with the ongoing Jesus movement. The temptation of others is to try to replicate a New Testament structural pattern perceived to be singularly approved by God.

Regarding the first temptation, it is important to remember that while legitimate movements *within* the church are part and parcel of its historical life, the church established by Jesus *is* a movement. Movements within the church come and go, but the Jesus movement is destined to continue to the end of time. Movements within the church serve the Spirit's purposes and then cease to exist, but the Jesus movement is empowered by the poured-out Spirit at Pentecost for the rest of time.

Movements within the church often retain a movemental vocabulary long after they cease functioning sociologically as one (see For Further Consideration). The more serious issue, however, is that they may fail to think of themselves as a dynamic part of the discipleship movement begun by Jesus.

For a church group to think of itself as a part of the two-thousand-year-old Jesus movement entails focusing all its energies on discipling the nations, serving as dramatic signs of the kingdom, and growing up in the image of Jesus Christ. To be a part of the Jesus movement is to pool our resources to get on with the missionary mandate of our Lord.

Regarding the second temptation mentioned above, namely, to try replicating a structural pattern perceived to be singularly approved of God, it is, in fact, impossible, with twenty centuries of history behind us, to wipe the slate clean and start over with a primitive pattern. Although many attempts at doing so have been made, they never succeed, first of all, because of the unrelenting pressure of contemporary circumstances, and second, because the collective, historical experience of the church inevitably influences whatever we do. It is impossible to extract ourselves from being who we are at a given time, influenced as we are by all that has transpired prior to that point. This position was stated well by P. T. Forsyth early this century when he said:

We cannot go back to the fountain head and simply ignore the 2,000 years of Christian evolution.... We cannot restore the exact conditions of the New Testament Church.... The normative in the New Testament is not a pattern. It is there in a historic context, not on a desert island.... We have not sufficient data about that very early state of affairs. Those who suggest such a thing are devoid of the historical sense.... To couple up directly with the Church order of the first century ... would be in truth to break with the past in its more inward reality. We may re-interpret and re-organize, but we cannot restore it.... All such attempts have been failures, and, more or less, waste. The future must grow out of all the past. Neither Church history nor Church piety is a continuous fall from the first century, where each age feels itself at the bottom, and must start scrambling up. Rather the whole of history converges and ascends through the present.... We have to solve our own problems as the whole past presents them.[11]

A New Testament Type of Movemental Church

The question, then, for the church to ask itself is not how to recreate a first century replica, but how to structure itself in the present century so that it can be a New Testament type of movemental church.

1) A Missionary Church with a Decisive Theology. A New Testament type of movemental church gives primary attention to the Christian mission. In the New Testament, mission is rooted in new theological understandings. To proclaim that Jesus is Lord, as the first century church did, is a *theological* proclamation. To teach that he is the Son of God and Savior of the world is a new *theological* teaching. To function with the conviction that all people need to hear the gospel about salvation through faith in Jesus Christ implies a *theological* framework for the work of the people of God. For the New Testament church, the Christian mission was an outgrowth of a new theological orientation; their

275

missiology grew out of their theology. Missiology and theology were inextricably bound together. Therefore, if the contemporary church is to be movemental in the New Testament sense, it can neither relegate theology to the academics in a seminary, nor consideration of the divine mission to one of several boards in a denominational structure. To do so is to split theology and mission. "What God has joined together let no one put asunder" should be the watch word for those who are involved in structuring the life of the church. A contemporary church is in spiritual continuity with the New Testament church only when New Testament theology and mission as a unit are at the forefront of everything it says and does. For a church to be structured movementally in harmony with the first-century Christian movement is for it to be structured in such a way that its central focus is on its theological mission and missionary theology.

2) A Nurturing Church That Cares about Persons. Those who are converted to Christ, as well as others, who though not converted are within the church's care, deserve to be nurtured either in the faith or toward the faith, as the case may be. As they grow and develop, make vocational choices, decide about marriage and singleness, face issues of life and death, and move through the stages of life, they need the guidance of the Christian faith. The Jesus movement, therefore, takes into account that those under its care are developing physically, spiritually, emotionally, and socially. That means that the church that structures itself movementally must concern itself not only with theology and mission, but with the nurture of those who either have already responded personally to the gospel or who are yet to respond. Its constituents will be treated not as impersonal cogs in an impersonal mission, but as recipients of personal care. A movemental church is structured in such a way that it can optimize its ministry for the spiritual conversion, growth, and development of every person in its fellowship.

3) An Interconnected Church. The church that structures itself movementally in harmony with the early Christian movement builds structures of interconnectedness with the whole church. God has only one church and only one mission. Contemporary structures that are harmonious with the one divine mission of the one church take seriously their responsibility to the whole church. It is God's whole church that is called to be on mission to God's whole world. A church group that does not pursue interconnectedness with all other Christians functions in fragmented fashion. For one tradition of Christians to disregard other traditions means probably one of two things: either it believes the other is not Christian, or it disregards the crucial importance of its interconnectedness to the whole church, in which case, sadly, it lives in contradiction to New Testament calls for unity.

The wider church includes those with whom any given church has great comfortability (e.g., a shared piety, a similar doctrinal emphasis, a common history) as well as those with whom it has great discomfort (e.g., foreign modes of worship, different organizational structures, contrary doctrinal emphases, dissimilar social locations). The Jerusalem church's distress with the Gentile churches is a first-century example. In fact, Judaizers from Jerusalem tried to convert the Galatian church to their way of thinking. Galatians 1 and 2 is a window into this conflict. In 2:11–14 Paul refers to his own sharp rebuke of Peter when he came to Antioch as a representative of the Jerusalem church. Nevertheless, the Jerusalem church took seriously its relationship to the Gentile churches, as we see in Acts 15, and Paul was committed to maintaining fellowship with the Jerusalem church, as we see in his stubborn earnestness to return there from his missionary work (see Acts 21:1–26) and his equally strong commitment to the gathering of an offering for them (1 Cor. 16:1–4; 2 Cor. 9).

It is crucial, therefore, for contemporary churches that seek to be in fellowship with the church depicted in the New Testament to ask themselves the following question: Do we have structures that facilitate the intentional and vigorous pursuit of interconnections with those Christian traditions with which we feel great comfortability as well as with those which cause us great discomfort? To the extent that churches can answer in the affirmative, they are to that extent in harmony with this dimension of the movemental church of the New Testament. (See chapter 13 for more discussion of Christian unity.)

A Movemental Structure

In summary, then, the following are the movemental principles growing out of these considerations. A church that thinks and acts movementally

1) is earnestly devoted to the Christian mission, instead of being devoted merely to the survival of its own organizational structures;

2) is infinitely flexible in its structured life as it responds to the Spirit, instead of being stymied in traditional structures that inhibit the accomplishment of its mission;[12]

3) is involved in grass roots discipleship, instead of being inundated by institutional intricacies;

4) is vigorously related to the whole church, instead

of trying to distance itself from it; and

5) is guided by missionary models instead of corporate business models.

One way of structuring church life movementally is for the body—whether it be a local congregation or a regional or confessional association—to organize its responsibilities in three arenas: theology and mission, Christian nurture, and internal and wider church relations. A coordinating entity would function to synchronize the work in each arena. Linked with this entity would be a parallel entity that would monitor how well the church body is doing as part of the Jesus movement, and address such questions as the following:

• How well is it (whether congregation, association, national or international organization or agency) doing at making disciples?

• Do structural changes need to be made in order to facilitate greater effectiveness in the care of souls?

• Is it in touch with the daily life of individual Christians?

• Is it establishing new relationships with other Christian traditions—both those very similar to their own and those very dissimilar?

• Is it functioning as God's missionary people, and with deep commitment to God's purposes and God's strategy?

Putting the questions more directly in line with an evaluation of organizational structures as such, the following would be asked:

• Do the organizational structures aid or hinder in communicating the gospel to more and more people?

• Do they help people to grow up into the fullness of Christ or inhibit their growth?

• Does the structured life reflect an eagerness "to maintain the unity of the Spirit in the bond of peace," or does it reflect a resistance to such a concern?

These are discipleship questions, and not financial questions, or questions having to do with institutional preservation, organizational expansion, the interrelatedness of corporate structures, or business matters. This is not to say that the latter questions are irrelevant, but that they are secondary, not primary. The secondary questions must never be allowed to overshadow the movemental questions regarding the making of disciples, the nurturing of disciples, and the interpersonal relatedness of disciples.

Bernard Thorogood, one-time general secretary and clerk of the General Assembly of the United Reformed Church in the United Kingdom has said:

> The church as institution is being challenged by the church as movement. We are not permitted to rest where we are, precisely because there is a pilgrimage of

faith, a calling towards a fuller unity and catholicity and holiness. All the major churches reveal an institutionalized concept of faith (witness how hard it is for them to deal with the independent churches of Africa) and therefore need to take very seriously the movement of people out of accustomed structures. The younger Christians, impatient with the institutions, lead the way towards more open grouping, more sacrificial giving, more awareness of the world church in which we live.[13]

Notes

1. John Jefferson Davis, *Handbook of Basic Bible Texts: Every Key Passage for the Study of Doctrine and Theology* (Grand Rapids: Academie, 1984), pp. 107–114.

2. Robert H. Lauer, *Social Movements and Social Change* (Carbondale: Southern Illinois University Press, 1976), p. xiii.

3. Ibid.

4. Ibid., p. 171. Lauer says that the following observation made by Gil Green in *The New Radicalism: Anarchist or Marxist?* is applicable to any movement if the word 'revolutionary' be omitted: "Without a common approach to strategy it is impossible to build a common Movement. A common approach to strategy is needed to help pull together the present disparate, amorphous, confused and divided Movement into a serious, ongoing and growing force for revolutionary change."

5. Ibid. p. 123.

6. Jo Freeman, (ed.), *Social Movements of the Sixties and Seventies* (New York: Longman, 1983), p. 2.

7. Ibid.

8. Ibid., p. 3.

9. Ibid.

10. Another major resource for definitions of social movements is Paul Wilkinson, *Social Movement* (New York: Praeger, 1971).

11. P. T. Forsyth, *Positive Preaching and Modern Mind* (London: Hodder and Soughton, 1907), pp. 143–145.

12. See Thomas Langford, *Practical Divinity: Theology in the Wesleyan Tradition* (Nashville: Abingdon, 1983): "There is a pernicious idolatry in sustaining an organizational form only in the interest of self-preservation. As the vitality of purpose within a movement declines, there is often an aggressive effort to reinforce the organizational structure that earlier served its dynamic life. A developed church order may be confused with the initiating and ultimate cause it was intended to serve; and by subtle shift, structure may be perpetuated in the name of the cause," p. 270.

13. Bernard Thorogood, "Local Ecumenism in England," *Mid-Stream: An Ecumenical Journal* XXVII, 2 (April 1988), 146f.

For Further Consideration

For an example of a church tradition with a movemental vocabulary, see Leroy Garrett, *The Stone-Campbell Movement* (Joplin: College Press, 1987).

The Church of God (Anderson), known in-house as a reformation movement, is another example. For a comprehensive history, see John W. V. Smith, *The Quest for Unity and Holiness*, (Anderson, Ind: Warner, 1982).

For a sociological analysis of the Church of God which contrasts with the description provided by Smith, see Val Clear, *Where the Saints Have Trod: A Social History of the Church of God Reformation Movement* (Chesterfield: Midwest Publications, 1977) .

13

Christian Unity

Overly Ambitious? Overly Idealistic?

Christian unity is a topic about which it is easy to be either overly ambitious in institutional matters or overly idealistic in preaching and teaching. The overly ambitious may fall into one of two traps: a heavy bureaucracy that attempts to make everyone conform to its views, or a broad tolerance that minimizes issues of truth and allows all sorts of viewpoints as long as the structures that permit disagreements are not called into question.

The overly idealistic may fall into other traps: either a doctrinal view (e.g., the church as the bride of Christ) that has little to do with the lived out experience of being the church, or a churchly spiritualization (e.g., the invisible church) that fails to deal with the practical and historical realities of church life. The overly ambitious run the risk of being political manipulators of church institutions, whereas the overly idealistic tend to ignore history.

The church, however, is both a spiritual reality that exceeds sociological structures and a historical reality that cannot exist apart from such structures. The New Testament tells the story not only of the church's victorious faith but also of its ongoing struggles.

Unity in the New Testament

Central among church themes in the New Testament are passages having to do with the spiritual unity that Christ both wills and gives—passages such as John 10:14–16 (one flock and one shepherd); chapter 17 (Jesus' prayer that they may all be one); 1 Corinthians 10:16–17 (the one body partakes of the one bread); 12:12–27 (one body with many members); 2 Corinthians 5:16–21 (a new creation reconciled to God and given the ministry of reconciliation); Galatians 3:27–29 (we are no longer Jew or Greek, slave or free, male or female for all are one in Christ); Ephesians 2:11–22 (Christ is our peace creating in himself one new humanity); and 4:1–16 (we are to make every effort to maintain unity; there is one body, one faith, one baptism).

Disunity in the New Testament Church

For those who accept Scripture as the authoritative guide for life and thought, the call to the experience of Christian unity should be no optional matter. The historical working out of that unity, however, has always been the great challenge.

The New Testament is not truth in general but truth in particular—that is, it is presented within the context of historical needs. One of the practical reasons the New Testament writers left us with the above mentioned passages on unity is that the first-century church needed them.

The early church, like the church today, was afflicted with division, strife, and tension. Witness the tension in the Jerusalem church between Hellenistic and Hebrew believers regarding the daily distribution of food to the Hellenistic widows (Acts 6:1).

Witness the criticism from circumcised believers in Jerusalem regarding Peter's preaching to and eating with uncircumcised Gentiles (11:1–3); and also the dissension between those who came from the church in Judea to the Gentile church in Antioch—a dissension so great that it necessitated convening the Jerusalem Council to address the issues (15:1–2).

Witness the sharp disagreement between Paul and Barnabas regarding whether John Mark should accompany them, leading, in the end, to separate missions (15:36-39).

In the epistles we see further evidence of the church's faltering ways and challenging struggles. It grappled with dissension within its ranks (e.g., Rom. 16:17-18), experienced division (e.g., 1 Cor. 1:10-13; 3:4; Titus 3:10-11), was afflicted with jealousy and quarreling (e.g., 1 Cor. 3:3), was plagued not only with false prophets (e.g., 2 Cor. 11:1-15) but also with confused and confusing teachers (e.g., Col. 2:4-5, 8, 16-23; 1 Tim. 1:3-7; 4:1-5; 6:3-5; 2 Tim. 2:17-18, 23-26; Titus 1:10-14) and deceitful letter writers (2 Thess. 2:2; cf., 3:17). It suffered open disagreements among its well known leaders (Gal. 2:11-14) as well as among its lesser known ones (e.g., Phil. 4:2-3), and knew the specter of unfaithfulness (e.g., 2 Tim. 1:15) and of hurtful relationships (2 Tim. 4:14).

Hebrews gives evidence of backsliding and apostasy (5:11−6:8). James reveals socioeconomic discrimination (2:1-7) as well as conflicts and disputes resulting from worldliness (4:1-10). Second Peter gives evidence of the threat of licentiousness invading the church (chap. 2). First John tells of the menace of antichrists proclaiming a distorted Christology (2:18-23; 4:1-6) and of lovelessness within the fellowship (4:20-21). Jude refers to those who shamelessly seek to pervert the life of the church (4, 8, 10, 12-13, 16, 19). Revelation speaks of churches troubled with an assortment of divisive people (chapters 2 and 3).

It is important for us to acknowledge that those who made up the first century church were constitutionally no different than we are. They experienced dissension, turmoil, and weakness, just as we do. It is not as though the first-century church was flawless whereas we have fallen from that ideal state. The church was never flawless in its ongoing historical life. Therefore, from the very beginning it has struggled to move from its flawed self to its new self in Christ.[1]

As the church moves toward fullness in Christ, it has two equally important challenges: both to pursue relationships of oneness, peace, and reconciliation and to be faithful to the God of truth. Focusing on the first without being equally concerned with the second may lead to a tepid relatedness; focusing on the second without being equally concerned with the first may lead to a smug separateness.

Christology at the Center

In the New Testament, the preponderant emphasis is on the person and work of Christ. Only in 3 John are the words "Jesus" or "Christ" not used, and yet, even there, reference is made to the name (v. 7), obviously referring to the name of our Lord. The New Testament, written as it was by different persons in a variety of localities, under diverse circumstances, addressing assorted needs and purposes and at various times, is nevertheless united in its allegiance to the person of Jesus Christ. Both the canon and the church are held together by Christ as the cohesive center.

The centrality of Christology for the unity of the church is seen clearly in 1 John: "We declare to you what we have seen and heard so that you also may have fellowship with us; and truly our fellowship is with the Father and with his Son Jesus Christ" (1:3). This epistle addresses two major Christological distortions: one has to do with the marginalization—if not the actual denial—of his humanity. Evidently some teachers held that while Jesus was divine, he only seemed to be human, thus only appearing to suffer and die. To such, 4:2–3 replies:

> By this you know the Spirit of God: every spirit that confesses that Jesus Christ has come in the flesh is from God, and every spirit that does not confess Jesus is not from God. And this is the spirit of the antichrist, of which you have heard that it is coming and now it is already in the world.

The other distortion was to stress the humanity of Jesus to the point of compromising his divinity. John, however, leaves no doubt about Jesus' divinity. In 1:1–2 where he refers to Jesus in the flesh—i.e., "what we have seen with our eyes, what we have looked at and touched with our hands"—he goes on to say that he is "the eternal life that was with the Father and was revealed to us." In 4:15 he declares that "God abides in those who confess that Jesus is the Son of God," and in 5:11 he says that "God gave us eternal life, and this life is in his Son."

First John contains in embryonic form the church's historical Christological confession that Jesus was fully human and fully divine, yet one person.[2] It is, John says, this Jesus whom "we declare to you ... so that you also may have fellowship with us" (1:3). In order for others to have fellowship with the church of the apostles, it was necessary for them to confess the same incarnate Christ confessed by the apostles. John leaves no doubt but that at the center of the Christian faith is Jesus Christ, eternal life in the flesh. Apart from this foundational understanding, there is no basis for a truly Christian fellowship.

For two millennia, the church has continued affirming this same apostolic understanding of Christ. With all of the differences between Roman Catholicism, Eastern Orthodoxy, and classical Protestantism, there is, nevertheless, a basic consistency in their confessional statements about Jesus Christ being fully human and fully divine, one Lord, only Savior. Even in Protestantism with its plethora of divisions one finds remarkable commonality regarding the doctrine of the person of Christ.[3]

The *first level* of the experience of Christian unity, then, is the common affirmation about the person and work of Jesus Christ. This does not mean that all Christians do, will, or must make their confessions of faith in the same words, but it does mean that the essence of what is said is the same. We already have remarkable unity at this all important foundational level. The church at large even with all of its diversity does not make Christological confessions that are mutually exclusive, e.g., one confession holding that Jesus was only a good man, while another that he was fully human and fully divine, and yet another that he was God in the flesh but not really human. Nor do we find in mainstream churches one holding that he was sinless, while another that he was not; or that he is one of many ways to God, while another that he is the only way to God. Apart from a basic commonality in Christological confession, Christian unity is impossible.

Worshiping with One Another

The *second level* of the experience of Christian unity is

worship with those of "like precious faith." Christians cross a major barrier to unity when they discover the rich variety that exists in our diverse traditions of corporate worship, and realize that there are many "right" ways to worship Christianly. It is in corporate worship that we discover the rich variety of expressions of the one faith.

Personal Note:

As an instructor in a seminary class on the theology of Christian worship, I take students on field trips to experience Christian worship in other traditions. In the course of a Sunday we worship in traditions as diverse as an African-American Disciples of Christ congregation where worship is the joyous gathering of Christian pilgrims, a Roman Catholic congregation where worship is the gathering under the sign of the cross, an Assembly of God where worship is the experience of the immediacy of the Holy Spirit, an Eastern Orthodox congregation where worship is the drama of redemption, and a noninstrumental Church of Christ where worship is a gathering for the study of Scripture. One of the observations that students typically make is that even though the forms of worship are significantly different, it is obvious that all of them honor the name of the Lord Jesus and are committed to what Scripture says about him.

Sometimes before we visit these churches, students

suggest that we attend a Jewish synagogue, a Mormon service, a Jehovah's Witnesses meeting, or a Christian Science gathering. I explain to them that this is a course in Christian worship and that none of those groups qualify because they either altogether reject Jesus as Savior and Lord or have developed a Christology that is contrary to the New Testament. Through this experience students begin to understand both the role that Christology plays in identifying the Christian community and that the community of Christian faith is identifiable by its Christological confession and not by a monolithic form of worship.

Worshiping with other believers in other traditions can enrich us in several ways:

1) It broadens our awareness of the wider Christian community.

Personal Note:

It was by participating in the worship life of other churches during my formative years in Mount Carmel, Illinois, that I came to realize both that the Christian community was larger than my local church and more variegated than my primary church tradition, and that I could be at home in many different traditions of Christian worship.

2) It can deepen our appreciation of our own mode of worship as we see it in relation to other modes.

Personal Note:

It was as an associate minister in the First Congregational Church of Hyde Park in Boston, Massachusetts, a church that did not have an altar call at the close of its services, that I gained a deeper appreciation of this practice in my own primary tradition.

3) It can enhance our own primary traditions with resources and practices of which we might not otherwise be aware.

Personal Note:

As Dean of the Chapel at Anderson University School of Theology, I take pleasure in introducing some practices from other Christian traditions into our own corporate worship, for instance, the passing of the peace and the use of the lectionary for the systematic reading of Scripture. These and other practices are received as gifts from other Christian traditions for the enrichment of our own. And as students from other traditions return to minister in their respective churches, they often introduce practices learned from us, e.g., foot washing.

Praying with and for Each Other

The *third level* in the experience of Christian unity is that of united prayer for concerns common to multiple traditions of Christians, and mutual prayer between differing traditions for the well being of each other. When Christians of different traditions unite in prayer for common concerns, the reality of being in the presence of a common Lord transcends our dividedness. As different traditions pray for the well being of each other, the spirit of competitiveness is more likely to subside.

Personal Note:

In 1992, our family spent six months in the little town of Charlbury, England where there are five churches — Anglican, Methodist, Baptist, Quaker and Roman Catholic. We soon noticed that each church prayed for the other four, calling out the names of the respective pastors or congregational leaders and offering intercessions for special needs in each congregation. Upon hearing this, I, as a newcomer, began to experience not five different communities of the Christian faith but one community with five different traditions.

Working with Each Other

The *fourth level* is that of cooperative action in areas that require a common Christian commitment, though not complete doctrinal agreement on all matters. Such cooperative action may take the form of concerted efforts in, for example, the distribution of the scriptures, community wide evangelistic efforts, combined vacation Bible schools, Christian counseling services. That which distinguishes these endeavors from cooperative efforts in general (e.g., keeping illegal drugs out of schools, controlling the open sale of pornography, collecting money for disaster relief) is that the first can accomplish their intended purposes only when sponsored and carried out on the basis of a Christian commitment whereas the latter do not require such a commitment.

Sharing Resources

The *fifth level* is the sharing of resources with those not of our own primary tradition. Paul led the Gentile churches in collecting an offering for the Jerusalem church even though in many ways it was very different. As 2 Corinthians 8 – 9 indicates, such sharing of resources is an expression of trust and confidence in the grace that is at work in traditions unlike one's own. Paul says that the churches in Macedonia were even "begging us earnestly for the privilege [Greek: *charis*, grace] of sharing in this ministry to the saints" (8:4).

If United Methodists were to write into their budgets causes sponsored by the Greek Orthodox Church, and if the Church of the Nazarene were to support causes sponsored by the Reformed Church in America, and if the Church of God (Cleveland, Tennessee) were to give to causes sponsored by the Episcopal Church, and if the African Methodist Episcopal Church were to support causes sponsored by the Mennonite Church, ad infinitum, it would be a significant opportunity for trusting each other with our resources, for developing a sense of spiritual interconnectedness, and for practicing mutual responsibility. Potentially, such a practice would be a sign that the church is truly the community of the Kingdom.[4]

The Authority of Scripture

We turn now to a consideration of the *sixth level* in the experience of Christian unity. If the church is to have a common Christology based on the Bible, it must, at least in that area, view the scriptures as the authoritative literary deposit of God's revelation. But what about the authority of Scripture in matters other than Christology? It is important not to overlook that the Bible is the only source of authority common to all Christians. Some traditions appeal to post-biblical writings as being authoritative, while others know little or nothing about them, or, if they do know and respect them, do not view them as in any sense authoritative for matters of faith and practice. Some appeal to particular teaching offices of the church as authoritative while for others they are not authoritative.

The only authority that is common to all Christians is the Bible (see the comment about differing canons in chapter 3). Unless we are willing to focus on the study of Scripture as the basis for what we believe and the way we live, there is little hope for Christian unity.

This is not to indicate a naive view that all issues are clearly settled in Scripture, nor that what it teaches is plain for all sincere people to see. On many matters of faith and practice equally devoted Christians differ radically about what the scriptures teach. Differences in principles of interpretation, historical experiences, and contemporary needs, all influence the way we read and understand them. The issue is not one of universal agreement about all matters of faith and practice; rather, it is one of universal agreement that the discussion of all matters of faith and practice must focus ultimately on what is common to all, namely, Scripture. The agreement to make the Bible the focus for the discussion provides a common reference point. This is in no way to indicate that extra-biblical material, historical traditions, and teaching offices are not helpful to the working out of our understandings regarding matters of faith and practice. In fact, we need them. The point is that they cannot be the ultimate court of appeal for any church that is serious about Christian unity. These other sources of authority may be shared with the wider church as it seeks greater understanding of issues, but, if the unity of the church is valued, no attempt should be made to impose on all what is not common to all.

Listening to what the Spirit Says to the Churches

The *seventh level* in the experience of Christian unity is the affirmation of the universal work of the Holy Spirit in the multiple traditions of the one church. Since the Spirit came upon the church as a whole on the day of Pentecost, it is the whole fellowship of Christ in whom and among whom the Spirit continues to work. That being the case, we should assume that the Spirit is at work among all traditions that confess, preach, teach, and live under the lordship of Christ. The Holy Spirit is at work among them doing what the Spirit always does, namely, leading them into the fullness of Jesus Christ (see John 14:26). To deny that the Holy Spirit is at work in a tradition, is, in a theological sense, to deny that it is in the Christian tradition, for as 1 Corinthians 12:3 says, "No one can say that 'Jesus is Lord' except by the Holy Spirit." A New Testament Christological confession of faith is the most basic sign of the work of the Holy Spirit. (Also see Rom. 8:9b and 15b–17.) Unless we believe that a group holds a Christology at variance with the New Testament, we are under theological obligation to view it as a tradition in which the Holy Spirit is at work.

If the Spirit is at work among all of Christ's people, we should be cautious about too quickly condemning their special concerns, whether they be matters of doctrine, social policy, piety issues, or polity. It is not being argued here that the Holy Spirit writes doctrinal statements, social policy, piety directives, and polity designs—we do that!—but that persistent concerns in the life of any tradition of God's people have something to do with the work of the Holy Spirit among them. It is not that the ways in which one tradition expresses its concerns are identical with the perfect will of the Spirit, but that as we listen prayerfully to what others *understand* as being of the Spirit, we may in the course of time come to a clearer understanding of what the Spirit is saying to all of us. Rex Koivisto, in his discussion of this issue, says: "Differences of opinion that are honestly held can lead to profitable and fruitful discussion out of which a fuller apprehension of the truth may emerge."[5]

For example, while some Christians may have major problems with what others teach about the eternal security of believers, listening appreciatively to their concern may lead the first group to think more carefully about our security in Christ. Conversely, while the second group may have significant difficulties with what the first group teaches about the possibility of losing one's salvation, listening appreciatively to their concern may lead them to think more carefully about our responsibility under God.

As one tradition listens attentively to the concerns of

other traditions, it avails itself of the opportunity to hear the Spirit speaking afresh in its own particular context. This, of course, does not mean that one tradition will simply capitulate to another, but that the one will be enriched by the others as together they seek to hear what the Spirit says to the churches (see Rev. 2—3).[6]

Intertradition Studies and Conversations

The *eighth level* in the experience of Christian unity is scholarly work that crosses the boundaries between different traditions of Christians. It is crucial that this work be done by those who are well informed by their own respective primary traditions. In order for this to be optimally fruitful, contemporary and representative viewpoints of each tradition need to be set forth with clarity. Since positions, arguments, and understandings change over the course of time, it is neither adequate nor charitable to know only what another tradition may at one time have held. Since every tradition has its ill-informed proponents who distort—either intentionally or out of ignorance—its concerns and positions, we need to listen to those who set forth another tradition in its best light.

The type of discussion being called for here takes place between those involved in biblical/historical/doctrinal/theological studies and who are charged by their respective traditions with the responsibility of representing that tradition. (See the discussion in chapter 11 on the ministry of the church's offices.) A major example of such studies are those conducted by the Faith and Order Movement which began during the early twentieth century.[7] Also, the Second Vatican Council (1963–65), while officially limited to Roman Catholic participation, invited observers from other Christian traditions who in turn became an integral part of the conversations in Rome. The value of this non-Roman influence is indicated by the title of a post-Council book, *The Catholic Rediscovery of Protestantism.*[8]

Equally important in the twentieth century are multilateral discussions involving three or more traditions and bilaterals between two traditions. These take place *between* major confessional families such as Pentecostals, Roman Catholics, Lutherans, and Reformed[9] or between two or more church groups *within* the same confessional family, such as among Lutheran bodies or Holiness denominations. Sometimes they take place between church groups that have special historical connections with each other, or which, though coming out of different historical traditions, share special doctrinal affinities on matters of common concern.[10]

Convergence of Understandings

The *ninth level* in the experience of Christian unity is both the convergence of understandings and the mutual appreciation for differences that continue to exist. The *Baptism, Eucharist and Ministry* document (BEM), published in 1982 by the Faith and Order Commission of the World Council of Churches, is a superb example of this. It reports the convergence of understandings resulting from some fifty-five years of study reflecting the participation of such divergent traditions as Eastern Orthodox, Oriental Orthodox, Roman Catholic, Old Catholic, Lutheran, Anglican, Reformed, Methodist, United, Disciples, Baptist, Adventist, and Pentecostal. Besides the points of convergence, BEM also identifies controversial issues still eluding convergence of thought; on these matters, the conversation can at least proceed with mutual respect for those having dissimilar understandings.

The theological and doctrinal conversations engendered by BEM elicited even broader participation by those not part of Faith and Order. In 1984, Anderson School of Theology hosted the Seventh Believers' Church Conference, an ad hoc conference of scholars from churches that practice believers baptism, for the purpose of providing them with the opportunity to respond to the BEM section on baptism. The conference affirmed eight points of agreement with BEM and then stated six points of disagreement.

The last part of the Anderson document lists two consequences which Believers Churches can draw from BEM for their relationships and dialogues with other churches and states four points of guidance that Believers Churches can take from BEM. The report concludes by giving three suggestions for the ongoing work of Faith and Order, one of which includes a statement related to the sixth level of the experience of Christian unity mentioned above. The Believers Churches conferees said, "Many of us would wish to add that Scripture is to be regarded as the sole source and criterion of Christian belief, standing as the authoritative corrective to our various traditions."[11]

The Ultimate Goal this Side of Heaven

The *tenth level* in the experience of Christian unity is a oneness of faith and order, life and work, mission and witness. This means unity at the Lord's table; a common identification; a united mission and witness; the integrative compatibility of services, structures, and ministries; and mutual love in diversity. We consider, now, each of these components — most with only a passing reference since they are discussed more fully elsewhere in this work, but one (i.e., common identification) more extensively because it is not discussed elsewhere.

Unity at the Lord's Table

Perhaps the only Christians who can fully appreciate the pain of disunity at the Lord's table are those who have been in services where some Christians are either barred from the table because they are not of the "right" Christian tradition, or where, even though all believers are welcome at the table, persons present from other churches are not free to participate due to restrictions imposed by their own churches. The Lord's table, which should be the central place for celebrating our unity in Christ has been made by us into a table of division. (See chapter 21 for a discussion of the Lord's supper.)

Common Identification

At the ultimate level of unity this side of heaven, individual Christian traditions would be willing to lay aside all narrow identifications related either to a church leader (e.g., Mennonite), church government (e.g., Presbyterian), church headquarters (e.g., Church of God—Anderson), a doctrinal distinctive (e.g., Baptist), a phenomenon (e.g., Quaker), an idealistic state (e.g., Reformed), a nation (e.g., the Church of England), or a function (e.g., Salvation Army), and identify themselves as closely as possible with the church of the New Testament.

According to the New Testament, the disciples of Jesus, in the course of time, came to be known by the general public as Christians: "And it was in Antioch that the disciples were first called 'Christians' " (Acts 11:26). In the Pauline epistles, however, the most common designation is church, *ekklēsia*. (See comments in chapter 9 regarding the use of this word for other than the Christian community.)

Given the fact that *ekklēsia* refers to an assembly in general and is not restricted to the assembly of Christians (for instance, the Septuagint's translation of Psalm 22:22 used in Hebrews 2:12), the word in and of itself is not sufficient for referring to the disciples of Christ, except when used within the Christian circle where it would be generally understood as a reference to themselves. Paul, for example, uses the word by itself when he refers to the following: a gathering for Christian worship (e.g., 1 Cor. 14:19), local communities of Christians (e.g., 1 Cor. 4:17, sometimes with locations added as in Rom. 16:1; also see Acts 8:1 and 3), house gatherings of believers (e.g., Rom. 16:5), and the universal body of Christians (e.g., 1 Cor. 12:28; Eph. 1:22; Phil. 3:6; also see Matt. 16:18).

In some cases, however, he is more descriptive of the kind of *ekklēsia* he has in mind. In reference to a plurality of local congregations he uses three different phrases: "churches of Christ" (Rom. 16:16), "churches of God" (1 Cor. 11:16 and 2 Thess. 1:4), and "churches of God in Christ Jesus" (1 Thess. 2:14). In reference to the local congregation at Corinth, he uses "the church of God" (1 Cor. 1:2; 11:22; 2 Cor. 1:1.)

Paul also speaks of the universal body of believers as the church of God (1 Cor. 10:32; 15:9; Gal. 1:13; see also Acts 20:28). First Timothy 3 urges that those who hold the office of overseer should be able to take care of the church of God (v. 5). Verse 15 is more expansive when it refers to "the household of God, which is the church of the living God, the pillar and bulwark of the truth."

It is clear that none of these terms were used in a modern denominationalistic sense. The churches of Christ were not distinguished from another group known as the churches of God, and from yet another known as the churches of God in Christ Jesus. The church of God was not a tag identifying one group of believers as over against another known as the church of the living God, the pillar and bulwark of the truth.

The church at the ultimate level of the experience of Christian unity seeks to find a way of identifying itself so that all communities and traditions of the one faith can readily recognize themselves as being members of the whole. At this level, none would use biblical terminology in any way that would exclude other Christian persons, communities, or traditions. All in each place who live under the lordship of Christ would be recognized as being members of one and the same community of faith. The second section of the New Delhi Statement on Unity adopted in India in 1961 reads:

> We believe that the unity which is both God's will and his gift to his Church is being made visible as all in each place who are baptized into Jesus Christ and confess him as Lord and Saviour are brought by the Holy Spirit into one fully committed fellowship, holding the one apostolic faith, preaching the one Gospel, breaking the one bread, joining in common prayer, and having a corporate life reaching out in witness and service to all and who at the same time are united with the whole Christian fellowship in all places and all ages in such wise that ministry and members are accepted by all, and that all can act and speak together as occasion requires for the tasks to which God calls his people. It is for such unity that we believe we must pray and work.[12]

In fact, at this ultimate level of unity, the church throughout the world would be identified as the one community of Christian faith.

Personal Note:

The story is told of my one time teaching colleague, the late John W. V. Smith, who, at an interdenominational meeting, was the first to introduce himself. "I am John Smith from the Church of God." The next man identified himself as being from the Presbyterian

Church of God. The next as being from the Baptist Church of God, and on it went around the table.[13] They were celebrating a common identity even within the context of their diversity.

United Mission and Witness

Not only would the church on the ultimate level have a common identification; it also would act together in a common mission and witness based on Matthew 28:18–20 and Acts 1:8. (For further discussion see chapter 1 on "Disciples Making Disciples," and chapter 12 on "The Church as the Jesus Movement.")

"Common mission and witness" does not require one way to conduct the life and work of the church at large. Rather, it calls for integrative compatibility of services, structures, and ministries. Some say unity but mean uniformity. They demand one way of serving God and others, one way to structure and govern the church, and one form of ministry for all. In order for the church to be in health, however, it needs a diversification of services (i.e., 1 Cor. 12:5), of structures (see chapter 12 on "The Church as the Jesus Movement"), and of ministries (see chapter 11 on "Ministry in the Church").

Monolithic sameness is not a sign of good health but of illness. Since the church is one in Christ, diversified services, structures, and ministries need to be compatible with each other so that each diversification is complementary to the whole, and none competitive with the others; thus the term, integrative compatibility.

Mutual Love in Diversity

Underlying all of this is the practice of mutual love in diversity. The placement of 1 Corinthians 13 in the middle of chapters having to do with diversity in the Corinthian church exhibits the theological importance of love for the well being of the church. As Paul says in Colossians 3:14: "Above all, clothe yourselves with love, which binds everything together in perfect harmony."

Finally at the Heavenly Throne

The *eleventh level* in the experience of Christian unity is eschatological. It will take place when finally the whole people of God are gathered at the throne of God, the Lamb (Christ Jesus) being at the center (Rev. 7:17). According to Revelation 7:9–12, in heaven—a reality so certain that it is referred to in the past tense—the church in all of its diversity will be gathered around its savior:

> There was a great multitude that no one could count, from every nation, from all tribes and peoples and languages, standing before the throne and before the Lamb, robed in white, with palm branches in their hands. They cried out in a loud voice, saying, "Salvation belongs to our God who is seated on the throne, and to

the Lamb!" And all the angels stood around the throne and around the elders and the four living creatures, and they fell on their faces before the throne and worshipped God, singing, "Amen! Blessing and glory and wisdom and thanksgiving and honor and power and might be to our God forever and ever! Amen."

Notes

1. This struggle in the first century is discussed helpfully in the following: Paul Achtemeier, *The Quest for Unity in the New Testament Church* (Philadelphia: Fortress, 1987); Carl S. Dudley and Earle Hilgert, *New Testament Tensions and the Contemporary Church* (Philadelphia: Fortress, 1987); J. D. G. Dunn, *Unity and Diversity in the New Testament* (London: S.C.M., 1977).

2. See chapter 6 for a discussion of the Chalcedonian Formula (451), which sets forth the classical doctrine of Christ, "same perfect in Godhead and the same perfect in manhood, truly God and truly man."

3. The following two statements coming from very different Protestant milieus illustrate the Christological unity that the church already has:

1) the *Westminster Confession of Faith* (1646) with its Calvinistic orientation: "The Son of God, the second person of the Trinity, being very and eternal God, of

313

one substance, and equal with the Father, did, when the fullness of time was come, take upon him man's nature, with all the essential properties and common infirmities thereof, yet without sin: being conceived by the power of the Holy Ghost in the womb of the Virgin Mary, of her substance. So that two whole, perfect, and distinct natures, the Godhead and the manhood, were inseparately joined together in one person, without conversion, composition, or confusion. Which person is very God and very man, yet one Christ, the only mediator between God and man" — chap. VIII, sec. 2. John H. Leith (ed.), *Creeds of the Churches: A Reader in Christian Doctrine from the Bible to the Present,* rev. ed. (Richmond: John Knox, 1973), p. 203f.

2) A twentieth-century charismatic statement: "Jesus Christ the Son is fully God and fully man: the only Savior for the sins of the world. He was the Word made flesh, supernaturally conceived by the Holy Spirit, born of the Virgin Mary, and was perfect in nature, teaching, and obedience. He died on the cross as the vicarious sacrifice for all mankind, rose from the dead in His own glorified body, ascended into heaven, and will return in glory. He is the Head of His body the Church, victor over all the powers of darkness, and now reigns at the right hand of the Father." *Doctrinal Statement, Melodyland School of Theology, California,* sec. V.

4. I made a proposal of this kind to my own church in

"On Being a Christian Unity Movement," *Vital Christianity,* Vol. 99, No. 4 (February 25, 1979), 2.

5. Rex A. Koivisto, *One Lord, One Faith: A Theology for Cross-Denominational Renewal* (Wheaton: BridgePoint, 1993), p. 100. See his fuller discussion on pp. 98–101.

6. I have discussed this more fully in "Christianity — In a Sectarian Mold or in a Wholistic One?" *Centering on Ministry,* VII, 2 (Spring 1982), 11–13. In the same issue, see the article to which mine is both a response and a continuation: Robert D. Brinsmead, "The Gospel Versus the Sectarian Spirit," 4–10, reprinted by permission from *Verdict,* IV, 3 (March 1981), 8–16.

7. At the 1910 World Missionary Conference held in Edinburgh, Scotland, the Protestant Episcopal Church of the United States proposed ongoing conversations between different Christian traditions regarding matters of faith and order. A preliminary meeting was held in Geneva, Switzerland, in 1920 which in time led to the First World Conference on Faith and Order in 1927 at Lausanne, Switzerland. The Second was held in 1937 at Edinburgh.

In 1948, Faith and Order became a commission within the World Council of Churches, but that did not mean that participation in the work of Faith and Order was thereby limited to member churches. The Faith and Order Movement continues to this day to be broader than the constituency of the WCC.

The Third Faith and Order Conference was held at Lund, Sweden, in 1952, the Fourth in Montreal, Canada, in 1963, and the Fifth at Santiago de Compostela, Spain, in 1993.

Interspersed between the conferences were other Faith and Order meetings: Oberlin, Ohio, USA in 1957; Aarhus, Denmark in 1964; Bristol, England in 1967; Louvain, Belgium in 1971; Accra, Ghana in 1974; Bangalore, India in 1978, all leading up to the meeting in Lima, Peru in 1982 that produced the *Baptism, Eucharist and Ministry* document, by far the most widely discussed document ever generated by Faith and Order. Since 1982, both member and nonmember churches have used it as a focus for discussing the three church-dividing issues identified in its title.

8. Paul M. Minus, Jr., *The Catholic Rediscovery of Protestantism* (New York: Paulist, 1976).

9. For example, see *Roman Catholic/Lutheran Joint Commission, Facing Unity* (Lutheran World Federation, 1985). Also, Ernest L. Unterkoefler and Andrew Harsanyi (eds.), *The Unity We Seek: A Statement by the Roman Catholic/Presbyterian-Reformed Consultation* (New York: Paulist, 1977).

10. Two examples are the theological discussions that took place in the1960's between the Church of God (Anderson, Indiana) and the Churches of God in North

America, the Church of the Brethren, the Brethren Church, and the Evangelical Covenant Church, all of which have some common understandings of the nature of the Christian life, and, in the case of the first two, a special historical connection (see Adam W. Miller and Fred D. Rayle (compilers), *Developments in Dialogue Between [the] Church of God (Anderson) [and the] Churches of God in North America* (Anderson, Ind, n.d.); also, the conversations conducted by the Open Forum Ad Hoc Committee of the Christian Churches and Churches of Christ, first, with the Christian Church (Disciples of Christ) with whom they share a common early history, and later, with the Church of God (Anderson) with whom they share a common concern for Christian unity.

11. For both the papers given at this conference and the response to BEM, see Merle Strege (ed.), *Baptism and Church: A Believers' Church Vision* (Grand Rapids: Sagamore, 1986). The response followed the suggested outline in the Preface of BEM (see For Further Consideration, Part II).

12. For the full Report on Unity, see W. A. Visser't Hooft, *New Delhi Report: The Third Assembly of the World Council of Churches, 1961* (New York: Association, 1962), pp. 116–134. Also, see the discussion in Koivisto, op. cit., pp. 275–282.

13. Told in an editorial of the *International Journal of Religious Education,* June 1967.

For Further Consideration

Part I. Introductory Reading on Unity

Emilio Castro, *Sent Free: Mission and Unity in the Perspective of the Kingdom* (Grand Rapids: Eerdmans, 1985).

Consultation on Doctrine, The Church: Its Nature, Mission, Polity, and Unity (Anderson, Ind: Executive Council of the Church of God, n.d.).

Paul A. Crow, Jr., *Christian Unity: Matrix for Mission* (New York: Friendship, 1982).

Christopher J. Ellis, *Together on the Way: A Theology of Ecumenism* (London: The British Council of Churches Inter-Church House, 1990).

Stanley Mooneyham (ed.), *The Dynamics of Christian Unity* (Grand Rapids: Zondervan, 1963).

J. Robert Nelson, *Criterion for the Church* (New York: Abingdon, 1962).

Geoffrey Wainwright, *The Ecumenical Moment* (Grand Rapids: Eerdmans, 1983).

Part II. A Model for Inter-Tradition Conversations

The *Baptism, Eucharist and Ministry* document sent to the churches in 1982 by the Faith and Order Commission of the World Council of Churches invited churches, whether members of the WCC or not, to respond according to the following guidelines. "The Faith and Order Commission now respectfully invites all churches to prepare an official response to the text at the highest appropriate level of authority, whether it be a council, synod, conference, assembly, or other body. In support of this process of reception, the Commission would be pleased to know as precisely as possible

• the extent to which your church can recognize in this text the faith of the Church through the ages;

• the consequences your church can draw from this text for its relations and dialogues with other churches, particularly with those churches which also recognize the text as an expression of the apostolic faith;

• the guidance your church can take from this text for its worship, educational, ethical, and spiritual life and witness;

• the suggestions your church can make for the ongoing work of Faith and Order as it relates the material of this text on *Baptism, Eucharist and Ministry* to its long-range research project 'Towards the Common Expression of the Apostolic Faith Today.'" p. x.

Part III. Two Nineteenth Century Unity Movements

Contrary to popular opinion, concern for Christian unity is by no means restricted to the twentieth century ecumenical movement. [For a history of which, see Harold E. Fey (ed.), *A History of the Ecumenical Movement*, Vol II. 1948–1968 (Philadelphia: Westminster, 1970); Also, Samuel M. Cavert, *On the Road to Christian Unity* (Westport: Greenwood, 1979).]

In the nineteenth century two movements emerged in the United States each of which had the oneness of the church at the center of its concerns. The earlier one known as the restoration movement was led by Thomas and Alexander Campbell and Barton W. Stone, and the later one known as the reformation movement was led by Daniel S. Warner. The first, having its origins among Presbyterians and Baptists, stressed a return to the faith and practice of the New Testament church as the only way to unity. It held that the contemporary church is to be a replica of the primitive church (see Henry E. Webb, *In Search of Christian Unity: A History of the Restoration Movement* (Cincinnati: Standard, 1990). The second, emerging primarily within the holiness movement, stressed the importance of God's work within the human heart as the only way that unity can be experienced (see John W. V. Smith, *The Quest for Holiness and Unity* (Anderson, Ind: Warner, 1980). Both of these emerged as grass roots movements for Christian unity. They remind us that the legacy of unity movements is not restricted to the ecumenical movement.

The reformation movement produced a sequence of writers who over the years theologized about Christian unity. In my "Experiential Salvation and Christian Unity in the Thought of Seven Theologians of the Church of God (Anderson, Indiana)" (unpublished Th.D dissertation, Boston University School of Theology, 1973), the central thought of each is identified as follows:

Daniel Sydney Warner (1842–95). His foundational idea was the ontological unity between Christ and the church. Christian unity is the mystical unity existing among all who experientially participate in the life of Christ.

Herbert McClellan Riggle (1872–1952). Basic to his thought was God's creative expansion of the realm of God's holiness. For him, Christian unity is the result of Christ's cleansing presence in the heart, eradicating all urges toward divisiveness.

Frederick G. Smith (1880–1947). He stressed the absolute authority of the Bible as the divine record of truths that must be adhered to by all who love God. Christian unity is possible only when Christians work for the reconstitution of the apostolic church in belief, practice, and structures.

Russell R. Byrum (1888–1980). Foundational for him is his doctrinal approach to Christian truth. The unity of the church is realized only as those in denominationalism understand that the denominational system is based on erroneous doctrine, and, rejecting the system as inherently sinful, affirm their membership in the universal church alone.

Charles Ewing Brown (1883–1971). His is a Christocentric relational theology worked out within the historical context of the radically faithful church. Christian unity is possible only as believers experience restoration to God through faith in Jesus Christ, forsake the sin of ruptured relationships, and overtly work for the establishment of love relationships with the rest of the Christian fellowship.

Earl L. Martin (1892–1961). His also is a Christocentric relational theology, but his view is worked out within the context of a vision of a new humanity on earth. Christian unity is made possible by a personal relationship with the God of love and unity who is revealed in Christ. It involves catching Christ's vision of a new humanity, developing attitudes of universal loyalty in place of narrow and small ones, being open to God's future, and walking courageously into it.

Albert F. Gray (1886–1969). He worked on the basis of the developmental, progressive, movemental nature of the church's experience, faith, thought, and structure. Christian unity is possible only as the denominationalistic view of Christianity is abandoned and the more biblically movemental, dynamic, and developmental view is embraced.

14

Disciples in a Pluralistic World

Paul in Athens

Acts 17:16–34 tells about Paul being in Athens where many views of God circulated. Some argued about the gods of philosophical speculation (see v. 18). Others believed in an unknown God (see v. 23). Still others worshiped gods made with their own hands (see v. 29).

In vv. 24–28, he says:

The God who made the world and everything in it, he who is Lord of heaven and earth, does not live in shrines made by human hands, nor is he served by human hands, as though he needed anything, since he himself gives to all mortals life and breath and all things. From one ancestor he made all nations to inhabit the whole earth, and he allotted the times of their existence and the boundaries of the places where they would live, so that they would search for God and perhaps grope for him and find him—though indeed he is not far from each one of us. For "In him we live and move and have our being."

After declaring that God is the creator and lord of heaven and earth, he ends by quoting with approval a sentence known by the Athenians, "In him we live and move and have our being." Paul is setting forth the idea that all of us, regardless of our religious orientation, have a God connection. It is impossible for us to be other than the creation of God. For this reason, followers of Jesus have a common basis for conversing with others about God. "He is not far from each one of us."

As believers, then, how should we relate to people of other religions, views, and orientations? This is the question that is uppermost in this chapter. We begin by remembering that even as creation is God's, even so the church is God's. Let's look at this as the basis for discussing our relationship to those outside the church.

The Church as a "Temporal Echo" of the Trinity

As Colin Gunton says, "If, with the New Testament, we are to speak of the church of God, the being of the church must be rooted in the being of God."[1] Since we are the church of *God*—the eternal community of three persons: Father, Son, and Holy Spirit—we should think of ourselves from the perspective of the nature of the

Trinity. According to Gunton, "The church is called to be the kind of reality at a finite level that God is in eternity,"[2] and again, the church is "a temporal echo of the eternal community that God is."[3]

Let us reflect, then, on the nature of the church in light of what was said about the thrice personal God in chapter 8, namely, that the First Person of the Trinity is the Person of mysterious depth, the Second is the self-imaged Person, and the Third is the Person in contact with all that is not God.

As a "temporal echo" of the First Person of the Trinity, the church is a community of mysterious depth which recognizes that there is more to itself than it can comprehend; it is a mystery greater than our understanding. The fact that so many different images of the church are found in the New Testament is testimony to this mystery. The church eludes having its meaning and nature completely encapsulated in any one concept or metaphor, for no one of them can fully explain it.

The practical implication of this is that we should continue growing in our understanding of the nature of the church, for it is always more mysterious than what we see on the surface, and more profound than any one concept or metaphor is adequate to communicate.

However, as a "temporal echo" of the Second Person of the Trinity, the church, though mysterious, does not need to drown in the depths of mystery, for it has the benefit of the biblical images of the church already discussed in chapter 9, i.e., the body of Christ, reconciled humanity, and the people of God. We can move forward in our understanding of the church with the assurance that the church in all its mystery is, nevertheless, congruent with what the church is according to these biblical images:

- it is a Christological body,
- a fellowship of Christian salvation, and
- an historical people of faith called into being by Christ. We know what we are, whose we are, and where we are in the historical process.

The practical implication of this is that we can have confidence about our self-understanding in that we have specific texts about ourselves. As we study and reflect on these texts, we can measure ourselves by them for the purpose of ordering and reordering our lives accordingly. When we discuss with others of the Christian faith what it means to be the church, we have common texts for the discussion; consequently, we are not left with the dilemma of merely chasing each other's elusive imaginations.

In no sense is this meant to imply that texts have only

one meaning for all to see. The multiple interpretations of the same texts is a fact of our life together. The point is that the discussion, frustrating though it may be, can at least have the common focus of particular texts.

As a "temporal echo" of the Third Person of the Trinity, the church is a community in touch with that which is beyond itself. To the degree that the church understands itself in this way, it will function not as though it were a self-enclosed entity, disconnected from that which is not itself, but as an outgoing community that is openly relational with those beyond the circle of Christian faith. It not only enjoys its own internal company but pursues the company of those beyond itself. The church which is a "temporal echo" of the Third Person of the Trinity is a community engaged at the deepest possible level with that which is not the church and with those who are not of faith.

The practical implications of this are that we are to be a responsive church that is touched by the needs of the world and a responsible church that is willing to lead the way in being good stewards of creation. We are to be a missionary church aglow with the Spirit for the spread of the gospel. In addition, we are to be a compassionate church that reaches out in love to all regardless of who they are. We are also to be a dialogically engaged church that is willing to enter into discourse with all regardless of their religious life or truth claims. It is to this issue we now turn.

Relating to those who Make Other Truth Claims

Truth is what we believe to be the case for all regardless of the perceptions others may have. To illustrate this with a nonreligious example, let us consider one who thinks that she can fly from one skyscraper to another a block away unaided by any mechanical devices. If a beloved relative were to attempt that, it is doubtful that one would say, "What is true for me may not be true for you." It is more likely that one would plead with the loved one not to pursue what would be viewed as a misconception.

The world buzzes with conversations about different truth claims. Some of them are mutually contradictory (e.g, the claim that a loving God is the source of life, as over against the claim that an egotistical satan is the source of life). Other truth claims are complimentary (e.g., divine love is self-sacrificing; the sacrifice of self may be a sign of emotional illness). Yet others are anticipatory of additional truth claims, (e.g., the nation of Israel is the fulfillment of God's promise to Abraham; Jesus Christ is the fulfillment of God's promise to Abraham). The particular issue that concerns us here is how the church of trinitarian faith should relate to those whose truth claims are contrary to ours.

The foundational question is whether we view Christian claims that God is Trinity and that Christ Jesus is the only divine savior as being merely options among many equally (or unequally) acceptable conceptions of God or whether we view them as being ultimately true. The watershed issue that decisively influences one's approach to people of other faiths is whether we are convinced that the trinitarian God is the only eternal God. Six major approaches to this matter can be identified, three of which view the trinitarian God as merely one of many equally (or unequally) acceptable conceptions of God, and three of which view the trinitarian God as the only true God.

First, we shall consider the three in the former category, and then the three in the latter category.

(1) Casual Interest

The first approach is that of a casual interest in diversity. The basic attitude in this approach is that all of us are historically and culturally formed and that our respective worldviews, being relative to those factors, are simply expressive of divergent historical and cultural experiences. Other worldviews, whether religious or secular, are equally as valid as our own. They are curiosities that are of interest in the same way that any other historical or cultural particularity is of interest.

We are enriched by getting acquainted with other ways of thinking about the world and God, but the issue of universal truth is not considered, and if, by chance, it is, it is only incidental. This attitude could be expressed as follows: Trinitarian thought is true for me, but whatever your view of God and the world is, is equally true for you. Since we each have curious ways of thinking about God and the world, getting acquainted with others broadens our understanding of the peoples of the world, and simply adds interest to life—nothing more.

(2) Zealous Dogmatism

A second approach is that of a zealous dogmatism about a new concept of God. This approach holds that there is a God beyond all religious understandings of God and that all such understandings are historical expressions of the God who is beyond any one historical understanding. For one to claim that one's own historical understanding of God is the truth for everybody is seen as being absurd and narrow. Those taking this approach have a very low tolerance level for those who claim, for instance, that the trinitarian God is the only eternal God. Making such a claim is viewed as being historically myopic and in need not only of enlightenment but of conversion to the more adequate view regarding the God-beyond-all-historical-understandings-of-God. This approach could be expressed like this:

Trinitarian thought is only one of many historical expressions of the God-beyond-all-historical-particularities. The way things really are is that the God-beyond-all-historical-particularities precludes the view that the trinitarian God is the only true God in that this, too, is a God of historical particularity.

(3) Dialogical Search for Truth

A third approach is the dialogical search for truth in which case trinitarianism is viewed as one among several great religious traditions all of which can learn from each other. The approach to others, then, is on a strictly egalitarian basis. We enter into the exchange with an openness to learn from others and to share our respective traditions in the hope that all of us might find something of value in what each has to offer. The key to genuine dialogue is the willingness to be changed in the process. Ultimate truth is understood as that toward which one is moving rather than that which one already has. This position could be expressed like this: We have a tradition that we gladly bring to the table of interchange, but we bring it to share, to be changed by what others share, and to be willing, if the evidence points in that direction, to move beyond the tradition out of which we come.

Raimundo Panikkar argues that "the very nature of truth is pluralistic."[4] He writes:

Religions reveal to us different facts of truth because truth itself is multifaceted. We are unable to bring different basic experiences of human beings into one single thought system because reality is that mystery which transcends not only our thinking but thinking as such. The variety of the ultimate human traditions is thus like the many colors of nature. We should be not monochromatically obsessed, but loving gardeners of all that grow on valleys, slopes, and peaks of that reality of which we are the human partners.[5]

The next three approaches are taken on the basis of the quite different conviction that the trinitarian God is the only true God.

(4) Withdrawal

Those of trinitarian faith who take the fourth approach, that of withdrawal, regard all other views of God and the world as being unworthy of consideration, perhaps even for informational purposes. They maintain a self-enclosed life within the confines of their own community without either seeking contact with those outside the community of faith or being willing to respond to those who initiate such contact.

This attitude could be expressed like this: We have the truth, and, to the degree that it is possible, want to withdraw from all who are not of the truth.

(5) Numerical Triumphalism

A fifth approach is that of numerical triumphalism. In this approach, the attempt is made to get more and more of those who see reality differently to convert, sometimes by whatever means, to one's own view. This attitude could be expressed like this: We have the truth, and you do not. Therefore, our one and only goal is to get more who agree with us than those who agree with you. By getting more on our side we will win the day for God.

(6) Dialogical Engagement

A sixth approach is that of dialogical engagement. In this approach, one comes to the discussion convinced that the trinitarian God is the only living God there is. This adherent realizes that others may see things very differently and that the world is a cacophony of conflicting truth claims, some of which are sophisticated systems of thought, others of which are not. The trinitarian participant in the conversation, while committed to the truth claim that God is Trinity, is, nevertheless, willing to enter into a relationship of respect for those whose truth claims are otherwise. She, however, enters into the discourse without denying who she is in the depths of her being but does so in such a way that the other is allowed to be who he is in the depths of his being as well. The result of the engagement might, of course, lead to *conversion* either way. Or, it may lead the participants to gain *new paradigms* for understanding their respective views of reality. As David Tracy observes, "Each dialogue is likely to make it possible to revise aspects of the tradition which need revision and to discover other forgotten, indeed often repressed, aspects of the great tradition."[6] Or again, dialogical engagement may lead participants to come to positions which in the last analysis are very different views of reality, and which, in effect, therefore, become *new truth claims.*

The difference between dialogical *search* for truth, referred to above, and dialogical *engagement* is the following. Dialogical search for truth *assumes from the outset* that one's views are relative to a truth beyond one's claims. In this approach, a basic presupposition about the *necessity* (as over against the possible need) to change in the pursuit of truth is foundational for the dialogue.

On the other hand, dialogical engagement makes no such presupposition about the *necessity* for change. (This does not mean that it rules out the *possible need* to change.) In dialogical engagement, no predialogical assumption exists that truth is other than what one holds to be the case. In fact, the opposite assumption is made, namely, that the truth claims being set forth are truth for all regardless of whether others accept them.

In dialogical engagement, the passionate conviction that the claims that one brings to the conversation (e.g., that the trinitarian God is the only eternal God and that this God has been revealed in Jesus Christ for the salvation of all) are ultimately true and, for that reason, necessary to fullness of life, places them in an evangelical category in which case conversion is sought. Indeed, according to Acts 17:18, some in Athens were converted. Paul pressed the case because he believed that his gospel was universally true, redemptively transforming, and eternally enriching. Otherwise, why disturb them? Why give them false hope? Why be so dedicated to the missionary cause? Convinced, therefore, that Christ was in fact the way, the truth, and the life, he was willing to disturb them, offer hope, and give of himself sacrificially.

Others in Athens, of course, evidently felt equally convinced about what they considered to be the truth. As a person of civility, though, there is no indication that Paul tried to deny them the right to share what they considered to be the truth. Faithful to what he was convinced was universally true, redemptively transforming, and eternally enriching, he engaged them in public conversation and was willing for God to do the rest.

If what we claim to be true actually is true, then we

do not have to worry about the ultimate outcome. In the end, God will vindicate the really true and the genuinely transforming and permanently enriching. Faith is the assurance that when all is said and done the God in whom we believe will vindicate the truth.

Summary Statement about Dialogical Engagement

Participants in dialogical engagement enter into discussion with those who make differing truth claims, and they do so both with the willingness to share truth as they see it and with respect for the views of others. They are willing to hear them out to such an extent that the same others are convinced that they have really been understood in regard to the nature of their differing truth claims. (We do not know whether this happened in Athens. Acts 17 is simply a text that moves in the direction of dialogical engagement; it is not an example of everything said here.)

In dialogical engagement, it is not enough for one party to say to another, "I know what your truth claims are"; instead, the goal is to come to that point when differing parties say to each other, "Yes, you really do understand what our truth claims are." Only then is it dialogical engagement at its best rather than merely an exercise in talking at each other.

The values of successful dialogical engagement are

1) that all partners feel that they have been heard and understood,

2) that each party has the opportunity to reevaluate its own truth claims, and

3) that each has the opportunity to come to grips with the reality of differing truth claims and to improve their understanding of them.

Harold Netland espouses this approach, calling it informal dialogue,[7] purposes of which include demonstrating "one's willingness to take the other person seriously as a fellow human being;"[8] evangelism;[9] and serving as "a mark of humility, sensitivity, and common courtesy to followers of other faiths."[10] He agrees with David Hesselgrave's rationale for such dialogical engagements: they can help in the promotion of freedom of worship and witness; they provide the opportunity for working out common approaches to issues having to do with physical and social well being; and they contribute to the breaking down of barriers of prejudice, distrust, and hatred between peoples of different religions.[11]

Netland maintains, however, that "the overriding concern throughout [dialogue] ... must be that the gospel of Jesus Christ is effectively communicated in a sensitive and gracious manner to followers of other religions."[12]

The Theological Rationale for
Choosing Dialogical Engagement

Is one approach preferable to the others? On the basis of the nature of the trinitarian God whose people we are, I say yes. Casual interest in diversity points in the right direction, but it is inadequate in that it does not focus on the God behind the diversity. Our trinitarian God is not only the creator, sustainer, and sanctifier of harmonious diversity as the stuff of God's world, but also the reconciler of destructive diversity. Mere casual interest in historical diversity is not a sufficient response to the trinitarian God who both creates and reconciles diversity for eternal purposes. We need to be engaged with the God behind the diversity and with the God who is at work in the diversity, instead of being satisfied with diverse religions as cultural curiosities.

I find the way of zealous dogmatism about a new way of thinking about God inconsistent with the trinitarian God who has been revealed definitively in Jesus Christ—a revelation understood to be the revelation of the only God there is. The church understands Scripture to teach that the First Person of the Trinity known by Jesus as Father, the Second Person revealed in Jesus as the Christ and the Third Person working in the world as the Holy Spirit are the one eternal God from whom, by whom and for whom all creation has its being. The Christian truth claim is that the trinitarian God is the only true God and that we are created in that trinitarian image. No God beyond the biblical God exists.

I find the way of dialogical search for ultimate truth inconsistent with the ultimacy of Jesus Christ who is the way, the truth, and the life. This does not mean that we are not to be searchers after truth, but that we search after proximate truth in light of the ultimate truth revealed in Christ. Nor does this mean that we do not grow in our understanding of Christ, for Christ is the inexhaustible fountain of God revealed. The Holy Spirit leads us to the Christ fountain for as long as we live. While we grow in our understanding of Christ, the fact of faith is that in him we have found ultimate truth beyond which nothing more can be discovered.

I find the way of withdrawal inconsistent with the nature of the trinitarian God who is the God of involvement with the world, incarnation in the world, and evangelization of the world.

I find the way of numerical triumphalism inconsistent with the nature of the trinitarian God who as the suffering God came to us in the humble and sacrificial life of Christ Jesus. God's way is not that of winning the day numerically, but of revealing truth incarnationally and, in the future, cosmically as well.

I choose, then, the way of dialogical engagement because the trinitarian God is a communion of interpersonal communicants who are united in the eternal truth that they are; they are not in pursuit of it as though it existed outside themselves. The trinitarian God is engaged with us for the purpose of converting us to the divine plan for human life.[13]

We are the church of *God* — Father, Son and Holy Spirit. As such, according to 1 Peter 2:9, "[we] are a chosen race, a royal priesthood, a holy nation, God's own people, in order that [we] may proclaim the mighty acts of him who called [us] out of darkness into his marvelous light."

The Bible is the record of the engaged God who calls us to be people who likewise are engaged in the lives of others, people who listen understandingly to all who have anything whatsoever to say. We also, however, are convinced that we have the good news of salvation, and, therefore, are "not ashamed of the gospel" because we are persuaded that "it is the power of God for salvation to everyone who has faith" (Rom. 1:16).

Notes

1. Colin E. Gunton, *The Promise of Trinitarian Theology* (Edinburgh: T and T Clark, 1991), p. 78. See chapter 4, "The Community. The Trinity and the Being of the Church."

2. Ibid., p. 81.

3. Ibid., p. 79.

4. Raimundo Panikkar, "Religious Pluralism: The Metaphysical Challenge," *Religious Pluralism*, ed. Leroy S. Rouner (Notre Dame: University of Notre Dame Press, 1984), p. 98.

5. Ibid., p. 114f. "Error entails isolation and breaking of relations. As long as there is dialogue, struggle, discussion, and disagreement we have conflicting opinions, different and even contradictory views; but all this appertains to the very polarity of reality.... From my vantage point my opponent is wrong, but not *absolutely* wrong *unless* the group or person in question breaks loose from ... the rest of us" (emphasis added) p. 114. Panikkar does think, therefore, in terms of absolute wrong, (eg., the loner), and absolute truth, (e.g., togetherness).

6. David Tracy, *Dialogue with the Other: The Inter-Religious Dialogue* (Grand Rapids: Eerdmans, 1991), p. 98.

7. Harold A. Netland, *Dissonant Voices: Religious*

Pluralism and the Question of Truth (Grand Rapids: Eerdmans, 1991), p. 296.

8. Ibid., p. 297.

9. Ibid., p. 298.

10. Ibid., p. 299.

11. Ibid., pp. 299–300.

12. Ibid., p. 301.

13. See Andrew D. Clark and Bruce W. Winter (eds.), *One God, One Lord: Christianity in a World of Religious Pluralism* (2nd ed.; Grand Rapids: Baker,1993); Lesslie Newbigin, *The Gospel in a Pluralist Society* (Grand Rapids: Eerdmans, 1989); also his *Trinitarian Faith and Today's Mission* (Richmond: John Knox, 1964).

IV
Salvation for Sinners

15

God's Will in the Face Of Evil and Suffering

Two Kinds of *Why* Questions

Some claim that evil is the surest proof that there is no God. While that is not the position taken here, the issue to be discussed is how one explains the reality of evil in light of the claim of biblical faith that God is both altogether good and all powerful. If God is altogether good, would God not want to have a world without evil, and if God is all powerful, is God not able to make such a world? According to John Hick, "the dilemma was apparently first formulated by Epicurus (341–270 B.C.), and is quoted ... by Lactantius (c. A.D. 260–c. 340)."[1] The word that has come into usage in discussions about this issue is "theodicy," from the Greek *theos*, God, and *dikē*, justice; a theodicy is an attempt to justify God. It is our defense of the claim that God is altogether good and all powerful even though we live in a world in which there is much evil. How do we reconcile the biblical view of God with our experience of evil? Why do we suffer? Whence comes evil? Why this kind of world?

It is important that we distinguish between two kinds of why questions. The first is the cry of emotional anguish. It is the anguished *why* that erupts out of the existential experience of tragedy, difficulty, and pain. In the midst of the turbulence of the experience, we lament that which has encroached on our lives. Though this is a genuine *why* question, the one crying out in anguish probably is not asking for a biblical, theological, or philosophical *answer* to the question, but simply for a *hearing*. The cry is for someone who will hear the lamentations of misery, not for someone who will speak words of explanation. It is the same kind of *why* question our Lord asked as he suffered on the cross: "My God, my God, why have you forsaken me?" (Matt. 27:46).

A second *why*, the intellectual and reflective one, is asked by those who are at an emotional distance from suffering. It may be asked by those who are more reflective after the shock of their own experience has to some degree been dealt with, or it may be asked by those who, though not existentially involved in the traumas of life at the present, are, nevertheless, interested in the human predicament. They ask: What kind of God is it who allows suffering to take place? This *why* calls for more than a comforting presence. It is a request for an explanation that makes sense of the experience of evil but that does not discount the scriptural claims about God. It is the second *why* that is the focus of this chapter.

The purpose here is to develop a biblically based theological framework regarding God and evil, within which we can function as we deal with both the emotional *why* and the intellectual one. As we attempt to relate to those who are in anguish, we need to have a conceptual structure that informs what we say and do even when we are not in an instructional mode but in an emotionally supportive one . What are our basic assumptions about God, the world, and evil as we "weep with those who weep"? What shall we say if and when the intellectual questions are raised?[2]

Beginning the Discussion at the Right Place: the Holy God

A matter that often hinders us as we approach this matter is that instead of beginning with the biblical God, we begin with abstract concepts of objective omnipotence and objective goodness that we view as standing outside of God, and by that even God is measured. We invite unnecessary problems when we begin with presuppositions about abstract power and abstract goodness instead of beginning with the biblical God who *is* the definition of power and goodness. The biblical God is not measured by external, abstract concepts. Instead of measuring God by our conceptions of external canons of power and goodness, it is crucial that we begin with none other than God who is the measuring rod for understanding power and goodness.

The God of the Bible says, "I AM WHO I AM" (Exod. 3:14),[3] reminding us as well as Moses that the living God is not our creation, but rather has created us and stands over against us in holiness, separate from all humanly contrived gods. That holiness is spoken of in Leviticus 11:44–45 in connection with the call for God's people to be separated from that which defiles them:

> For I am the LORD [Yahweh] your God; sanctify yourselves therefore, and be holy, for I am holy. You shall not defile yourselves with any swarming creature that moves on the earth. For I am the LORD [Yahweh] who brought you up from the land of Egypt, to be your God; you shall be holy, for I am holy.

According to this passage the people of God are unlike any other people, and for that reason are not to pollute themselves with what is displeasing to God. Yahweh, the eternal I AM,[4] is the one who sets the standard as to what is clean and unclean, acceptable and unacceptable. Just as it was on the basis of I AM's own mysterious will — and not according to some external influence — that God decided to create the world, even so, it is according to I AM's own mysterious will that certain things are clean and others unclean. Likewise, just as it was on the basis of I AM's own inscrutable will that the descendants of Abraham were chosen to be God's people, even so it is according to that same inscrutable will that some things are declared to be acceptable and others unacceptable. Therefore, it is not our prerogative to decide what is acceptable in God's sight and what is not; I AM decides that. It is our responsibility to accept in faith the ways of the holy God, just as Abraham did when he answered the call to enter into a covenant for which he and his people were mysteriously chosen.

The holiness of God is dramatically portrayed in Isaiah's worship experience in the temple: "In the year that King Uzziah died I saw the Lord sitting on a throne, high and lofty; and the hem of his robe filled the temple" (6:1). And the seraphs uttered words of worship, saying "Holy, holy, holy is the LORD of hosts; the whole earth is full of his glory" (v. 3). Isaiah's response in the presence of the holy God was, "Woe is me! I am lost, for I am a man of unclean lips; yet my eyes have seen the King, the LORD of hosts!" (v. 5). After the prophet was cleansed of his sin, he heard the divine invitation to be the Lord's emissary, to which he replied, "Here am I; send me!" (v. 8).

It was not Isaiah who set the standards, but the holy God. This same emphasis on God as the one who sets the standards is seen also in Hosea when it was expected that God would abandon God's people because of their unfaithfulness. Nevertheless, what people expected was not what God was willing to do. God's way was not to be determined by standards of acceptability established by humanly devised criteria. In Hosea 11:9, God says, "I will not execute my fierce anger; I will not again destroy Ephraim; for I am God and no mortal, the Holy One in your midst, and I will not come in wrath [as per the people's expectations]." In other words, God will do what God determines is good.

First Peter 1:14–16 picks up on this Old Testament theme of the holy God who sets God's own standards for calling a holy people who will be faithful to those standards:

Like obedient children, do not be conformed to the desires that you formerly had in ignorance. Instead, as he who called you is holy, be holy yourselves in all your conduct; for it is written, "You shall be holy, for I am holy."

The beginning point for our getting at the issue of

theodicy is to realize that we are in the presence of the holy God whose ways are not necessarily our ways. It is the holy God who is the eternal, all-wise determiner of good and evil. We see this in graphic form in the first creation story in Genesis 1–2:4a where after each of the stages of creation, God declares its goodness (1:4, 10, 12, 18, 21, 25), and then, according to v. 31, "God saw everything that he had made, and indeed, it was very good." The creation is good because the holy God said so, not because it was measured against some neutral standard of goodness and found acceptable. As Claus Westermann says, "In God's sight the entire creation is good, in spite of all that seems incomprehensible, cruel, and terrible to human beings. The goodness of creation is based solely on God's authority; what it is good for, such as it is, only God knows."[5]

Again, in the second account of creation found in 2:4–25, it is the holy God who is the determiner of the distinction between good and evil. One of the trees mentioned in v. 9 is "the tree of the knowledge of good and evil." This tree, along with "the tree of life," represents God's will for us.

The tree of life represents God's gift of eternal life, as 3:22 makes clear: "Then the LORD God said, 'See, the man has become like one of us, knowing good and evil; and now, he might reach out his hand and take also from the tree of life, and eat, and *live forever'* " (emphasis added).

The tree of the knowledge of good and evil represents God's prerogative knowledge, as the same verse makes equally clear: "the man has become like one of us, knowing good and evil." (See For Further Consideration for contemporary biblical scholarship regarding this tree.)

The point is that it is only the omniscient God who determines what is good and what is evil; we do not determine that, nor, as we have said above, is the criterion for determining good and evil some standard by which even God is measured. Only God has the prerogative of creating a world and declaring it good; only God has the prerogative of declaring something unclean and therefore unacceptable. This knowledge of good and evil is a mystery rightfully belonging to God alone; it is not the divine will for us to know this mystery. The whole of reality as only God knows it is the reality of good and evil; no reality is neutral.

According to vv. 16 and 17, God commands

You may freely eat of every tree of the garden; but of the tree of the knowledge of good and evil you shall not eat, for in the day that you eat of it you shall die.

Contrary to this command, however, Adam and Eve

did partake (3:6); the consequence was that God barred them from the tree of life. Their invasion into the divine mystery resulted in God's prohibition of their partaking of eternal life. As Gerhard Von Rad points out, the reference to the knowledge of good and evil

> signifies at one and the same time knowledge of all things and the attainment of mastery over all things and secrets, for here good and evil is not to be understood one-sidedly in a moral sense, but as meaning 'all things.'...By endeavoring to enlarge his being on the godward side, and seeking a godlike intensification of his life beyond his creaturely limitations, that is, by wanting to be like God, man stepped out from the simplicity of obedience to God. He thereby forfeited life in the pleasant garden and close to God. What remained to him was a life of toil in the midst of wearying mysteries, involved in a hopeless struggle with the power of evil, and, at the end, to be, without reprieve, the victim of death.[6]

The idea set forth in Genesis is that God offered eternal life but not God's prerogative knowledge. While, according to 3:8, God entered into fellowship with the created order, intrusion into the mysterious knowledge of God was strictly off limits. By partaking of the forbidden tree, Adam and Eve transgressed not only a commandment, but the very personhood of God. This primal transgression can be understood analogically from our own experience. Each of us has a depth of personal mystery that we do not want anyone else to invade, not even those with whom we are most intimate; to do so is to violate one's personhood.

The human condition is that we have invaded the mystery of God's personhood, and as a result we do have some invasive understandings—though partial, broken, and distorted—of God's comprehensive knowledge of good and evil. With this partial knowledge, though, we can say at least something about matters of good and evil: On the basis of God calling good everything that was created, we can assume that good is whatever God creates, and that evil is whatever is brought into existence by other than God, in opposition to God and as a misuse of creation. Evil is opposition to God through the distorted use of creation; it is the creature's invention of that which is disharmonious with the Creator and creation.

The Roots of Evil

In the commandment not to eat of the tree of the knowledge of good and evil (2:16-17), it is assumed that the human creature has the capacity to choose to be obedient to God. If that is not the case, then the commandment is the charade of a fiction, but such is not in keeping with the kind of God found in the Bible. When God commands something, it is assumed that we have the capacity to obey by choice.

The Genesis account, however, is often misread at this point as though God placed before humans two options, one evil and one good. The picture is that of humans standing in a neutral position considering first one option and then the other, both of which were created by God, and then, tragically, choosing the option of evil.

This notion is to misread the account, for there is no evidence that evil is an option created by God alongside another option called good. The human creature does not have two options; instead God has given only one, that of choosing freely to worship God through loving obedience. God does not say, "Here are two options, take what you will"; instead, God says, "Here is the one option you have, choose this and live."

It is much like being a parent who gives the keys of an automobile to a new driver in the family. A wise parent would not say to the new driver, "You have two options: either be a good driver, be courteous, and obey all rules of the road, or, if you want, be a poor driver, be discourteous and disobey the rules." No, the parent gives the youth only one option, that of choosing to be a good driver. The parent, of course, knows that the young person may manufacture another option contrary to the one given. The fact that the youth is not a robot but a volitional agent prompts the parent to give the one option in the first place. If the new driver were a robot, no instructions would be necessary; but since she is not, the parent is dependent on her to choose good driving practices. She is capable of choosing a contrary option devised by herself because she is by divine design a volitional creature. To choose an opposite option is inherently possible but not one given to her by her parents.

So, to choose that which is contrary to the expressed will of God is a structurally inherent possibility but not an intentionally objective option. The difference between the two can be seen, for instance, in matters such as mulling over whether to murder another. It is obvious that even to consider the possibility is evil. In Matthew 5:27–28, Jesus makes this kind of assumption in reference to lust:

> You have heard that it was said, 'You shall not commit adultery.' But I say to you that everyone who looks at a woman with lust has already committed adultery with her in his heart.

That murders and adultery can be committed is obviously the case since they do actually occur in our world.

Most human beings have the structurally inherent capability of pulling the trigger on a gun, for instance. We are made in such a way that such can be done. But that is very different than an intentional option that one mulls over: "Shall I murder him?" There are many things that structurally we can do but which are never options that we even for the slightest moment consider. Many of us love family members, for instance, without ever giving any consideration whatsoever to the possibility of not loving them. To love is a volitional relationship, but that does not necessarily mean that we ever consider the contrary structural possibility of doing them harm.

Volitional choice does not necessitate two or more objective options. God has created us as volitional creatures with the structurally inherent capacity for making contrary decisions, but God has not set before us objective options for making those volitional decisions. We devise those options. The origin of evil is a human invention; it is rooted in the human decision to transgress the prerogative knowledge and mysterious personhood of God.

But what about the serpent? The Genesis account leads to the following observations about it:

1) According to 3:1 "the serpent was more crafty than any other wild animal the LORD God had made."

Understood within the context of this passage, the serpent was one of the wild animals made by God, and was the most "astute"[7] of them all. The serpent, then, was not an invader from another sphere of reality, but was of the created order itself. (See For Further Consideration, Part III.)

2) According to 3:1–5, the serpent had the capacity to communicate with the human creature. In our own association with the animal kingdom, we know that there are gradations of communications between human beings and the animal kingdom. We experience, for instance, more communication between a seeing eye dog and a human being, than between an ant and a human. Just as we see the vast difference in communication levels between ants and dogs, even so, according to this account, a vast difference existed between the unique serpent spoken of here and the other wild animals. In the Genesis story, this creature had communication skills peculiar to itself in the animal kingdom.

3) In 2:18–20, the loneliness of the man is considered. All of the animals were brought to him for naming, but, as v. 20 says: "There was not found a helper as his partner." According to Westermann: "Here 'helper' is meant in its broadest sense—not only for work or procreation, but for mutual help in all spheres of human existence."[8] Since the serpent was one of the animals, it also was rejected as the man's partner—a helper for "mutual self-understanding in conversation, in silence, in openness to one another."[9]

4) In the canonical text as it now stands (in an earlier tradition, 2:18-24 was a continuation of 2:8 and chapter 3 was a continuation of 2:9, 15-17)[10] immediately after the woman was created as the man's partner—all animals having been rejected for this role—the serpent initiated conversation with the woman and assumed the role of antagonist to God.

5) In 3:14-15, God pronounces a curse on the serpent, placing enmity between it and the woman and demoting the unique serpent to snakehood, i. e., "upon your belly you shall go" (v. 14). A curse is a pronouncement that something is no longer fit for its original purpose and is therefore permanently banned from its original status.[11] "That the serpent was cursed from the animals … means that it was put outside their community."[12]

This, then, is a summary of what the text itself says about the serpent. The issue facing us, however, is the theological significance of the serpent. Four points emerge: first, the serpent is nonhuman creation gone sour; second, the serpent is nonhuman creation presenting itself as an option for worship over and against God, God thereby being lowered in human eyes to the position of being merely one of two possible options. (Think of the unacceptability of treating one's spouse as merely one of two options for marital devotion. Even to consider another option alongside the spouse is to elevate the other to an undeserved level and is to lower the spouse to an inappropriate level.) Third, the serpent is nonhuman creation in an unholy alliance with the human order in common opposition to God; and fourth, the serpent is nonhuman creation banned from fulfilling God's original purpose.

What Is a Holy God to Do?

What, then, was the holy God to do, given the fact that the human order and the nonhuman order, represented by the unique serpent, had originated an option other than that given by God—the option of enmity toward God?

1) God could have annihilated the whole creation. If God had done that, God would have destroyed that which, by God's own declaration, is good. It is not creation itself that is evil but the options invented by the members of the created order. For God to have annihilated creation would have meant that God would have destroyed what is good.

2) God could have done nothing about the joint antagonism of the human and nonhuman created order. If God had taken that approach, God would have mar-

ginalized such antagonism and minimized the seriousness of sin.

3) God could have brought judgment, devoid of salvation, upon the antagonistic creation. If God had taken that course, all that could have been done would not have been done.

4) God could have offered the charade of salvation devoid of judgment. I say charade because no actual salvation is possible apart from judgment in that the very work of salvation implies the conclusion that something is wrong and needs to be rectified; salvation is implicitly a judgment (unless, of course, one saves another incidentally without any knowledge of the other's plight, but such does not apply to an omniscient God). A charade, then, would be a matter of God acting in a saving manner for personal pleasure but without it ever actually affecting the created order; in this case, God would act privately without the created order knowing anything about it. It would be somewhat like a person transgressed against who never confronts the transgressor about it for fear of making him feel uncomfortable. The person, therefore, acts as though everything is all right when actually it is not. He deals with the transgression in and of himself without ever letting the transgressor know that anything was ever wrong. If God had taken that approach, the created order would have gone its merry way unaware that any problem existed.

5) The approach actually taken by God was that of judgment linked with the offer of salvation. The judgment set forth in Genesis 3 is threefold: First, God's presence in the garden was in and of itself a judgment upon the sinfulness of the human pair. According to v. 8 they "hid themselves from the presence of the LORD God among the trees of the garden." Second, as we have already said, the serpent was cursed; and third, God established a cleavage (a disjointedness, a disharmony) between the human order and the nonhuman order of creation.

This cleavage was established in multiple dimensions of life:

a) It was established between the human order and the cursed serpent, i.e., the enmity placed between the serpent and the woman (v. 15). Instead of the relationship of security between the two, it is now a relationship of fear between the human being and the physical offspring of the serpent.

b) It was established between the natural process of biological reproduction and the human desire not to experience pain, i.e., the pain of giving birth is increased (16a).

c) It was established between persons in what had

been the natural partnership of human relationships; the marital relationship was frustrated so that what evidently had been created as an egalitarian love relationship was turned into a hierarchical one (v. 16b).[13]

d) It was established between the God-given responsibility that humans have to take care of the created order (1:26–30) and the human desire for pleasure (3:6, "it was a delight to the eyes"). In 3:17–19 the harmonious relationship between care taking and pleasure is disrupted, for, as v. 17 says, "in toil you shall eat of it [the ground] all the days of your life."

e) It was established in the disjointedness between the nakedness of the created order as such and the nakedness of the human pair. Whereas the human pair had been naked along with the rest of the natural order, a separation was established between the nonhuman created order and the human order. As a result, the human order, now experiencing itself as being naked, clothed itself (3:7). Clothing bespeaks the separation now existing between the two orders.

f) The ultimate separation is seen in 3:22–24 when the human order is driven out of Eden lest the tree of life be partaken of and the human order live forever in opposition to God. A separation was established between the environment created by God (i. e., Eden), on the one hand, and volitional decisions made by the human pair, on the other. Whereas the environment had been created as a synchronized context for the volitional decisions of the human pair, that synchronized context was no longer available to them. Consequently, all of us now live outside the garden! The human order and the created are no longer synchronized. According to v. 24, God "drove out the man, and at the east of the garden of Eden he placed the cherubim, and a sword flaming and turning to guard the way to the tree of life."

Why the Cleavage?

The establishment of the cleavage in chapter 3 implies that prior to God's judgment and sentence, the basic divine design was (and still is) that of a harmonious whole. We see this same created solidarity between the differing dimensions of creation in other parts of the scriptures also, as, for instance, in the Psalms, which point to the interconnectedness of the human order with the wider created order (e.g., Pss. 96 and 98) and in New Testament passages such as Romans 8:18–23 (v. 19 of which speaks of the creation waiting "with eager longing for the revealing of the children of God") and Colossians 1:15–20 with its emphasis on "all things" being reconciled through Christ. We see, then, that according to divine plan, both the human order and the nonhuman created order are all of a piece. Both the human order and the nonhuman created order were created to be a synchronized whole with all dimensions being interrelated in reciprocal support. Why, then, the sentence of disjointedness?

According to Genesis, it is due to the fact that the two orders—the prototypical nonhuman order (represented by the unique serpent) and the prototypical human order (Adam and Eve)—were united in opposition to God. God, however, graciously broke the union of antagonism by establishing a cleavage between the two orders for salvation purposes. The rest of the book of Genesis is the story of God's covenantal salvation taking place within the context of such a world.

The cleavage between the two orders is the way we experience the world. The whole biblical story assumes that it is in the midst of this cleavage that God works to the end that we will know that God alone is Lord—the one whom we are to love wholeheartedly. Deuteronomy 6:4-5:

Hear, O Israel: The LORD is our God, the LORD alone. You shall love the LORD your God with all your heart, and with all your soul, and with all your might. (cf., Matt. 22:34-40; Mark 12:28-34; Luke 10:25-28.)

Theological Reflection on Disjointedness

Paul in Romans 8:20 speaks of this disjointedness when he refers to the creation being subjected to futility. The Greek word is *mataiotēs* meaning vanity, folly, emptiness, frailty, uselessness. The New International Version translates the word as "frustration." This passage, 8:18–25, is crucial to our understanding:

I consider that the sufferings of this present time are not worth comparing with the glory about to be revealed to us. For the creation waits with eager longing for the revealing of the children of God; for the creation was subjected to futility, not of its own will but by the will of the one who subjected it, in hope that the creation itself will be set free from its bondage to decay and will obtain the freedom of the glory of the children of God. We know that the whole creation has been groaning in labor pains until now; and not only the creation, but we ourselves, who have the first fruits of the Spirit, groan inwardly while we wait for adoption, the redemption of our bodies. For in hope we were saved. Now hope that is seen is not hope. For who hopes for what is seen? But if we hope for what we do not see, we wait for it with patience.

God frustrated the relationship between the human order and the nonhuman created order not for the purpose of giving us trouble, but for the purpose of breaking up the union of antagonism against the Creator. In this space of disjointedness between the human order that desires wholeness, harmony, and the idyllic and the nonhuman order that provides the environment for such wholeness and harmony — in this space human beings can discover the tragedy of their sinfulness and the misadventure of their antagonistic league with the created order. This space allows humans to turn away from the worship of the creature to the worship of the Creator. The space gives them opportunity to participate in the gracious work of the God who is making all things new (see Rev. 21:5).

Without this cleavage between human desire and natural environment, we would be insufferably ignorant of our degenerative unity of antagonism toward God. We would be dreadfully satisfied with our worship of the creature. We would be woefully unknowing of the grace of salvation.

God's subjection of the creation to futility is not primarily punitive but saving, not essentially wrathful but loving, not basically retaliatory but redemptive. It is in this gracious space of disjointedness between the human order and the created order that we get in touch with ourselves, and that God gets our attention. It is here that we experience grace through the incarnation of God in Christ Jesus. It is in the midst of this gracious

369

circumstance that the divine purpose of developing holy volitional lovers of God takes place. It is in this kind of world that Jesus Christ came to seek and save the lost.

Christ Jesus

The incarnate Christ was the unique person of holy volitional love in the created order. He was what the human pair were created to be. He was the eternal guarantee that God's purpose for creation would be realized regardless of the direction taken by the human pair. Acts 2:23 refers to him as being part of the "definite plan and foreknowledge of God." First Peter 1:20 says that "he was destined before the foundation of the world, but was revealed at the end of the ages for your sake."

This eternal guarantee became the incarnate guarantee. He entered into the created order where he participated in the divinely designed disharmony, even to the depths of despair and death. He became the man of sorrows who in the abyss of gloom cried out from the cross: "My God, my God, why have you forsaken me?" (Mark 15:34). But as Hebrews 2:18 says: "Because he himself was tested by what he suffered, he is able to help those who are being tested." Hebrews 4:15 continues, "For we do not have a high priest who is unable to sympathize with our weaknesses, but we have one who in every respect has been tested as we are, yet without sin."

Christ Jesus, the eternal and incarnate guarantee of holy volitional love in the created order, will also, according to Scripture, be the consummate guarantee at the end of the age. We are assured by 1 Corinthians 15:21–22: "Since death came through a human being, the resurrection of the dead has also come through a human being; for as all die in Adam, so all will be made alive in Christ." When he has brought all things under subjection to him, then "the Son himself will also be subjected to the one who put all things in subjection under him, so that God may be all in all" (v. 28). According to this, the human and nonhuman created order will be redeemed at the close of the age because of the work of Christ. Revelation 7:9–17 says that at the end of history the four living creatures (v. 11) — referring to the whole of the created order — will join the redeemed of the Lord in the worship of God in the glory of the eternal consummation at the center of which is Christ the Lamb (v. 17).

Some Theological Ramifications

Several theological ramifications of this perspective are as follows:

1) The goal of creation is not simply that we will be happy, pain-free individuals, but that we will be the holy people of God. The divine goal is that we become persons who know that our origin is from the holy God, who worship the holy God, and who are living as God's holy people. As 1 Peter 1:14–16 puts it:

> Like obedient children, do not be conformed to the desires that you formerly had in ignorance. Instead, as he who called you is holy, be holy yourselves in all your conduct.

2) The capacity to suffer is inherent in our being created in the image of the God who has the capacity to suffer. According to Genesis 6:6, "the LORD was sorry that he had made humankind on the earth, and it grieved him to his heart." The God of both the Old and New Testaments is the suffering God.[14] The capacity to suffer, therefore, is by definition good in that it is part of the nature of God.

3) Our relationship to God determines whether the experience of suffering is good or evil.[15] On the basis of our definitions of good and evil stated above, we conclude that suffering is good when it is experienced in a relationship of love for God (love, being of God, is good since by definition whatever is of God is good); it is evil when it is experienced in a relationship of antagonism to God (since evil is whatever has its origin from other than God).

4) Our suffering, whether good or evil, is brought about by

a) the randomness of natural occurrences that all persons, regardless of their relationship to God, experience by virtue of living in the cleavage between the two orders (see Matt. 5:45),

b) the overt work of Satan who seeks to destroy us (e.g., 2 Cor. 12:7),

c) the evil works of others who intend to hurt us (e.g., Acts 12:1–5), and

d) by our own lack of self-control (see Mark 9:42–48).

5) For disciples of Christ, suffering is also the result of our decision to take up the cross for the sake of Christ (e. g., Matt. 16:24–26). Paul speaks of Christian volitional suffering in Philippians 3:10 where he says, "I want to know Christ and the power of his resurrection and the sharing of his sufferings by becoming like him in his death." In Colossians 1:24, he writes, "I am now rejoicing in my sufferings for your sake, and in my flesh I am completing what is lacking in Christ's afflictions for the sake of his body, that is, the church." (See also 1 Cor. 11:16–33.)

6) As disciples, we are to be teachers of the faith who declare to others the message of assurance that God has dealt redemptively with sin and evil in the person of Jesus Christ. (See chapter 5 on "Christ Jesus, the Kingdom, and Eschatology" and chapter 6 on "The Person and Work of Christ Jesus.") We have a teaching function to inform others about the new perspective revealed in Christ, on the issues of sin and evil.[16]

7) Also, we are to be agents of love who, as participants in the historical process, struggle and suffer along with every one else. We are called to be Christ's people who not only help fellow sufferers but also seek remedies for the tragic occurrences of life. We work in the spirit of the good Samaritan (Luke 10:25–37) about whom Jesus said that we should "go and do likewise."[17]

8) In addition to this, we are to be sharers of hope who influence others by the confidence we have in the divinely glorious consummation of the whole creative enterprise.[18] What God set out to do will be accomplished, namely, to establish a fellowship of holy volitional lovers who know that their origin is from the holy God, who worship the holy God and who are devoted to being the holy people of God.

9) By divine design this is a transitional world. It is a world having a beginning and an ending. It is not the ultimate world; the ultimate lies beyond the world as we know it. Revelation 21:1 says, "Then I saw a new

heaven and a new earth; for the first heaven and the first earth had passed away." Verse 5: "And the one who was seated on the throne said, 'See, I am making all things new.' " The disappointments that we experience in relation to this world's difficulties are often the result of our failure to be in touch with the transitional nature of where we now exist. Our experience of not-yetness is part of being creatures in a transitory world.

This view of transitoriness could, of course, lead to both the devaluation of the importance of this world and the shirking of responsibility for making it better. This is likely to happen if the biblical perspectives on the goodness of creation (Gen. 1), the human responsibility to care for it (Gen. 1: 26ff.), and the Christological nature of it (Col. 1:15–20) are not taken seriously. Such passages do not allow for indifference toward making this a better transitional place in which to live until the time comes for us to dwell in the new heavens and new earth. In some mysterious way, the good that we have done in, to, and for this transitional world will be included in the new world, and that which is ignoble will be excluded (See Rev. 21:26; cf., vv. 24, 27; 22:3, 15).

Summary

In summary, then, by divine design, this is a good transitional world. Though by creaturely choice it is afflicted with evil, nevertheless, by God's gracious judgment, it is subjected to frustration between the human order and the nonhuman created order. As such, it is the arena for God's equally gracious salvation, and is itself being redeemed by the suffering God in covenant with God's suffering people.

Some practical consequences of this view are

a) sensitive solidarity with humanity as a whole,

b) commitment to redemptive suffering,

c) humble joy in the hope already revealed in Jesus Christ, and

d) the willingness to be signs of the kingdom of God, which kingdom will be brought to consummation at the end of this transitional world. The end of this transitional world will come when, according to Matthew 24:14, "this good news of the kingdom will be proclaimed throughout the world, as a testimony to all the nations; and then the end will come."

Notes

1. John Hick, *Evil and the God of Love* (San Francisco: Harper and Row, 1978), p. 5.

2. Examples of theologies of suffering are D. A. Carson, *How Long, O Lord? Reflections on Suffering and Evil* (Grand Rapids: Baker, 1990); Daniel Liderbach,

Why Do We Suffer? New Ways of Understanding (New York: Paulist, 1992).

3. Or, "I AM WHAT I AM" or "I WILL BE WHAT I WILL BE."

4. See Exod. 3:14 where God says to Moses, "Thus you shall say to the Israelites, 'I AM has sent me to you.'"

5. Claus Westermann, *Genesis: A Practical Commentary,* trans. David E. Green (Grand Rapids: Eerdmans, 1987), p. 11f.

6. Gerhard Von Rad, *Old Testament Theology,* Vol. I, trans. D. M. G. Stalker (New York: Harper and Row, 1962), p. 155.

7. See Victor P. Hamilton, *The Book of Genesis Chapters 1–17* (Grand Rapids: Eerdmans, 1990), p. 187. This is his translation of the word, *'ār^um,* which appears only here in Genesis. He points out that it is frequently used in Proverbs as a commendable trait of prudence, shrewdness, cleverness and is contrasted with being foolish (12:16, 23; 13:16; 14:8) or with the simple (14:15,18; 22:3; 27:12). In Job, however, the word is used pejoratively (5:12; 15:5). Hamilton's conclusion, therefore, is that it is "an ambivalent term that may describe a desirable or undesirable characteristic." "It appears best to take 'astute, clever' as an appropriate description of the snake, one that aptly describes its use of a strategy of prudence when it engages the woman in dialogue," p. 188.

8. Westermann, op. cit., p. 21.

9. Ibid.

10. See Claus Westermann, *Genesis 1 – 11: A Commentary,* trans. John J. Scullion (Minneapolis: Augsburg, 1984), pp. 225ff., 236ff.

11. See Ibid., p. 258f.

12. Johs Pedersen, *Israel, Its Life and Culture, I–II* (London: Geoffrey Cumberlege, Oxford University Press, 1964), p. 452.

13. Westermann does not see this passage as being simply punitive (and neither do I, but I do see it as a gracious sentence for the sake of salvation); nevertheless, he does note the theological importance of the difference between the egalitarian relationship established between man and woman in Gen. 2:21–24 (coming as it does from one tradition used in the canonical text) and the hierarchical one spoken of in 3:16b (coming from another tradition): "In contrast to the temporary subordination of the woman [3:16] stands the permanent relationship between man and woman [2:21–24]: the difference between them is a part of human existence that will always remain" (Eerdmans), p. 26. I maintain that in the canonical text as we now have it, while the hierarchical relationship is part of the gracious sentence, it is not reflective of the order of creation as such. In Christ, though, the good ordering of human relationships is restored (see Gal. 3:28).

14. See Paul S. Fiddes, *The Creative Suffering of God*

(Oxford: Clarendon, 1988). For an assessment that calls into question his view, see Frances Young, *Face to Face: A Narrative Essay in the Theology of Suffering* (Edinburgh: T and T Clark, 1990), pp. 237–239. Young says that we need to reclaim the insight "that God is 'beyond suffering' in the sense that he is not emotionally involved in a self-concerned way—rather he is that ocean of love that can absorb all the suffering of the world and purge it without being polluted or changed by it," p. 239.

Also, Joseph M. Hallman, *The Descent of God: Divine Suffering in History and Theology* (Minneapolis: Fortress, 1991).

15. See Young, op. cit.

16. See Richard F. Vieth, *God, Where Are You? Suffering and Faith* (Cleveland: United, 1989).

17. For a provocative discussion of the parable of the good Samaritan in relation to the topic under consideration, see Arthur C. McGill, *Suffering: A Test of Theological Method* (Philadelphia: Westminster, 1982), chap. 6. Also see Stanley Hauerwas, *Naming the Silences: God, Medicine and the Problem of Suffering* (Grand Rapids, Eerdmans, 1990).

18. See M. Scott Peck, *People of the Lie: The Hope for Healing Human Evil* (New York: Simon and Schuster, 1983).

For Further Consideration

Part I. Selected Reading on Theodicy

Norman L. Geisler, *The Roots of Evil* (Grand Rapids: Zondervan, 1978).

John Hick, *Evil and the God of Love* (San Francisco: Harper and Row, 1978).

C. S. Lewis, *The Problem of Pain* (New York: Macmillan, 1948).

Lucien Richard (ed.), *What Are They Saying About the Theology of Suffering?* (Mahwah: Paulist, 1992).

Alvin Plantinga, *God, Freedom, and Evil* (Grand Rapids: Eerdmans, 1982).

Marguerite Shuster, *Power, Pathology, Paradox: The Dynamics of Evil and Good* (Grand Rapids: Zondervan, 1987).

Part II. The Tree of the Knowledge of Good and Evil

See Claus Westermann, *Genesis 1 – 11: A Commentary*, trans. John J. Scullion (Minneapolis: Augsburg, 1984), p. 234. "The function of the object of 'to know' is not to separate, but to bring together: a whole is described by the two extremes [of good and evil]. This explanation of [J.] Wellhausen has also been taken up by a number of scholars and clarified further, especially by P. Pidoux, 'a means of expressing totality.' " "These explanations of Wellhausen that 'good and evil' have (a) a functional and (b) an all-embracing sense can be presumed. They accord with the meaning of the text."

For another review of classical interpretations and a critique of each, see Victor P. Hamilton, *The Book of Genesis Chapters 1 – 17* (Grand Rapids: Eerdmans, 1990), pp. 162–166. While Hamilton rejects the theory that the tree of the knowledge of good and evil is a symbol of omniscience, he does understand it to be a symbol of the divine prerogative: "What is forbidden to man is the power to decide for himself what is in his best interests and what is not. This is a decision God has not delegated to the earthling.... Man has indeed become a god whenever he makes his own self the center, the springboard, and the only frame of reference for moral guidelines. When man attempts to act autonomously he is indeed attempting to be godlike," p. 166.

Also see Hugh C. White, *Narration and Discourse in the Book of Genesis* (Cambridge: Cambridge University Press, 1991), pp. 117–119. White understands the tree of the knowledge of good and evil to be a symbol of "knowledge, wisdom, or intellectual discernment" (p. 118). The two trees "*offer* human beings the chief qualities of divinity: eternal life and autonomous selfhood" (p.119; emphasis added). While the concept of autonomous selfhood is reflective of the text, the idea that the tree of the knowledge of good and evil is a symbol of a divine *offering* is not, for to partake is explicitly prohibited in 2:17.

Part III. Satan

See Victor P. Hamilton, *The Book of Genesis Chapters 1–17* (Grand Rapids: Eerdmans, 1990), p. 188. "Regarding the serpent's origin, we are clearly told that he was an animal made by God. This information immediately removes any possibility that the serpent is to be viewed as some kind of supernatural, divine force. There is no room here for any dualistic ideas about the origins of good and evil."

For opposing positions, see Harold G. Stigers, *A Commentary on Genesis* (Grand Rapids: Zondervan, 1976), p. 73, i.e., the serpent is not an animal but another kind of fallen being; Gerhard von Rad, *Genesis* (Philadelphia: Westminster, 1973), p. 87, i. e., the serpent is a literary device for speaking about "the impulse to temptation."

My view is that the serpent should be understood within the context of the text itself and not in light of later biblical understandings. That the serpent is connected with Satan in Revelation 20:2 must not be allowed to intrude on the interpretation of this text as such; otherwise, we do not allow every part of the Bible to speak with clarity its own message in the canonical symphony. I, therefore, disagree with Stigers who, in my view, disallows Genesis having its own clear sound in the canonical symphony, but I also disagree with von Rad who, it seems to me, distorts—perhaps as an over reaction to the view represented by Stigers—the obvious shape of the text in which the serpent is part of the created order that is external to the human pair, rather than a symbol of an internal impulse.

It is my theological view (to be distinguished from an exegetical view of the Genesis passage itself) that Satan is the ongoing spirit of the unique serpent. Since the unique serpent was cursed, its physical progeny is the reptile family devoid of the original spirit of the unique serpent. The original spirit of the unique serpent is still with us but without body. What Revelation 20:2 refers to as "the dragon, that ancient serpent, who is the Devil and Satan" is a bodiless spirit of militant antagonism to God.

Other Helpful Resources:

Rivkah Schärf Kluger, *Satan in the Old Testament* (Evanston: Northwestern University Press, 1967).

James Kallas, *Jesus and the Power of Satan* (Philadelphia: Westminster, 1968).

William Robinson, *The Devil and God* (New York: Abingdon-Cokesbury, 1945).

16

Sin

Sin is both the root cause of evil and the moral expression of it. Whereas evil is both personal and impersonal, sin is strictly personal. Evil has to do with the structure of the whole created order, but sin has to do strictly with volitional life. Sin is the human being's basic predicament, the devil's only commitment and God's central reason for the incarnation and atonement.

We gain an adequate understanding of the nature of sin only when we view ourselves in light of Christ who came "to take away sins, and in him there is no sin" (1 John 3:5). He is the great high priest "who in every respect has been tested as we are, yet without sin" (Heb. 4:15).

The sinless Jesus of Nazareth was totally committed to God's will for the world and God's mission in it. Our predicament is that while we were created for the same commitment, we are born not knowing what God's will and mission are.

In the New Testament, three different words express this human predicament: *hamartia*, i.e., missing the mark, translated as sin (e.g., Luke 11:4a; Rom. 5:12-13; 14:23; James 4:17; 1 John 3:4; 5:17); *paraptōma*, i.e., a false step, usually translated as trespass (e.g., Matt. 6:14-15; Mark 11:25-26; Rom. 4:25; 5:15ff; 11:11-12; 2 Cor. 5:19; Gal. 6:1; Eph. 1:7; 2:5; Col. 2:13)[1]; and *anomia*, i.e., against law, usually translated as lawlessness, wickedness or iniquity (e.g., Matt. 7:23; Rom. 6:19; 2 Cor. 6:14; 2 Thess. 2:3 and 7; Titus 2:14; Heb. 1:9; 1 John 3:4).

The church's theological and doctrinal life has been greatly influenced by its differing views of sin. In order to find our own location on the theological landscape, therefore, it may be helpful to review major historical developments on the subject.

Foundational Views in the Eastern and Western Churches

Although in the early centuries of the Christian era, the Eastern church was primarily devoted to discussions about the nature of Christ and of the Trinity, two theologians who did gave significant attention to the doctrine of sin were Origen (ca. 185–ca. 254) and Gregory of Nyssa (ca. 330–ca. 394).

In Origen's major work, *On First Principles* (II, 9, 1–6), he argues that sin and evil came into existence as the result of the exercise of the free will of created souls prior to the creation of the material world.[2] This purely speculative argument never commended itself to the church at large.

Gregory wrote about our corruption, which is the result of our turning away from God. God is at work both throughout our life and in death to remove this corruption from us. Death is the way by which we are, "like a clay pot ... dissolved into earth again—so that the filth which has become a part of him may be separated out and he may be refashioned in his original form through the resurrection" (*Catechetical Oration*, 8).[3] Origen sees sin as a cosmic aberration, and Gregory sees it as creational pollution.

The more technical discussions about the nature of sin took place in the Western church. Whereas the East had viewed it more as an alien influence in the human being, the West came to view it more as a radical depravity of the human being. We see this, for instance, in Tertullian of Carthage (ca. 160–ca. 220) who proposed a so-called truducian view (from the Latin phrase *tradux animae, tradux peccati,* i.e., transmission of the soul, transmission of sin) by which he meant that the soul along with sin is transferred from parent to child in the act of conception. In Adam all are afflicted with sin by virtue of seminal inclusion.[4]

The fuller explication of this Western emphasis was to await Augustine (354–430). His conversion in 387 was in no small part due to the influence of Ambrose of Milan who, like Tertullian, had given major attention to the subject of sin.

By 395, Augustine had become bishop of Hippo in North Africa where his own view of sin was worked out in opposition to that espoused by a British monk, Pelagius (ca. 360–ca. 420)[5] who held that each human being, when born, has the same standing before God that Adam originally had, and, therefore, conceivably might not sin. He did, however, admit that in the course of the world's history this has become highly unlikely, given the cumulative influence of sin. Pelagius saw sin primarily as a problem of social influence rather than as a dilemma resident in the human being as such; accordingly, we have the ability in and of ourselves as the good creatures of God to be obedient to God's commands.

Pelagius propagated his teaching in Rome from 409 until 411; from there it spread to the North African church mainly through his disciple, Caelestius, and to the Palestinian church through Pelagius himself.

Augustine, concerned about the spread of this view,

argued that since we are born with sin, it is structurally impossible for us to love God as we ought. His schema of human history from creation to consummation is that the human being was created with the ability not to sin (*posse non peccare*). However, because of Adam's sin, we are now in a dismally different state characterized by the inability not to sin (*non posse non peccare*[6]). Because of the atoning work of Christ, though, we have the promise that in the future life we shall have the inability to sin (*non posse peccare*). He writes,

> Therefore the first liberty of the will was to be able not to sin, the last will be much greater, not to be able to sin; the first immortality was to be able not to die, the last will be much greater, not to be able to die; the first was the power of perseverance, to be able not to forsake good — the last will be the felicity of perseverance, not to be able to forsake good. (*A Treatise on the Merits and Forgiveness of Sins, and on the Baptism of Infants*, Book I, chap. 11 [x].)[7]

Augustine took a corporate view of the human family. That means that when Adam sinned, all individual members of the human family participated — "all were that one man" (*Treatise on Rebuke and Grace*, chap. 33).[8] All of us, then, by virtue of being members of the human race are guilty of Adam's sin. Furthermore, our total being fell into degradation leaving us with no natural resources for coming to God. We see the dire state of which Augustine speaks, for example, in his *Treatise on the Merits and Forgiveness of Sins* where he describes our fallen state as follows:

> When ... Adam sinned by not obeying God, then his body ... lost the grace whereby it used in every part of it to be obedient to the soul. Then there arose in men affections common to the brutes which are productive of shame.... Then also, by a certain disease which was conceived in men from a suddenly injected and pestilential corruption, it was brought about that they lost that stability of life in which they were created, and, by reason of the mutations which they experienced in the stage of life, issued at last in death (chap. 21 [xvi]).[9]

Accordingly, we are totally unable to do anything whatsoever that is of any value to salvation; we are saved from our hopeless state of bondage by nothing less than the grace of God. This grace so works on our wills that they do, in fact, volitionally love God, this being possible, not because the sinful will is able to love God, but because God has elected some to be saved from universally fallen humanity, the so-called *massa perditionis*, the mass of perdition. As Augustine explains in *A Treatise on Nature and Grace, Against Pelagius* (chap. 5 [v.]),

The entire mass, therefore, incurs penalty; and if the deserved punishment of condemnation were rendered to all, it would without doubt be righteously rendered. They, therefore, who are delivered therefrom by grace are called, not vessels of their own merits, but "vessels of mercy." But of whose mercy, if not His who sent Christ Jesus into the world to save sinners, whom He foreknew and foreordained, and called, and justified, and glorified? Now, who could be so madly insane as to fail to give ineffable thanks to the Mercy which liberates whom it would? The man who correctly appreciated the whole subject could not possibly blame the justice of God in wholly condemning all men whatsoever.[10]

Since some have been elected to salvation, they are, by virtue of that election, thereby capable of volitionally loving God. It is important to note, however, that this volitional capacity is not a capacity that is intact in spite of the fall—for that was completely lost in the fall—but that it is restored as a benefit of election to salvation. Sin has so thoroughly depraved us that nothing remains that is able to respond to the grace of God. We do not experience God's grace because we have faith; we have faith because of God's grace. Since there is nothing in us to which the grace of God responds, our election to salvation is according to the sovereign choice of God. Out of the *massa perditionis*, God elects some to be saved, leaving all others in the state of perdition where, in fact, all of us deserve to be.

In the course of the intellectual battle between Augustinianism and Pelagianism, the former gained ascendancy. In North Africa, where Augustine had been bishop for twelve years, Caelestius, in 412 at Carthage, was declared a heretic. Although Pelagius was tried for heresy at two synods (Jerusalem and Diospolis) in Palestine (414–416), he was not actually condemned until his views were considered by two other synods in 416, one of which was at Carthage and the other at Milevum where Augustine was present.[11] Later in 431 at the Council of Ephesus, his views were again condemned. John Ferguson in his study of Pelagius writes:

> Augustine lays his stress upon the divine initiative, Pelagius upon the human response. In any real meeting of God and man there must be both. Augustine won in part because the Church, seeing how God is greater than man, and the divine initiative greater than the human response, felt that his emphasis was right. But as Augustine formulated his full theory of predestination he left no room for human freedom. Pelagius' emphasis was not objective; it did not arise from any denial of the initiative or power of God. Indeed Pelagius in some ways made more of the power of God than Augustine, for he saw in Augustine's denial of the possibility of

sinlessness a derogation from God's power. Pelagius was accepting as common ground with Augustine the initiative of God. But upon that common ground he wished also to assert man's free response.... It is hard to see that he was wrong.[12]

A mediating position eventually emerged, known in the history of the church's intellectual life, as Semi-Pelagianism, a name that belies the attitude of those calling it by the name of a man whose views had been officially condemned. Regardless of the pejorative tag, its concern was to maintain, on the one hand, Augustine's emphasis on the universality and pervasiveness of sin in the human race, and on the other, Pelagius's emphasis on human responsibility. Its view of the human condition was not as severe as the Augustinian: the human being was severely and adversely affected by sin but not to the degree that human response to God is impossible. Divine grace linked with human faith was seen as the basis for salvation.[13]

The Council of Orange in 529 condemned this view also, and a somewhat modified form of Augustinianism was propounded. Greater emphasis was given to sacramental grace that enables people to overcome their innate sinfulness. While salvation is of grace, it is channeled through the sacramental life of the church and is not, therefore, strictly a matter of the predestination of God. Instead of emphasizing the unmediated grace of predestination, it placed the emphasis on the mediated grace of the church's sacramental life. In this view, then, some human agency—the church—is necessary for salvation.

Medieval Views

Anselm of Canterbury (1033–1109) revived Augustinian themes in his *Cur deus homo? (Why the God-Man?)*. Like Augustine, he argued that original sin is not confined to the sin of Adam, but is the condition into which all persons are born, and of which they are guilty:

> Inexcusable is man, who has voluntarily brought upon himself a debt which he cannot pay, and by his own fault disabled himself, so that he can neither escape his previous obligation not to sin, nor pay the debt which he has incurred by sin. For his very inability is guilt, because he ought not to have it.... As it is a crime not to have what he ought, it is also a crime to have what he ought not ... For it is by his own free action that he loses that power [to avoid sin], and falls into this inability [to do right, avoid sin, and restore the debt he owes for sin].... Man's inability to restore what he owes to God ... does not excuse man from paying; for the result of sin cannot excuse the sin itself. (Book I, chap. 24.)[14]

We are born into a spiritual dilemma from which there is absolutely no escape except by virtue of the gracious sacrifice, on our behalf, of the God-man, Jesus Christ. None but a human being needs to make the sacrifice, but none but God can make sufficient satisfaction through sacrifice. The only solution to the dilemma is the God-man. (See Book II, chaps. 6–7.)[15]

Prior to the reformation, however, scholastic theologians developed the view that the human situation is not quite so dismal. Sin was seen as being the wrong exercise of our innate ability to choose the good, an ability that, in their view, was not destroyed by the sin of Adam and Eve. That which was changed as a result of their sin was the loss of the divine gift of grace making obedience easier.

The scholastics stressed the idea that God had created the human being with a lower and a higher nature. Since the two are in tension, conflict between them arises. Therefore, God, at the time of creation, added a gift that was not part of the human being's nature as such.[16]

The purpose of this gift was to keep the flesh in subservience to the spirit, and the whole person in obedience to God. Thomas Aquinas, for instance, speaks of "the reason being submissive to God, the lower powers to the reason, the body to the soul."[17]

He goes on to argue that

> it is plain that submission of body to soul and lower
> powers to reason was not by nature; otherwise it would
> have persisted after sin, since even the demons' natural
> endowments have remained after sin.... From this it is
> plain that that primary submissiveness in which the rea-
> son put itself under God was not something merely nat-
> ural either, but was by a gift of supernatural grace.[18]

While it is the case, then, that with Adam's sin this supernatural grace was lost, it is also true that nothing having to do with our natural endowment was lost. In his consideration of God's image, Thomas maintains that "man's natural aptitude [not to be confused with the actuality] for understanding and loving God, an aptitude which consists in the very nature of the mind" is found in all persons as persons.[19] This image, which is principally "an intelligent nature," *intellectualem natu-ram*,[20] is not destroyed by Adam's sin. After the fall, human beings were left in the natural state that belonged to Adam prior to receiving supernatural grace. The significance of this for medieval thought was that sin did not bring about the total depravity of the human being as originally created. Since we still have the innate ability to turn to God, our salvation is the result of the working together of God and humans, i.e., it is synergistic, as over against the Augustinian monergistic view that salvation is strictly the work of God and in no sense whatsoever ours.

Reformation Views

This medieval view of God and humans working together (in what might be called a synergism) was in theological ascendancy at the time of the sixteenth-century reformation. However, the reformers rejected that view and revived the Augustinian (or monergistic) tradition that places all of the emphasis on God.

John Calvin (1509–1564) took the older Augustinian way of thinking to the more radical conclusion that the fall so depraved human beings that their total being, including their volitional powers, thinking processes, and actions, are thoroughly evil in relation to God. "He who perverted the whole order of nature in heaven and earth," Calvin writes, "deteriorated his race by his revolt."[21] Expanding on the degradation into which the human family has fallen, he says:

> After the heavenly image in man was effaced, he not only was himself punished by a withdrawal of the ornaments in which he had been arrayed — viz. wisdom, virtue, justice, truth, and holiness, and by the substitution in their place of those dire pests, blindness, impotence, vanity, impurity, and unrighteousness, but he involved his posterity also, and plunged them in the

same wretchedness. This is the hereditary corruption to which early Christian writers gave the name of Original Sin, meaning by the term the depravation of a nature formerly good and pure.[22]

All of us, then, are descended from the impure seed of Adam so that "before we behold the light of the sun we are in God's sight defiled and polluted."[23] Every part of the human being is affected by original sin, "from the intellect to the will, from the soul even to the flesh."[24] The title of Book II, Chapter 3 of the *Institutes* states it boldly, "Everything Proceeding from the Corrupt Nature of Man [is] Damnable."[25]

All three major reformers—Calvin, Martin Luther (1483-1546), and Ulrich Zwingli (1484-1531)—stressed Augustinian monergism. As so often happens, one extreme breeds another. The extremes of Calvinism evoked the extreme views of the Socinians—so called after their leaders Lelio Sozzini (1525-1562) and his nephew Fausto (1539-1604)—in their revival of Pelagianism. Sin, for them, is the result of weakness, which for the morally strong should not occur.

A much different response to the reformation's revival of Augustinian monergism was made by Philipp Melanchthon (1497-1560), systematizer of Lutheran theology and ecumenist who sought to bring about a degree of reconciliation between the Catholic church and the reformation. Troubled about monergistic thinking, he argued that salvation is experienced when the human being, upon hearing the gospel, does not refuse God's grace. As one Melanchthon scholar has pointed out, "the Holy Spirit and the word are first active in conversion, but the will of man is not wholly inactive; God draws, but draws him who is willing, for man is not a statue."[26]

This does not mean, however, that he in any way minimizes the devastating consequences of Adam's sin on the whole human race. In his systematic work, *Loci Communes*, he maintains a clearly Augustinian and reformed view. For example: "To be in original sin is to be in God's disgrace and wrath, to be damned on account of the fall of Adam and Eve." In the same passage he goes on to speak of "our perverted, evil tendencies" (chap. VI).[27]

Having established the dire need of the human soul for God's grace, he, then, speaks of the importance of personal faith, as when he refers to our "childlike fear toward God [which] is in *the heart*." Faith, he says, is a laying hold of the promise of grace; but not only does it lay hold of the *promise*, but also "in the midst of terror [it] lays hold of grace [itself]" (XXV).[28] In his chapter on faith, Melanchthon describes it as "the means by which we behold the Lord Christ and by which *we* apply and appropriate his merit to ourselves" (XI), (emphasis added)[29]. In yet another place, he speaks about faith being "heartfelt trust in the Son of God" (XIII).[30] Another important passage is in chapter VII, "Of Divine Law," in which he says that there "must be a beginning [of love for God], even though, unfortunately, in all men it is very weak."[31] He then goes on to say:

> This beginning occurs when the heart, truly terrified before God's wrath against our sin, hears the gospel through which God, for the sake of the Lord Christ and through him, gives forgiveness of sins and also gives the Holy Spirit. Then, through faith in the Son of God, the heart is snatched out of anxiety and hell. Thus the heart knows God's wrath and also his mercy.[32]

Melanchthon propounded the universal offer of forgiveness and faith for all. While his view of the *need* for salvation was thoroughly Reformed, his view of the universal *offer* anticipated the Wesleyan revival, e.g.,

> *All* men in their corrupted nature have sin, and God truly hates sin in *all men*.... On the other hand, the preaching of grace in the gospel is also *universalis*, and promises forgiveness, mercy, justification, the Holy Spirit, and eternal blessedness for *all* who accept this grace *with faith* and trust in the Lord *Christ*. [Emphases his.]

Continuing this line of thought, in reference to Matthew 11:28 where Jesus says "Come to me, all who labor and are heavy laden, and I will give you rest," he comments that "In the number 'all' everyone should include himself, and with faith in the Lord Christ should ask for help" (IX).[33]

While Melanchthon was careful to argue that the will is not the agent of salvation, he emphasized the importance of a heartfelt faith response. We do genuinely cooperate with God's grace, although even our cooperation itself is made possible by grace at work in us. In Melanchthon, then, radical monergism was called into question.

Another mediating influence in the late sixteenth and early seventeenth centuries was that of the Dutch Calvinist, Jacobus Arminius (ca. 1559–1609), who, in the course of time, took exception to the extreme views of his mentor Theodore Beza (1519–1605), Calvin's successor at Geneva. He raised questions about both the view that grace is limited to those who are predestined to salvation and the view that sin had so adversely damaged the human will that no power remains for the acceptance of grace.

Following his death in 1609, those who further developed the views that his influence had unleashed — especially Simon Episcopius, leader of the Remonstrants, as they came to be known—were called to task in 1618 by the States General of the Netherlands, at the Synod of Dort.[34] Dort declared against the five points of the Arminian Remonstrance, namely, election that is conditional on human response, the universal offer of redemption, the capability of willfully accepting or rejecting God's offer of salvation, the resistibility of grace, and the possibility of apostasy. In doing so, Dort reaffirmed its views about total depravity (i.e., the inability of the human being to make any movement of faith in relation to God), unconditional grace (i.e., predestination to salvation which is in no way the result of human volitional decisions), limited atonement (i.e., Christ died only for those predestined to salvation), irresistible grace (i.e., those who are predestined to salvation cannot resist grace) and the perseverance of the saints (i.e., the saved will never fall away from salvation).

Regarding the doctrine of sin, Arminians held that Adam's sin had an evil influence on all of his descendants, not as an imputation of guilt but as a spiritual pollution affecting the whole human race. This spiritual disease makes it impossible for us, in and of ourselves, to come to God; what God does, therefore, is graciously to enable us to respond to the Spirit and the Word. While we may indeed reject the gospel, we may, on the other hand, by God's grace, respond in faith. Rejection, however, is due to the exercise of our own human will, not to the predetermined election of God unto damnation. On the other hand, the response of faith is the result of God's grace. By putting it this way, Arminians sought to place the priority on grace without marginalizing the genuineness of human response; they also wanted to value the role of human response without treating us as though we were initiators of salvation.

Eighteenth-century Wesleyanism promulgated Arminian views, though with renewed commitment to preserving the Augustinian emphasis on the divine priority.[35] On the question of guilt, they held, like the sixteenth century reformers, that the guilt of Adam was indeed imputed to the whole human race, but, departing from them, held that in the atoning work of Christ, it was canceled. Furthermore, on the question of volition, they maintained, with the reformers, that the consequence of the fall renders us incapable of taking any initiative whatsoever in relation to salvation, but, unlike the reformers, held that God, through enabling grace, has made it possible for whosoever will to respond to the gospel. (See John Wesley's essay on "Justification by Faith.")[36]

On June 25, 1744, at The First Annual Conference of his societies, John Wesley (1703–1791), in answer to a question about Adam's sin being imputed to all, set forth his view about the results of the fall: "In Adam all died—i.e. (1) our bodies then became mortal; (2) our souls died—i.e. were disunited from God; (3) and hence we are all born with a sinful, devilish nature, by reason whereof (4) we all are children of wrath, liable to death eternal." He goes on to say, however, that "by the merits of Christ all men are cleared from the guilt of Adam's actual sin" and an "actual seed or spark" of "a capacity of spiritual life" is recovered.[37]

Conclusion

In the history of the church three major lines of thought, therefore, can be identified regarding sin. One is the Eastern, Semi-Pelagian, Catholic, Melanchthonian, Arminian, Wesleyan line, which sees sin as the universal plague of humanity. The second is the Augustinian, Anselmian, Reformation, Dort line, which sees it as the ontological fall of humanity. The third is the Pelagian, Socinian line, which sees it as the unnecessary failure of individual humans.

Pelagianism picks up on the biblical theme of human responsibility but fails to do justice to the corporate nature of humanity and the profundity of God's grace. Augustinianism picks up on the biblical theme of the corporate nature of humanity and the profundity of grace, but marginalizes the equally biblical emphasis on human responsibility. Only the Wesleyan line of thought takes into account all emphases in the biblical material and gives all themes full weight without marginalizing any of them. Such an approach may not result in the most airtight logical system (as is the case with the other two), but it does reflect the realistic dynamism of the Bible.

And so, it is within this tradition that I propose the following schema regarding primordial sin, systemic sin, individualized sin, and devilish sin.

Primordial Sin

Primordial sin is the sin of Adam and Eve in the garden of Eden (see my discussion in chapter 15). In both of the Genesis creation accounts, human beings were given specific instructions for fulfilling their role in the garden. In 1:26, God says:

> Let us make humankind in our image, according to our likeness; and let them have dominion over the fish of the sea, and over the birds of the air, and over the cattle, and over all the wild animals of the earth, and over every creeping thing that creeps upon the earth.

Again in v. 28, after receiving God's blessing, they are told, "Be fruitful and multiply, and fill the earth and subdue it; and have dominion." In the second creation account, 2:15 also speaks of a divine commission: Adam is to till and keep the garden.

However, instead of fulfilling this mission to have dominion over the created order, Adam and Eve allowed the created order—in the form of the serpent—to have dominion over them. They, thereby, volitionally rejected God's will for life in Eden by forsaking the divine mission. Making themselves unfit for life in the edenic environment, they were, therefore, deprived of it by God's gracious sentence of expulsion (vv. 23–24).

Primordial sin was volitional rejection of God and of God's purpose in the created order and of God's mission. This primordial sin set the stage for the whole of human history.

Systemic Sin

This leads us to consider the sin of the whole human family, what we shall call systemic sin. Romans 5:18–19 says that "one man's trespass led to condemnation for all," and that "by one man's disobedience the many were made sinners." Again in 3:23, "All have sinned and fall short of the glory of God."

Having made it clear that sin is a universal human dilemma, Paul, however, does not tell us in what sense all are sinners; consequently, the door is left open for much disagreement, as we have seen in our historical review of this issue. Since the how question is not answered in the Bible text, strictly exegetical explorations will not help us. Therefore, we can either ignore the question, or we can think about it theologically within a framework of thought broader than the context of Romans.

The danger in this approach is that we may become merely speculative. The guideline that helps to guard against unbridled speculation is to consider the issue from the perspective of other relevant passages of Scripture. That approach commends itself to us, especially since in Romans Paul himself refers to the story of sin in Genesis 3; therefore, we, also, do well to consider the question of how it is that primordial sin affected the whole human family by considering the question from the perspective of that same story.

As we have seen, the sin of the first pair resulted in their being driven from the garden. Human life, since that time, has existed outside of Eden. William Willimon's book title, *Sighing for Eden*, expresses the nature of the human condition spoken of here.[38] To live outside of Eden is to exist apart from the perfect environment. It is to live where the original will, purpose, and mission of God for the human family are not immediately known; it is to live where the accomplishment of the divine will, purpose, and mission is not augmented by a created order that is in perfect harmony with such work. All of us are progeny of those who live outside of

Eden. (See the discussion in chapter 15.)

Adam and Eve forfeited the blessings of being in the garden, which was the synchronized environment created by God for the fulfillment of God's will for the human family. The fact that our forbears squandered the blessings of Eden is foundational to our history as human beings.

Whereas primordial sin was the overt, volitional rejection of God and of God's will, purpose, and mission, systemic sin is humankind's corporate existence outside of the synchronized environment of Eden and apart from the immediate knowledge of God's will, purpose, and mission. Primordial sin was obstinate action; systemic sin is a negative condition. Primordial sin was active; systemic sin is passive. Primordial sin was like being an overt renegade in an ideal family; systemic sin is like being a passive member of a dysfunctional family—the former doing what is wrong under ideal circumstances, the latter participating unwittingly in a sick system.

A parable that may help has to do with a family's expulsion from Planet A to Planet B. Because they had transgressed so radically the way of life on Planet A they were taken to Planet B with no means of returning to Planet A. The progeny born in this alien environment are still creatures of Planet A, and in that sense they have an indelible relationship with it. Being the progeny of those who had rejected the ways of Planet A, they inevitably transgress the ways of Planet A, not because they have a genetic flaw but because they are the progeny of those living apart from Planet A. They do not know the ways of Planet A except through the distorted view given to them by their exiled forebears. Measured by the ways of Planet A, then, they fall short of living accordingly; their falling short is the result of being the progeny of those in exile. Systemic sin, then, as in this parable, really is our sin, in the sense that we function as volitional creatures who are the progeny of those expelled from Eden.

Systemic sin is corporate sin; it is the result of the fact that the human family is an interdependent whole. Nothing that any one individual does is strictly private. Every "private" act is social in that each person is part and parcel of the whole of humanity. Therefore, when the original pair rejected both the mission and the benefits of Eden, the whole of their progeny from that point on suffered the consequences.

Each of us was born outside of Eden, and therefore do not have immediate knowledge of the mission of God for the human family; it is only by virtue of the grace mediated through new birth in Christ that we come to know that divine purpose and mission.

Individualized Sin

This brings us to a consideration of individualized sin. As we saw in chapter 7 on "The Universal Work of the Holy Spirit," God in the person of the Spirit has immediate access to every individual (e.g., Ps. 139:7–12; Rev. 5:6).

Besides this, we have an inherent awareness of God through creation. Romans 1:19–20:

> For what can be known about God is plain to them, because God has shown it to them., Ever since the creation of the world his eternal power and divine nature, invisible though they are, have been understood and seen through the things he has made. So they are without excuse.

Furthermore, written on the conscience of each individual is the awareness of God's law, for "what the law requires is written on their hearts" (Rom. 2:15). There is, then, even in the corporate state of expulsion from Eden, sufficient awareness of God, sufficient knowledge of God's law, and the sufficient ministry of the Holy Spirit to make every person, regardless of his or her level of intelligence or proximity to the proclamation of the gospel, responsible to God. Though in a state of expulsion, every person is provided with sufficient awareness to make either a turning toward or a turning against God their own choice. When we personally reject the God made known to us in the created order, reject the law written on our hearts, and reject the Spirit who works upon us, then it is that the systemic condition of implicit alienation takes on the character of individualized rebellion.

The New Testament defines this spirit of personal antagonism toward God in *four different ways:*

1) It is *anomia*, (lawlessness, iniquity, wickedness) — 1 John 3:4; it does what it wants to do, with no thought given to God or others.

2) It is *adikia*, (unrighteousness, wrongdoing) — 1 John 5:17; it pursues its own way regardless of what it knows about God.

3) It is knowing the right thing to do but failing to do it — James 4:17.[39]

4) It is "whatever does not proceed from faith" — Romans 14:23; it is living apart from faith in God.

In all four, then, sin is pursuing one's own way instead of God's.[40]

For all persons — regardless of whether they have been confronted with the gospel — systemic sin is life outside of Eden, and individualized sin is rebellion against the revelation God gives outside of Eden. In relation to the gospel, systemic sin is lack of understanding regarding God's call to the human mission in the world, and individualized sin is rejection of God's call in Christ to the gospel mission.

Devilish Sin

The final consideration is devilish (or satanic) sin.[41] First John 3:8 says that "the devil has been sinning from the beginning." The essence of the devil's existence is total commitment to the antithesis of the will, purpose and mission of God.

Primordial sin is the active rejection of God and God's will, purpose, and mission. Systemic sin is passive alienation from the same. Individualized sin is active antagonism toward the same; but devilish sin is total commitment to that which is antithetical to God and to God's will, purpose, and mission. Human sin says *no* to God; devilish sin is total commitment to that which is other than God. Human sin is the soul divided between God and something or someone else; devilish sin is the soul united in antipathy toward God. Human sin is the sin of alienation; devilish sin is the sin of antithesis. Human sin is the act of running from God; devilish sin is the act of attacking God.

Humans can pursue their own way over against God's to such an extent that their sin becomes devilish, as in the case of Judas. Luke 22:3 says that Satan entered into him.

Devilish sin is to sin against the Holy Spirit. Jesus says that

> people will be forgiven for every sin and blasphemy, but blasphemy against the Spirit will not be forgiven. Whoever speaks a word against the Son of Man will be forgiven, but whoever speaks against the Holy Spirit will not be forgiven, either in this age or in the age to come [Matt 12:31–32].

The sin against the Holy Spirit is the condition of being so completely committed to the devil that one is in total moral confusion, calling good evil and evil good. Scripture usually speaks of devilish sin in terms of being possessed of demons (*daimōn*), (e.g., Mark 5:1–20). This kind of sin is the merging of one's will with the devil's to the point of wholeheartedly delivering one's entire volitional capabilities to him. To be possessed of a demon is to sell one's soul to the devil.

Christ came to cast down, to cast out, and to destroy devilish sin (e.g., Matt. 12:28; Mark 1:39; Luke 10:18; Rev. 20:7–10). He came to forgive us of individualized sin and to redeem us from it (e.g., Eph. 1:7; 1 John 1:9). He came to take away systemic sin (e.g., John 1:29). He came to reverse primordial sin (e.g., Rom. 5:12–21; Rev. 21:1 – 22:5).

Notes

1. In Romans 5:20, both *hamartia* and *paraptōma* are used: "But law came in, with the result that the trespass [*paraptōma*] multiplied; but where sin [*hamartia*] increased, grace abounded all the more." Also, Ephesians 2:1: "You were dead through the trespasses [*paraptōmasin*] and sins [*hamartiais*]."

2. Maurice Wiles and Mark Santer (eds.), *Documents in Early Christian Thought* (Cambridge: Cambridge University Press, 1975), pp. 96–101.

3. Ibid. p. 108f.

4. For a guide to Tertullian's treatment of sin, see Reinhold Seeberg, *Textbook of the History of Doctrines*, trans. Charles E. Hay (Grand Rapids, Baker,1966), Vol. I, p. 122f.

5. See John Ferguson, *Pelagius* (Cambridge: W. Heffer and Sons, 1956).

6. See Richard A. Muller, *Dictionary of Latin and Greek Theological Terms* (Grand Rapids: Baker, 1985), p. 203: "Also described as *impotentia ben agendi,* the inability to do good. This condition does not imply an absence of moral responsibility.... The nature, as such, remains free to act according to the limit of its abilities, apart from any external coaction or coercion, and has lost only the ability to make a choice ... of the good. In addition, since the loss of that ability is the result of the original sin of

Adam and not of any act of the divine Law-giver, the responsibility of man before the moral law and the divine promise of fellowship in return for perfect obedience remain unblemished despite human inability."

7. Philip Schaff (ed.), *A Select Library of the Nicene and Post-Nicene Fathers of the Christian Church, Vol. V: Saint Augustin: Anti-Pelagian Writings* (Grand Rapids: Eerdmans, 1956), p. 19.

8. Ibid., p. 485.

9. Ibid., p. 23.

10. Ibid., p. 123.

11. Ferguson, op. cit., p. 93.

12. Ibid. p. 175.

13. Chief proponents of Semi-Pelagianism were John Cassianus of Marseilles (d. ca. 435) and Faustus of Riez (d. ca. 495). For a summary of the literature, see Seeberg, op. cit., Vol. I, pp. 368–382.

14. St. Anselm, *Basic Writings*, trans, S. N. Deane (La Salle, Illinois: Open Court, 1962), p. 248.

15. Ibid., pp. 258–260.

16. The so-called superadded gift, *donum superadditum*, discussed by medieval theologians, was given to human nature after creation but before the fall. According to Muller, "[Thomas] Aquinas [ca. 1217–1274] maintained that the *donum superadditum* was part of the original constitution of man [that is, it

was God's original gift to us but not *innate* to our nature as humans] and that its loss was the loss of the original capacity for righteousness. Since the superadded grace was not merited in the beginning, it cannot be regained by merit after the fall. Franciscan theology, particularly as mediated to the later Middle Ages by [Duns] Scotus [ca. 1266–1308], argued that the *donum superadditum* was *not* [emphasis added] part of the original constitution or original righteousness of man, but was to be considered truly as a gift *merited* [emphasis added] by a first act of obedience on the part of Adam performed by Adam according to his *purely natural capacities* [emphasis added].... Since Adam could, by doing a minimal or finite act, merit the initial gift of God's grace, fallen man might, by doing a minimal act, also merit the gift of first grace." See Muller, *op.cit.*, p. 96f.

17. Thomas Aquinas, *Summa Theologia, Vol. XIII: Man Made to God's Image* (Question 95, Point 1, 6), (London: Eyre and Spottiswoode, 1963), p. 109.

18. Ibid.

19. Ibid. (Question 93, Point 4, 3), p. 61.

20. Ibid., p. 60.

21. John Calvin, *Institutes of the Christian Religion (Book II, chap. 1, 5), Vol. I,* trans. Henry Beveridge (London: James Clarke and Company, 1957), p. 214.

22. Ibid.

23. Ibid.

24. Ibid. (II, 1, 9), p. 218.

25. Ibid., p. 248.

26. Clyde L. Manschreck, *Melanchthon on Christian Doctrine: Loci Communes 1555* (New York: Oxford University Press, 1965), p. xiii. Supportive references for Manschreck's conclusion are in *Corpus Reformatorum*, 21:271–274, 330; 1:637.

27. Ibid., p. 75.

28. Ibid., p. 240.

29. Ibid., p. 159.

30. Ibid., p. 165.

31. Ibid., p.87.

32. Ibid.

33. Ibid., p. 145.

34. See Carl Bangs, *Arminius: A Study in the Dutch Reformation* (Nashville: Abingdon, 1971).

35. For a study of the influence of Arminianism on the English church, see Nicholas Tyacke, *Anti-Calvinists: The Rise of English Arminianism, c.1590–1640* (Oxford: Clarendon, 1990).

36. Albert C. Outler (ed.), *John Wesley* (New York: Oxford University Press, 1964), pp. 198-209.

37. Ibid. p. 139.

38. William H. Willimon, *Sighing for Eden: Sin, Evil, and the Christian Faith* (Nashville: Abingdon, 1985).

39. For a fuller discussion of James's view of sin, see

my "Salvation in the General Epistles," *An Inquiry into Soteriology from a Biblical Theological Perspective,* ed. John E. Hartley and R. Larry Shelton (Anderson, Ind: Warner, 1981), p. 200f.

40. See my discussion of *hamartia mē pros thanaton* (sin not unto death) and *hamartia pros thanaton* (sin unto death), in Hartley and Shelton, pp. 216–218.

41. Used synonymously in Revelation 20:2: "He seized the dragon, that ancient serpent, who is the Devil [*diabolos*] and Satan [*satanas*], and bound him for a thousand years."

17

Discipleship Faith

Four Ways to Look at Faith

The opposite of sin is faith. God through Christ has redeemed us from the life of sin and introduced us to the life of faith. In the New Testament, the noun *pistis* is translated either as faith or belief, and the verb *pisteuō*, either to have faith or to believe.

These words are used in at least four different ways:

1) as trust in a person, i.e., faith in;

2) as acceptance of that which is taught, i.e., faith about;

3) as confidence that something will happen, i.e., faith that; and

4) as the sacred tradition, i.e., the faith.

The first has to do primarily with a personal relationship, the second with a conviction that what is being taught is true. The third has to do with an assurance that something will take place, and the fourth with an

418

established way of thinking and living. (See For Further Consideration for a bibliography on "faith.")

1) Faith In

At the heart of the New Testament message regarding salvation is the understanding that salvation is a matter of personal trust in Christ. An example is John 3:16, which says "that everyone who believes in him may not perish but may have eternal life." John 4:39 says that "many Samaritans from that city believed in him." Believing in the name of Jesus, (e.g., 2:23), is another way of expressing trust in the person of Jesus, for in biblical thought the name represents the essence of a person. This emphasis on faith as trust in the person of Jesus is found also in Romans 4, which stresses that it is not by being religious that we are saved, but by trusting Christ. (See also such passages as Acts 10:43 and 14:23.)

2) Faith about

In addition, faith as a relationship of trust in Christ presupposes belief in his teachings, and later, in the church's confessions about him. No split exists in the New Testament between a trusting relationship with Jesus and an acceptance of his teachings as though one were possible without the other. To trust Jesus was to be a learner at his feet, his teachings being integral to his personhood. Christopher Marshall, in his study of faith in Mark, concludes that

Mark sees them [belief as mental conviction and trust as existential commitment] as inseparably bound together under the general conception of faith. For Mark, faith is rooted in belief (or, better, in insight into God's presence in Jesus) and fructifies [produces fruit] in trusting reliance upon him. One attitude calls for the other. Belief which does not lead to trust is sterile and does not experience the power conveyed by Jesus (cf. 8:27–30 and 9:18ff). Trust, which requires at least a minimum of belief to come into being, must be accompanied by a growth in understanding (4:13) or it will fail in dire circumstances (4:35–41).[1]

Being a disciple was not a matter of having a fuzzy, positive feeling about him. It meant trusting him not just simply as a preacher and teacher but as preacher and teacher of the gospel, as establisher of the kingdom, as fulfiller of the divine promises, and as founder of a new community of belief.

It was precisely his teachings that led to his crucifixion. John 18 and 19 tell of Pilate wrestling with what to do with Jesus; his struggle centered on whether Jesus was a political revolutionary, as was being charged. Jesus answered: "My kingdom is not from this world. If my kingdom were from this world, my followers would be fighting to keep me from being handed over to the Jews. But as it is, my kingdom is not from here" (18:36). Even though Pilate could find no sufficient accusation against Jesus as a person (18:38; 19:4, 6), he submitted to the will of the religious culture which found Jesus' teachings unacceptable. He condemned him to die, not because he was a bad person, but because of political considerations regarding those who opposed his teachings. Furthermore, the confession that Jesus is the Christ led to the establishment of the church (see Matt. 16:15–18). In fact, the Gospels came into existence as the early church's testimony that the Jesus in whom they trusted was a man whose teachings were to be believed. In them, Jesus and his teachings are presented as being inseparable; he is not a nondescript figure devoid of conceptual content.[2] As Alister McGrath puts it:

> It is impossible to speak about Christians copying the private relationship of Jesus to his Father (a classic belief of the "Christianity without doctrine" school) without noting that Jesus spells out, in sermon and parable, what that relationship presupposes, expresses and demands.[3]

The Gospels serve as a control factor for the who, when, what, and where of Jesus of Nazareth. They assume that one cannot have faith in the historical Jesus apart from who he was and what he taught. We see this, for instance, in John 12:48 where Jesus says: "The one who rejects me *and does not receive my word* has a judge; on the last day *the word that I have spoken* will serve as judge" (emphasis added).

In Paul, the content in which believers have faith are the confessions about Jesus. We find not only the simple confession, "Jesus is Lord" (1 Cor. 12:3), but also more expansive ones that elaborate on the person and work of Christ (see Phil. 2:6–11, Col. 1:15–20 and 1 Tim. 3:16).[4]

Christian faith is personal trust in Jesus and belief both in his teachings and in the church's confessions about him. His "thatness" (i.e., the historical figure who gains a following) is always related to his "whoness" (i.e., his identity), and his "whoness" determines the significance of his "whatness" (i.e., his teachings). Others have lived the sacrificial life even to the point of death, have performed miracles, and have told parables as good as the one about the prodigal son (Luke 15), for instance, but it is who Jesus is that raises his particular life, ministry, teachings, and death to the level of ultimacy and finality. Helmut Thielicke, in his discussion of this matter, writes:

> Since the being of his person (as the Lord who has authority and the Brother who is in solidarity) is always the element which gives meaning to his words and works, these words and works come under severe misunderstanding if they are ever detached from his person.[5]

3) Faith That

In the New Testament, faith is also spoken of as the full assurance that it is God's will for something in particular to happen. Hebrews 11:1 says: "Now faith is the assurance of things hoped for, the conviction of things not seen."

The Gospels include many references to faith as a spiritual exercise of intense confidence that Jesus will do some mighty work, as we see, for example, in the Matthew 9:28b–29 account of his healing two blind men:

> Jesus said to them, "Do you believe [*pisteuete*] that I am able to do this?" They said to him, "Yes, Lord." Then he touched their eyes and said, "According to your faith [*pistin*] let it be done to you."

The passage that emphasizes perhaps most graphically this particular view of faith is Matthew 17:20. To the disciples' question as to why they had not been able to heal the epileptic boy, Jesus answers, "Because of your little faith. For truly I tell you, if you have faith the size of a mustard seed, you will say to this mountain, 'Move from here to there,' and it will move; and nothing will be impossible to you' " (cf. Mark 9:28–29 and Luke 17:6).

We see this same concept of faith in Jesus' response to

the disciples' question about his withering of the fig tree. In Matthew 21:21-22, he says,

> If you have faith and do not doubt, not only will you do what has been done to the fig tree, but even if you say to this mountain, 'Be lifted up and thrown into the sea,' it will be done. Whatever you ask for in prayer with faith, you will receive (cf. James 1:6).

4) The Faith

The New Testament also speaks of faith as the tradition of belief and practice handed down from one generation to another. First Timothy 4:6 says: "If you put these instructions before the brothers and sisters, you will be a good servant of Christ Jesus, nourished on the words of the faith [*tēs pisteōs*] and of the sound teaching that you have followed." In fact, the whole of chapter 4 is an exhortation to teach the received tradition instead of, as v. 7 says, "profane myths and old wives' tales" (see also 6:20-21).

Jude 3 makes an appeal for the church "to contend for the faith that was once for all entrusted to the saints," and in v. 20, he enjoins them to build themselves up on their "most holy faith."

Jesus' Call to Discipleship Faith

The view of faith exhibited by Jesus' call to discipleship includes all four of the components identified above: the invitation to trust him, the instruction to learn from him, the summons to exercise confidence in his power, and the directive to be devoted to his will and way. To be his disciple meant that a person's heart was "strangely warmed" in his presence, but it also meant that one's mind was engaged with his teachings, that one's whole life was oriented around his power, and that one accepted his way of life and was willing to be engaged in his mission. The New Testament portrays faith in Jesus as being relational, conceptual, confident, and devoted.

These four components are identifiable in Mark 3:13–15, which says that Jesus

> went up the mountain and called to him whom he wanted, and they came to him. And he appointed twelve, whom he also named apostles, to be with him, and to be sent out to proclaim the message, and to have authority to cast out demons.

The disciples were in a personal relationship of trust in Jesus to the degree that they were willing to follow him up the mountain; they knew the message of the kingdom well enough to preach it; they were called, as apostles, to be his devoted emissaries; they were empowered by the same power that they saw at work in him. For the Twelve, to be in faith was to know God in Christ, to learn from Jesus, to do his will and to remain devoted to his ways and mission.

Correctives and Developments in the New Testament Itself

From the first century of the Christian era to the present, the church has been confronted with the problem of one or more of these components being emphasized at the expense of the others, necessitating, therefore, corrective work. We see this even as early as Mark, which exhibits caution about an overemphasis on faith expressed as miraculous power. His approach is to contrast Jesus the miracle worker who astounds us with Jesus the suffering savior who calls us to take up the cross and follow him. For example, in the account about the woman healed of prolonged hemorrhaging (5:24–34), Jesus says to her, "Daughter, your faith has made you well" (v. 34). This was in response to her intense confidence that "if I but touch his clothes, I will be made well" (v. 28), and to be sure, he honored her faith. However, Mark makes clear that faith is more than intensity of confidence. The faithful are to trust Jesus regardless of the circumstances of life—even to the point of death. It is significant that in the account of Peter's confession of Jesus as the Christ, 8:31 says that Jesus began to teach them that the Son of man must suffer many things, be rejected, be killed, and rise. Verse

32: "And he [Jesus] said all this quite openly. And Peter took him aside and began to rebuke him." Then, in v. 34, Jesus says to his disciples, "If any want to become my followers, let them deny themselves and take up their cross and follow me."

George Montague argues that

> for a long time the Markan church had known the presence of the spirit in praise, deliverance, healings and miracles. But now something more than these "success stories" was being asked of them. Could they prove by their death what they experienced in their life?[6]

Even though faith as intensity of confidence in God's power to do miracles is certainly part of the Gospels, Mark's message is that faith is primarily a relationship of trust in Jesus irrespective of whether miraculous release from pain and suffering takes place. Discipleship faith includes the willingness to assume pain and suffering for the sake of the cause for which Christ came. This is the kind of faith that wins the world to Christ. Montague writes:

> What wins from the Roman centurion the confession, "Truly this was the Son of God' is the *way in which Jesus died* (15:39).... Thus for Mark, men, even Jesus' disciples, do not understand the language of the miracles (cf. Mark 8:17–21). The taunting Jews are even more "put

off" by the absence of signs on the cross (15:29–32). But the centurion who makes the full Christian confession, has understood the language of Jesus' death.[7]

James and Paul provide additional evidence that forces were at work in the first century church leading to a shrinking of the full orb of faith. James addresses what he views as a serious reduction when he speaks against the idea that one can have faith as relational trust and as acceptance of certain teachings without it finding expression in one's daily life. He writes, "Show me your faith apart from your works, and I by my works will show you my faith" (2:18), and, in v. 26, "For just as the body without the spirit is dead, so faith without works is dead."[8]

Likewise, Paul, who speaks so much about faith being the gift of God, nevertheless, drives home the point that the believer's new relationship with God through Christ calls for a radically new orientation to life. He calls for the people of God to live out the implications of the grace that they have experienced through faith. No longer are they to live according to the "works of the flesh" but according to "the fruit of the Spirit" (Gal. 5:16–25). His message is this: "If we live in the Spirit, let us also walk in the Spirit" (v. 25).[9] Throughout the Pauline epistles, the indicative of the gospel gift requires the imperatives of gospel living. As

Herman Ridderbos puts it, "every imperative [in Paul] is an actualizing of the indicative."[10]

The New Testament is evidence not only that Christian faith was viewed in a variety of ways by the first-century church, but also that there was a developmental expansion, refinement, maturing, and rounding out of the understanding of what it means to live in faith.

Sacred tradition became increasingly important in the life of the church as the original community of faith passed away. During the earliest years, faith was primarily relational, conceptual, and confident in Jesus' power. In the course of time, however, as the incarnation was more of a story told than a life experienced, sacred traditions became essential. When the church felt endangered by the intrusion of ideas that were incompatible with the original message, experience, and expressions of faith, the importance of passing on, intact, the apostolic heritage increased. Consequently, even in the New Testament church, the idea of faith as the sacred tradition emerged.

As the church expanded numerically and continued in time, there was a greater need to standardize the sacred heritage. The development of the four Gospels represents the dynamic process whereby some degree of regularization took place. Matthew explicitly states that his intention is to set the record straight: "Now the birth of Jesus the Messiah took place in this way" (1:18). Mark is committed to telling the story of Jesus' public ministry in a straightforward manner. Luke begins his two-volume work (Luke-Acts) to Theophilus with the explicit purpose "that you may know the truth concerning the things about which you have been instructed" (1:4), and John 21:24 calls for acceptance of the sacred tradition as it has been set forth in that Gospel: "This is the disciple who is testifying to these things and has written them, and we know that his testimony is true."

Paul has the same concern for the sacred tradition. We see it expressed in such passages as 1 Corinthians 15:3, "For I handed on to you as of first importance what I in turn had received," and 2 Thessalonians 2:15, "So then, brothers and sisters, stand firm and hold fast to the traditions that you were taught by us, either by word of mouth or by our letter." (See also Gal. 1:6–9.)

Faith as the sacred tradition is stated most explicitly, however, in the Pastoral Epistles. In 1 Timothy 1:10–11, reference is made to what is "contrary to the sound teaching that conforms to the glorious gospel of the blessed God, which he entrusted to me." Reference already has been made to 4:6 which speaks about the received tradition as "the faith," and 6:3, which speaks about "the sound words of our Lord Jesus Christ." (See also 1 Tim. 1:3 and 15, 3:16, 5:8, and 6:20.)

The other two Pastorals have the same emphasis: 2 Timothy 1:13–14 says:

> Hold to the standard of sound teaching which you have heard from me, in the faith and love that are in Christ Jesus. Guard the good treasure entrusted to you, with the help of the Holy Spirit living in us. [See also 2 Tim. 2:17–18, 23–25; 3:14–17; 4:3–4.]

Titus 1:4 refers to Titus as "my loyal child in the faith we share," and v. 13 stresses the necessity of rebuking those who teach falsehood "so that they may become sound in the faith [*en tē pistei*]." In 1:9, Titus is instructed to appoint elders who "have a firm grasp of the word that is trustworthy in accordance with the teaching," so that they "may be able both to preach with sound doctrine and to refute those who contradict it." (See also Titus 2:2.)

The way by which the sacred tradition was preserved for the church of later generations was through the collection, preservation, transmission, and use of the materials that finally came to be known as the New Testament. In the course of time this emerging body of literature was accepted as the vehicle whereby the faith of the original community of faith was transmitted to later generations. It was the written canon by which the sacred tradition was preserved and passed on; it served as the measuring rod for testing later claims, teachings, and developments in the life of the church.

George Lindbeck in *The Nature of Doctrine* argues for the necessity of having a written tradition if a religion is to survive. He writes:

> In oral cultures there is no transpersonal authority to which the experts on tradition can refer their disputes. This helps explain why purely customary religions and cultures readily dissolve under the pressure of historical, social, and linguistic change, but it also suggests that canonical texts are a condition, not only for the survival of a religion but for the very possibility of normative theological description.[11]

If faith — originally relational, conceptual, confident, and devoted — is to be passed on to future generations, in faithful continuity with the past, the development of a sacred tradition is inevitable. The sacred tradition provides the line of continuity between the originating community of faith and the ongoing community. The danger, of course, always exists that the tradition will replace faith as personal and relational trust, but for this to happen is to misunderstand the genesis of tradition. The driving force is not that it will become a substitute for the living God, but that it will serve both as a sure reference point for later generations and as the means by which they, too, may experience personal faith with the same freshness and purity as did the original community of faith.

The Need for a Full Orb of Faith

Throughout the history of the church, the same challenge that faced the New Testament church has persisted, namely, the ascendancy first, of one emphasis regarding the nature of faith, and then another (see For Further Consideration, Part II). We should be alert to the following tendencies:

• Faith primarily as personal trust, with only secondary attention given to other emphases, often leads to subjective experientialism. Pietism and revivalism have to guard against this truncated view.

• Faith primarily as the making of right confessions, with only secondary attention given to other emphases, often leads to argumentative intellectualism. Lutheran orthodoxy and fundamentalism have to guard against allowing this to happen.

• Faith primarily as the intensity of confidence that the Lord is going to do something miraculous, with only secondary attention given to other emphases, often leads to prideful spiritualism. Pentecostalism and the charismatic movement have to guard against this.

• Faith primarily as the sacred tradition, with only secondary attention given to other emphases, often leads to constrictive institutionalism. Eastern orthodoxy and Roman catholicism have to guard against this.

Even though historical examples of tendencies toward truncation have been given above, such tendencies are by no means so strictly limited. Incomplete views of Christian faith may emerge in any church tradition. It needs also to be said that just because a tradition has a likelihood for a particular truncation does not mean that it actually yields to that propensity. Any Christian tradition, regardless of its historical propensities, can rise to the New Testament challenge of living in the full orb of faith.

On the basis of the foregoing, I conclude that from this point in history, Christian faith is basically a relationship of trust in Jesus Christ as Savior and Lord, as proclaimed by the biblical tradition. It is the heartfelt desire to sit at the feet of the Christ revealed in the scriptures, and to do so in company with the historic community of faith. Furthermore, it is the willingness both to witness for Christ by the way we think, live, suffer, and die, and to open ourselves to his power for the accomplishment of divine purposes.[12] Put another way, to be in faith is to trust in Jesus Christ as Savior and Lord, to think in harmony with the revelation of

God recorded in the Christian scriptures (Old and New Testaments), to live in covenant with the whole people of God, and to pray in the confidence that he is able "to accomplish abundantly far more than all we can ask or imagine" (Eph. 3:20).

Or, again, to be in faith is to be related to Christ Jesus in salvation, to be informed by the Christian scriptures in understanding, to be committed to Christian service in life and work, and to be empowered by the Spirit in worship and witness.

To be in faith is to know Jesus, to think Christianly, to live in confident hope in the power of God, and to accept the biblical tradition as authoritative for faith and practice.

Notes

1. Christopher D. Marshall, *Faith as a Theme in Mark's Narrative* (Cambridge: University Press, 1989), p. 56.

2. See Gerhard Ebeling, *The Nature of Faith*, trans. Ronald Gregor Smith (London: Collins, 1961), pp. 49–57 for a discussion of the Gospels as the vehicles whereby the teachings of Jesus are passed on to the community of faith in Jesus. In this connection he writes:

> These elements in the message of Jesus: the nearness of the rule of God, the clarity of his will, and the simplicity

of discipleship, with joy, freedom, and lack of anxiety —
are the interpretation of one thing, the call to faith. But
it is all seen in the context of the remarkable authority
of the Person of Jesus. If discipleship means sharing in
the way of Jesus, then understanding his preaching of
the will of God means sharing in his freedom, and
understanding his message of the rule of God means
sharing in his joy, his obedience, and his courage in face
of the nearness of God.... What Jesus says cannot be separated from his Person, and his Person is one with his
way."

p. 56

3. Alister McGrath, *Understanding Doctrine: Its
Relevance and Purpose for Today* (Grand Rapids:
Zondervan, 1990), p. 100.

4. For a concise treatment of the confessions in the
New Testament, see Ralph Martin, *Worship in the Early
Church* (Grand Rapids: Eerdmans, 1974), chaps. 4 and 5.

5. Helmut Thielicke, *The Evangelical Faith,* Vol. II: *The
Doctrine of God and of Christ,* trans. and ed. Geoffrey W.
Bromiley (Grand Rapids: Eerdmans, 1977), p. 300. For a
fuller discussion of this issue, see his chap. 20.

6. George Montague, *The Holy Spirit: Growth of a
Biblical Tradition* (New York: Paulist, 1976), p. 252.

7. Ibid., p. 251f.

8. See my *Living as Redeemed People: Studies in James
and Jude* (Anderson, Ind: Warner, 1976), chap. 5. "In this
passage [2:14–26], James is correcting those who have

the right ideas about God but who do not go beyond that. Their ideas are not translated into action" p. 29. Also, my "Salvation in the General Epistles," *An Inquiry into Soteriology,* ed. John E. Hartley and R. Larry Shelton (Anderson, Ind: Warner 1981), pp. 195-224. "The fetus of faith is brought to birth in the womb of obedience," p. 197.

9. King James Version, which is closer to the Greek text.

10. Herman Ridderbos, *Paul: An Outline of His Theology,* trans. John Richard De Witt (Grand Rapids, Eerdmans, 1975), p. 257. See his full discussion, pp. 253-258.

11. George Lindbeck, *The Nature of Doctrine: Religion and Theology in a Postliberal Age* (Philadelphia: Westminster, 1984), p. 116.

12. For another full orb of faith approach, see Donald G. Bloesch, *Essentials of Evangelical Theology, Volume One: God, Authority, and Salvation* (San Francisco: Harper and Row, 1978), pp. 223-252.

For Further Consideration

Part I. Introductory Reading on Faith

For biblical studies of faith, see Gerd Theissen, *Biblical Faith: An Evolutionary Approach* (Philadelphia: Fortress, 1985); Frank R. VanDevelder, *The Biblical Journey of Faith* (Philadelphia: Fortress, 1988).

For post-biblical historical treatments, see Paul Giurlanda, *Faith and Knowledge: A Critical Inquiry* (Lanham: University Press of America, 1987).

For a Jewish theology of faith, see Louis Jacobs, *Faith* (New York: Basic, 1968).

For a Christian theology of faith, see Gerhard Ebeling, *The Nature of Faith,* trans. Ronald Gregor Smith (London: Collins, 1961).

For philosophical treatments, see John Hick, *Faith and Knowledge* (2d ed.; Ithaca: Cornell University Press, 1966); Richard Swinburne, *Faith and Reason* (Oxford: Clarendon, 1981). Also see H. Richard Niebuhr, *Faith on Earth: An Inquiry into the Structure of Human Faith,* ed. Richard R. Niebuhr (New Haven: Yale University Press, 1989).

For pastoral studies, see Jeff Astley and Leslie Francis (eds.), *Christian Perspectives on Faith Development* (Grand Rapids: Eerdmans, 1992).

Part II. Historical Views of Faith

Paul Giurlanda, *Faith and Knowledge: A Critical Inquiry* (Lanham: University Press of America, 1987), pp. 180–255. Giurlanda discusses the views of the following: *Augustine* who held that faith was a rational decision and a gift from God; he "found himself justifying the rationality of faith to the pagan world and, more importantly, arguing with Pelagius over its gratuity" (p. 180); *Anselm* for whom, as Giurlanda puts it, "faith, by its nature, moves us out toward the delight of knowledge" (p. 192); *Thomas Aquinas* about whom he concludes that *"faith is an action of both intellect and will which is explainable by neither faculty working alone nor by both of them working together, but by God's grace,* that unexplainable free gift" (p. 203, author's emphasis); *Martin Luther* about whom he says that "talk of the will seems [to Luther] to deny ... the joyous fact that we are not saddled with the burden of saving ourselves. The act of faith is precisely giving up that burden of will, and not even by an act of permissive will, which we allow God to take over, for will is will, and as soon as there is will there is self justification" (p. 220); *Immanuel Kant* and his view of a utilitarian faith which is not dependent on revelation. Giurlanda, in reference to Kant's "abyss of a mystery," says that "to such an incomprehensible mystery an attitude of reverence is appropriate, and the word faith is also appropriate, as expressing the reality that 'it may well be expedient for us merely to know and understand that there *is* such a mystery, [but] not to comprehend it' " (p. 226, emphasis added); *Friedrich Schleiermacher* for whom faith is the experience of total dependence on God. Giurlanda writes:

> What is new about Schleiermacher's understanding is that he has dispensed with objective language about God as the essence of faith. Faith is not the belief *that* certain promises of God will be kept in the future, nor is faith the belief *in* the trustworthiness of God grounding those promises. Faith is not about promises at all, not about propositions at all, and is therefore not an act of the intellect properly understood. It is the beginning of the new life, the moment when the new life of Christ— the God-consciousness which is his and which only his church can communicate—begins to be appropriated.

Continuing, he says that "though faith is not intellectual, it is nevertheless certain, for there is nothing more certain than one's own experience" (p. 232f.).

Speaking about the "major fault line" that divides Protestants and Roman Catholics, Giurlanda says that "if faith is an act with an intellectual and communal component and a volitional and individual one, then the Catholic tradition has tended to emphasize the former, the Protestant tradition the latter, aspects of faith" (p. 245).

He concludes that although the Christian tradition does not speak with one voice about faith, "one thing which is very much common to all uses of the word is that *faith is a gift of God.* There seems to be no one who wants to deny this who is in the main stream of the tradition, either Protestant or Catholic. All agree, as well, that faith has something to do with the *will,* by which the gift of God is somehow appropriated" (p. 243).

18

The Gift of a New Identity

Salvation: A Biblical Overview

The Greek word *sōtēria* means deliverance, preservation, salvation, safety. It is the word used in the
Septuagint, the Greek translation of the Hebrew Bible,
for *yashá*, the basic meaning of which is spaciousness.
According to John Hartley in his study of salvation in
the Old Testament, *yashá* "also correlates with words
that mean 'broad' or 'expansive.'" He refers to Psalm
18:19 as an example, "He brought me forth into a broad
place; he delivered me, because he delighted in me,"
and then continues by saying:

> Further support for the identification of spaciousness
> with salvation comes from use of the image of a broad
> open place, where expansion may take place, to depict
> an era of salvation. For instance, Isaiah images Israel's
> great prosperity after the nation's confinement in cap-

442

tivity in terms of spaciousness: 'Enlarge the place of your tent, and let the curtains of your habitations be stretched out; hold not back, lengthen your cords and strengthen your stakes. For you will spread abroad to the right and to the left' (Isa. 54:2-3). This root meaning is evident, too, in that ...[it] stands in contrast to words for 'narrowness and confinement,' as *sārar* 'be narrow, cramped' (Judg. 2:15-16).[1]

Salvation in the Old Testament is God's decisive action (e.g., the Exodus) and ongoing work of bringing God's people to a spacious place of peace, freedom, service, and wholeness. It is God's work of delivering them from bondage, protecting them from enemies, and establishing them in peace, prosperity, plenty, and righteousness.

In the Synoptics, salvation has to do with the appearing, growth, and consummation of the kingdom of God. In John, it has to do with the gift of eternal life. Even though the Synoptics and John speak of salvation in different modes, in both, one finds the same basic theme, namely, that in Christ, perfect righteousness is revealed and established on the earth (e.g., Matt. 3:15; John 16:8-11).

From that basic theme flow other parallel messages from the Synoptics and John:

Parallel Messages

Topics	Synoptics	John
• God delivers us from bondage	Mark 1:21–28	John 2:13–17
• God protects us from that which has the power to destroy	Mark 4:35–41	John 10:11–15
• God establishes us in Christ who gives divine peace	Luke 2:14	John 14:27
• God gives spiritual prosperity	Matthew 5:1–11	John 4:13–14
• God provides for our bodies	Mark 6:30–44	John 2:1–11

In the Pauline epistles, salvation is understood as the justification, sanctification, and glorification of human life by God's grace working through faith. Justification is a legal term which refers to our acquittal before God; sanctification is a religious term which refers to our being made holy for God's use; and glorification is a devotional term which refers to our becoming like God. (See For Further Consideration, Part I.)

Throughout the Bible, salvation has a very strong corporate or communal character. In the Old Testament, it is a national people, the emphasis being on the salvation of all who are physical descendants of Abraham. In the Synoptic Gospels, it is a kingdom people, the emphasis being on all who yield to Christ's reign. In John, it is a newly born people, the emphasis being on all who believe in Jesus. In Paul, it is a people incorporated into Christ, the emphasis being on grace working through faith. It is equally clear that none of this takes place apart from personal faith. When we speak of the corporate, as we have above, it obviously consists of persons responding to God. In the Old Testament, it is in terms of obedient trust in the God of Israel. In the Synoptics, it is a matter of being a disciple of Jesus. In John, it is belief in Jesus. In Paul, it is God-enabled faith.[2]

Paul's emphasis on righteousness and justification is rightly understood in connection with the divine will expressed as law. Righteousness has to do with obedience to the divine standard whereas justification has to do with acquittal in relation to it.

The human dilemma is that we are guilty of disobedience. Romans 3:23 says that "all have sinned and fall short of the glory of God." As was pointed out in chapter 16 on "Sin," all of us have been born into the spiritually dysfunctional family of Adam and Eve. Part of this dysfunctionality is that there is no possibility that any of us can rectify the situation. Sin has brought about such extensive confusion in the spiritual life of the human family that this confusion bleeds over into all other dimensions of life as well. We are ignorant and confused about God's will for and mission in the world. We are in a muddle regarding our role in the divine economy. Paul speaks of the radical nature of this confusion when in Romans 7:14–15, he says: "For we know that the law is spiritual; but I am of the flesh, sold into slavery under sin. I do not understand my own actions. For I do not do what I want, but I do the very thing I hate." Verse 24 is the resultant cry of anguish: "Wretched man that I am! Who will rescue me from this body of death?"

Whereas Romans 7 sets forth the human plight, Romans 8 declares the good news that what we could not do for ourselves has been done for us by Jesus Christ. Consequently, "There is therefore now no condemnation for those who are in Christ Jesus" (8:1). The essence of salvation is that we, though members of a sinful, dysfunctional human race, have been acquitted by God's grace.

We have not been acquitted because God winked at our plight, nor because we were tried and found innocent. We have been acquitted because, on the basis of grace working through faith, we are identified with Jesus Christ, the perfectly righteous one. In the midst of the dysfunctional human race, the new man — the God-man — Jesus Christ came once and for all to live as a human being in a way that was perfectly pleasing to God, to assume the consequences of our sin upon himself and to break its destructive cycle. All who are in Christ by faith are justified by virtue of being spiritually identified with the perfectly righteous one. In him we are justified because our identity is no longer an Adam-identity but a Christ-identity. By faith we belong to Christ, the eternally elected one, who is altogether righteous. By virtue of being his, we are divinely elected people who stand justified before God. In vv. 33–34, Paul writes,

> Who will bring any charge against God's elect? It is God who justifies. Who is to condemn? It is Christ Jesus, who died, yes, who was raised, who is at the right hand of God, who indeed intercedes for us.

In Christ, we have a new identity. No longer are we members of the condemned race of Adam, but of the righteous race of Christ. In Romans 5 where Adam and Christ are contrasted, Paul says in v. 19, "For just as by the one man's disobedience the many were made sinners, so by the one man's obedience the many will be made righteous."

The fundamental character of our salvation in Christ is that we are given the new identity of being Christ-people. No longer are we to think of ourselves primarily as members of Adam's fallen race, but as members of Christ's body.

Grace is the source of our new identity; faith is the means of receiving it; repentance is the attitude for experiencing it; water baptism is the Lord's designated way for it to be declared.[3] To these considerations we now turn.

Grace: The Source of Our New Identity

Our new identity is a gift from God, and is in no sense earned. It is grounded in God's foreknowledge that some would respond in faith to Christ (i.e., "those whom he foreknew," Rom. 8:29). It is based on God's decision prior to creation that, as human beings, our true destiny is to live in conformity to Christ (i.e., "he ...predestined to be conformed to the image of his Son, in order that he might be the firstborn within a large family," v. 29). It is offered to us by the call of God, the implied corollary of which is our response of faith (i.e., "those whom he predestined he also called," v. 30); it gives us a new standing before God when indeed we do respond in faith to the call of God (i.e., "and those whom he called he also justified," v. 30). It reaches its culmination at the end of the age when we shall be like him (i.e., "those whom he justified he also glorified," v. 30).

Regarding the grace which bestows this new identity, Ephesians 2:4–10 says:

But God, who is rich in mercy, out of the great love with which he loved us even when we were dead through our trespasses, made us alive together with Christ—by grace you have been saved—and raised us up with him and seated us with him in the heavenly places in Christ Jesus, so that in the ages to come he might show the immeasurable riches of his grace in kindness toward us in Christ Jesus. For by grace you have been saved through faith, and this is not your own doing; it is the gift of God, not the result of works, so that no one may boast. For we are what he has made us, created in Christ Jesus for good works, which God prepared beforehand to be our way of life.

Faith: The Means of Receiving the New Identity

It is by faith that we receive this gift of a new identity (see chapter 17 on *Discipleship Faith*). Furthermore, faith itself is of grace in that it depends fully on God's work: it is possible only because the capacity to have faith was created by God and the response of faith is inspired by God. The acceptable way for living out one's faith is superintended by God, and the biblical story and content of faith are preserved by God. While faith is genuinely our own volitional response, it is, nevertheless, of God, from beginning to end. It is God who created us in such a way that we can make volitional decisions, God who calls us to faith, and God the Holy Spirit who convicts us of sin, points us to Jesus and inspires us to faith (see chapter 7 on "The Universal Work of the Holy Spirit"). Faith, Paul says, "is not your own doing; it is the gift of God—not the result of works, so that no one may boast." All that we can claim as originating with us is the No of unbelief; the Yes of faith originates with God.

Repentance: The Attitude for Experiencing the New Identity

According to 2 Peter 3:9, God is patient "not wanting any to perish, but all to come to repentance" (cf., Rev. 9:20-21; 16:9,11). In order to experience God's gift of a new identity, we must repent of our sins. The Greek word is *metanoia*, meaning a change of mind or purpose. In the New Testament, it refers to a change of mind and heart about God; we turn away from the old way of life which dishonors God and embrace the new which brings honor to God.[4]

The core of Jesus' proclamation was: "Repent, for the kingdom of heaven has come near" (Matt. 4:17; cf., Mark 1:15)[5], and his disciples, likewise, "proclaimed that all should repent" (Mark 6:12). Jesus taught that there is "more joy in heaven over one sinner who repents than over ninety-nine righteous persons who need no repentance" (Luke 15:7; cf., v. 10). Furthermore, in Luke 17:3-4, he teaches the necessity of repentance and forgiveness as the ongoing standard of life among the disciples (cf., 2 Tim. 2:5; Rev. 2:5, 16, 21–22; 3:3, 19). And before his ascension, he commissioned the disciples "that repentance and forgiveness of sins is to be proclaimed ... to all nations" (Luke 24:47).

After Pentecost, Peter instructed those desiring to be saved, saying, "Repent, and be baptized every one of you in the name of Jesus Christ so that your sins may be forgiven" (Acts 3:38). Acts records multiple references to both Peter and Paul preaching that repentance is necessary for salvation (see Acts 3:19; 5:31; 8:22; 11:18; 17:30; 20:21; 26:20. Cf., Heb. 6:1, 4).

In both Romans and 2 Corinthians, Paul writes about the importance of repentance. In Romans 2:4, he speaks of God's kindness which "is meant to lead you to repentance," and in 2 Corinthians 7:9–10 of a grief that leads to repentance: "for godly grief produces a repentance that leads to salvation" (12:21 speaks of the urgency of repentance within the church).

Water Baptism and the New Identity

Water baptism is the Lord's designated way for the new identity to be declared (see For Further Consideration, Part II, on immersion as the New Testament mode). The commission of our Lord to the disciples was: "Go therefore and make disciples of all nations, baptizing them in the name of the Father and of the Son and of the Holy Spirit, and teaching them to obey everything that I have commanded you" (Matt. 28:19-20). As we have already noted above, Peter instructs respondents to the gospel to repent and be baptized (Acts 2:38). Throughout Acts, believers are baptized: in 8:12, the Samaritans are baptized; in 8:38, the Ethiopian eunuch is baptized; in 9:18, Paul is baptized by Ananias; in 10:47, Peter instructs new believers to be baptized; in 16:15, Lydia is baptized; in 16:33, the Philippian jailer is baptized along with his whole family, and 18:8 says that "many of the Corinthians who heard Paul became believers and were baptized."

References in Acts to baptism in the name of Jesus Christ (2:38; 10:48), or in the name of the Lord Jesus (8:16; 19:5), call attention to the fact that these persons had become Jesus-people as over against those who still had not come to faith in him. In Acts, no dominical (having to do with instructions from our Lord) formula for baptism (as in Matt. 28:19) is found. Instead, Acts simply contains a description of the *identifying mark* of Christian baptism, namely, belief in Jesus as the Messiah, whereas Matt. 28:19 gives the *dominical formula* for it. [6]

Paul's major theological passage on baptism is in Romans 6:3-4. Even though he does not speak here explicitly of water baptism, such imagery is in the forefront of his thought:

Do you not know that all of us who have been baptized into Christ Jesus were baptized into his death? Therefore we have been buried with him by baptism into death, so that, just as Christ was raised from the dead by the glory of the Father, so we too might walk in newness of life.

In this passage Paul speaks of our spiritual identification with the death and resurrection of Jesus Christ. It is that identification which serves as the basis for his appeal in vv. 5–23 for them to live in a qualitatively different way so as to give testimony to their relationship to Christ. In v. 11 he says, "So you also must consider yourselves dead to sin and alive to God in Christ Jesus."

We know both from Acts and Paul's letters that water baptism was a part of his own personal experience (Acts 9:18) and ministry (Acts 16:15, 33; 18:8; 19:5; 22:16). Even in two problematic passages in Paul, we, nevertheless, have additional evidence of the significance of water baptism in the life of the church. The first, in 1 Corinthians 1:10–17, deals with the pride of allegiance to different baptismal parties. Paul appears to be overly zealous about distancing himself from such parties, so much so that it is only with reluctance that he even allows himself to remember those whom he has baptized in Corinth. In his strong reaction to baptismal partyism, he stresses the all-important priority of the proclamation of the gospel. It is the gospel that is at the center of the Christian mission, and not allegiance to baptismal parties. Regarding this passage, G. R. Beasley-Murray in his study of baptism concludes that Paul's subordination of the administration of baptism to the proclamation of the gospel is consistent with baptism itself. "For the latter follows the proclamation of Christ and draws its meaning from the gospel." He goes on to say that "Paul's insistence that he was sent to preach, rather than to baptize, reflected his consciousness of the essential priority of his work if there were to be any baptisms at all!"[7]

And the second problematic passage, 1 Corinthians 15:29 which is part of his discussion about the resurrection of the dead, refers to "baptism on behalf of the dead" — the meaning of which, though obscure to us, does, at least, point to the importance of baptism. Five interpretations include the following: (a) that it was a way to refer to a regular baptism with its emphasis on the Christian hope that they would be raised from the dead; (b) that it was a spiritual baptism of suffering or death as in Luke 12:50; (c) that it had to do with a Corinthian practice of baptism taking place over the graves of dead believers whereby they gave witness to their spiritual fellowship with the dead in Christ; (d) that it referred to our being baptized on behalf of ourselves as being dead in sin; and (e) that some new converts had died prior to water baptism, and therefore, others in the Christian fellowship submitted to proxy baptism on their behalf in order to give witness to the faith in which some had died prior to baptism.

On the basis of what Paul says in 1 Corinthians 1:13–17 to distance himself from water baptisms, and on the basis of such passages as Romans 10:9 ("If you confess with your lips that Jesus is Lord and believe in your heart that God raised him from the dead, you will be saved"), it is clear that his priority is on personal faith in Jesus Christ and not on the liturgical act of baptism. This, however, should not lead to the theological denigration of the dominical (i.e., the words of our Lord in Matthew 28:19) and ecclesial (i.e., practices of the young church recorded in Acts) traditions of water baptism. Rather, what Paul says should be understood as a pastoral caution against allowing the liturgical act in and of itself to replace the spiritual substance of the relationship of which water baptism speaks.

Who, What, and How of Baptism

Water baptism is the Bible's approved way of announcing our allegiance to the Lord. It declares who we are in the sight of God (We are Christ-people), what we confess to the world (We believe that Jesus was crucified for our sins and raised from the dead to give us life), and how we understand our daily vocation (We are to be dead to sin and alive to God; as the baptized, we are to "walk in newness of life").

Water baptism is part of God's plan for salvation. To reject it is to reject God's plan. The assent of believers to this God-ordained way provides evidence of trust in Jesus Christ. It is in that sense that 1 Peter 3:21 speaks of baptism saving us "not as a removal of dirt from the body, but as an appeal to God for a good conscience." Water baptism is the basic external testimony of the internal testimony of the Spirit (Rom. 8:16) that we are children of God. For one to refuse to follow the Lord in baptism must be viewed as a spiritual crisis of major proportions.

The question which inevitably arises is that of the status of believers who die prior to water baptism. Are they lost? It is important to keep in mind the difference between God's regular plan of salvation which we are obligated to teach and practice, on the one hand, and God's gracious prerogative, on the other.

It is critical that we resist the temptation to write theology on the basis of exceptional cases. It is our responsibility to theologize on the basis of the revealed will of God, leaving all special cases in God's hands, realizing that God is bound neither to our theology nor to the regular plan of salvation as we know it.[8]

We take note of the fact that in Acts 10:44, the Holy Spirit fell on those who heard the gospel while Peter was still preaching. The sign of divine blessing was bestowed prior to water baptism. Subsequently, however, they were baptized (vv. 47–48). It was not baptism that brought the blessing of the Holy Spirit, but hearing and believing the gospel. Would they have been lost had they died between the time of believing and their baptism? If we take seriously, as we do, that it is the Spirit's role to confirm that we are children of God, the answer would be No. We conclude, then, that the Spirit's falling upon them was God's way of confirming that they were the children of God even prior to baptism.

The fact is that they did not die prior to baptism. They were, therefore, under divine obligation as the children of God to follow the Lord in water baptism. Verses 47–48:

Then Peter said, "Can anyone withhold the water for baptizing these people who have received the Holy

Spirit just as we have?" So he ordered them to be baptized in the name of Jesus Christ.

What if they had refused water baptism? That would have been a major crisis in their spiritual lives. In this passage, baptism is treated not as optional, but as the normal course of action for those coming to faith in Jesus Christ. Water baptism is the announcement of the new identity we have by virtue of God's grace.[9]

Foundational Sanctification

Salvation, first of all, then, is the experience of having a new identity given to us by God. No longer are we to be known as Adam-people (i.e., sinners, aliens to God) but as Christ-people (believers, children of God).

Romans 9:25–26:

As indeed he [God] says in Hosea, "Those who were not my people I will call 'my people,' and her who was not beloved I will call 'beloved'" And in the very place where it was said to them, 'You are not my people,' there they shall be called children of the living God."[10]

This new identity is the result of God's initial, foundational sanctification. The word, sanctification, *hagiasmos,* signifies the process of being made holy.[11] In the New Testament, there are several dimensions of sanctification, the first having to do with the subject of this chapter—God's gift of a new identity which provides a new basis on which God appeals to us.

This is the dimension of sanctification found in 1 Corinthians 1:2 where Paul addresses Christians as "those who are sanctified in Christ Jesus, called to be saints [*hagioi*]." The sanctification of which he speaks has to do with the fact that the Corinthians had been chosen in Christ to be God's special people in the world. It does not refer to a special class of spirituality within the church, for it is the whole church—including those with serious relational, moral, and ethical problems—which is being addressed in this passage. All, regardless of their degree of maturity or immaturity, are referred to as the "sanctified in Christ Jesus." It is on the basis of this new status, then, that Paul addresses their shortcomings. Even though their problems are much like those of the population in general, he speaks not to Corinthians in general but to the community of Christian faith at Corinth. Why them in particular? Because they have been "sanctified in Christ Jesus." On the basis of the indicative of who they are by the grace of God, he proceeds to address them with the imperatives of the gospel.

We see this same basic dimension of sanctification in 6:11, "But you were washed, you were sanctified, you were justified in the name of the Lord Jesus Christ and in the Spirit of our God." Here Paul uses three ways of referring to the same salvation reality—washing (from the natural realm), sanctification (from the religious realm), and justification (from the legal realm). He addressed them as persons having taken a bath, as persons set apart for divine service, as persons of right standing. These are not three different steps of salvation, but three ways of viewing their new identity. At conversion, not only were they washed in Christ's righteousness and justified before God, but also they were sanctified for the divine mission in the world. They became members of the church of God. They were the *hagioi*, i.e., the holy ones, or saints. In fact, Paul understands his mission to the Gentiles to be that "they may receive forgiveness of sins and a place among those who are sanctified by faith in me [Christ]" (Acts 26:18).

Christians are no longer aliens to God, but friends; no longer sinners in need of salvation, but believers in need of perfection; no longer outsiders to the divine mission in the world, but participants in it; no longer strangers and enemies to the household of faith, but members of it. Their unique status in the divine economy is that they are "the sanctified in Christ Jesus" (see also Acts 20:32 and Heb. 10:10, 14).

Notes

1. John E. Hartley, "The Message of Salvation in the Old Testament," *An Inquiry into Soteriology from a Biblical Theological Perspective*, eds. Hartley and R. Larry Shelton, Vol. I: *Wesleyan Theological Perspectives* (Anderson, Ind: Warner, 1981), p. 3.

2. For other treatments of salvation in the New Testament, see in *Inquiry into Soteriology*, Wayne McCown, "Such a Great Salvation," pp. 169–194, e.g., "The most profound and unique contribution of Hebrews to Christian soteriology [is] the declaration of Jesus as our (high) priest," p. 173; my "Salvation in the General Epistles," pp. 195–224, e.g., "There is no saving faith that is not obedient faith," p. 222; and Fred D. Layman, "Salvation in the Book of Revelation," pp. 225–263, e.g., "Eschatological salvation is experienced by Christians in the present as liberation from sin and alien spiritual powers and as conquest in spiritual conflict." Believers, therefore, "have become participants in the 'already' of eschatological salvation," p. 233.

Also, see Ronald A. Ward, *The Pattern of Our Salvation* (Waco: Word, 1978) in which Ward uses a grid for his discussion of salvation in all books of the New Testament other than the Gospels. The grid consists of the following: the nature of God; our being against God, i.e., sin; God being against us, i.e., judgment; the other side, i.e., God's salvation; God at work for us, i.e., objective salvation; and God at work in us, i.e., subjective salvation.

3. For an historical and theological treatment of the different dimensions of conversion, see Bernhard Citron, *New Birth: A Study of the Evangelical Doctrine of Conversion in the Protestant Fathers* (Edinburgh: University Press, 1951). In chapter VI on "The Elements of Conversion" he deals with faith, repentance, and the new will. In the next chapter, he considers baptism as a promise and a pledge. Also, Walter E. Conn (ed.), *Conversion: Perspectives on Personal and Social Transformation* (New York: Alba, 1978).

4. Citron points out that in scripture repentance appears in three distinct forms: return to God, turning away from evil deeds and mortification. Op. cit., pp. 94-98.

5. Also, see Matt. 4:17; 11:20-21; 12:41; Luke 5:32; 10:13: 11:32; 13:3-5. (Cf. the ministry of John the Baptist, 3:2–11; Mark 1:4; Luke 3:3, 8; Acts 13:24; 19:4.)

6. For an exegetical study of references in Acts to baptism in the name of Jesus and of the trinitarian passage in Matt. 28:19, see G. R. Beasley-Murray, *Baptism in the New Testament* (Grand Rapids: Eerdmans, 1973), pp. 77–92, 100–104.

For a discussion of this issue from the standpoint of

Christian worship, see Keith Watkins, (ed.), *Baptism and Belonging* (St.Louis: Chalice, 1991), pp.140–142. "In the earliest period, converts came from Judaism. They already believed in God. What was distinctive about their new religious condition was their belief in Jesus as the Messiah. Thus they were directed to be baptized 'in the name of Jesus Christ so that your sins may be forgiven' (Acts 2:38). Soon thereafter, converts from non-Jewish sources came to be baptized and the name used at baptism was enlarged. The baptismal name stated in Matt. 28:19 is based on this later development: 'in the name of the Father and of the Son and of the Holy Spirit," p. 140.

7. Beasley-Murray, op. cit., p. 180.

8. Robert O. Fife in an unpublished paper entitled "Why Must I Be Baptized?" delivered at the North American Christian Convention, July 11, 1984, Atlanta, Georgia, puts it this way: "God is not bound to the sacraments, though man is," and concludes that "we must take care not to presume upon the grace of God by thinking that because 'God is not bound to the sacraments,' neither are we. Likewise a congregation dare not neglect its responsibility to teach and observe the terms of pardon given on Pentecost, simply because God in His freedom may extend His grace as He wills," p. 3.

9. For a balanced historical and theological study of

Eastern, Western and Baptist patterns regarding baptism, see Geoffrey Wainwright, *Christian Initiation* (Richmond: John Knox, 1969). On the issue of children and baptism, see Marlin Jeschke, *Believers Baptism for Children of the Church* (Scottdale: Herald, 1983).

10. Also John 11:52; Rom. 8:16-17, 21; Gal. 3:26-29; Eph. 1:5; 5:1, 8; 1 Thess. 5:5; Heb. 12:5-6.

11. *Hagiasmos* is an active verbal noun (e.g., Rom. 6:19, 1 Cor. 1:30, 1 Thess. 4:3 and 7, 2 Thess. 2:13, Heb. 12:14, 1 Peter 1:2). Other related words are *hagiadsō*, to make holy, consecrate, sanctify (e.g., Matt. 6:9, John 10:36, 17:17 and 19, Acts 20:32, 1 Cor. 6:11, 2 Tim. 2:21, Heb. 2:11, 9:13, 10:10, 13:12, 26:18); *hagios*, dedicated to deity, sacred, holy (e.g., Matt.24:15, Mark 6:20, Luke 1:49 and 70, Acts 4:30, 9:13 — translated as saints, Rom. 1:7, 1 Cor. 7:14, Eph. 1:4, 3:5, Heb.6:10 — translated as saints or as God's people, 9:1 — translated as sanctuary); *hagiotēs*, the quality of sanctity or holiness (i.e., 2 Cor. 1:12 and Heb. 12:10); *hagiōsunē*, the resultant state of holiness (e.g., 2 Cor. 7:1, 1 Thess. 3:13).

For Further Consideration

Part I. Justification, Sanctification, and Glorification in Paul

R. Larry Shelton, "Justification by Faith in the Pauline Corpus," *An Inquiry into Soteriology from a Biblical Theological Perspective*, eds. John E. Hartley and Shelton, Vol. I: *Wesleyan Theological Perspectives* (Anderson, Ind: Warner, 1981), pp. 97–132. "The justification and union with Christ concepts are parallel rather than successive. They are different metaphors, 'justification' dealing with acquittal of the sentence of condemnation and 'union with Christ' dealing with deliverance from the bondage and power of sin," p. 99. "Paul closely relates justification and sanctification and emphasizes the totality of salvation rather than fractionalizing it into stages. No aspect of newness of life is optional nor is any element of salvation allowed to be unimportant in this life," p. 125.

Bert H. Hall, "The Pauline Doctrine of Sanctification," Ibid., pp. 133–154. "It seems clear ... that Paul uses the term *hagiasmos* to indicate a process, a sloughing off of the sins of the past so that the Christian may walk not in 'uncleanness but in sanctification.' This process begins the moment one is born again. As John Wesley states, 'We grant that the term sanctified is continually applied by St. Paul to all that were justified' [John Wesley, *The Works of John Wesley* (Kansas City, Mo: Nazarene Publishing House, Lith. from ed. of 1872),

VIII, p. 294. Used by permission.]." p. 138f.

Robert W. Wall, "Glorification in the Pauline Letters," Ibid., pp. 155–167. "For Paul, God's salvation and therefore his glory was revealed 'in Christ'.... That is, the old 'glory of God' formula was recast into a new 'in Christ' formula that proclaimed the advent of God's presence back to earth in the incarnation of Jesus and in his dying and rising. God's election of a people was retold as something that happened 'in Christ' (Eph. 1:3–14); the new community of 'true' Israel was understood as a people whose existence was 'in Christ'; indeed, the promised future of this new eschatological people was sealed by Christ's Spirit 'in him.' God's glory, then, is located in the Son; and the Son's people, the church, which has assumed Christ's presence on earth, also basks in the exalted glory of its Lord (Eph. 1:19b–23)," p. 158f.

Part II. Immersion

It is generally agreed among biblical scholars, regardless of their ecclesiastical allegiances, that New Testament baptism always means immersion. The Greek word, *baptidzo* means to dip, immerse, or sink.

The Baptism section of *Baptism, Eucharist and Ministry,* Faith and Order Paper No. 111 (Geneva: World Council of Churches, 1982), recognizes the emphasis on immersion in the New Testament: "By baptism, Christians are immersed in the liberating death of Christ where their sins are buried, where the 'old Adam' is crucified with Christ, and where the power of sin is broken.... Fully identified with the death of Christ, they are buried with him and are raised here and now to a new life in the power of the resurrection of Jesus Christ, confident that they will also ultimately be one with him in a resurrection like his," p. 2. Regarding believers baptism, the document states that "baptism upon personal profession of faith is the most clearly attested pattern in the New Testament documents," p. 4.

Also, see an article by George E. Rice, "Baptism in the Early Church," *Biblical Archeology*, reprinted in *Ministry* (March 1981), p. 22, in which he shows that "the archeological evidence overwhelmingly testifies to immersion as the usual mode of baptism during the first ten to fourteen centuries."

19

The Experience of a New Spirit

In the New Testament, salvation is not only a gift from God but also the experience of the Holy Spirit. Romans 7:6 speaks of "the new life of the Spirit," and 8:2 says that "the law of the Spirit of life in Christ Jesus has set you free from the law of sin and of death."

Salvation as the Holy Spirit's Work
(Foundational Sanctification)

Salvation is the work of the Spirit from beginning to end. Regarding its beginning, Jesus says to Nicodemus that "no one can see the kingdom of God without being born from above" (John 3:3) by which, as he indicates in subsequent verses, he means the Spirit; to be born from above is to be born of the Spirit. Apart from the work of the Spirit it is impossible to enter into salvation, spoken of here as the kingdom of God.

In 2 Thessalonians 2:13, Paul says to the church: "God chose you as the first fruits for salvation *through sanctification by the Spirit* and through belief in the truth," and 1 Peter 1:2 refers to Christians as those who have been *"sanctified by the Spirit* to be obedient to Jesus Christ and to be sprinkled with his blood" (emphases mine in both cases; see also Rom. 15:16). This is what in the last chapter we called foundational sanctification. Before going on to other considerations, we simply call attention here to the fact that this foundational sanctification is the work of the Spirit.

The Indwelling of a New Presence (Edifying Sanctification)

The same Spirit who brings about foundational sanctification continues to indwell believers in order to build up both individual believers and the church as a whole. One could call this edifying sanctification. Regarding this ongoing sanctification of believers, a nineteenth century article says: "Sanctification is the maintenance and progression of a new life, imparted to the soul, by a direct agency of the Spirit of God, in regeneration or the new birth."[1] It goes on to say: "This antecedent, fundamental, causative presence of the Holy Spirit, is, according to the Scripture, the secret of the beginning, progress, and end of the work of sanctification."[2]

According to the letters of Paul, the Spirit indwells believers from conversion onward. It is not as though the Spirit brings us to the experience of new birth and then departs until at some future time we invite the Spirit to return. In Paul's treatise in Romans 8 on the Spirit's work in believers, the life of salvation is understood as being synonymous with the experience of the Spirit. To receive salvation as the gift of a new identity is in and of itself to begin experiencing the ongoing work of the Holy Spirit within us. Paul says to Christians in general: "You are in the Spirit, since the Spirit of God dwells in you. Anyone who does not have the Spirit of Christ does not belong to him" (v. 9). Not to experience the indwelling Spirit is the same as not being a Christian. In v. 14, he says that "all who are led by the Spirit of God are children of God."

Let us consider the benefits of the indwelling Spirit:

1) According to Paul, we would not even know ourselves to be God's children apart from the internal witness of the Holy Spirit (see v. 16). The Spirit gives us the assurance of being children of God, "and if children, then heirs, heirs of God and joint heirs with Christ" (v. 17). The same emphasis on the Spirit's confirmation of believers in their new identity is found in Ephesians 1:13 which refers to their being "marked with the seal of the promised Holy Spirit" when they believed. Verse 14 says that "this is the pledge of our inheritance toward redemption as God's own people." In 1 John 4:13 the same theme is found: "By this we know that we abide in him [Christ] and he in us, because he has given us of his Spirit." The indwelling Spirit confirms whose we are.

2) In 1 Corinthians 12:3 Paul says that "no one can say 'Jesus is Lord' except by the Holy Spirit," and in Galatians 4:6, "because you are children, God has sent the Spirit of his Son into our hearts, crying, 'Abba! Father!'" The indwelling Spirit, therefore, also inspires Christ-centered worship and fellowship with God (see chapter 21 on "Worshiping People" for a discussion of Christ-centered worship).

3) In addition, the indwelling Spirit produces the fruit of the Spirit (see Gal. 5:22–23), and

4) is manifested in the charismata at work in and through us for the edification of the church; these are manifestations of the Spirit for the common good (see 1 Cor. 12:4–11).

5) Another work of the indwelling Spirit is that of giving us a foretaste of future glory when our bodies will be redeemed. Romans 8:23 says that it is because Christians have "the first fruits of the Spirit" that they "groan inwardly" while waiting "for adoption, the redemption of ... [their] bodies."

The Spirit, then, is at work bringing sinners into salvation and believers to maturity. After introducing us to Christ, the Spirit indwells us, giving us confidence about whose we are, inspiring Christ-centered worship, producing the fruit of the Spirit, ministering through us for the edification of the church, and giving us a foretaste of the consummation at the end of the age.

Provision for a New People
(Effusive Sanctification)

Acts 2 speaks of a work of the Spirit which is not implicit in the gift of salvation. It is an effusive (pouring forth without reserve) work. This outpouring on the day of Pentecost catapulted the church into the world-wide mission of Christ:

> And suddenly from heaven there came a sound like the rush of a violent wind, and it filled the entire house where they were sitting. Divided tongues, as of fire, appeared among them, and a tongue rested on each of them. All of them were filled with the Holy Spirit and began to speak in other languages, as the Spirit gave them ability (vv 2–3).

Pentecost was the fullness of time for the divine empowerment (i.e., wind) and purification (i.e., fire) of the church for witness in the world. Because of the outpouring and infilling work of the Holy Spirit, disciples in Jerusalem on the day of Pentecost experienced the bursting forth of their potential for worldwide mission and service. Pentecost revealed that the externally demonstrative Spirit was also the internally filling Spirit; that the wind-like Spirit was also fire-like; that the Spirit for the whole gathering was also the Spirit for each individual.

The result of the pentecostal outpouring was the ongoing witness of the church "in Jerusalem, in all Judea and Samaria, and to the ends of the earth" (1:8). Pentecost transformed a mere company of learners at the feet of Jesus (i.e., a discipleship church) into being also a company of emissaries on foot for him (i.e., an apostolic church).

The church was empowered both to increase numerically and to live a new quality of life. Acts includes not only quantitative dimensions of the early church's story (e.g., 1:15; 2:41; 4:4; 6:1,7; 11:26; 13:44; 14:1; 17:12), but also qualitative dimensions, as we see, for instance, in the statement about the converts on the day of Pentecost devoting themselves to "the apostles' teaching and fellowship, to the breaking of bread and the prayers" (2:42). Verses 44–47 give an additional description of the quality of their church life:

> All who believed were together and had all things in common; they would sell their possessions and goods

and distribute the proceeds to all, as any had need. Day by day, as they spent much time together in the temple, they broke bread at home and ate their food with glad and generous hearts, praising God and having the goodwill of all the people.

When sin was discovered in the fellowship, it was treated as a serious threat to their integrity as the new people of God. Ananias and Sapphira were a case in point. They had lied both to the church and to the Holy Spirit about the proceeds from the sale of their property and were confronted by the church and by God. The result of the divine judgment was their untimely deaths (see 5:1–11). It was assumed that the church of "pentecostal grace"[3] would be one of personal holiness and righteousness.

Another tradition regarding the coming of the Spirit, John 14:15 — 16:15, contains Jesus' promise regarding the coming of the Spirit for the spiritual edification of his disciples. In 14:16, he says, "And I will ask the Father, and he will give you another Advocate, to be with you forever." The Lord tells them that the Spirit "will be in you" (14:17), testifying on his behalf (15:26) and guiding believers "into all the truth" (16:13) by taking what is his and declaring it to them (v. 15). The Holy Spirit was promised for the purpose of nurturing the disciples in the truth revealed in Christ.

The Spirit's effusive work subsequent to the incarnation was for the purpose of empowering, cleansing, and instructing the church for Christ-centered living and mission.

Realignment for a New Purpose (Developmental Sanctification)

Throughout the New Testament, great emphasis is placed on the re-ordering of lives for the purpose of bringing glory to the name of Christ. The church is to be both a company on mission to the world and a fellowship being developed into the image of Christ. Believers are to experience both an outward thrust and inward growth.

Not only is this realignment made possible by the grace of God and the power of the Spirit, but responsibility for it also resides with believers themselves, as we see in such passages as 1 Thessalonians 4:3–8 where Paul, speaking of the importance of living a life pleasing to the Lord, says "For this is the will of God, your sanctification: that you abstain from fornication" (v. 3). Also, in 2 Timothy 2:14–26 where instructions are given for being workers who are approved by God, v. 21 says: "All who cleanse themselves of the things I have mentioned will become special utensils, dedicated and useful to the owner of the house, ready for every good work." Again, in Hebrews 12:1 believers are enjoined to "lay aside every weight and the sin that clings so closely." When in 1 Corinthians 6 Paul addresses the issue of sex relationships with prostitutes, he asks in v. 19:

> Do you not know that your body is a temple of the Holy Spirit within you, which you have from God, and that you are not your own? For you were bought with a price; therefore glorify God in your body.

The onus of responsibility is on believers to abstain from certain practices, to cleanse themselves from certain ways of living, to lay aside that which keeps them from serving God well, in order more fittingly to glorify God.

Romans 6:19 reminds believers that just as in former times they had presented themselves "as slaves to impurity and to greater and greater iniquity," so now as Christians, they should present themselves "as slaves to righteousness for sanctification [*hagiasmon*, i.e., the process of being made holy]."

Second Corinthians 7:1 calls on believers to cleanse themselves "from every defilement of body and spirit, making holiness [*hagiōsunēn*, the state of holiness already given] perfect [*epitelountes*, bringing it to its ultimate goal] in the fear of God." And, Hebrews 12:14 says "Pursue peace with everyone, and the holiness [*hagiasmon*, i.e., the process of being sanctified] without which no one will see the Lord." New Testament imperatives for right living imply that such is our personal responsibility, and Pentecost provides Holy Spirit power and cleansing for it. Living the Godly life begins as a result of the Spirit's work from the moment of conversion, and it is intensified by the experience of the pentecostal effusion.

We turn now to issues often raised regarding Holy Spirit baptism.

Issue 1:
Holy Spirit Baptism and the Indwelling of the Spirit

The work of the indwelling Spirit spoken of in Paul is a consequence of our faith response to the gospel. The work of the infilling Spirit spoken of in Acts is a consequence of our faith response to the promise of the Lord who, prior to his ascension, said, "But you will receive power when the Holy Spirit has come upon you; and you will be my witnesses." (Acts 1:8). In the first instance, the Spirit at work in us is the implicit benefit of yielding to Christ; in the second, the Spirit's empowerment and purification depends on our yielding to the Spirit's work for that purpose. The Spirit does not empower and purify believers for witness and service apart from their volitional response to the divine offer to do so. The work of the Spirit as indwelling presence has to do with our constitutive life in Christ; the work of the Spirit as infilling power has to do with our missionary life for Christ. The indwelling Spirit leads us to the Spirit's own unrestrained work of "pentecostal grace." The outpoured and infilling Spirit is none other than the one who already indwells us awaiting our yes to Christ's promise about Spirit-baptism.

In Acts, this emphasis on our volitional desire for Spirit-baptism is seen in 1:14 where the 120 devoted themselves to prayer in preparation for the historical outpouring on the day of Pentecost, in 8:15 which says that the new believers in Samaria received the Holy Spirit, and in 19:1–7 where the not so new believers in Ephesus had to be instructed before availing themselves of the benefits of the Spirit.

The account in Acts 10 about the house of Cornelius is another case, though not as clear. Cornelius sent for Peter to further explain the gospel, to which, though dimly understood, he and his household evidently had already responded (i.e., the centurion knew enough about it to send for a gospel preacher). That they were already accepted is implied in Peter's sermon to them, for he says that "in every nation anyone who fears him [God] and does what is right is acceptable to him" (v. 35), and he affirms that they "know the message he [God] sent to the people of Israel, preaching peace by Jesus Christ" (v. 36). Evidently Peter's function, therefore, was to clarify what they had heard and believed from afar. In his message, he summarized the good news about Jesus, by telling about Jesus' being endowed with the Spirit, and about his ministry, crucifixion, resurrection, commission to the church, and his forgiveness of sin.

As Peter preached, what the house of Cornelius had previously heard in muted tones was amplified. It seems that they already possessed in embryonic form the faith of which Peter was an authoritative proponent. Verse 44 says that "while Peter was still speaking, the Holy Spirit fell upon all who heard the word."

Apparently the house of Cornelius wanted all that God had for them. Consequently, God did the same mighty work in them which he did for the disciples at Pentecost. When at the Jerusalem council (see Acts 15), Peter defended his ministry to the house of Cornelius, he said:

> And God, who knows the human heart, testified to them by giving them the Holy Spirit, just as he did to us; and in cleansing their hearts by faith he has made no distinction between them and us (8–9).

In all of the above mentioned texts, it is assumed that an additional divine work, predicated on the volitional response of believers, is needed subsequent to belief in Jesus Christ.

Issue 2:
Whether Spirit-Baptism is Optional

The theological conclusion called for by the fact that the Pauline emphasis on the indwelling Spirit and the Lukan emphasis on the outpoured Spirit exist in the same scriptures is that Christian experience is to be informed by both. Therefore, Christians should not be satisfied with the benefits of the indwelling Spirit without opening themselves also to the benefits of the outpoured and infilling Spirit, for they are one and the same Spirit. When believers resist the infilling of the outpoured Spirit, they grieve none other than the indwelling Spirit. Paul says: "Do not grieve the Holy Spirit of God, with which you were marked with a seal for the day of redemption" (Eph. 4:30). His instruction is that Christians should "be filled with the Spirit" (5:18b). In 2 Thessalonians 5:19, his word is, "Do not quench the Spirit." If all the Bible's teaching regarding the Holy Spirit is accepted, then resistance to the pentecostal effusion is resistance to none other than the indwelling Spirit. Such resistance is a form of grieving and quenching the Spirit.

Issue 3:
The Location of the Spirit

Often the issue is raised as to how the Spirit who already indwells us could come from heaven to fill us;

that sounds like a contradiction. We do well, however, to remember that the Holy Spirit is not to be thought of as being at one place but not at another, for, by nature, the Spirit is everywhere. Therefore, words in Scripture which imply movement from one place to another are to be understood not as having to do with space but with relations, functions, activities, and works. Spirit-infilling is not to be understood as the Spirit coming where before the Spirit had not been, but as the Spirit's special working in a place where the Spirit had been all along.

Mark Rutland, an evangelist with the United Methodist Church, comments:

> Only those who know him [Christ] and recognize his presence with them are candidates to receive the Holy Spirit in them.... [Believers] are to receive a new work done by the Spirit they already know.

I find the classical Wesleyan terminology especially helpful at this point. The Wesleyans speak of a second work of grace. John Wesley used grace interchangeably with the Holy Spirit. Therefore, Wesley speaks of two works of the Holy Spirit. Many who are doubtful that receiving the Holy Spirit is for those who are already saved, might be helped to realize that it is not a matter of receiving a Spirit which they feel they already have. It is receiving a work not already done.[4]

Issue 4:
The Use of Different Words
Regarding the Spirit's Coming

The infilling of the Spirit is spoken of in the New Testament in a variety of ways, a fact which points to the mutually enriching perspectives on the same reality. We see this most clearly in Acts 11:15-16 where Peter tells the Jerusalem church about the outpouring of the Spirit on Gentiles. He says: "And as I began to speak, the Holy Spirit *fell* upon them just as it had upon us at the beginning [which is referred to in 2:4 as a *filling*]. And I remembered the word of the Lord, how he had said, 'John baptized with water, but you will be *baptized* with the Holy Spirit'" (emphasis in the quotation itself also mine).

We see this interchangeability of terms also in Acts 8:15-16 where Peter and John pray that the new Samaritan Christians might receive the Holy Spirit, for, as v. 16 says, "the Spirit had not *fallen*[5] upon any of them; they had only been *baptized* in the name of the Lord Jesus [implying that they needed Holy Spirit baptism]" (emphasis added).

We may conclude, therefore, that the multiple terms point to the same definitive event, namely, the effusion of the Spirit on the day of Pentecost. This effusion was the fulfillment of the Lord's promise that they would be baptized with the Spirit, and it was experienced by those on the day of Pentecost and at other times as an infilling, later experienced also as a great power which fell on them, but, nevertheless, an experience to be received.

In Acts, the effusion of the Spirit is understood as an ongoing reality, and not as a one time experience which, with the passage of time, is left in the past. It was a continuing experience for both the church (see 4:31; 13:52) and individuals (see 4:8; 13:9).

Issue 5:
The Timing of the Spirit's Work

Another issue which often comes up in discussions of this subject is whether one must wait awhile for Spirit baptism, in obedience to the Lord who before his ascension told his disciples "to wait there [in Jerusalem] for the promise of the Father."

That we should wait, however, overlooks the context of the Lord's instruction. The instruction to wait was given to the original disciples so that they would not proceed with their own agenda prior to the fulfillment of the promise to send the Spirit. They were not to get ahead of the divine timetable, but to wait for the fullness of time when the divine promise would be historically and publicly fulfilled according to divine plan.

Since, however, for us, the divine agenda has already been fulfilled (i.e., on the day of Pentecost), there is, therefore, no further need for believers to wait. In this connection, it is instructive to note that after Pentecost, Acts says nothing about waiting for the infilling of the Holy Spirit; the emphasis is always on the urgency of their receiving what had already been poured out.

Pentecost was the historical time when the Spirit was poured out for the empowerment and purification of the church, and, in light of the Johannine tradition, also for instructing the church about Christ. This outpouring is still part of the divine economy for the church in the same way that the incarnation is. Christians, therefore, are to avail themselves of its benefits just as they avail themselves of the benefits of the incarnation. Even as sinners are called to embrace by faith the atoning work of the incarnate Lord, even so believers are called to embrace by faith the empowering, purifying, and instructive work of the pentecostal Spirit.

While the infilling of the Holy Spirit is subsequent to belief in Jesus Christ as Savior and Lord, it does not follow that we need to concern ourselves with the issue of a waiting period. Its subsequent nature is primarily one of relationships rather than of time. Subsequent to belief in Christ as Savior and Lord, believers are to be introduced to the effusive work of the Holy Spirit which will empower them for witness, purify them for service, and instruct them in Christ. The message for believers at this point in history is never, "Wait," but, "Be filled."

Issue 6:
Evidence of the Spirit's Work

Another consideration which emerges in such discussions has to do with the identifiable moment when Holy Spirit baptism takes place. How does one know when it has happened? The rise of modern pentecostalism was in no small part in response to this question; its answer is that tongues speaking is the initial evidence of Holy Spirit baptism.[6]

Those who reject tongues speaking as the basic evidence, as do many holiness denominations, tend to turn in another direction and place undue weight on being able to identify the time and place when they experienced Spirit-baptism; in this case the date and location of an experience serves as the basic evidence in much the same way that tongues speaking does for pentecostalists. Each of these approaches, however, sidesteps the all-important issue of the present-day reality of living in the cleansing, missionizing, and instructive power of the Spirit. The fundamental question is not primarily *what* happened (a pentecostal hazard), nor *when* it happened (a holiness hazard), but *that* it is happening.

The lesson of Acts is that the pentecostal effusion is a continuing reality. The crucial issue is the reality issue. Do we know ourselves, here and now, to be living in the power of the Spirit for the purpose of Christian witness and service? Do we know ourselves, here and now, to be the recipients of the purifying fires of the Spirit? Do we know ourselves, here and now, to be disciples who are also apostles, learners who are also teachers, recipients of the gospel who are also sharers of the gospel, beneficiaries of grace who are also growing in grace? If the answers are in the affirmative, we can be sure that we have in fact experienced Holy Spirit baptism. We can know the answer in terms of the reality in the here and now rather than in terms of what and when in the then and there. If the present reality is right, one can be certain that the baptism has taken place, but if the present reality is not right, one can be equally certain that the baptism which may indeed have taken place at some previous time, regardless of how definitive and memorable it may have been, is, however, no longer valid.

Summary Statement

The Spirit as indweller establishes us in Christ. The Spirit as empowerer, purifier and instructor prepares us for Christ's mission to the world.

The Holy Spirit is at work in our salvation from beginning to end; the old spirit (Rom. 8:2 calls it "the law of sin and death") is replaced by a new Spirit, who although not new in the sense of having just been recently created is new for us who believe. This is the Spirit of new birth, the Spirit continually renewing us, the Spirit providing a foretaste of the eternal newness awaiting us in the consummation. The Spirit's salvation work is one of foundational, edifying, effusive, developmental sanctification, and, as we shall see in the next chapter, also of anticipatory and entire sanctification.

Notes

1. *The Princeton Review* Vol. XXXIX, No. IV (October 1867), p. 537. Although this article falters by saying nothing about Spirit baptism subsequent to conversion, it is, nevertheless, helpful in its treatment of the work of the Holy Spirit in the ongoing life of believers.

2. Ibid., p. 543.

3. Phrase borrowed: Laurence W. Wood, *Pentecostal Grace* (Wilmore: Francis Asbury, 1980).

4. Mark Rutland, *The Finger of God* (Wilmore: Bristol, 1988), p. 103.

5. The NRSV translates *epipeptōkos* as "come" but then indicates in a footnote that the Greek means "fallen."

6. See, for example, Stanley Horton, "The Pentecostal

Perspective," *Five Views on Sanctification* (Grand Rapids: Zondervan, Academie Books, 1986): "We [pentecostals] recognize ... that speaking in tongues is only the initial evidence of the baptism of the Holy Spirit. It marked the filling of the Spirit on the Day of Pentecost. It was the convincing evidence at the house of Cornelius ('for they heard them speaking in tongues,' Acts 10:46)," p. 130.

It ought to be noted that pentecostal theologians do not teach that the *gift* of tongues is the initial evidence. A distinction is made between the initial evidence in Acts 2:4 and the gift of tongues in 1 Cor. 12:28–30. Persons may have the initial evidence but never again speak in tongues because they do not have the gift.

For Further Consideration
Introductory Reading on the Spirit and Sanctification
The Spirit and Salvation

Thomas C. Oden, *Life in the Spirit; Systematic Theology: Volume Three* (San Francisco: Harper, 1992).

H. Wheeler Robinson, *The Christian Experience of the Holy Spirit* (London: Nisbet, 1952).

Leonard I. *Sweet, New Life in the Spirit* (Philadelphia: Westminster, 1982).

The Indwelling Spirit

G. C. Berkouwer, *Faith and Sanctification* (Grand Rapids: Eerdmans, 1952).

Walter Marshall, *The Gospel-Mystery of Sanctification* (London: Oliphants, 1956).

Stephen Neill, *Christian Holiness* (New York: Harper, 1960).

Kenneth Prior, *The Way of Holiness* (Downers Grove: InterVarsity, 1967).

Thomas A. Smail, *Reflected Glory: The Spirit in Christ and Christians* (Grand Rapids: Eerdmans, 1975).

Sanctification and Spirit Baptism

Russell R. Byrum, *Holy Spirit Baptism and the Second Cleansing* (Anderson, Ind: Gospel Trumpet, 1923).

F. G. Smith, *Sanctification and the Baptism of the Holy Spirit* (Anderson, Ind: Gospel Trumpet, n.d.).

Daniel Steele, *The Gospel of the Comforter* (Kansas City: Beacon Hill, 1960).

D. S. Warner, *Bible Proofs of the Second Work of Grace* (Goshen: E. U. Mennonite Publishing Society, 1880).

Laurence W. Wood, *Pentecostal Grace* (Wilmore: Francis Asbury, 1980).

The Spirit and the Reordering of Life

James C. Fenhagen, *Invitation to Holiness* (San Francisco: Harper and Row, 1985).

Holiness Alive and Well: The Meaning of Holy Living in Twentieth-Century Life (in the Aldersgate Dialog Series; Kansas City: Beacon Hill, n.d.).

Earnest Larsen, *Holiness* (New York: Paulist, 1975).

W. T. Purkiser, *Interpreting Christian Holiness* (Kansas City: Beacon Hill, 1971).

Hannah Whitall Smith, *The Christian's Secret of a Happy Life* (New York: Revell, 1916), and *Living in the Sunshine* (New York: Revell, 1906).

George Allen Turner, *Christian Holiness in Scripture, in History, and in Life* (Kansas City: Beacon Hill, 1977).

20

The Culmination of a New Reality

Christian salvation is a movement from the predicament of not having one's life integrated around God to the blessing of having it totally integrated around God. On the one hand, this total integration has to do with glorification, and, on the other, with entire sanctification. We speak here not of two different salvation experiences, but of two dynamics taking place in salvific life, bringing to culmination the new reality which is ours by grace through faith.

Glorification of a New Being
(Anticipatory Sanctification)

Glorification has to do with our being changed to become like Jesus Christ.[1] The *locus classicus* for the idea of glorification is 2 Corinthians 3:18:

491

And all of us, with unveiled faces, seeing the glory of the Lord as though reflected in a mirror, are being transformed into the same image from one degree of glory to another; for this comes from the Lord, the Spirit.

In the verses leading up to v. 18, Paul refers to the story in Exodus 34:29–35 of Moses who had beheld the glory of God at the top of Sinai. According to Paul's interpretation in 2 Corinthians 3:13, Moses, upon descending the mountain, put a veil over his face in order to keep the people of Israel from gazing at the fading glory. Jesus is different: instead of being a holy man who goes up to where the glory of God is and then descending from the glory, he is the eternal glory of God, who, having descended to us, reveals the divine glory which never fades (see also 1 Cor. 11:7 and 2 Cor. 4:6). Even though, as risen Lord, he has ascended to the right hand of the Father, the Spirit continues revealing his glory as brilliantly as it was during the days of the incarnation. Through the Spirit, then, we continue beholding the glory of God in the face of Jesus Christ. The former glory continued to diminish for the people of God the further they moved in history from the time of Moses' encounter with God on the mountain. The present glory continues to increase in those who live in the Spirit. Those who by the power of the Holy Spirit are in an ongoing personal relationship with God through Christ, are, thereby, "being transformed into the same image [of Christ] from one degree of glory to another."

This process of glorification goes on until the end of the age when, according to 1 Corinthians 15:43, even our bodies will be "raised in glory," for "just as we have borne the image of the man of dust [Adam], we will also bear the image of the man of heaven [Christ]" (v. 49).

Glorification has to do with our complete restoration into the image of Jesus Christ. In our glorified state of heavenly existence, we shall finally arrive at the eternal goal for human life, namely, perfect communion with our Lord, nothing whatsoever hindering it. The glorification taking place now as we keep our spiritual eyes on Jesus is a process which will never end prior to the Lord's return.

Divine provisions for this process to take place are the Gospels, the Lord's Supper, gatherings in the name of Jesus, and the washing of the saints' feet:

1) The Gospels are the definitive record of our Lord's life, teaching, and ministry. It is only as we read and meditate on them and as we hear them read and taught that we are able to keep our spiritual eyes on Jesus.

2) Regular communion at the Lord's table is the divinely approved way for us to be reminded again and again of the price of our salvation, to be rekindled again and again in our anticipation of the eternal banquet with him, and to be blessed again and again by his living presence here and now (see chapter 21, "Worshiping People"). According to Luke 24:30–31, it was in the breaking of bread that the disciples at Emmaus beheld their risen Lord.

3) We see him in the fellowship of the church, for Jesus said, that "where two or three are gathered in my name, I am there among them" (Matt. 18:20).

4) In serving others, we behold Jesus. In John 13, after Jesus washed the feet of his disciples, he instructed them to do the same (vv. 14–17). Washing feet is the liturgical way by which we continue seeing Jesus as God's servant bringing us to salvation (see Phil. 2:1–11). According to the judgment scene of Matthew 25, it is in service to others that we see Jesus; in v. 40, he says: "Just as you did it to one of the least of these ... you did it to me." (See chapter 23, "Foot Washing People.")

This process of glorification will be completed only with resurrection at the end of the age (see 1 Cor. 15:35–57). Daniel Steele (1824–1914), sometime professor of theology at Boston University and influential intellectual in the holiness movement, wrote:

> You may mend a pitcher by the application of cement, so that it will hold water; but when you strike it there is

no ring. To regain the ring of a perfect vessel, you must hand it over to the potter to be ground to powder and to be reconstructed. So it is with us in the present life. Jesus, if we will submit our shattered vessels to him, can mend us up so that we may be filled with the Spirit, but we shall not on earth regain the true Adamic ring of absolute perfection. We must be handed over to death to be reduced to dust and be built up again by the Divine Potter, when we shall be presented faultless, not in the obscure twilight of some distant region, but faultless in the meridian splendors "of the presence of his glory."[2]

Until that time, we experience the future glory only in the Spirit to whom Paul refers as the *arrabōn*, the earnest or pledge of that which is to come. Second Corinthians 5:1–5 says:

> For we know that if the earthly tent we live in is destroyed, we have a building from God, a house not made with hands, eternal in the heavens. For in this tent we groan, longing to be clothed with our heavenly dwelling, if indeed, when we have taken it off we will not be found naked. For while we are still in this tent, we groan under our burden, because we wish not to be unclothed but to be further clothed, so that what is mortal may be swallowed up by life. He who has prepared us for this very thing is God, who has given us the Spirit as a guarantee [*arrabōn*; see also 2 Cor. 1:22 and Eph. 1:14].

Oneness with a New Cause
(Entire Sanctification)

The *locus classicus* for the culmination of sanctification is Paul's benediction in 1 Thessalonians 5:23–24:

> May the God of peace himself sanctify you entirely [*holotelēs*]; and may your spirit and soul and body be kept sound [*holoklēros*] and blameless at the coming of our Lord Jesus Christ. The one who calls you is faithful, and he will do this.

The word *holotelēs*, translated here as "entirely," is used only once in the New Testament. It is derived from two words: *holos*, meaning whole, entire, or complete, and *telos*, meaning the end or goal of an act or state of being, the final aim or purpose of a process (e.g., 1 Tim. 1:5: "But the aim [*telos*] of such instruction is love that comes from a pure heart, a good conscience, and sincere faith").

The combination of these words, then, indicates a condition in which all the parts of the whole are working together to fulfill their ultimate purpose; all the parts are centered on the one goal and the one goal has permeated all the parts. In comparison to *holoklēros*, meaning "complete," used in the same verse, *holotelēs*, "draws more special attention to the several parts to which the wholeness spoken of extends, no part being wanting or lacking in completeness."[3]

This Thessalonian benediction is that Christians will be sanctified entirely at some point in the future.[4] The sanctification spoken of here is one in which all dimensions of life — "spirit and soul and body" — are to be brought to ultimate, purposeful wholeness so that the divine goal will be attained and we will be found "sound and blameless at the coming of our Lord Jesus Christ."

Entire Sanctification for Historical Existence

The issue about which church people disagree has to do with when this entire sanctification is to take place in the future: Is it to take place prior to death? or, at the time of the believer's death? or, at the time of Christ's return?[5]

Since the text itself does not give a conclusive answer to the question, it is helpful to take into account another important consideration, namely, the function of the holy throughout the scriptures. It is informative to note that in the Old Testament, holy places, utensils, offerings, people, and days were always for the purpose of fulfilling the mission of God in history. The same is true in the New Testament, which refers to places as being holy (see Matt. 24:15 and also Heb. 9:1 where the word is translated as sanctuary) as well as prophets (see Luke 1:70), apostles (see Eph. 3:5), and Christians in general (see Acts 9:13; Rom. 1:7; Heb. 6:10; Rev. 5:8). In every case, these places and people are made holy for the purpose of God's work in history. For instance, 1 Peter 1:15

says: "As he who called you is holy, be holy yourselves in all your conduct," and then in 2:9 the historical purpose for this mandate is given: "But you are a chosen race, a royal priesthood, a holy nation, God's own people, *in order that you may proclaim the mighty acts of him who called you* out of darkness into his marvelous light" (emphasis added). Being made holy is for the purpose of accomplishing the divine mission in history.

There is no compelling reason to hold, therefore, that Paul in 1 Thessalonians 5:23 thinks otherwise than that sanctification is for the purpose of accomplishing the divine mission during the historical life of God's people. The blessing of entire sanctification is for this life so that the mission of God can proceed with strength. That this experience is for Christians "in this world" is central to the theological understanding of John Wesley who wrote in *A Plain Account of Christian Perfection*: "Yea, we do believe that He will *in this world* so 'cleanse the thoughts of our hearts by the inspiration of His Holy Spirit, that we shall perfectly love Him, and worthily magnify His holy name'" (emphasis added).[6]

While entire sanctification is inextricably bound up with glorification, it is not identical with it. Entire sanctification has to do with the complete oneness of the total self with Christ for the purpose of fulfilling his mission on earth whereas glorification has to do with the complete oneness of the total self with Christ for the purpose of unbroken and eternal communion (see Rev. 4 and 5). The culmination of glorification takes place only at the end of historical time when the Lord returns; the culmination of sanctification, on the other hand, takes place prior to the end of time as believers yield wholeheartedly to their Lord. Each is a distinctive dimension of God's salvation plan .

Stephen as an Example

Stephen, the first Christian martyr, serves as an example of the kind of entire sanctification for which Paul prays in 1 Thessalonians 5:23. Following Stephen's message before the Sanhedrin (see Acts 7:2–53), "they became enraged and ground their teeth at Stephen. But filled with the Holy Spirit, he gazed into heaven and saw the glory of God and Jesus standing at the right hand of God." Rushing at him, they "dragged him out of the city and began to stone him" (v. 57), during which he prayed "Lord Jesus, receive my spirit" (v. 59). Kneeling down, he "cried out in a loud voice, 'Lord, do not hold this sin against them.' When he had said this, he died" (v. 60).

"The God of peace himself" had sanctified Stephen *holotelēs.* The whole of his being was totally integrated around the person and mission of Christ, which integration took place obviously prior to both his own death and the return of Christ, so that when death did come, he was ready.

It was not death that entirely sanctified him; instead,

it was entire sanctification that prepared him for death as a martyr. His whole being was complete and blameless, so that in the midst of the stoning he had no fear in the presence of his Lord, only joy. He was ready to be in the divine presence on the other side of death. (See also Eph. 5:25–27, 2 Peter 3:10–14, and 1 John 4:17–18 each of which speaks of a culmination of readiness for the return of the Lord.)

Stephen is testimony to the sanctifying work of God which was so entire that nothing whatsoever had the power to persuade him to turn his back on Christ. No set of circumstances could distract him from his whole-hearted and single-minded devotion to the Christian mission. In 1 Thessalonians 3:13, Paul says: "And may he [the Lord] so strengthen your hearts in holiness that you may be blameless before our God and Father at the coming of our Lord Jesus with all his saints." Stephen was one who had been strengthened in holiness so that he was blameless before God. He saw Christ standing at the right hand of God—perhaps an indication of divine approval.

Presenting Ourselves as Living Sacrifices

Since, according to 1 Thessalonians 5:13–24, entire sanctification is God's work, the question arises as to whether we have any role to play in it. In Romans 12:1–2, Paul speaks about our responsibility:

I appeal to you therefore, brothers and sisters, by the mercies of God, to present your bodies as a living sacrifice, holy and acceptable to God, which is your spiritual worship. Do not be conformed to this world, but be transformed by the renewing of your minds, so that you may discern what is the will of God—what is good and acceptable and perfect [*teleion*].

While according to 1 Thessalonians 5:23-24, it is God who brings us to the point of entire sanctification, according to Romans 12:1-2, it is we who are responsible for (a) presenting ourselves as a living sacrifice to God, (b) not conforming to the world, and (c) yielding to the transforming power of God, all to the end that we may "discern what is the will of God—what is good and acceptable and perfect [*teleion*]." In other words, God wants us to know and do that which is in conformity with God's ultimate goal, i.e., the *telos*. We are to offer ourselves in such a way that we come to the point of discerning the *telos*, but ultimately it is only God who can bring all dimensions of our lives together for the purpose of serving that *telos*. Only we can give ourselves as a living sacrifice to God's *telos*; only God can sanctify us *holotelēs* for it.

For All or for a Few?
Monastic religious orders were developed for the

purpose of taking seriously the entire sanctification to which Christians are called. Robin Maas calls monasticism the way of those who make the pursuit of whole-hearted love of God "a full-time occupation."[7] The whole of monastic life is integrated around the service and worship of God; time and activities in their entirety are regulated according to what is perceived to be the ultimate purposes of God.[8]

In light of the church's history of too often ignoring the call of God for personal sanctification for all believers, the monastic movement is to be commended for its commitment to this lost emphasis. However, two serious shortcomings of this approach are the mandatory withdrawal from natural associations such as marriage and family and the assumption that the life of entire sanctification is only for a special class of Christians.

The monastic approach is taken even in Protestantism by those who assume that the totally consecrated life is only for the few, but certainly not for all Christians. The New Testament, however, teaches otherwise: both of the passages under consideration were addressed to Christians in general who were still involved in natural relationships and in the normal responsibilities of life. All believers were called to consecrate themselves to God, the end result being the divine work of entire sanctification. It is within the context of such consecration that God brings about the total integration of the self around God's purposes.

As one writer has said:

> A mature person in either a psychological or biblical sense is integrated, has a purposeful or goal-directed quality about his life, is open to himself and others, while the immature person is disorganized, having either conflicting goals or no goal, and is unaware and unaccepting of various aspects of himself and others.[9]

A life entirely sanctified is a life centered on its divine vocation. It is a life with all of its parts integrated around the person of Christ and his mission in the world. Steele refers to a Dr. Payson who speaks of three kinds of Christians, ranged in concentric circles around Christ:

> Some value the presence of their Saviour so highly that they cannot bear to be at any remove from him. Even their work they will bring up, and do it in the light of his countenance, and while engaged in it will be seen constantly raising their eyes to him, as if fearful of losing one beam of his light. Others, who, to be sure, would not be content to live out of his presence, are yet less wholly absorbed by it than these, and may be seen a little further off, engaged here and there in their various callings, their eyes generally upon their work, but often looking up to the light which they love. A third

class, beyond these, but yet within the life-giving rays, includes a...multitude, many of whom are so much engaged in their worldly schemes that they may be seen standing sidewise to Christ, looking mostly the other way, and only now and then turning their faces toward the light.[10]

Entire sanctification is, as Albert Outler puts it, "having no other gods of our own, since the First Commandment is also the last!"[11] Or, as Maas says, "Perfect love is, in the first place, the whole-souled love of God, our Maker."[12]

Henry Ward Beecher had the right idea when he made the following observation:

This, then, is my estimate of sanctification. It is that state into which men come when every part of their nature has been developed, and when the faculties have been subordinated in their real gradations. When the faculties have all come to have affinities with the central controlling elements of Divine and human love in the soul; when that love is the center from which power goes out and stimulates every faculty, — then men are perfect.[13]

The strength of this definition is that it rightly stresses the integration of the total person around God. However, Beecher goes on to say that he cannot find such people. He, thereby, stumbles on the same stone which troubles so many: he makes no distinction between *behavior* which is flawless and *love* which is perfect. That is, love which, though it may have flawed behavior, is, nevertheless, focused in single-hearted devotion on the beloved. Entire sanctification does not mean flawless behavior; it means single-hearted devotion to the God of our salvation—a devotion which only the "God of peace himself" is able to evoke from us.

Since God does the work, the knowledge of the extent of that work is known conclusively only by God. We do well to leave the bookkeeping there. Our responsibility is to consecrate ourselves wholeheartedly to the Lord; the Lord will take care of the work of sanctifying entirely. Ours is a trustworthy God: "The one who calls you is faithful, and he will do this."

Implications for the Care of Souls

The last three chapters raise issues having to do with the care of souls in relation to salvation. On the basis of what has been said, the following ten way marks can be identified as indicators both to the people of God and to their shepherds as to where persons are in their Christian pilgrimage. I list these not as though they were a sequential check sheet or as though each were a self-enclosed entity unrelated to all the others. Instead, I list them for the pastoral care of souls. I have in mind not only those who hold a pastoral office, but all disciples who care about their own spiritual life and that of others. Recognizing that the Lamb's Book of Life belongs to God and that we neither enter names nor erase them, we do as believers, nevertheless, have responsibility for the care of souls. What, then, are major indicators that one has entered into and is maturing in the life of faith revealed in "Jesus the pioneer and perfecter of our faith" (Heb. 12:2)? The evidences may be set forth as follows:

Evidences of the Birthing and Establishing Operation of Grace

- Faith/repentance/water baptism;
- Assurance of being a child of God;
- Devotion "to the apostles' teaching and fellowship, to the breaking of bread and the prayers";
- Fruit of the Spirit;
- Building up the body of Christ;
- Openness to the infilling work of the Holy Spirit.

Evidences of the Empowering and Perfecting Operation of Grace

- Consecration of oneself as a "living sacrifice" to God;
- The experience of the Spirit's ongoing empowerment, cleansing, and instruction for the sake of the Christian mission;
- Self-cleansing of all that hinders one's usefulness for Christ's mission;

• Christ-likeness;

• The sense of being so wholly integrated in the totality of one's being around the purposes of God that nothing diverts one from Christ and his mission;

• The Maranatha prayer, "Our Lord, come!" (1 Cor. 16:22).

Notes

1. For a theology of glorification, see Bernard Ramm, *Them He Glorified: A Systematic Study of the Doctrine of Glorification* (Grand Rapids: Eerdmans, 1963).

2. Daniel Steele, *Love Enthroned* (Reprinted Salem: Schmul, 1961), p. 58.

3. G. Milligan, *St. Paul's Epistles to the Thessalonians* (Macmillan, 1908) as quoted in G. Abbott-Smith, *A Manual Greek Lexicon of the New Testament* (New York: Charles Scribner's Sons, 1936), p. 316.

4. The verb, *hagiasai*, being 1st aorist active optative, refers to an action which is to be brought to completion in the future.

5. For a presentation of the major answers to this question, see *Five Views on Sanctification* (Grand Rapids: Zondervan, 1986): the Wesleyan answer given by Melvin E. Dieter, the Reformed by Anthony A. Hoekema, the Pentecostal by Stanley M. Horton, the

Keswickian by J. Robertson McQuilkin and the Augustinian-Dispensational perspective by John F. Walvoord. One of the strengths of this work is that after each makes his own presentation, each of the others responds.

6. John Wesley, *A Plain Account of Christian Perfection* (London: Epworth, 1952), p. 111.

7. Robin Maas, *Crucified Love: The Practice of Christian Perfection* (Nashville: Abingdon, 1989), p. 32.

8. See R. Newton Flew, *The Idea of Perfection in Christian Theology* (London: Oxford University Press, 1934) for his treatment of monasticism as well as other Christian movements which emphasize the entire sanctification of life.

9. John D. Carter, *Wholeness and Holiness*, ed. H. Newton Maloney (Grand Rapids: Baker, 1983), p. 192.

10. Steele, op. cit., p. 8.

11. Albert Outler, *Theology in the Wesleyan Spirit* (Nashville: Tidings, 1975), p. 85.

12. Maas, op. cit., p. 60.

13. Henry Ward Beecher, *Yale Lectures on Preaching*, (Boston: Pilgrim, 1874), p. 298.

For Further Consideration
"Entire Sanctification"

Charles Ewing Brown, *The Meaning of Sanctification* (Anderson, Ind: Warner, 1945).

Brian W. Grant, *From Sin to Wholeness* (Philadelphia: Westminster, 1982).

Harold Lindstrom, *Wesley and Sanctification* (London: Epworth, 1946).

Asa Mahan, *Christian Perfection* (Reprinted Salem: Schmul, 1962).

Robin Maas, *Crucified Love* (Nashville: Abingdon, 1989).

Theodore Runyon (ed.), *Sanctification and Liberation* (Nashville: Abingdon, 1981).

John A. Sanford, *Healing and Wholeness* (New York: Paulist, 1977).

H. E. Schmul (ed.), *Christian Perfection: A Compilation of Six Holiness Classics in One* (Salem: Schmul, 1974).

Daniel Steele, *Love Enthroned* (Salem: Schmul, 1961).

Laurence W. Wood, *Pentecostal Grace* (Wilmore: Francis Asbury, 1980).

Mildred Bangs Wynkoop, *A Theology of Love: The Dynamic of Wesleyanism* (Kansas City: Beacon Hill, 1972).

V

Human Life for Divine Purposes

21

Worshiping People[1]

The essence of sin is the refusal to worship God. Salvation is both God's rectification of this refusal and empowerment for us to become the worshiping beings we were created to be.

Worship in the Old Testament

Adam's and Eve's basic sin was the refusal to worship their Creator; instead, they worshipped the fruit of the Lord's creation (see Gen. 3). The rest of the Old Testament reflects the struggle of the people of God to turn from the worship of the created order to the worship of the Creator. High points along the way were the call of Abraham (Gen. 12:1-9), Moses at the burning bush (Exod. 3-4:17), the triumphant words of Moses and Miriam (15:1-21), the Israelites at Mount Sinai (19-20), tabernacle worship during the pilgrimage in the wilderness (see especially the reference to the cloud and the glory in 40:34-38), and the song of Moses (Deut. 31:30−32:47). Additional high points include the commissioning of Joshua (1:1-9), Hannah's prayers in the house of God (1 Sam. 1−2), the call of Samuel (1 Sam. 3), David's joyous celebration when the ark of God was brought to Jerusalem (2 Sam. 6:1-19), and Solomon's dedication of the temple (1 Kings 8). As we continue reviewing this pilgrimage, we are reminded of Josiah's renewal of the covenant (2 Chron. 34:29-33), Ezra's reading of the law following the Babylonian exile (Neh. 8:1-12), the Psalms, Isaiah's temple vision (chapter 6), Ezekiel's visions, and Jonah's prayer in the belly of a whale (chap. 2). These and other passages mark the journey of the people of God toward the time of the perfect worship of God.

Alongside these high points of worship, however, were also the low points of rebelliousness. In fact, national calamity is consistently linked to their refusal to worship God with purity of heart (e.g., Dan. 9:4-19). According to Jeremiah and Ezekiel, the only solution to this dilemma is for God to give new hearts to the people. Ezekiel 36:26 says: "A new heart I will give you, and a new spirit I will put within you, and I will remove from your body the heart of stone and give you a heart of flesh" (See also Jer. 31:33).

The Perfect Worshiper and Us

Enter Jesus Christ.

Our Lord came with new spirit and heart. He did not merely go to particular places from time to time to worship God; his whole earthly life was the worship of God. He loved the courts of the Lord, accepted fully his divine vocation, resisted all temptations of the devil, dwelt in unbroken communion with his heavenly Father, lived according to the standards of the heavenly kingdom, and was obedient to the divine mission even to death on the cross.

He came, however, not only to worship as a fully human being, but to make it possible for us also to live in God's presence worshipfully. Jesus, who was physically born by the power of the Holy Spirit, came that we might be spiritually born by the power of the same Spirit. He who was raised from the dead came that we, too, might experience the power of the resurrection in our own lives. Jesus Christ, the perfect worshiper of God, came with the new heart spoken of by the prophets so that we, also, might have hearts pleasing unto God.

He came to transform us into worshipers who love the courts of the Lord, accept God's vocation, resist the devil, dwell in unbroken communion with God, live according to the standards of God's kingdom, and are obedient to the divine mission even to the point of death.

The worship to which Christians are called is not simply the performance of rituals at stated times and places. Instead, we are called to the reorientation of the whole of life around Jesus Christ, his kingdom, and his mission in the world.[2] We see this particularly in Paul who "views the entire activity of Christian life in general and his apostleship in particular as worship that must be accorded to God."[3]

Worshiping Lives and Worship Services

Such a perspective, however, is not to be construed to mean that specified times and places for worship are of little significance. We see their great importance in the fact that our Lord's life included participation in both temple gatherings and synagogue meetings. Furthermore, he often gathered his disciples in order to teach them, and assemblies of needy people were drawn to him for healing. Jesus was not a spiritual recluse; instead, the way he functioned affirmed the crucial part gatherings play in the divine plan for God's people.

Evidence of the importance ascribed to worship services is seen in the following: on the night before his crucifixion, Jesus gathered the Twelve for a worship meal; after the resurrection "the eleven disciples went to Galilee, to the mountain to which Jesus had directed them" (Matt. 28:16). Note also that it was at a gathering on the day of Pentecost that the Holy Spirit came upon the church.

It is also important to note that no small part of Paul's Corinthian correspondence has to do with the kind of gatherings the church should have (see 1 Cor. 11—14), and that the writer to the Hebrews, in 10:24-25, explicitly encourages believers not to neglect church services when he says, "And let us consider how to provoke one another to love and good deeds, not neglecting to meet together, as is the habit of some, but encouraging one another, and all the more as you see the Day approaching."

As stated above, Christians are called to live in the worship of God all the time. We are called to assemble ourselves together not as though worship begins and ends with our entrance into and departure from particular places, but because it is in the gathering that we can be renewed in the worshipful life to which we have been called in Christ. Worship services should be times of rejuvenation for worshiping lives.

In the New Testament, two services which are pivotal for understanding the nature of Christian gatherings are the holy meal in the upper room, and Spirit-baptism on the day of Pentecost. Our identity as the church of Jesus Christ will be enhanced to the degree that the significance of these two gatherings is appreciated. The spiritually healthy church is the continuation of upper room communion and of pentecostal power. Understood within this context, any and all of our worship services should be times of communion with the crucified, risen, reigning, and coming Lord, as well as times of empowerment for the mission to which he calls us.

Worship Services as
Times of Communion with Our Lord

Services of Christian worship are times of communion with the Lord. Jesus' holy meal with the Twelve on the night before his crucifixion is described in Matthew 26:17–30, Mark 14:12–26, Luke 22:7–23, and 1 Corinthians 11:23–26; (cf. John 13:1–20). This pivotal gathering leads to the following observations:

1) The Lord himself was the host of the gathering. The Twelve were there by virtue of his invitation. He was to be listened to by all present, including the aspiring leaders among them. Even though, at his direction, the disciples had made preparations for the meal, once the gathering began, he was the one in leadership; his was the dominant presence.

2) It was a gathering in which the past was honored. Who they were as disciples could be understood only in relation to the history of God's people through the centuries. The fact that it was a passover meal was in and of itself a connection with this history.

3) The central focus of the gathering was the salvation wrought by Christ. He was the fulfillment of all salvation history, the eternal passover, the Lamb of God who takes away the sin of the world. He was spiritual life, health, and nourishment. He was the agent of the new covenant of grace.

4) The service was designed for the purpose of renewing the disciples' relationship with their Lord. According to Paul's account, Jesus said, "Do this in remembrance of me" (1 Cor. 11:24–25). The meaning of the Greek word, *anamnēsis*, translated here as "remembrance," has to do with more than simple memory; it has to do with ongoing participation in the saving reality established in the past. In a discussion of *anamnēsis*, Herman Ridderbos, the Pauline scholar, says:

> The Lord's Supper is herewith qualified as a redemptive-historical commemorative meal. It is not a question here only of the commemoration of what has once taken place in the past, but no less of its abiding, actual redemptive significance. Christ's self-surrender is now, as hitherto the exodus of Israel out of Egypt, the new and definitive fact of redemption which in the eating of the bread and in the drinking of the wine the church may accept as such again and again...from the hand of God.[4]

5) It was an anticipatory service. Being marred by the defection of Judas and possibly also by the dispute as to which one of the disciples was the greatest (see Luke 22:24), the service certainly was not without flaws. The Lord, however, pointed beyond the gathering with all of its flaws, to the consummation of the Kingdom. According to Matthew 26:29, he said, "I tell you, I will never again drink of this fruit of the vine until that day when I drink it new with you in my Father's kingdom." (See also Mark 14:25; Luke 22:16; and Paul's reference to the return of the Lord in 1 Cor. 11:26.) *The Baptism, Eucharist and Ministry* document says:

> The anamnēsis in which Christ acts through the joyful celebration of his Church is thus both representation and anticipation. It is not only a calling to mind of what is past and of its significance. It is the Church's effective proclamation of God's mighty acts and promises.[5]

6) Jesus conducted it as a time of thanksgiving. All four accounts of the holy meal refer to the Lord giving thanks. The Greek word for giving thanks, *eucharesteō* has given rise to the practice in some Christian traditions of calling the holy meal, the Eucharist. Our Lord saw this as an occasion for thanksgiving.

7) It was a service of preparation for the divine work of redemption. The meeting in the upper room led beyond the room to the public arena where the decisively redemptive events of crucifixion and resurrection would take place, i.e., "When they had sung the hymn, they went out to the Mount of Olives" (Matt. 26:30).

Questions that Emerge Out of the Upper Room Service

The holy meal stands at the summit of Jesus' life in the flesh with his disciples, and at the base of his atoning work. It summarizes his incarnational life and introduces his atoning work. It is the bridge between the disciples' knowledge of Jesus as earthly teacher and their experience of him as crucified, risen, reigning, and coming Lord. Consequently, it provides us with the right questions to ask regarding our worship services in the present:

1) Is Jesus the dominant presence in our services, or do we get in the way? Are we—all of us whether preachers, singers, instrumentalists, or whatever—in a secondary role, or have we moved to the center, thus leaving the Lord's presence to be experienced in a secondary way?

2) Is the past honored as the story of faith in which we, too, become participants? Are the scriptures read and taught, and is the long history of the faith celebrated? Or, on the contrary, is the connection with the church's story downplayed in an attempt to be contemporary?

3) Is Christ's salvation at the center of every gathering? Or, is the saving work of Jesus Christ treated merely as one among several possible themes which simply might be at the center of services of worship? The reason that some Christian traditions participate in the holy meal every Lord's Day has to do with the importance they ascribe to keeping the saving work of Christ at the center, instead of treating it as merely one among several possible emphases for a service.

4) By participating in the services, are believers renewed in their life in Christ? Or, does it deplete them of life and cause them to stumble in the faith?

5) Is anticipation of the Lord's future engendered, or is all the attention on the past or the present? Is attention drawn to the hope that is in Christ for the coming of the kingdom in us, in the world, and in consummation at the end of world history? Or, on the other hand, is all the attention on the "Judases" and on the church's immaturity?

6) Are worship services times of praise, gratitude, and thanksgiving for the goodness of God in creation and in God's sustaining love and saving grace? Or, are they times of lamentation about how bad the world or the church is?

7) Do the services lead to our participation in Christ's mission in the public arena? Is Christ's redemptive work seen as God's work for the benefit of the whole world, and is the function of the church understood as being that of making disciples of all nations? Or, quite to the contrary, is the service seen as a private affair for Christians, accomplishing its goal merely by making those in attendance feel good and wanting to come back for a repeat? Is the service seen simply as the satisfaction of the soul, or is it seen, also, as preparation for mission?

Worship Services as Times of Spirit Empowerment

Not only are services of Christian worship times of communion with the Lord; they are times of empowerment for mission, as well. Pentecost was the occasion when the post-resurrection church gathered for the inauguration of its mission (see especially Acts 2:1–4).

That inaugural worship service, like the holy meal in the upper room, was a pivotally transitional service in that it was at the summit of resurrection glory and at the base of the church's mission. The glory of that service is maintained by the power of the Holy Spirit for the church in all ages and places. The mission for which the church at Pentecost was empowered is still in place.

We can bask in the same glory which those at Pentecost enjoyed in that the glory of the resurrection has not diminished. The Lord wills that the church continue being at the summit of resurrection glory for as long as time continues.

In addition, the fundamental mission has not changed, namely, to be the Lord's "witnesses in Jerusalem, in all Judea and Samaria, and to the ends of the earth." While obviously we are no longer at the beginning of this mission, the fact that the Lord has not returned makes it equally obvious that the mission is not yet finished, for, as Jesus says in Matthew 24:14, "This good news of the kingdom will be proclaimed throughout the world, as a testimony to all the nations; and then the end will come."

This inaugural service of resurrection glory, then, is not to be mimicked as though it had no continuity into the present—it is not a relic of the past! Since the outpouring of the Holy Spirit has never been recalled, it is still a continuing reality which we either enter into or refuse to enter. The question for the church in every subsequent time is whether it will embrace the reality of the outpoured Spirit or whether it will avoid it. To be sure, one finds examples of groups which give little or no indication that they desire either the cleansing fire of the holy flame or the empowerment of the holy wind. For whatever reason, they have not entered into the reality of the outpoured Spirit and consequently are not on mission to "Jerusalem,... Judea and Samaria, and to the ends of the earth." On the other hand, one finds many other examples of churches which have entered that reality and consequently are alive in the Spirit and vigorous in mission.

A great difference exists between, on the one hand, services which are designed as reproductions of Pentecost, and, on the other, those understood as continuations of Pentecost. Copy services focus on replicating the same external phenomena read about in Acts 2, whereas continuation services focus on both the cleansing fire in the lives of individual believers and the empowering wind authorizing the whole church to proceed with the mission. I use the word "authorizing" because of Acts 1:4: "While staying with them [the apostles], he [the resurrected Lord] ordered them not to leave Jerusalem, but to wait there for the promise of the Father." In other words, they did not have divine authorization to proceed with the mission until the Spirit was poured out. The pentecostal outpouring, therefore, both empowered and authorized the church in all times and places to proceed with its historical mission.

Questions Emerging from the Service of the Outpoured Spirit

The church on the day of Pentecost consisted not only

of the original eleven but also of the newly chosen twelfth and the extended company of those who were faithful to the resurrected Lord. Even as Luke wrote his Gospel to Theophilus (a Greek name meaning lover of God) so that he and presumably all God-lovers might "know the truth concerning the things about which you have been instructed" (1:4), likewise, it was for the same purpose that in his second volume, he gave the account of Pentecost and the early history of the church of the outpoured Spirit. The fact that Acts found its way into the Christian scriptures is evidence that the church after the day of Pentecost was being urged to enter into the reality of the outpoured Spirit in the same way that they had entered into the reality of the incarnation of Christ Jesus.

New Testament writings are not documents of irrelevant historical facts; they are invitations to faithful participation in God's drama of grace. The story of the outpoured Spirit, therefore, is not a bit of cold information, but an invitation to enter into the reality of which it speaks. Since it is part of the church's scriptures, it is not acceptable for us to ignore it. Neither is it any more permissible to try either to reproduce or to supersede Pentecost than it is to attempt to reproduce or to supersede the birth of Christ. The church's obligation of faith is to enter into the spiritual reality already established.

Our services of worship, then, should be continuations of Pentecost. If we are serious about that, we will ask questions growing out of what we know about it. Such questions as these, therefore, emerge:

1) Are we planing and leading services on the assumption that God's gracious Spirit is already poured out, or are we planning and leading them on the false assumption that we have to conjure up the Spirit? The former option leads to calm trust in God's ability to do superabundantly beyond all that we ask or think. The latter leads to manipulative procedures and orchestrated plans for creating desired moods in services. That some leaders are skillful enough to bring about particular moods and responses is obviously the case; but that is crowd control and not sensitivity to the Spirit. The Spirit poured out on the day of Pentecost was the Spirit of divine surprise, and still is.

2) Are the holy fire and holy wind preparing the people of God for divine mission? Or, to the contrary, are God's people using the fire and wind for their own enjoyment? Are they being empowered for the missionary task of the church, or are they being overwhelmed by the astonishing phenomena of the Spirit?

The account of the outpouring on the day of Pentecost should be seen in the context of the whole book of Acts in which the outpouring led to witness beyond the space of the service itself. We see this first of all in the fact that the great throng of visitors gathered in Jerusalem for the Jewish celebration of Pentecost were attracted to the scene of the outpouring where they heard of "God's deeds of power" (2:11). "That day about three thousand persons were added" to the church through repentance and water baptism (see 2:37–41).

Pentecost led, also, to the ongoing nurturing of the faithful. Verse 42 says, "They devoted themselves to the apostles' teaching and fellowship, to the breaking of bread and the prayers."[6]

It led furthermore to the ever widening witness to which their Lord had commissioned them. Acts tells about their witnessing in Jerusalem, Judea, Samaria, and beyond.

In summary, the worship service on the day of Pentecost did not turn the participants inward; it turned them outward in evangelism, nurture, and mission "to the ends of the earth."

3) Additional questions are these: Do our services of worship get us beyond our walls with the good news? Do they have an evangelical consequence? Do they serve as the impulse for committed study, fellowship, communion, and prayer? Do they catapult us into the divine mission in ever widening circles of witness? Or,

on the other hand, do they keep us insulated from the wider world? Are they private services for our own personal enjoyment? Do they downplay the importance of such matters as disciplines of the Spirit, growth as a covenant community of faith, and being schooled in the heritage of the faith? Do they simply make us want to come back for more of the same kind of experience instead of sending us forth to dissimilar kinds of people?

A Word about Singing

Colossians 3:16 says, "with gratitude in your hearts sing psalms, hymns, and spiritual songs." Psalms are poetic recitations about the ways of God; hymns are musical confessions about the nature of God; spiritual songs are melodious articulations about the experience of God. Paul does not present these as options, but as the wholesome range of the church's singing. It is assumed that our singing should include all three: poetic recitations about the ways of God, the more didactic and presumably carefully crafted confessions of faith, and devotionally expressive articulations which, springing from the heart, as they do, give less thought to poetic style or didactic content and more to personal experience. The spiritually robust church will have all three: the songs of the poets, the songs of the theologians, and the songs of the testifiers. It needs the songs of the Bible, the songs of the ages, and the songs of the moment. It needs the songs of pilgrimage, the songs of revelation, and the songs of experience. It needs songs that express the soul, songs that stretch the mind, and songs that rejoice the heart. It needs Bible songs, hymn-book songs, and chorus songs. It needs songs from its own tradition, songs from other traditions, and songs of no tradition.

A Word about the Reading of Scripture

We often forget that the books of the Bible were written for public reading to the people of God. In Colossians 4:16 Paul instructs: "And when this letter has been read among you, have it read also in the church of the Laodiceans; and see that you read also the letter from Laodicea." Indications of the importance of the role of public reader are found in passages such as Matthew 24:15 which parenthetically says, "Let the reader understand," and Revelation 1:3 with its special blessing: "Blessed is the one who reads aloud the words of the prophecy, and blessed are those who hear and who keep what is written in it."

The private reading of scripture is an additional blessing which by God's grace we modern people enjoy, but we do well not to leave it at that. Scripture is experienced in a different way when it is addressed to the people of God, i.e., to Israel and to the church, as was originally the case. We all need to have the biblical message addressed to us within the context of the gathering of God's people, for then it is that we may begin hearing it not as a private word addressed to us individually but as the public word to God's people as a whole.

Those churches are to be commended which place a high priority on the public reading of the scriptures in their services of worship. Many churches read through all segments of the Bible in the course of a three year period. They follow what is known as a lectionary, which is a list of compatible readings for every week of the year. Quite often the combination is a reading from the psalms, a reading from other books in the Old Testament, a reading from the Gospels, and a reading from one of the other books in the New Testament.[7]

A Word about Proclamation

When we speak of proclamation in connection with worship services, we usually think first and foremost of the sermon, and that certainly is understandable. (See chapter 10 on *The Church Preaching the Good News*.) However, those who strictly limit proclamation to the sermon alone need to be reminded that the New Testament speaks also of the Lord's supper as a proclamation. In 1 Corinthians 11:26 Paul says, "For as often as you eat this bread and drink the cup, you proclaim the Lord's death until he comes."

The Lord's supper is a proclamation by the church as a whole. It is not a private devotional exercise as is implied by a practice recently developed in some churches, of so-called "come and go communion" which treats the Lord's supper as though it were a private devotional experience. Instead, the holy meal is a corporate proclamation of the church's faith in the redemptive work of Christ.

The Lord's supper serves to remind us of the essential character of all truly Christian preaching, namely, that regardless of the subject, text, concern, or occasion, it is to be a proclamation of the good news of the redemptive work of Christ.

A Word about Prayers

Corporate prayer is the church's direct conversational communion with the Lord. New Testament instructions about prayer (e.g., Eph. 6:18–19; Phil. 4:6; Col. 4:2; 2 Tim. 2:1–2), requests for prayer (e.g., 2 Thess. 3:1–2), commitments to prayer (e.g., Eph. 3:14–21), examples of prayers (e.g., Acts 4:24–30; Eph. 3:16–21), and benedictory prayers (e.g., 1 Thess. 5:23; Jude 24–25) — all remind us of the importance of prayer in the life of the New Testament church.

The biblical assumption is that even when one person is voicing the prayer in a public service, it is to be an expression not simply of that one individual, but of the whole church. The Hebrew word "Amen," meaning "firm" or "established," was the Jewish congregation's way to participate in the prayer. It indicated that they claimed the prayer, though spoken by one individual, as their own. For instance, we find in Nehemiah 8:6 that when Ezra blessed the Lord, all the people answered, "Amen, Amen," thereby signifying that it was not merely Ezra's private prayer in a public place, but theirs.

In the New Testament, we see the continuation of the congregational use of the Amen. Paul, addressing the Corinthians about the inappropriateness of prayers which are unintelligible to others in the congregation, asks in 1 Corinthians 14:16: "If you say a blessing with the spirit, how can anyone in the position of an outsider say the 'Amen' to your thanksgiving, since the outsider does not know what you are saying?"

Those churches are to be commended which use the participatory Amen in prayer, whether it is a spontaneous Amen uttered by individuals during the prayer itself, or the unified congregational Amen at the close of the prayer, or both. It is unfortunate when congregations no longer participate in public prayers by using the biblical Amen. Often the result of this absence is that the congregation tends to think that even the pastoral prayer is little more than the prayer of an individual offered in a public place; consequently, the corporate experience of the whole church being at prayer is almost always lost.

A Word about the Offering

Second Corinthians 8 and 9 is a treatise on the stewardship of resources in relation to the life of the church. To be sure, it is a discourse about the collection of money for those in need, but it is much more; it is a statement about the priority of giving oneself to the Lord.

Too often it is the case that offering time is simply money time; that, however, is to overlook the New Testament teaching about the giving of oneself and the whole of one's resources. In 8:5, Paul, referring to the Macedonian believers, says that "they gave themselves first to the Lord and, by the will of God, to us." This, of course, is in line with Paul's plea in Romans 12:1 for us to present our bodies as a living sacrifice, holy and acceptable to God, which, he says, is our spiritual worship. Some Christian traditions emphasize this by having an altar call usually near the end of the service. Growing out of the American camp meeting tradition, it is an invitation both to Christian discipleship and for consecrating oneself to the Lord. The strength of this tradition is that it places high priority on the offering of the self. The weakness is that the monetary offering is disconnected from the offering of the self, so that offering time degenerates into little more than an interlude during worship for the collection of money. It is possible, of course, for both times to be opportunities for personal response. In some instances, churches have placed the monetary offering at the end of the service along with the altar call in order to maintain the connection. Understood from a biblical perspective, offering time is for the renewal of the covenant of Christian discipleship which is, as Mark emphasizes, to take up one's cross and follow the Lord.

A Word about the Passing of the Peace

In the New Testament, the word of peace is an important component of interpersonal relations among Christians. First Peter 5:14 instructs the church, saying, "Greet one another with a kiss of love. Peace to all of you who are in Christ." (Other passages indicating the importance in biblical religion, of the word of peace are especially Num. 6:24–26, and in the New Testament: Luke 10:1–12; 24:36; John 14:27; 20:19, 21, 26; Rom. 1:7; 15:33; 1 Cor. 1:3; 2 Cor. 1:2; Gal. 1:3; Eph. 1:2; 6:23; Phil.

1:2; Col. 1:2; 1 Thess. 1:2; 2 Thess. 2:2; 3:16; 1 Tim. 1:2; 2 Tim. 1:2; Titus 1:4; Philem. 3; 1 Peter 1:2; 2 Peter 1:2; 2 John 3; 3 John 13; Jude 2; Rev. 1:4.)

Those churches are to be commended which teach their people how to give each other the greeting of peace. In many churches, an important element of every service is the "passing of the peace," during which time the worship leader says to the congregation something like, "The peace of the Lord be with you" and the congregation responds, "And with you." Then the leader says, "Let us share the peace of Christ with each other," after which the whole assembly immediately begins moving about saying to each other, "The peace of Christ be with you," and giving signs of peace such as clasping hands, embracing, giving holy kisses. This general movement of the congregation proceeds sometimes for as long as two or three minutes.

This distinctive greeting serves as a reminder that the church is more than a group of people who are merely being friendly with each other as they say a casual, "Hello, how are you?" The passing of the peace in the name of Christ is a mark of a Christian gathering.

A Word about Good Order

As Paul dealt with the disorder in the Corinthian church, he gave a pronouncement that has served the church well ever since: "All things should be done decently and in order" (1 Cor. 14:40). From the approach taken in the section leading up to this verse we conclude that he did not mean to rule out spontaneity; rather, his purpose is to insist that spontaneity should always build up the church and never be simply for the purpose of personal satisfaction, regardless of how gratifying it may be for some in the church. The sufficient question never is, Does someone want to do thus and so? but, Will this build up the church as a whole?

Good order should not rule out spontaneity, nor should spontaneity ever be unedifying to the church as a whole. Paul's words strike a wise balance: "When you come together, each one has a hymn, a lesson, a revelation, a tongue, or an interpretation. Let all things be done for building up" (1 Cor. 14:26).[8]

The church at services of worship is called to be a gathering of disciples in communion with their Lord—the only one whose worship is flawless; it is to be the congregation of those who are open to the Spirit's empowerment for becoming the worshiping beings they were created to be.

Notes

1. The general schema of this chapter is found also in my "Biblical Foundations for Worship," *Worship the Lord Hymnal Companion* (Anderson, Ind: Warner,1992), p. A37–49.

2. See Peter Brunner, *Worship in the Name of Jesus,* trans. M. H. Bertram (St. Louis: Concordia, 1968), Introduction.

3. Ibid. p. 12f. Also, Theodore W. Jennings, *Life as Worship: Prayer and Praise in Jesus' Name* (Grand Rapids: Eerdmans, 1982).

4. Herman Ridderbos, *Paul: An Outline of His Theology,* trans. John Richard De Witt (Grand Rapids: Eerdmans, 1975), p. 421.

5. *Baptism, Eucharist and Ministry, Faith and Order Paper No. 111* (Geneva: World Council of Churches, 1982), p. 11.

6. For a study of this passage, see J. Robert Nelson, *Criterion for the Church* (New York: Abingdon, n.d.).

7. One of many places to find a lectionary is in Robert E. Webber, *Worship Old and New* (Grand Rapids: Zondervan, 1982), pp. 213–222. Also, Reginald Fuller, *Preaching the Lectionary* (Collegeville: Liturgical, 1984).

8. See *Biblical Guidelines for the Local Church, The Report of the Study Committee on Glossolalia (Tongues),* Adopted by the General Assembly of the Church of God, June

1986, Anderson, Indiana. Published by Warner Press. Includes six general guidelines for maintaining good order when dealing with issues of corporate worship.

For Further Consideration

A. Theology

The cruciality of worship in all dimensions of theology is underscored by Geoffrey Wainwright who has written a systematic theology through the prism of worship: *Doxology: The Praise of God in Worship, Doctrine, and Life* (New York: Oxford, 1980).

B. Old Testament

For an excellent treatment of Old Testament worship, see Walter Brueggemann, *Israel's Praise* (Philadelphia: Fortress, 1989). Another excellent resource which includes a chapter on worship in the Old Testament as well as a more extensive treatment of worship in various portions of the New Testament (e.g., Acts, Paul, Hebrews, Revelation) is David Peterson, *Engaging With God: A Biblical Theology of Worship* (Grand Rapids: Eerdmans, 1992).

C. New Testament

New Testament worship is treated helpfully in Ralph P. Martin, *Worship in the Early Church* (Grand Rapids: Eerdmans, 1976).

D. Historical Works

Two definitive historical works regarding the liturgical life of the church are Dom Gregory Dix, *The Shape of the Liturgy* (Westminster: Dacre, 1954) and Bard Thompson, *Liturgies of the Western Church* (New York: New American Library, 1961); two much shorter historical works are James F. White, *Introduction to Christian Worship* (Nashville: Abingdon, 1990) and Robert Webber, *Worship: Old and New* (Grand Rapids: Zondervan, 1994). Additional resources are Webber (ed.), *The Renewal of Sunday Worship* (Nashville: Star Song Group, 1993), Vol. 3 in his seven volume *Complete Library of Christian Worship,* and White, *Documents of Christian Worship: Descriptive and Interpretive Sources* (Louisville: Westminster/John Knox, 1992). Also, for ethnic studies, see Melva Wilson Costen and Darius Leander Swann (eds.), "The Black Christian Worship Experience: A Consultation," *The Journal of the Interdenominational Theological Center* Vol. XIV, Nos. 1 and 2 (Fall 1986/Spring 1987), and Costen, *African American Christian Worship* (Nashville: Abingdon, 1993).

E. Holy Meals

For a study of two different traditions of holy meals in the New Testament, one emphasizing the joy of the Lord's presence and the other, his salvific work, see "The Meaning of the Lord's Supper in Primitive

Christianity" by Oscar Cullmann, in *Essays on the Lord's Supper*, trans. J. G. Davies (Atlanta: John Knox, 1958). In the same volume is a helpful monograph titled "This Is My Body" by F. J. Leenhardt. He writes:

> Jesus Christ chooses this bread to serve as an expression of His will to continue His presence with His disciples beyond the separation. He will be seen no more, but His presence will continue, and it will continue to be as now, corporal. By the choice which He makes of it and the will which He expresses in regard to it, this bread becomes the organ of expression of His person and of its communication to others, His body.
>
> (p. 42)

For another approach to the differing traditions of holy meals in the new Testament, see chap. 3, "The New Testament Banquet: Improving on a Common Theme" in Dennis E. Smith and Hal E. Taussig, *Many Tables: The Eucharist in the New Testament and Liturgy Today* (Philadelphia: Trinity Press International, 1990). While their application to the present state of the church is, in my view, seriously flawed, their discussion of the New Testament material itself is enlightening.

Also, see the Eucharist section of *Baptism, Eucharist and Ministry, Faith and Order Paper No. 111* (Geneva: World Council of Churches, 1982).

Other helpful resources are: Horton Davies, *Bread of*

Life and Cup of Joy (Grand Rapids: Eerdmans, 1993); Alasdair I. C. Heron, *Table and Tradition* (Philadelphia: Westminster, 1983); Joachim Jeremias, *The Eucharistic Words of Jesus*, trans. Norman Perrin (Philadelphia: Fortress, 1966); Gary Macy, *The Banquet's Wisdom: A Short History of the Theologies of the Lord's Supper* (New York: Paulist, 1992); I. Howard Marshall, *Last Supper and Lord's Supper* (Grand Rapids: Eerdmans, 1980); Max Thurian, *The Mystery of the Eucharist: An Ecumenical Approach*, trans. Emily Chisholm (Grand Rapids: Eerdmans, 1983).

A reference book containing representative articles generated within the restoration movement—associated with the names of Thomas and Alexander Campbell and emphasizing the importance of coming to the Lord's table each Lord's Day—is Charles R. Gresham and Tom Larson, (eds.), *The Lord's Supper: Historical Writings on Its Meaning to the Body of Christ* (Joplin: College Press, 1993).

For a theological analysis of a group which does not give high priority to weekly participation, see my "The Lord's Supper and the Church of God," *Centering on Ministry*, published by The Center for Pastoral Studies, Anderson University School of Theology. Vol. 12, No. 3 (Spring 1987), 2–4. Also published under the title, "A Thankful Review of Communion," VITAL CHRISTIANITY,

Vol. 106, No. 18 (November 23, 1986), 10–12.

For the eschatological dimension of the Lord's Supper, see Geoffrey Wainwright, *Eucharist and Eschatology* (New York: Oxford University Press, 1981).

F. The Public Nature of Corporate Worship

Patrick R. Keifert, *Welcoming the Stranger: A Public Theology of Worship and Evangelism* (Minneapolis: Fortress, 1992).

Frank C. Senn, *The Witness of the Worshiping Community: Liturgy and the Practice of Evangelism* (New York: Paulist, 1993).

G. Components of Worship

For a consideration of various components of worship services, see C. Welton Gaddy, *The Gift of Worship* (Nashville: Broadman, 1992). In Part III, Gaddy discusses the following: gathering, praising, listening, praying, confessing, proclaiming, singing, offering, and departing.

H. Music

Fred R. Anderson, *Singing Psalms of Joy and Praise* (Philadelphia: Westminster, 1982).

Friedrich Blume, *Protestant Church Music: A History* (London: Victor Gollancz, 1975).

Harry Eskew and Hugh T. McElrath, *Sing with Understanding: An Introduction to Christian Hymnology* (Nashville: Broadman, 1980).

DeVon W. Helbling, *A Story of Christian Song* (Portland, OR: Bible Press,1991).

Donald P. Hustad, *Jubilate! Church Music in the Evangelical Tradition* (Carol Stream: Hope, 1981).

Calvin M. Johansson, *Discipling Music Ministry: Twenty-first Century Directions* (Peabody: Hendrickson, 1992).

James Rawlings Snydor, *Hymns and Their Uses: A Guide to Improved Congregational Singing* (Carol Stream: Agape, 1982).

Jan Michael Spencer, *Protest and Praise: Sacred Music of Black Religion* (Minneapolis: Fortress, 1990).

I. Scripture Reading

Thomas Edward McComiskey, *Reading Scripture in Public* (Grand Rapids, 1991).

E. H. Van Olst, *The Bible and Liturgy*, trans. John Vriend (Grand Rapids: Eerdmans, 1991).

William H. Willimon, *The Bible: A Sustaining Presence in Worship* (Valley Forge: Judson, 1981).

J. Prayer

A classic practical theology of corporate prayer is Andrew W. Blackwood, *Leading in Public Prayer* (New York: Abingdon, 1958). Superb examples of pastoral prayers are those by James A. Jones, *Prayers for the People* (Richmond: John Knox, 1967) and James G. Kirk, *When We Gather* (Philadelphia: Geneva, 1983, 1984).

22

Praying People

The Christian's deepest relationship with God, strongest link with others and greatest contribution to the upbuilding of the body of Christ is prayer. It is our way of being connected to God for the good of the world; it is God's design for divine-human partnership; it is the divine way for us to participate in heavenly plans for earthly purposes. Prayer is that activity by which we live up to our full potential as creatures in the image of God. As Eugene Peterson puts it: "The primary use of prayer is not for expressing ourselves, but in becoming ourselves."[1]

Eight Definitions of Prayer

In this chapter we shall consider eight definitions of Christian prayer.

1. Prayer as an Overflowing Fountain

Prayer is an overflowing fountain of praise, adoration, and thanksgiving to God. This is the kind of prayer we find Mary the mother of Jesus offering during her visit with Elizabeth. Mary had been "much perplexed" (Luke 1:29) about being chosen for the special vocation of serving as the mother of our Lord. Having submitted to the divine plan, she visited Elizabeth who was pregnant with John the Baptist.

As the two women greeted each other, the child in Elizabeth's womb "leaped for joy" (v. 44), after which Mary offered a prayer of jubilation — the so-called Magnificat, first word in the Latin hymnic translation of it — about the mighty deeds of God (see Luke 1:46–55). She expressed amazement at the providential care of God who had surprised her by divine grace, had blessed her beyond measure, and had poured out favor upon her with such abundance that her soul could not contain it. In grateful response, she burst forth with lyrics of gratitude and exultation: "My soul magnifies the Lord, and my spirit rejoices in God my Savior."

This kind of prayer erupts without hesitation from the soul. One does not have to make oneself do it, for it comes as naturally as breathing. Mary's exultation in God's presence was in response to the Spirit's work (1:35), was guided by the divine word (vv. 30–33), and was in continuity with the history of faith (vv. 32–33).

When, on the day of Pentecost, the disciples were filled with the Holy Spirit, Acts 2:11 says that the visitors in Jerusalem heard them speaking in all the languages represented there "about God's deeds of power" (v. 11). From all indications, it was not a formal liturgy of prayer, but an eruption of love for God; it was the gushing forth of exultation from hearts enkindled by the divine Spirit (2:4) and from minds attuned to the divine word (1:3) and from wills devoted to living in continuity with the divine history of faith (1:4-8,14; 2:1).

This kind of prayer becomes a regular and dynamic part of one's life only to the extent that one is open to the Spirit and Word and open to the challenge of living in the flow of God's plan. It is only the Holy Spirit who can burst one's heart with praise; it is only the hearing of God's Word that can stimulate one's mind with adoration; it is only the awareness that this is a divine moment in history and the willingness to be a part of it that can bring one into truly humble exultation. "The breath that God breathes into us in daily pentecosts is breathed out in our prayers, 'telling in our own tongues the mighty works of God.'"[2]

2. Prayer as Disciplined Communion

Prayer is disciplined communion with God. We find

547

this in the model prayer which Jesus gave to his disciples, commonly referred to as the Lord's Prayer (Matt. 6:9–13 and Luke 11:2–4; see For Further Consideration, Section C). In Luke, the prayer is given after one of the disciples makes the request, "Lord, teach us to pray, as John taught his disciples" (v.1).

It was commonplace in Jesus' day for rabbis and other religious leaders to teach their followers how to organize their prayers and to give instructions about their content. These so-called "Index Prayers,"[3] served as outlines for what were considered to be well-rounded prayers.

In this model prayer, Jesus gives his disciples an "index" for disciplined communion with God. It is to include:

1) the recognition that God is our heavenly Father,

2) worship and adoration of God,

3) readiness and willingness for the reign and rule of God,

4) submission to the divine will and purposes,

5) recognition of our dependence on God for the supply of our daily needs,

6) humble acceptance of God's forgiveness linked with our forgiveness of others,

7) the solemn plea for God's watchcare as we encounter the devil's temptations.[4]

This, then, is our Lord's index for disciplined prayer. The mere repetition of the words, however, is not sufficient. Instead, we are to fulfill the prayer by sincerely relating to God as loving parent, by faithfully worshiping and adoring God, by confidently opening ourselves to the heavenly kingdom, by trustingly submitting our lives to God, by genuinely relying on God to supply our daily needs, by wholeheartedly believing that God forgives and expects us to be forgiving people, and by assuredly counting on God to keep us from the wiles of the devil. The Lord's Prayer is not a magical formula for good luck, but a guide for the kind of disciplined prayer life his followers are to have.

3. Prayer as the Flow of Divine Energy

Prayer is the flow of divine energy to the needs of others. We see this preeminently in the life of our Lord who was able to speak words of healing to the sick and distressed, thereby bringing to them strength and wholeness. Mark 7:31–35 says:

> Then he [Jesus] returned from the region of Tyre, and went by way of Sidon towards the Sea of Galilee, in the region of the Decapolis. They brought to him a deaf man who had an impediment in his speech; and they begged him to lay his hand on him. He took him aside in private, away from the crowd, and put his fingers

into his ears, and he spat and touched his tongue. Then looking up to heaven, he sighed and said to him, 'Ephphatha,' that is, 'Be opened.' And immediately his ears were opened, and his tongue was released, and he spoke plainly.

Our Lord, being in perfect communion with the heavenly Father, was the channel by which healing energy flowed into the deaf man's body, making him well.

Jesus' sighing, spoken of in v. 34, is of interest in relation to the prayerful sighing mentioned in Romans 8:26 where Paul refers to the Holy Spirit in us interceding "with sighs too deep for words." Our Lord sighed in his intercessory work in the same way that the Holy Spirit sighs in intercessory work in and through us. Mark, in his description of Jesus' intercessory work, says that "looking up to heaven, he sighed." Then when Jesus spoke words of grace, divine healing flowed into the body of the deaf man so that "immediately his ears were opened, his tongue was released, and he spoke plainly."

What may be our role in such praying? Even though we are not eternal sons and daughters of God, can we, nevertheless, be prayer channels through which the divine energy flows to the needs of others? Acts indicates that we can be. Chapter 9 tells the story about Peter going to the town of Joppa where a disciple named Tabitha—her Aramaic name, Dorcas being her

Greek name—had died. When he arrived on the scene, he put all of the mourners out of the room whereupon he "knelt down and prayed. He turned to her and said, 'Tabitha, get up.' Then she opened her eyes, and seeing Peter, she sat up. He gave her his hand and helped her up. Then calling the saints and widows, he showed her to be alive." Peter at prayer became a channel through which divine life flowed into the body of Tabitha, raising her from death.

In chapter 28 we find another example of this kind of occurrence. When Paul, having been shipwrecked, found himself on the island of Malta, he visited Publius, the leading man of the island, whose father was ill with a fever and dysentery. Verse 8 says that "Paul visited him and cured him by praying and putting his hands on him." Verse 9 reads: "After this happened, the rest of the people on the island who had diseases also came and were cured."

In both instances, prayer was the flow of divine energy to the needs of others. Just how strong this flow was is indicated by two other remarkable accounts. Acts 5:15 tells about people bringing the sick and placing them on cots and mats in the street "in order that Peter's shadow might fall on some of them as he came by." The same kind of phenomenon took place in relation to Paul's prayer life. According to Acts 19:11–12,

"God did extraordinary miracles through Paul, so that when the handkerchiefs or aprons that had touched his skin were brought to the sick, their diseases left them, and the evil spirits came out of them."

Of course, this kind of phenomena can be counterfeited. Jesus, in Matthew 7:15–16a, says "Beware of false prophets, who come to you in sheep's clothing but inwardly are ravenous wolves. You will know them by their fruits." Some who give the appearance of having the same kind of divine power spoken of in Acts do not bear the fruit of Christ. While they appear to perform miracles, the way they live does not conform to the pattern of humble discipleship. Instead of being under the discipline of Christ and his church, they are independent of all biblical authority and function as free-lance manipulators of the miraculous for personal gain, popularity, and self-interest. They are wolves in sheep's clothing.

All Christians, regardless of popularity or status, are to be measured by Galatians 5 which lists the works of the flesh as "fornication, impurity, licentiousness, idolatry, sorcery, enmities, strife, jealousy, anger, quarrels, dissensions, factions, envy, drunkenness, carousing." Such people, the apostle says, "will not inherit the kingdom of God." The works of the flesh are evidence that persons are not of God.

Instead, it is the fruit of the Spirit which verifies Godliness: "love, joy, peace, patience, kindness, generosity, faithfulness, gentleness, and self-control." Whereas Paul refers to the works (plural) of the flesh, he refers to the fruit (singular) of the Spirit. Any one of the works identifies one as being not of God, but to be truly of the Spirit means that all characteristics of the fruit are in evidence, for they are all of a piece.

Assuming the foregoing about the fruit of the Spirit, we feel free, therefore, to hold that truly faithful disciples, characterized by the fruit of the Spirit, are to be channels of divinely miraculous power so that others will experience a positive change when in their presence. Does anyone want to lie in our "shadows" as they did Peter's? Do we make any positive difference on "Maltas" the way Paul did? It all depends on whether our prayer life is inspired by the Holy Spirit, is rooted in the biblical word, and is in continuity with God's work through God's people. That is the secret to being conduits of the healing and helping power of God.[5]

4. Prayer as the Struggle of the Soul

Prayer is the struggle of the soul in relation to God.[6] Genesis 32:22–32 tells about Jacob wrestling with a divine emissary at Peniel. In v. 28, the emissary says to him, "You shall no longer be called Jacob, but Israel, for you have striven with God and with humans, and have prevailed." In fact, in the struggle between Jacob and the divine emissary, Jacob's hip socket was put out of joint causing him to leave Peniel with a limp.

Prayer is not always a pretty business. It sometimes leaves us with a limp. In Job, we find another man who, in a mighty struggle of soul, developed a "limp"; in 42:6 he says, "Therefore I despise myself, and repent in dust and ashes."

The Psalms contain many examples of this kind of prayer. For instance, Psalm 88 is from beginning to end a prayerful expression of a struggling soul. Verses 1-3 read: "O Lord, God of my salvation, when, at night, I cry out in your presence, let my prayer come before you; incline your ear to my cry. For my soul is full of troubles, and my life draws near to Sheol." The prayer ends with a spiritual "limp" in v. 18 when the psalmist says to God "You have caused friend and neighbor to shun me; my companions are in darkness."

In the New Testament, we find the same kind of prayer. Both Mary and Joseph struggled with God about the unusual circumstances surrounding her pregnancy (see Matt. 1:18–25 and Luke 1:26–38); after Jesus' birth, they continued struggling with God as to what they should do about Herod's attempt to kill their child (see Matt. 2:13–23).

However, it is preeminently our Lord who experienced this kind of prayer. On the night before he was crucified, he cried out as he struggled in Gethsemane, saying, "My Father, if it is possible, let this cup pass from me, yet not what I want but what you want" (Matt. 26:39). He told his disciples, "I am deeply grieved, even to death" (v. 38). The next day, the struggle continued on the cross when in the darkest moment of human history, Jesus cried out "My God, my God, why have you forsaken me?" (27:46).

Even as Jacob left Peniel limping with a hip out of joint, even so our Lord was wounded in the midst of the most momentous struggle since the beginning of time, and he, also, had marks to show for it. When Thomas doubted that Christ was indeed risen from the dead, Jesus stretched forth his hands and showed him the nail scars, whereupon Thomas cried out, "My Lord and my God!" (John 20:28). It was the wounds suffered in the struggle that led Thomas to faith.

We find another example of this kind of prayer in 2 Corinthians 12 where Paul speaks of his thorn in the flesh. Verses 8 and 9 describes his struggle: "Three times I appealed to the Lord about this, that it would leave me, but he said to me, 'My grace is sufficient for you, for power is made perfect in weakness.'" Thus, Paul, like his Lord, knew that prayer was, among other things, also the struggle of the human soul with God. In his prayer life, he was very much in company with Mary and Joseph and with the troubled psalmist and with forefather Jacob who ended up with a limp.

He was in prayer fellowship with both Job and all others who struggle mightily in prayer. He came to realize that from time to time these struggles leave us limping, wailing, and perhaps even crucified for the sake of the kingdom. In fact, sometimes the struggle is so great that we cannot sort it out well enough even to put the struggle into words. Prayer at those times is simply the wordless anguish of the soul in the presence of God, as in Romans 8:26–27:

> Likewise the Spirit helps us in our weakness; for we do not know how to pray as we ought, but that very Spirit intercedes with sighs too deep for words. And God, who searches the heart, knows what is the mind of the Spirit, because the Spirit intercedes for the saints according to the will of God.

5. Prayer as the Mind Seeking God's Mind

Prayer is the human mind seeking the mind of God. James 1:5–8 says:

> If any of you is lacking in wisdom, ask God, who gives to all generously and ungrudgingly, and it will be given you. But ask in faith, never doubting, for the one who

doubts is like a wave of the sea, driven and tossed by the wind; for the doubter, being double-minded and unstable in every way, must not expect to receive anything from the Lord.

Even though God will give heavenly wisdom to us "generously and ungrudgingly," in order to have it, we must "ask in faith." In James, the opposite of faith is doubt. Doubt is a matter of coming to God double mindedly. Those who approach God not quite certain whether God exists, and even if such is the case, are not sure whether God actually answers prayer, and even if perchance God does answer, they are not convinced that they are important enough for the divine will to be made known to them, and even if God does make the divine will known, they wonder whether it would be good news or bad—those who approach God in this way "must not expect to receive anything from the Lord."

In Matthew 7:7–8, Jesus says:

Ask, and it will be given you; search, and you will find; knock, and the door will be opened for you. For everyone who asks receives, and everyone who searches finds, and for everyone who knocks, the door will be opened.

There are times when prayer is primarily a matter of

depleted feelings, and other times when it is a matter of an inquiring mind. The first is God praying through us; the second is God speaking to us. The first is the soul in a stupor; the second is the soul in puzzlement. The first is the prayer of last resort; the second is the prayer of initial choice. The first has to do with the feeling that there are no options; the second has to do with the desire to know which option. Whichever is the case at any particular time, we can be sure that God is always willing to meet us when we come in earnestness of spirit. Jesus taught that we "need to pray always and not to lose heart" (Luke 18:1).

6) Prayer as Intercession[7]

Prayer is intercession to God on behalf of others. In a general sense, to intercede is to put ourselves in the place of others and to plead their case before one who can help them. In intercessory prayer, therefore, appeal is made to God who can make a difference for the good.

In Mark 2, we have an example of enacted intercession. Jesus had returned to Capernaum. Upon hearing that he was back, a great crowd gathered at the house where he was staying. Verses 3–5 read:

> Then some people came, bringing to him a paralyzed man, carried by four of them. And when they could not bring him to Jesus because of the crowd, they removed

the roof above him; and after having dug through it, they let down the mat on which the paralytic lay. When Jesus saw their faith, he said to the paralytic, "Son, your sins are forgiven."

Later, in v. 11, he says to the same man, "Stand up, take your mat and go to your home." Verse 12 says that "he stood up, and immediately took the mat and went out before all of them."

That was intercessory prayer in action. Those who brought the paralytic were convinced that Jesus could heal him; therefore, they did for him what he could not do for himself. They were persistent about bringing him into the presence of Jesus, so much so that when they could not gain entrance through the door, they tore up the roof. They had the faith, did the work, and were the intercessors; the paralytic was the beneficiary of their faith and of the Lord's grace.

Matthew 4:24 points to other intercessors when it says, "So his [Jesus'] fame spread throughout all Syria, and they brought to him all the sick, those who were afflicted with various diseases and pains, demoniacs, epileptics, and paralytics, and he cured them." Many needy people were made whole because a company of intercessors brought them to the Lord for his compassionate touch. Intercessory faith linked with Christ's healing grace made the difference.

Basic to all of our work as disciples is that of coming to the Lord to intercede on behalf of those in need of saving, keeping, and healing power. In Ephesians 1:19, Paul speaks of "the immeasurable greatness of his power for us who believe." Verse 20: "God put this power to work in Christ when he raised him from the dead and seated him at his right hand in the heavenly places." His point is that the power which raised Jesus from the dead is ours through faith in him. Furthermore, according to 2:18 we have access to the divine source of this resurrection power, and 3:12 says that we can come to God "in boldness and confidence through faith in him [Jesus Christ]."

Christians have the privilege of participating in the divine fellowship of intercession–a fellowship consisting of Jesus Christ who intercedes at the right hand of God (see Rom. 8:34), and the Holy Spirit who intercedes from within those who believe (see Rom. 8:26–27). We have the privilege of joining this intercessory fellowship to intercede for others.

James 5:13–16 reflects the importance of this intercessory work in the life of the first century church. The sick were instructed to call for the elders of the church to anoint them with oil in the name of the Lord and to pray the prayer of faith on their behalf.[8]

Christian intercessory prayer takes place in league

with Jesus Christ, in league with the Holy Spirit, and in league with the worldwide fellowship of believers who are committed to the same intercessory work of the kingdom. While Jesus Christ is at the place of greatest power and the Holy Spirit is at the place of greatest need, we are at the place of greatest faith. This intercessory fellowship brings about heavenly good for earthly benefit. In this divine covenant, Christ, the Spirit, and believers bring together ultimate power, deepest need, and sincerest faith; that is the secret of answered prayer. Prayers are answered by virtue of the "the immeasurable greatness of his power" (Eph. 1:19) linked with the Spirit's "sighs too deep for words" (Rom. 8:26) in conjunction with our "boldness and confidence through faith in him" (Eph. 3:12).

Probably the longest intercessory prayer meeting in history started on August 27, 1727, when twenty-four male and twenty-four female Moravians agreed to spend one in every twenty-four hours in intercessory prayer. Within a short while, the wider membership of the Moravian church entered into this practice, called the "Hourly Intercession," which continued for over a hundred years. John Wesley was greatly influenced by the praying Moravians during a storm at sea enroute to Georgia for missionary service. And it was at a Moravian meeting on Aldersgate Street in London on

May 24, 1738 that he felt his heart "strangely warmed." This period of concerted intercessory prayer was paralleled by great missionary outreach, spiritual revival, and social witness.

7. Prayer as Petition to God

Prayer is petition to God for our own needs. Petitionary prayer which is truly Christian asks God for that which we are convinced is in accordance with the divine will. It is generous in spirit in that personal needs are prayed about in conjunction with concern for the well being of others.

The New Testament teaches the following about petitionary prayer: *First, that God knows what we need even before we ask.* In Matthew 6:7–8, our Lord says:

> When you are praying, do not heap up empty phrases as the Gentiles do; for they think that they will be heard because of their many words. Do not be like them, for your Father knows what you need before you ask him.

Our prayers do not have to be detailed documents with all of the specifications spelled out as to exactly what we need and why we need it. We do not have to be experts at composing long requisitional essays. In our daily lives we often have to expend a great deal of time and energy making our case to others in hopes that they will give us what we think we need, but not so with God. Before we ask, God knows what we need.

Second, God wants us to ask for that which is good. In Matthew 7:11, Jesus says, "If you then, who are evil, know how to give good gifts to your children, how much more will your Father in heaven give good things to those who ask him." We can take it from this that if we ask for something which is not granted, it must not be good for us.

Third, we are to ask in the name of Jesus. John has a great deal to say about this. In 14:13–14, Jesus says, "I will do whatever you ask in my name, so that the Father may be glorified in the Son. If in my name you ask me for anything, I will do it." To ask in the name of Jesus is not a matter of using his name as a magical fetish. Instead, it is to be so attuned to the life of Christ that our hearts are at one with his heart, our minds with his mind, our purposes with his purposes, and our desires with his desires. To ask in Christ's name requires us to be in spiritual harmony with him; it means that we ask for that which God wills to accomplish through us as persons committed to the continuation of the incarnational ministry of Jesus Christ.

All of this, of course, assumes that we are lively branches of the Christ vine spoken of in John 15. Verse 7 says, "If you abide in me, and my words abide in you,

ask for whatever you wish, and it will be done for you."
To ask in the name of Christ is to ask as one who is
abiding in Christ and through whom, therefore, the
Christ life is flowing. If we are not members of the
Christ vine, the mere tacking on of the words "In the
name of Jesus" at the end of a petitionary prayer has no
power whatsoever. To pray in the name of Jesus is to
pray under the weight of his cross; it is to pray with
Gethsemane relinquishment, "nevertheless not my will
but thine be done"; and at times it is to pray even as he
did on the cross when he cried out, " My God, My God,
why have you forsaken me?"

We must remember, however, that the story of Jesus
continues on to Easter morning. Therefore, to pray in
the name of Jesus is also to pray in resurrection
power—power which can defeat evil, power which
gives birth to newness of life, power which brings healing and wholeness.

*The fourth lesson about petitionary prayer is that we have
not because we ask not.* James deals with this issue when
in chapter 4 he speaks about the selfish desires of
Christian people. They work feverishly to have those
desires gratified and for evil purposes. In condemning
them for such greediness, he calls them "adulterers" (v.
4). He says: "You do not have, because you do not ask.
You ask and do not receive, because you ask wrongly,

in order to spend what you get on your pleasures." Often we have not that which is good because we do not ask for it; we are too busy asking for that which is selfish. God wills for us to have that which is good, but God wants us to want it.

8. Prayer as Watchful Communion with the Lord

Prayer is watchful communion with the Lord, which communion keeps us from yielding to temptation. On the night before his crucifixion, our Lord said to the disciples: "Keep awake and pray that you may not come into the time of trial; the spirit indeed is willing, but the flesh is weak" (Mark 14:38). Later that night the disciples deserted their Lord (v. 50), and Peter openly denied him (vv. 66–72).

To watch and pray is work; we need to do more than simply have noble spiritual intentions about not yielding to temptation. To be sure, Peter, on the night of Jesus' arrest, expressed noble intentions about not deserting him, but the problem was that neither he nor the others were watching and praying. They were too weary to be spiritually vigilant.

Paul says that we should pray without ceasing (1 Thess. 5:17) and then, a few verses later, urges us to "test everything; hold fast to what is good; abstain from every form of evil." To live that kind of life is to discover what it means for prayer to be watchful communion with the Lord; it necessitates praying without ceasing. Only in this way are disciples kept from yielding to temptation.

Conclusion

The life of prayer is multidimensional. The trouble is that some of us want one or more dimensions but not all. For instance, we may want to experience prayer as the flow of divine energy to others but not prayer as the struggle of the soul. That is to deny the fullness of the prayer life to which we are called. Such a denial inevitably leads to a sub-Christian experience of prayer. As disciples of our Lord, we are called to a full orbed prayer life including both the effervescence of its power and the trepidation of its struggles. In a full orbed prayer life we experience both respite and challenge, both joy and anguish, both confidence and questions, both knowns and unknowns, both light and darkness. Jesus invites us to the life of prayer in all of its fullness.

To have a prayer life that is pleasing to God is to have one's eyes opened to the glory of God; it is to care about God's whole world; it is to be connected with resources beyond our human resources; it is to be united both with God and with persons far beyond our immediate locations. It is to be in a position to be surprised by the

One to whom Paul prayed in Ephesians 3:20-21: "Now to him who by the power at work within us is able to accomplish abundantly far more than all we can ask or imagine, to him be glory in the church and Christ Jesus to all generations, forever and ever. Amen."

Notes

1. Eugene H. Peterson, *Answering God: The Psalms As Tools for Prayer* (San Francisco: Harper, 1991), p. 19.

2. Ibid.,p. 60.

3. A term used by F. J. Burgess and D. B. Proudlove, *Watching unto Prayer* quoted in Herbert Lockyer, *All the Prayers of the Bible* (Grand Rapids: Zondervan,1979), p. 192.

4. For this general schema I am indebted to Herbert Lockyer who identifies seven voices in the Matthean prayer: (1) The Voice of the Son – "Our Father in heaven," (2) The Voice of the Saint – "Hallowed be your name," (3) The Voice of the Subject – "Your kingdom come," (4) The Voice of the Servant – "Your will be done," (5) The Voice of the Suppliant – "Give us this day our daily bread," (6) The Voice of the Sinner – "Forgive us our debts" and (7) The Voice of the Sojourner – "Do not bring us to the time of trial," op. cit., p. 192.

5. For a philosophical and historical critique of the idea of miracle, see Colin Brown, *Miracles and the Critical Mind* (Grand Rapids: Eerdmans, 1984).

6. See Donald G. Bloesch, *The Struggle of Prayer* (San Francisco: Harper and Row, 1980).

7. For a helpful treatment of this subject, see the chapter titled "Represented by Counsel (Intercession)" in Charles Ewing Brown, *The Way of Prayer* (Anderson, Ind: Warner, 1940), pp. 135–155. Also, the classic, Andrew Murray, *The Ministry of Intercession* (New York: Revell, 1898).

8. See Morris Maddocks, *The Christian Healing Ministry* (London: SPCK, 1981), pp. 88ff., 116ff.

For Further Consideration

A. Historical

Roberta C. Bondi, *To Pray and Love: Conversations on Prayer with the Early Church* (Minneapolis: Fortress, 1991).

Joseph A. Jungmann, *Christian Prayer Through the Centuries*, trans. John Coyne (New York: Paulist, 1978).

Perry LeFevre, *Understandings of Prayer* (Philadelphia: Westminster, 1981). Introductions to various theologians' views on prayer, including Karl Barth, Paul Tillich, Dietrich Bonhoeffer, Karl Rahner, and Abraham J. Heschel.

A. L. Lilley, *Prayer in Christian Theology: A Study of Some Moments and Masters of the Christian Life from Clement of Alexandria to Fénelon* (London: Student Christian Movement, 1925).

William O. Paulsell, *Rules for Prayer* (New York: Paulist, 1993). An introduction to the various "rules for prayer" developed throughout Christian history.

Robert L. Simpson, *The Interpretation of Prayer in the Early Church* (Philadelphia: Westminster, 1965).

B. Theological Classics of the Twentieth Century

E. M. Bounds, *Purpose in Prayer* (New York: Revell, 1920).

George Arthur Buttrick, *Prayer* (New York: Abingdon-Cokesbury, 1942).

Albert Edward Day, *Existence Under God* (New York: Abingdon, 1958).

P. T. Forsyth, *The Soul of Prayer* (London: Independent, 1954).

O. Hallesby, *Prayer*, trans. Clarence J. Carlsen (Minneapolis: Augsburg, 1939).

Georgia Harkness, *Prayer and the Common Life* (New York: Abingdon-Cokesbury, 1958).

James Hastings, *The Christian Doctrine of Prayer* (Edinburgh: T. and T. Clark, 1915).

C. The Lord's Prayer

Karl Barth, *Prayer According to the Catechisms of the Reformation*, trans. Sara F. Terrien (Philadelphia: Westminster, 1952).

Joachim Jeremias, *The Prayers of Jesus*, multiple translators (Naperville: Allenson, 1967).

Daniel L. Migliore (ed.), *The Lord's Prayer: Perspectives for Reclaiming Christian Prayer* (Grand Rapids: Eerdmans, 1993).

23

Foot-Washing People

John 13:1–20 tells about Jesus washing the feet of his disciples—an enacted condemnation of Judas' mode of life, a dramatic lesson for Jesus' disciples about the divine approach to life, and the establishment of a liturgical observance for spiritual renewal.

Enacted Condemnation

The historical context for what Jesus did in John 13 is Judas Iscariot's sin. Judas had allowed his own ideas about salvation to get the upper hand. Convinced that Jesus was an imposter rather than the true bearer of salvation, he took matters into his own hands thus placing himself above the authority of Jesus. By so doing, he betrayed his Lord. Judas refused to submit himself to Jesus as Jesus had submitted himself to his heavenly Father.

The redemptive plan of God was dependent on loving and trusting subordination. For the eternal Word (John 1:1, 14) to have insisted on his own way would have been contrary to the divine nature, and likewise, for a disciple of the incarnate Word to insist on his own way was antithetical to the divine plan, also.

Jesus' condemnation of Judas' insubordination pervades the whole chapter. It is his spiritual plight that introduces the narrative about Jesus washing feet:

> The devil had already put it into the heart of Judas son of Simon Iscariot to betray him. And during supper Jesus, knowing that the Father had given all things into his hands, and that he had come from God and was going to God, got up from the table, took off his outer robe, and tied a towel around himself. Then he poured water into a basin and began to wash the disciples' feet and to wipe them with the towel that was tied around him [John 13:2–5].

The issue of Judas' sin figures also in vv. 10–11. When in response to Peter, Jesus says that not all of them are clean, John explains that he is referring Judas. The issue of Judas figures also in vv. 16–30 when, following the washing of his disciples' feet, Jesus, in his explanatory commentary, says:

> Very truly, I tell you, servants are not greater than their master, nor are messengers greater than the one who

sent them. If you know these things, you are blessed if you do them. I am not speaking of all of you; I know whom I have chosen. But it is to fulfill the scripture, "The one who ate my bread has lifted his heel against me." I tell you this now, before it occurs, so that when it does occur, you may believe that I am he.

Verses 21–30, then, proceed to tell about Judas partaking of the bread offered by Jesus, whereupon Judas leaves to carry through with his plans for betrayal.

Judas acts as though the servant is greater than the master, and the messenger than the sender. This attitude is so diametrically opposed to Jesus' own relationship with his heavenly Father for whom he is servant unto salvation that it has to be openly and decisively condemned. (The term "servant unto salvation" will become clearer as we continue this discussion.) Jesus enacts the truth that Judas rejects, namely, that "servants are not greater than their master, nor are messengers greater than the one who sent them." In so doing he also enacts his condemnation of Judas' mode of life. Just as Jesus was in submission to his heavenly Father as servant unto salvation, even so his disciples are to submit themselves to him in a servant role for the same purpose.

Dramatic Lesson

Interwoven with the condemnation of Judas' mode of life is Jesus' dramatic demonstration of the way his people are to live. They are to be willing to lay aside their cloaks of respectability for the sake of God's redemptive work in the world. The message in John 13 is that his disciples are to take care that they do not follow Judas' way of non-servanthood, but Jesus' way of servanthood. Rudolf Schnackenburg writes:

> The disciples are to understand Jesus' action as their master's deliberate act of humiliation, by means of which he aims to give them an example of humble service.... The obligation of the disciples to perform a similar service among themselves follows from the action of the Lord and Master.[1]

Philippians 2:1–11 is a Pauline parallel to this Johannine theme of Jesus' servanthood unto salvation. According to vv. 6–8, he is the one

> who, though he was in the form of God, did not regard equality with God as something to be exploited, but emptied himself, taking the form of a slave, being born in human likeness. And being found in human form, he humbled himself and became obedient to the point of death — even death on a cross.

In the incarnation Jesus disrobed himself of heavenly glory in order to enter into the earthiness of human life; he "emptied himself, taking the form of a slave." In John 13 we see Jesus' dramatic demonstration of the incarnation for the sake of redemption: he "got up from table [the place of dignity], took off his outer robe [the sign of dignity], and tied a towel around himself [the sign of servanthood]" (v. 4), and "began to wash the disciples' feet and to wipe them with the towel that was tied around him [the act of servanthood]" (v. 5). As George R. Beasley- Murray puts it:

> The footwashing is rightly seen as denoting the *kataba-sis*, the 'descent,' of the Word.... [which] is a descent to the death of the cross, that the world may be delivered from sin–its defilement, guilt, and bondage, and so released for life in the kingdom, which entails adoption of the pattern of service displayed in the Redeemer.[2]

Jesus' enactment is also an enactment of resurrection and ascension. His confidence in the divine plan for victorious ascent following the incarnational descent is indicated in v. 1: "Jesus knew that his hour had come to depart from this world and go to the Father." The same confidence is expressed in v. 3: "Jesus, knowing that the Father had given all things into his hands, and that he had come from God [the incarnational descent] and was going to God [the victorious ascent]." Knowing this, he acted out not only the incarnational descent and crucifixion by disrobing and washing feet, but also the victorious resurrection and ascent by putting on his robe again and returning to the table, the place of respectability.

A. M. Hunter, as well as others, sees a parallel between the action here and the sacrificial act of the Good Shepherd in chapter 10: "Consider...the verbs which John uses to describe Jesus' actions. Jesus 'lays aside' his garments and, the washing over, 'takes them again.' These are the very verbs which the Good Shepherd had used of his death and resurrection (10:11,15,17f.)."[3] The dramatic lesson regarding the descent, however, is what startled Peter. He found it difficult to recognize his Lord in a menial role marked by girding himself with a towel, the mark of a slave. Edwyn Hoskyns explains further why the action which Jesus took was so surprising, at least to Peter:

> To wash the feet of their masters belonged to the duties of slaves (I. Sam. 25:41). According to Rabbinic teaching, slaves of Jewish birth were not bound to perform this menial action, though wives were expected to wash the feet of their husbands.[4]

Accordingly, Jesus shocked the disciples on two scores, first, in that not even Jewish slaves had to perform such a task—therefore, Jesus, Jewish man that he was, certainly was not expected to do such work—and second, when it was performed, it was the role of a woman.

Having astounded them with the truth about the nature of his incarnational life, he returns to the table, not only to demonstrate the victorious ascent, but also to assume his more recognizable role as a teacher giving verbal instructions. But, having washed their feet, he is now a teacher with a difference; he is a teacher who has stooped as a slave ministering the divine hospitality of salvation.

Henry Ward Beecher called Jesus' washing of his disciples' feet "one of the proofs ... of Christ's divinity."[5] To say the least, it was a jolting paradigm shift for the Twelve (and for us!). The incarnational, slave-like descent was contrary to their presuppositions about God.

Not only was it a paradigm shift about the nature of God, but also about what it means to be the people of God. In both John 13 and Philippians 2 Jesus as the servant unto salvation is the basis of appeal regarding the way disciples are to live. In John 13:15, Jesus says, "I have set you an example, that you also should do as I have done to you," and in Philippians 2:5, Paul says, "Let the same mind be in you that was in Christ Jesus."

These two passages are the basis for the song "He Washed His Servants' Feet," the first stanza of which reflects Philippians and the others John:

> Disrobed of all His heav'nly dress, The Savior came to earth; Clothed in a veil of mortal flesh, And bowed His head in death.

> That awful night in which betrayed, He introduced the feast, Which we, my friends, have seen displayed, Where each has been a guest.

> The solemn scene about to close, To make the whole complete, He meekly from communion rose And washed His servants' feet.

> "To each," He said, "let others do As I your Lord, have done: The heav'nly pattern still pursue, In form as I have shown."

> Since Christ has the example set, Recorded in His Word; We'll humbly wash each other's feet, Obedient to our Lord.[6]

The servanthood mode of existence for followers of Jesus is a theme found throughout the New Testament. In Matthew 23:11–12, Jesus says: "The greatest among you will be your servant [*diakonos*]. All who exalt themselves will be humbled, and all who humble themselves will be exalted." Again, in Mark 9:35, Jesus says to the Twelve, "Whoever wants to be first must be last of all and servant [*diakonos*] of all."

In Matthew 20:25–28, in reference to the way of "the rulers of the Gentiles" who "lord it over" others, Jesus says that it must not be so among his followers, for "whoever wishes to be first among you must be your slave [*doulos*]; just as the Son of Man came not to be served but to serve, and to give his life a ransom for many." (Parallel, Mark 10:42–45.)

In the epistles the use of the word *doulos* in reference to one's relationship to Christ is quite common: Romans 1:1, "Paul, a slave[7] of Jesus Christ"; Philippians 1:1, "Paul and Timothy, slaves of Christ Jesus"; Colossians 4:12, "Epaphras ... a slave of Christ Jesus"; Titus 1:1, "Paul, a slave of God"; James 1:1, "James, a slave of God and of the Lord Jesus Christ"; 1 Peter 2:16, "As slaves of God, live as free people"; 2 Peter 1:1, "Simon Peter, a slave and apostle of Jesus Christ"; Jude 1, "Jude, a slave of Jesus Christ"; Revelation 1:1, "The revelation of Jesus Christ, which God gave him to show his slaves what must soon take place"; and 19:5, "And from the throne came a voice saying, 'Praise our God, all you his slaves."

The song by S. B. McManus summarizes the lesson which Jesus taught about the mode of life to be pursued by his disciples:

Love serves, yet willing, stoops to serve,
What Christ in love so true

Hath freely done for one and all,
Shall we not gladly do?[8]

Liturgical Observance

To begin this section let us summarize the different cultural and religious facets of the foot-washing practice:

1) It was an eastern Mediterranean custom connected with personal hygiene and refreshment (e.g., Gen. 18:4; 19:2; 24:32; 43:24; Judg. 19:21; Song of Sol. 5:3).

2) It was also used from time to time as an act of hospitable service in which one washed the feet of another (e.g., 1 Sam. 25:41), or at least provided water for one to wash one's own feet. We see evidence of this in Luke 7 when the woman in the house of Simon the Pharisee bathed Jesus' feet with her tears. In response to Simon's criticism that Jesus would allow her to do so, Jesus says, "I entered your house; you gave me no water for my feet, but she has bathed my feet with her tears and dried them with her hair" (v. 44). Evidently Simon had not performed the most basic hospitable act of providing water so that Jesus could wash his own feet.

3) In the just mentioned account as well as in John 11:2 and 12:3 another factor appears; it is an expression of thanksgiving and devotion to Jesus. Those washing Jesus' feet use the water of tears, the towel of one's hair, and the precious liquids of oils and perfumes.

4) In the Old Testament it was also part of the preparation for temple duty. According to Exodus 30:17–21:

> The LORD spoke to Moses: You shall make a bronze basin with a bronze stand for washing. You shall put it between the tent of meeting and the altar, and you shall put water in it; with the water Aaron and his sons shall wash their hands and their feet. When they go into the tent of meeting, or when they come near the altar to minister, to make an offering by fire to the LORD, they shall wash with water, so that they may not die, They shall wash their hands and their feet, so that they may not die: it shall be a perpetual ordinance for them, for him and for his descendants throughout their generations [see also 40:31].

It was this cultural practice of personal hygiene and refreshment, this act of hospitable service, this cultic preparation for temple duty which Jesus reshapes for his own purposes.

That Jesus considered what he did as more than a mere act of hospitable service is indicated by his instructions concerning it. When Peter objects to having the Lord wash his feet, Jesus replies, "Unless I wash you, you have no share with me" (v. 8). These words are the first indication that the washing is more than an act of hospitality; it has to do with Peter's ongoing relationship to Christ. According to v. 8, refusing to allow

Jesus to wash his feet would have led to acute spiritual consequences for Peter (see For Further Consideration, Part I, for additional commentary).

Peter, realizing that to reject Jesus' washing of his feet was to forfeit spiritual fellowship with him, responds: "Lord, not my feet only but also my hands and my head!" (v. 9). In his comprehensive study of John 13, John Christopher Thomas argues that Peter's mention of hands and head is more than an incidental reference to his whole body in general. The hands are always in need of being washed, a matter which was crucial in the religion of the Pharisees (cf., Matt. 15:1-21, Mark 7:1-23, Luke 11:37-44), the rigid observance of which elicited Jesus' condemnation of it. "When Peter requests that his hands be washed, he is suggesting that if any part of the body is in constant need of washing, it is the hands."[9] Jesus is not dealing here, however, with physical or ritual cleanliness, and therefore it is not Peter's hands which need to be washed.

Neither did his head need washing. Thomas argues that "in ancient Greek *kephalē* came to represent the whole person, life itself.... Peter's request that his head be washed expresses the view that the head represents the person."[10] Peter, therefore, was requesting that Jesus do an all inclusive work on his whole life.

The point of the narrative, though, is that Peter needs neither a hygienic or ritual cleansing of the hands, nor a cleansing of the self as self; he has already experienced the cleansing of the self as self by virtue of his faith in Jesus. As one has put it:

> Peter is already sitting at the Lord's Table. His impulsive and emotional change of attitude shows that he is bathed already in the Love so soon to die, and now — what he could not yet understand and therefore rejects — this love is kneeling at his feet in service. He has yielded himself in spirit to Christ; he must further yield himself in action. This love must wash his feet, remove life's travel-stains, and manifest its results in the common ways of life.[11]

In light of the spiritual context indicated both by v. 8 where Jesus says, "Unless I wash you, you have no share with me," and by v. 11 where Judas' spiritual plight is clearly in view, it is reasonable, therefore, to conclude that v. 10 is to be understood within the same spiritual context, in which case the meaning would be: "One who has [spiritually] bathed [*louō*] does not need to [spiritually] wash [*niptō*], except for the [spiritual] feet, but is entirely clean [spiritually]." Accordingly, Jesus' washing of the disciples' feet was not what in other New Testament passages would be understood as the initial bath of regeneration. (See Titus 3:5 which uses *loutron* in relation to regeneration. The same word is used in 1 Cor. 6:11; Eph. 5:26; Heb. 10:22 where in each case the reference is to a spiritual bath.) Instead, the water event of John 13 is a subsequent washing for spiritual renewal, without which, Jesus says, Peter can "have no share" with him (see For Further Consideration, Part II, for further discussion of v. 10).

This emphasis on the spiritual necessity of remaining in an ongoing vital relationship with Jesus is consistent with other passages in John. For instance, the promise in 14:18 where Jesus says, "I will not leave you orphaned," and the warning in 15:6 that "whoever does not abide in me is thrown away like a branch and withers".

It is Thomas' conclusion that foot washing in those churches especially influenced by John was understood as the liturgical rite established by Jesus for the purpose of maintaining this vital spiritual relationship with his disciples. It was understood as being a liturgical practice in the same way that baptism and the Lord's Supper was.[12] Even as baptism signified their entrance into the circle of disciples, even so foot washing signified their continuing life of discipleship. Thomas writes:

> The disciples are not being initiated into belief [as in baptism] in this passage, but are continuing in their belief. Their earlier baptism, which the community probably understood as being at the hands of John (1:19-39) or possibly Jesus (3:22, however cf. 4:1-2),

would designate initial belief and fellowship with Jesus, whereas footwashing would signify the continuance of that belief and fellowship. As a sign of preparation for Jesus' departure, footwashing signifies the disciples' spiritual cleansing in preparation both for a continuing relationship with Jesus and for taking on his mission in the world.[13]

Jesus' washing the feet of his disciples is not the end of the matter, however. He instructs the disciples to wash each other's feet: "You also ought to wash one another's feet" (v. 14); "You also should do as I have done to you" (v. 15); "If you know these things, you are blessed if you do them" (v. 17).

That the practice of foot washing had been established in the early church is indicated in 1 Timothy 5:10 which refers to the washing of the saints' feet as one of the qualifications for women to be placed on the church's official list of widows. That this was other than simple hospitality is implied by the fact that the qualification immediately preceding is that of showing hospitality, and the one immediately following is that of helping the afflicted. Washing the saints' feet, therefore, is identified as a practice distinguishable both from showing hospitality and from helping the afflicted.

Evidence of a foot-washing liturgy, the *pedilavium*, is found throughout the church's history.

Regarding early Christianity, Thomas writes:

> The evidence from early Christianity demonstrates that a number of people read the text [John 13] in just such a fashion [as a religious rite to be continued]. Not only is the geographical distribution of the evidence impressive–in that it comes from North Africa (Tertullian), Egypt-Palestine (Origen), Asia Minor (I Timothy, Martyrdom of Polycarp, John Chrysostom), Italy (Ambrose, Augustine), and Gaul (Caesarius)—but the diverse contexts in which the commands were obeyed are also noteworthy, in that they range from the church, to the monastery, to the home.[14]

As we see in the examples below, foot washing is in some cases a communal liturgy as, for instance, among the Anabaptists; in others it is a representative liturgy as, for instance, the practice of the Roman pontiff's washing of feet on Maundy Thursday. In some cases it is a reenactment of what Jesus did, while in others it is understood as providing some means of grace to the participants. In some instances it is an expression of Christian hospitality, while in others it is understood as having to do with our spiritual relationship to Christ.

First century
• John 13 and 1 Timothy 5:10
Third century
• c. 211, Tertullian in *De Corona* 8 indicates that it was a part of Christian worship[15]

• "In Spain the rite must have existed in the third century, since it was abolished by the forty-eighth canon of the Council of Elvira, A.D.305: 'Nor are the feet of the baptized to be washed by the priests or by any of the clergy.'"[16]

Fourth century

• later half of the century, the *Apostolic Constitutions* 3.19 sets it forth as a role for deacons[17]

• c. 366-373, Athanasius in his canons, chap. 66 sets it forth as the duty of a bishop[18]

• c. 391, John Chrysostom in *Homilies on John* 71 urges Christians to do it[19]

• Ambrose (d. 397) in *The Sacraments* 3.5 expresses his personal commitment to it as an important liturgical practice to which his church is faithful even though Rome is not[20]

Fifth century

• 404, Monastic Rules 51–52 associated with Pachomias says that visiting clerics and monks are to be received at the monastery by the washing of feet[21]

• Augustine (d. 430),in *John: Tractate* 58.4 encourages the practice[22] and in *Homilies on John* 56.5; 58.5; 59.5 he connects it with spiritual cleansing for Christians[23]

• John Cassian (d. 435) in *Institute of the Coenobia* 4.19 refers to it as a practice in his community[24]

Sixth century

• Caesarius of Arles (d.542) in *Sermon* 202 defends the practice[25]

Seventh century

• 694, the Seventh Synod of Toledo censured its non-observance on Maundy Thursday[26]

Thirteenth century

• Mabillon's tenth *Ordo Romanus* indicates that when the Maundy Thursday Mass came to be celebrated in the morning, the Pedilavium remained as a separate service confined to cathedral and abbey churches[27]

Sixteenth century

• Anabaptists institute the practice of foot washing in obedience to Christ[28]

Seventeenth century

• 1647, publication of the Greek liturgy of the Divine and Sacred Basin, edited with a Latin translation, which describes the practice in the Greek church[29]

Eighteenth century

• "In England, the sovereign, or in his stead the Lord High Almoner [an official in the royal household charged with the distribution of alms], used to do this ceremony until 1731."[30]

Nineteenth century

• Some holiness and pentecostal churches in the United States revived the practice of foot washing as an ordinance, and, in some instances, developed theological treatises on the subject.[31]

Twentieth century

• Pope Pius XII (1939–1958) recommended its observance in all churches[32]

• Introduction of foot-washing liturgies into Protestant denominations that heretofore had not practiced the rite, as, for instance, in the worship book of the United Church of Christ.[33]

Conclusion

Since the foot washing in John 13 took place in a corporate gathering, its continuation—if thought of as being in conformity with that original liturgy—also should be a corporate experience for disciples. It is a communal rite in the same way that water baptism and the Lord's supper are. It is a liturgical/spiritual foot washing alongside the liturgical/spiritual bath and the liturgical/spiritual meal.

Just as baptism is not a washing of physical dirt from the body,[34] but rather the physical acting out of the cleansing work of Jesus Christ, even so Jesus' washing of feet is the physical enactment of an ongoing cleansing of all that keeps us from being what God wants us to be. Just as the Lord's supper is not for the purpose of filling stomachs,[35] even so foot washing is not for the purpose of providing physical refreshment, but for giving spiritual renewal to disciples during their pilgrimage of faith (see For Further Consideration, Part III, for additional commentary).

On the basis of the multidimensional character of John 13, it may be concluded that this ongoing cleansing leading to renewal is threefold:

1) We are renewed in the willingness to live in submission to Christ for redemptive purposes even as Christ submitted to his heavenly Father for the purpose of bringing salvation to the world;

2) We are renewed in the life of mutual service to each other, both by receiving the priestly service of others who extend the ministry of Christ to us, and by giving this priestly service to others; and

3) We are renewed for the walk of faith.

Foot washing has as much basis for being a liturgical act with spiritual significance for disciples as does baptism and the Lord's supper. It, too, is grounded in the redemptive work of Jesus, was instituted by him, is connected directly with the corporate worship life of the church, and is understood in Scripture as having an ongoing place in the life of the church.[36]

This offering of spiritual renewal is extended to us by Christ through the common members of the church. In the foot washing fellowship, we are both recipients of

Christ's renewing grace working through others and agents of his grace in our service to others. Foot washing has the potential of being the major liturgical act of the priesthood of all believers. In this service disciples as disciples serve as nothing less than the designated agents of Christ for the spiritual benefit of other disciples. P. T. Forsyth said it well: "If you wash his disciples' feet it must be not merely as a poor serving brother [or sister] but with the kind dignity of the agent and apostle of Christ."[37] In the service of foot washing, every disciple—regardless of official capacities in the church or length of time as a disciple—is a functioning priest.

As with other liturgical acts, when the spiritual reality is separated from the acts themselves, they degenerate into little more than empty religious rituals. The case of Judas reminds us that liturgical acts in and of themselves do not work in a mechanical fashion to bring about a renewal in faith. As Raymond Brown observes:

> Verse 10b and vs. 11 make clear that Judas had not been changed by the footwashing. Peter had protested to Jesus but had quickly accepted the footwashing when Jesus pointed out its salvific purpose. But Judas' heart (vs. 2) was already filled with evil intent, and he had not opened himself up to the love that Jesus was extending toward him.[38]

However, when the liturgical acts do express a vital spiritual relationship through faith in Jesus Christ, they become corporate expressions of grace. In other words, they are *ex opere operantis* ("from the work of the worker" — that is, their effects depend on the faith and love of the participants) and not *ex opere operato* ("from the work performed" — that is, their effects being guaranteed by the liturgical action in and of itself).

These liturgical acts are designated by the Lord as ways by which we, if we have faith, experience grace in the corporate life of the church. In baptism we experience, in communion with others, the grace of God which brings us to conversion. In the Lord's supper we experience, in communion with others, the grace of God which blesses us with the presence of the risen Lord. In foot washing we experience, in communion with others, the grace of God which renews us as disciples of Christ.

Foot washing indicates the form of life which the pilgrim people of God are to assume. We are servants unto salvation; we are priests each to the other; we are beneficiaries of the grace of God made available to us through the ministries of others. We are in constant need of being renewed in faith, refreshed for service, and refocused on the incarnation and the salvation which it brought.

Picking up on this theme, one songwriter urges us to "put on the apron of humility; serve each other, washing feet, that you may walk in the way of the Lord, refreshed, refreshed."[39]

Notes

1. Rudolf Schnackenburg, *The Gospel According to St. John:* Volume Three, Commentary on Chapters 13–21 (New York: Crossroad, 1982), p. 23f.

2. George R. Beasley-Murray, John, Vol. 36 in *Word Biblical Commentary* (Waco: Word, 1987), p. 239.

3. A. M. Hunter, *The Gospel According to John* (Cambridge: University Press, 1965), p. 134.

Raymond E. Brown says that "a deliberate parallel is not out of the question" between the use of *tithēmi,* to lay down, in v. 4 and its use in 10:11, 15, 17, 18, and the use of *lambanō,* take up, in v. 12 and its use in 10:17, 18. *The Gospel According to John (XIII-XXI)* in *The Anchor Bible* (London: Geoffrey Chapman, 1971), p. 551. Also, see his extensive treatment of various interpretations of this whole passage as well as his own, esp. pp. 558–572.

Edwyn Clement Hoskyns: "In the Greek the words *layeth aside his garments* and the corresponding words in v. 12 *had taken his garments,* are strikingly significant, since the verbs *lay aside* and *take* have been previously used with reference to the death and resurrection of

Jesus... (10:17, 18, cf. 11, 15, 13:37, 38, 15:13; 1 John 3:16)." *The Fourth Gospel*, Vol. II (London: Faber and Faber, 1950), p. 512.

4. Hoskyns, op. cit., p. 513.

5. Henry Ward Beecher, *Yale Lectures on Preaching, Third Series* (Boston: Pilgrim, 1874), p. 149.

6. *Worship the Lord: Hymnal of the Church of God* (Anderson, Ind: Warner, 1989), No. 382.

7. In all references in this paragraph I translate *doulos* as slave, instead of as servant as does the *New Revised Standard Version*. Other references to the Christian community as a fellowship of slaves are 1 Cor. 7:22: 2 Cor. 4:5; Eph. 6:6. In each of these instances the NSRV does translate *doulos* as slave.

8. S. B. McManus, "Love Consecrates the Humblest Act," *Worship the Lord*, No. 383.

9. John Christopher Thomas, *Footwashing in John 13 and the Johannine Community*, No. 61 in the *Journal for the Study of the New Testament Supplemental Series* (Sheffield, England: JSOT Press, 1991), p. 96.

10. Ibid. In support of his argument, Thomas cites K. Munzer on the subject of the "Head" in *New International Dictionary of New Testament Theology*, Vol. II (Grand Rapids: Zondervan, 1978), p. 159: "In wanting to have his head washed ... Peter wanted his whole life to be cleansed."

11. R. H. Strachhan, *The Fourth Gospel: Its Significance*

and Environment (London: Student Christian Movement Press, Third Edition 1941, Reprinted 1955), p. 267.

12. Thomas, op. cit., pp. 174-177.

13. Ibid., p. 105. Thomas discusses foot washing as the inaugural event of the so-called *Book of Glory* (chaps. 13-21), the first part of John being the so-called *Book of Signs* (chaps. 1 – 12).

14. Ibid., p. 147. Thomas presents a comprehensive history of the practice. For a short overview, see Hoskyns, op. cit., pp. 520–524, "Detached Note 7: The Liturgical Use of the Pedilavium or the Washing of the Feet."

15. Thomas, op. cit., p. 129.

16. Hoskyns, op. cit., p. 521.

17. Thomas, op. cit., p. 131f.

18. Ibid., p. 130.

19. Ibid. p. 130f.

20. Ibid., p. 178 where Ambrose is quoted as saying: "We are not unaware of the fact that the Church of Rome does not have this custom.... There are some who ... try to allege in excuse that this is not to be done in the mystery, nor in baptism, nor in regeneration, but the feet are to be washed as for a guest. But one belongs to humility, the other to sanctification: 'If I wash not thy feet, thou shalt have no part with me.' So I say this, not that I may rebuke others, but that I may commend my

own ceremonies. In all things I desire to follow the Church in Rome, yet we too, have human feelings; what is preserved more rightly elsewhere we, too, preserve more rightly."

21. Ibid., p. 132.

22. Ibid., p. 131.

23. Ibid., p. 159f.

24. Ibid., p. 132.

25. Ibid., p. 133f.

26. "In the third canon of the seventeenth Council of Toledo (A.D.694), the non-observance of the practice of the washing of the feet on the Thursday in Holy Week was censured, and a strict performance of the ceremony was enforced both as an example of humility and as an act of preparation for the Supper of the Lord, with which the ceremony was closely associated. Disobedient priests were ordered to be excluded from Communion for two months. Further, since the penitents were publicly reconciled at the Paschal season, the liturgy of the Pedilavium had special reference to the remission of sin after baptism." Hoskyns, op. cit., p. 524.

27. *The Oxford Dictionary of the Christian Church* (London: Oxford University Press, 1974), p. 1057.

28. "The early Lutheran church rejected the ritual as a Roman Catholic attempt at righteousness by ceremonial works. It was elected as a preferred practice by

Protestant sectarians after the Reformation, especially by Anabaptists and Mennonites, who saw in it a sign of brotherhood and humility." William H. Gentz, ed., *The Dictionary of Bible and Religion* (Nashville: Abingdon,1986), p. 366.

29. Hoskyns, op. cit., p. 523.

30. J. H. Bernard, *St. John,* Vol. II in *The International Critical Commentary* (Edinburgh: T. and T. Clark, 1928), p. 465f.

31. An example is the Church of God (Anderson, Indiana) which emerged in the early 1880s. Reflective of the position held are Russell R. Byrum, *Christian Theology* (Anderson, Ind: Gospel Trumpet Company, 1925, Third Edition 1950), pp 583–591; H. M. Riggle, *Christian Baptism, The Lord's Supper and Feet-Washing* (Anderson, Ind: Gospel Trumpet Company, 1909), chap. 3; and F. G. Smith, *What the Bible Teaches* (Anderson, Ind: Gospel Trumpet Company, 1920), chap. 15.

32. "Pope Pius XII's Holy Week Ordinal placed it in the restored evening Mass immediately after the Gospel and recommended its observance in all churches. During the singing of antiphons, twelve men are led into the sanctuary, where the celebrant solemnly washes and dries the feet of each in turn. When the ceremony was observed apart from the Mass, it began with the recital of the Gospel narrative (Jn. 13)." *Oxford*

Dictionary of the Christian Church, p. 1057.

33. *The Book of Worship* (St. Louis: Church Leadership Resources, 1986), pp.197-206.

34. 1 Peter 3:21, "And baptism ... now saves you—not as a removal of dirt from the body, but as an appeal to God for a good conscience."

35. 1 Cor. 11:22 asks "Do you not have homes to eat and drink in?"

36. For Thomas' argument regarding its sacramental character, see op. cit., p. 177.

37. P. T. Forsyth, *Positive Preaching and Modern Mind* (London: Hodder and Stoughton, 1907), p. 123.

38. Brown, op. cit. p. 568.

39. Shirley Lewis Brown, "The Foot-Washing Song," *Sing and Rejoice!* (Scottdale: Herald), No. 110.

For Further Consideration

Part I. More Than an Example

A. M. Hunter: "Was the whole episode, as some hold, simply an acted parable whose theme was the glory of service? This is part of the truth, but far from the whole of it—or else in that mysterious dialogue with Peter Jesus is simply obscuring the parable's plain lesson." *The Gospel According to John* (Cambridge: University Press, 1965), p. 134.

D. Guthrie: "The washing of the feet was more than

an example. It was a means by which the disciples could participate in the Lord's humiliation. This brings cleansing. Nothing more is needed." *The New Bible Commentary, Revised* (London: Inter-Varsity, 1970), p. 957.

Edwyn Clement Hoskyns: "As Origen well perceived, these words ["You do not know now what I am doing, but later you will understand" (v. 7)] mark the mysterious nature of the action of Jesus. It is no mere action of humility, such as would have been the case if Jesus had undertaken to perform a normal act of feet-washing before a meal.... The meal has already been begun, if not concluded, when Jesus rises to perform an act so impressive and symbolic that the disciple can understand its meaning only in the light of later events." *The Fourth Gospel,* Vol. II. (London: Faber and Faber, 1950), p. 513.

Part II. John 13:10

According to Jean Owanga-Welo, *The Function and Meaning of the Footwashing in the Johannine Passion Narrative: A Structural Approach* (Ann Arbor: University Microfilms International, 1980), John 13:10, "makes the point to the disciples on the need to have one's feet washed.... It is not always the case that a man who has bathed needs no further washing. Even in the tradition-al bath houses or places, the regular bath was almost always followed by anointing.... It is even reported that the bath (by immersion), in order to be complete, must be followed by a passage or stay in the sudatorium for transpiration, and by the application of ointment to the legs and arms.... These are indications of the care given to the members of the body after a bath," p. 240f.

A point of disagreement among biblical scholars is whether v. 10 should follow some ancient texts which include the phrase "except for the feet" or others where it is missing. John Christopher Thomas, for example, argues for the longer text [see *Footwashing in John 13 and the Johannine Community, No. 61 in the Journal for the Study of the New Testament Supplemental Series* (Sheffield, England: JSOT Press, 1991), chap. 2], whereas Raymond E. Brown argues for the shorter [see *The Gospel According to John* (XIII-XXI) in *The Anchor Bible* (London: Geoffrey Chapman, 1971), p. 567f]. Owanga-Welo argues for the longer text and concludes that the above mentioned cultural background "gives added support to our argument in favor of the longer reading," p. 241.

Part III. Theological Significance of Foot Washing

B. F. Westcott: "The limited cleansing [of foot washing] ... is all that is needed [after the bath of baptism]. He who is bathed needs, so to speak, only to remove the stains contracted in the walk of life; just as the guest, after the bath, needs only to have the dust washed from his feet when he reaches the house of his host.... The partial and superficial defilements, of hands, or head [but see Thomas above] or feet, do not alter the general character. The man, as a whole, the man as man, is clean." *The Gospel According to St. John* (Grand Rapids: Eerdmans, 1958), p. 191f.

Edwin Clement Hoskyns: "The Pedilavium was ... originally both an example of Christian humility and a means of post-baptismal sanctification." *The Fourth Gospel,* Vol. II (London: Faber and Faber, 1950), p. 524.

John Christopher Thomas: "By following the ancient banquet practice to its completion the deeper meaning of the footwashing comes into view. The one who travels any distance at all on the dusty paths in the ancient orient accumulates dust which must be removed. If, in the analogy Jesus uses, *louō* represents baptism, then it makes best sense to take the function of the footwashing as an additional act of cleansing." *Footwashing in John 13 and the Johannine Community, No. 61 in the Journal for the Study of the New Testament Supplemental Series* (Sheffield, England: JSOT Press, 1991), p. 104.

Also, Thomas: "In a sense, footwashing is an extension of baptism, for it signifies the washing away of post-baptismal sins in Peter's (the believer's) life." p. 106.

24

People in Full-Orbed Relatedness

We do not have relationships; we are relationships. The Bible is the story of the God who is the eternal relationship, creating a world of relationships, working within those relationships to redeem them from destructive powers, and bringing the world of relationships to consummation in heavenly jubilation. The Christian life is best characterized as that of a full-orbed relatedness including God, ourselves, families, others both inside and outside the church, the whole created order, our particular resources, and the oppressed. We turn now to a consideration of each of these dimensions of our new relatedness.

Our Saving Relationship to God

Sin is the disruption and distortion of our relationship to God; salvation is the healing of the relationship. Those who live out this salvific relationship do so in worship, prayer, and service. The life to which we are called is one of basking in God's love revealed in Christ, of intercessory prayer in the name of Jesus, and of yearning for more and more of God. It is a life of listening to God's call and answering in faith, responding with wholehearted love, and yielding with joyous trust. It is a life in which we are so completely in love with God that nothing whatsoever has sufficient power to cause us to reject God. It is a life of readiness for Christ's return, knowing that for those who are completely at one with him, there is nothing to fear at his appearance, for "perfect love casts out fear" (1 John 4:18).

The Christian life is to have what Adam and Eve forfeited by their sin, namely, to hear with joy "the sound of the LORD God walking in the garden at the time of the evening breeze" (Gen. 3:8). Because of the redeeming work of Christ Jesus we have no need to hide from God, as the original couple did. The saving relationship which is ours by obedient faith enables us to join with John and all the saints in saying—not only "at the time of the evening breeze" but also as we anticipate the end of the age—"Amen. Come, Lord Jesus!" (Rev. 22:20).

The Healing of Relationships Within Ourselves

Salvation has to do not only with a new relationship to God, but also within ourselves. On the basis of the trinitarian understanding of God (see chapter 8, on "The Trinitarian God") in whose image we are created, we say that the human being consists of three persons: the mysterious person of private depth, the imaged person of one's own perception, and the interactive person in contact with reality other than one's self-image.

The mysterious person of private depth is who we are down deep inside. It is the person who leads us to make such comments as: "I don't know why I said that"; "I'm surprised at myself"; "I can't figure out why I did that." It is this person whom we seek to understand when we turn to counselors and therapists for help. It is this person who continually surprises us—a person so mysterious that neither we nor any other human being, not even professional analysts, can ever fully comprehend the mystery.

The imaged person of one's own perception is who we think ourselves to be; it is our self-image which includes the assumptions we make about our strengths and weaknesses. Others see us functioning on the basis of this imaged self and refer perhaps to our low self-image or to our inflated ego, as the case may be.

This is the self which leads some to do crazy deeds, others, noble ones. It is the self which prevents some from doing what otherwise they would have been able to do, while for others, it motivates them to stretch to the far limits of their possibilities. It is the self which has the potential of stimulating some to aspire to the heights, while it plunges others into despair.

The interactive person in contact with reality other than one's self-image is that to which we refer as ourselves running into stone walls—we thought we could do something which a hard reality determines that we cannot do. An example is that of Branwell Brontë, brother of the famous English writers, Emily and Charlotte, who wasted away at an early age. His biographer, who did an extensive study of his tragic personality, describes the dissonance near the end of his life:

> The dream world, in whose atmosphere he had lived since boyhood dissolved about him, and the anguish of living in the real world with a live sorrow was more than he could face. He recognized instinctively its power to kill him...."My wretchedness," he wrote...on the day of awakening, "is not about castles in the air, but about stern realities."[1]

Not only does such reality serve as a non-negotiable No to what we had thought and perhaps continue to think we are able to do; it also serves as a liberating Yes to that which we had thought we could not do. In this case, reality other than our self-image conveys that we are more than we see in ourselves.

We are, therefore, the interrelationship between the mysterious person of private depth, the imaged person of one's own perception, and the interactive person in contact with reality other than one's self-image. Sin, however, distorts harmonious relatedness between the three persons, so that who we perceive ourselves to be is not in harmony with the mysteriousness of our inner being nor with who we actually are in relation to other reality. A dissonance exists within the human being between the depths of the soul, the soul's self-understanding, and the soul interacting with other reality.

Salvation, however, brings about the healing of the soul in that we receive the gift of a new identity, a new self-image, a new self-understanding. We come to know ourselves as being beloved children of God, created in God's image and members of "a chosen race, a royal priesthood, a holy nation, God's own people" who are challenged with the divine responsibility of proclaiming "the mighty acts of him who called ... [us] out of darkness into his marvelous light" (1 Peter 2:9).

Not only do we receive a new perception of the self; we also receive forgiveness of that within us which is far too complicated for us to understand. Paul, speaking of the mysterious turmoil within, said, "I do not understand my own actions. For I do not do what I want, but do the very thing I hate" (Rom. 7:15). And again, "For I do not do the good I want, but the evil I do not want is what I do" (v. 19). He ends by crying out "Wretched man that I am! Who will rescue me from this body of death? Thanks be to God through Jesus Christ our Lord," following which, he proclaims the gospel: "There is therefore now no condemnation for those who are in Christ Jesus" (8:1).

First John, dealing with the ongoing mysteriousness of the inner self which continues to confound even Christians, says: "My little children, I am writing these things to you so that you may not sin. But if anyone does sin, we have an advocate with the Father, Jesus Christ the righteous" (2:1).

Not only, however, do we have the benefit of this mediatorial work of Jesus Christ for as long as we live, but also the benefit of the intercessory work of the Holy Spirit who "helps us in our weakness; for we do not know how to pray as we ought, but that very Spirit intercedes with sighs too deep for words" (Rom. 8:26). Paul goes on to explain in verse 27 that "God, who searches the heart, knows what is the mind of the Spirit, because the Spirit intercedes for the saints according to the will of God."

We experience blessed relationships within ourselves when, knowing ourselves forgiven and perfectly understood by God, we function on the basis of being the beloved children of God, endowed by and guided by the Spirit to minister in the name of Christ to others.

Family Relationships

Jesus taught a new concept of family when his mother and brothers came asking to see him. Pointing to his disciples, he said, "Here are my mother and my brothers! For whoever does the will of my Father in heaven is my brother and sister and mother" (Matt. 12:49–50; parallel Mark 3:34–35).

The Bible assumes that every person needs relationships of spiritual intimacy, and Jesus' teaching is that the place to find such intimacy is among those whose primary desire is to live according to the will of God. He redefines the essence of family as being a social unit of spiritual intimacy existing among those whose greatest desire is to do the will of God.

This social unit may, of course, be a physical unit of marriage and natural relationships, but such natural relationships are no guarantee that those in them will live in obedience to the will of God. On the other hand, those who are disassociated from natural family life may, nevertheless, have the blessing of the familial relationships spoken of by Jesus.

The ideal family unit as defined by Jesus is a spiritual unit of those on mission for God. This, then, also applies to the natural family: the ideal natural family is one in which each sees the other not merely as natural mother, daughter, father, son, brother, sister, husband, wife, but primarily as servant of God and then secondarily as a natural relative. The ideal natural family is one in which each is both encouraged to discover his or her vocation under God and helped to fulfill it; it is one in which the vocation of the whole family unit is that of fulfilling the will of God. For instance, in the case of Priscilla and Aquila who took Apollos aside and "explained the Way of God to him more accurately" (Acts 18:26), they were working as a unit to fulfill their vocation as a married couple.[2]

The ideal natural family is an *ecclesiola in ecclesia*, a little church within the church; one thinks of the *ecclesiola in ecclesia* established in Lydia's house in Philippi (Acts 16:14–15, 40), and the one established at the midnight hour in the Philippian jail (27–34).

In the Christian view, both marriage and singleness are gifts of God (see 1 Cor. 7:7). Our Lord was committed to the single life, as was Paul, but there is no indication that those who did not have the gift of the single life were either spiritually superior or inferior based on the mere fact of their singleness.

As far as marriage is concerned, the New Testament teaches that it is a covenant intended to remain in effect until either the covenant is irreparably broken by unchastity or until the separation which death brings. Regarding unchastity, the Greek word used in Matt.

5:32 is *porneia*, which can also be translated as fornication or marital unfaithfulness. It reads: "But I say to you that anyone who divorces his wife, except on the ground of unchastity, causes her to commit adultery; and whoever marries a divorced woman commits adultery" (also in 19:9). The parallel passage in Mark 10:11 differs in that it 1) does not include the exceptive clause, and 2) addresses the issue of the wife divorcing the husband: "Whoever divorces his wife and marries another commits adultery against her; and if she divorces her husband and marries another, she commits adultery." (For Paul's instructions about sexual abstinence within marriage, remarriage, divorce, and the special issue of the relation between believing and non-believing spouses, see 1 Cor. 7:1-16, 25-40.) Regarding death, Paul in 1 Corinthians 7:39 writes: "A wife is bound as long as her husband lives. But if the husband dies, she is free to marry anyone she wishes, only in the Lord" (also, see his analogical references in Rom. 7:1-3).

The Christian single who decides that marriage is his or her gift is under obligation to marry another Christian and not to be "mismatched with unbelievers" (2 Cor. 6:14) in an arrangement which, by its very nature, cannot be a covenant in Christ (see 1 Cor. 7:39). However, if one spouse becomes a Christian after marriage, he or she is not to take that as license for divorcing the unbeliever, but to see it as an opportunity for evangelism (see 7:12–16; also 1 Peter 3:1–7).

The Christian household has a special vocation, namely, that of serving as a living symbol of the sacrificial love of God revealed in Christ (see Eph. 5:21 — 6:9; also Col. 3:18 — 4:1; Titus 2:1-15; 1 Peter 2:18 — 3:7). When passages such as the immediately foregoing are used legalistically, their meanings are distorted. The purpose of these instructions is not to encumber households with rigid rules as though mere obedience in and of itself satisfies God; rather, their purpose is to encourage whole Christian households to live together in loving relationships in such a way that they give witness to the world about what God has done in Christ.[3] The Christian family is called to be a circle of Christ's peace, a fellowship of Christly reconciliation, a hostel of divine hospitality, a haven of Kingdom-oriented healing, a sanctuary for holy empowerment, a center for learning how families as a whole as well as the individual members can best fulfill their respective vocations under God.

Addressing the church, Paul says in 1 Corinthians 3:16-17, "Do you [plural here and throughout] not know that you are God's temple and that God's Spirit dwells in you? If anyone destroys God's temple, God will destroy that person. For God's temple is holy, and you are that temple." Not only, we assume, is the congregation of believers the dwelling place of the Holy Spirit, but also the Christian family as an *ecclesiola in ecclesia*.

The Christian family is a sacrosanct unit within the economy of God. As a little church within the church, it is the place where the faith is lived out, tested, proved, experienced in the most intimate of ways, learned, and passed on. When not all members are believers, it still is sanctified by the presence of even one believer in the family unit (see 1 Cor. 7:14). This sanctification means that the family unit is a special arena of grace. It is made holy by virtue of the fact that at least one believer is a member of it—one who both prays for others within the family circle and lives as an example of the grace of God, to the end that God will bring the whole household to faith. The Christian family, whether a spiritual unit with no natural family ties or a natural unit spiritually sensitized, is the most basic social unit of Christian relatedness. It provides the most crucial quality-testing there is of the restored relationships which we have in Christ. (See For Further Consideration for a selected bibliography.)

Relationships with People in General

By God's grace we are gifted for service in the church and for mission in the world (see 1 Cor. 12). Our relationships, whether for service or for mission, are blessed of God to the extent that they are loving. For those within the circle of faith, it is an edifying love which does all it can to build them up in Christ (e.g., John 13:34–35, 15:12,17; Rom. 12:10; Eph. 4:15–16; Col. 1:4; 1 Thess. 3:12; Heb. 10:24; 1 Peter 1:22, 2:17; 1 John 3:18, 4:7–21; 2 John 5). For those outside the circle of faith, it is a compassionate love desiring their salvation (e.g. Matt. 5:43–48, 28:19–20). For all people, regardless of whether they are inside or outside the circle of faith, it is a caring love which responds in Christ-like fashion to human need (see Matt. 19:19, 22:39; Luke 10:30–37).

The church, in fact, is to be known by its love. John 13:35 says, "By this everyone will know that you are my disciples, if you have love for one another," and 1 John 4:16b affirms that "God is love, and those who abide in love abide in God, and God abides in them."

The kind of love spoken of throughout the New Testament is defined by the life and death of Jesus Christ. As Paul says, "Let the same mind be in you that was in Christ Jesus" (Phil. 2:5).

Since the love relationship we have with others is not to be legalistically regulated, it requires constant review and readjustment. Its goal, however, is never in doubt; it is that we relate to others as God in Christ relates to us. First John 4:19 says that "we love because he first loved us."

The Christian Way of Relating
to the Whole Created Order

Not only do Christians have a special calling to relate to other persons in conformity to Christ's love for us, but also they are challenged to develop a Christ-centered way of relating to the whole created order. Colossians 1:16–20 teaches that in Christ "all things in heaven and on earth were created, things visible and invisible, whether thrones or dominions or rulers or powers–all things have been created through him and for him." Furthermore, Christ is the sustainer of the whole created order: "In him all things hold together" (v. 17). In addition, he is the reconciler; as v. 20 says, "through him God was pleased to reconcile to himself all things, whether on earth or in heaven, by making peace through the blood of his cross." According to Raymond Van Leeuwen:

> This passage stands against every sinful Christian attempt to divide reality into secular and sacred realms. All of reality is Christ's good creation, all of reality is redeemed by him; therefore, all of reality is the responsibility of God's people. Since the church is now Christ's body, his visible presence in this world, it is the church's job to continue the reconciling, cosmic work of Christ until he comes again.[4]

Christ is at the center of God's creative work. He is

the goal of all creation, and its cohesive substratum. He is the agent of reconciliation between the created order and God. According to Colossians, the one who created human beings, created every thing else as well. The one whom Christians worship is the same one to whom the whole created order brings glory and praise. The one who sustains the life of human beings is the same one who sustains the whole of creation. The one who reconciles does so for the benefit not only of human beings but for the benefit of the whole created order.

Whenever we misuse the created order, we sin against the Christ who saves us, for he is the same Christ who pervades the whole of creation in sustaining grace. Salvation has to do not merely with the human family; it has to do with the whole of creation. The Lord of human hearts is the Lord of history and of creation as well.

We see this intimate interrelatedness between the human order and the whole order of creation both in Genesis 3 where human sin and divine condemnation affect both orders, and in Romans 8:18-25 which assumes that there is an interrelatedness between the salvation of the human family and the salvation of creation as a whole. Verse 19 says that "the creation waits with eager longing for the revealing of the children of God," and verse 21 that "the creation itself will be set free from its bondage to decay and will obtain the freedom of the glory of the children of God." (See a fuller discussion of this interrelatedness in chapter 5 on "Christ Jesus, the Kingdom, and Eschatology" and in chapter 15 on "God's Will in the Face of Evil and Suffering.")

Christians give witness to Christ by living in harmony with the created order, taking care of it, enjoying its goodness, and using it for Christly purposes.[5] As a contemporary evangelical theologian, Millard Erickson, has observed: "Since the major emphasis of evangelical Christianity is transforming persons, God's regenerating and sanctifying grace becomes a major resource for us to accomplish the ethics of ecology."[6]

The Stewardship Relationship

Christ's disciples are to be good stewards of the world, for, as pointed out above, it is created, sustained, and redeemed by the same Christ who creates, sustains, and redeems us. We are to be good stewards of our resources and possessions, for all that we have comes from the hand of God. We are to be good stewards of our bodies, for they are temples of the Holy Spirit.

The Greek word translated as steward is *oikonomos*, the manager of a household or estate. The word is used in Luke 12:42 where Jesus teaches his disciples that they have responsibility to manage well that which they have been given as his followers. The lesson to be learned is set forth in v. 48: "From everyone to whom much has been given, much will be required; and from the one to whom much has been entrusted, even more will be demanded." Christ's disciples, as stewards of the superabundant grace of God revealed in Christ, have a great responsibility because they have been given so much from the hand of God.[7]

The word is used again in 16:1–13 in the parable about the steward who upon being told that he is going to be dismissed because he has squandered his property proves himself to be a shrewd manager. He calls in his master's debtors and reduces their debt–perhaps the amount of interest which they owe, an amount the manager himself would have received.[8] If that is, in fact, what he did, he would thereby have shown obedience to the Old Testament strictures against charging interest on loans. It may be that the reason he is referred to as a "dishonest" steward who is nevertheless to be commended is because he made amends by eliminating the exorbitant interest which had gained him the censure of being dishonest.

In what is admittedly a difficult passage to interpret, the main points seem clear enough: disciples are to act responsibly with the "true riches" they have in Christ (see v. 11), and they are to focus on spiritual resources which are given to them by divine grace with as much creativity as the steward in the parable dealt with monetary issues. They are reminded that the riches of Christ, which come to us as the gift of God, are of ultimate importance over and above any monetary resources we accumulate for ourselves, i.e., we "cannot serve God and wealth."

The word is used again in 1 Corinthians 4:1–2 where Paul refers to the ministry of the apostles as being that of "stewards of God's mysteries," following which he says that "it is required of stewards that they be found trustworthy." Also, Titus 1:7 refers to a bishop as being "God's steward."

First Peter 4:1–11 is the most comprehensive passage regarding Christian stewardship. It speaks of all Christians as being stewards of God's grace. Verse 10 says: "Like good stewards of the manifold grace of God, serve one another with whatever gift each of you has received."

The manifold grace of God includes all the ways God blesses us whether in creation, sustenance, or redemption. Whatever we have is placed in our care for the purpose of extending blessing beyond ourselves. God's grace is for the benefit of the whole of creation (e.g., John 3:17 and Rom. 8:19, 21–22). Therefore, whatever blessings we have are not simply for our own personal enjoyment but for wider benefit. The "owner" of the blessings is God; we are to be good stewards of that which belongs to God. The way we function as good stewards is by serving "one another with whatever gift each ... has received." This includes our natural endowments, that which we have inherited from others, and that which we have as a result of the investment of our God-given resources of time, energy, ingenuity, opportunity, talents, and expertise.

The Christian question is always this: How can we extend beyond ourselves and our own self interest, the benefits of that which we have from the hand of God? Christian stewardship has been defined as "the receiving and sharing of God's bounteous gifts, managing them for the best promotion of God's purposes in the world."9

Second Corinthians 8 and 9 is the *locus classicus* about the Christian stewardship of resources. Paul calls attention to the way of Christ when in 8:9 he says: "For you know the grace of our Lord Jesus Christ, that though he was rich, yet for your sakes he became poor, so that you through his poverty might become rich."10 The principle derived from Christ's self-giving is spelled out in 9:8: "And God is able to provide you with every blessing in abundance, so that by always having enough of everything, you may share abundantly in every good work."

Christian stewardship has to do not only with what we have, but also with who we are under God. We are created in the image of God (Gen. 1:27) with bodies to be used as temples of the Holy Spirit (1 Cor. 6:15, 19). As such, we are not our own. Paul says, "You were bought with a price, therefore glorify God in your body" (v. 20).

The way we use our bodies is basic to Christian stewardship. We are to use them for the purpose of living in holiness before the Lord. The seriousness with which the holy life is emphasized throughout the New Testament is evident from the fact that every book has something to say about it.[11] Romans 12:1 summarizes the point well: "I appeal to you therefore, brothers and sisters, by the mercies of God, to present your bodies as a living sacrifice, holy and acceptable to God, which is your spiritual worship."

Liberating Relationships Leading to Divine Jubilee

At the beginning of Jesus' public ministry he gave an inaugural message based on Isaiah, at the synagogue in Nazareth. According to Luke 4:18–19, he read:

> The Spirit of the Lord is upon me, because he has anointed me to bring good news to the poor. He has sent me to proclaim release to the captives and recovery of sight to the blind, to let the oppressed go free, to proclaim the year of the Lord's favor.

This passage is relatively close to our Isaiah 61:1–2 and 58:6. In the latter chapter, the people of Israel are being condemned for their rigorous food fasts which are little more than religious rituals devoid of ethical implications. Verse 3: "'Why do we fast [the people ask God], but you [God] do not see? Why humble ourselves, but you do not notice?' [They are answered with the words:] Look, you serve your own interest on your fast day, and oppress all your workers." In v. 6, the kind of fast which does please God is described: "Is not this the fast that I choose: to loose the bonds of injustice, to undo the thongs of the yoke, to let the oppressed go free, and to break every yoke." When that kind of social responsibility obtains, then, as v. 9 says, "You shall call, and the LORD will answer; you shall cry for help, and he will say, Here I am."

Isaiah 61 announces a future glorious jubilee of both national release from the encumbrances of the past and restoration to wholeness of life. According to Leviticus 25, every fiftieth year was to be a jubilee during which the land was to rest, ancestral possessions were to be returned to those who had been forced to sell them due to poverty, and liberty was to be proclaimed to all Israelites held in bondage by their fellow citizens.

The purpose of Jesus' message in Luke 4 is to declare that he is the fulfillment of Isaiah's promise of a divine jubilee. Jesus is the bringer of justice. His is the religion of helping and healing. His is the spirit and power of liberation from the bondage of Satan, fear, sickness, sin, and self. Jesus ushers in that glorious time of jubilee when the poor hear good news, the brokenhearted are healed, captives of evil hear the message of freedom, and prisoners of destruction hear the message of release.

When he left Nazareth Jesus proceeded to put into practice what he had declared there. In the synagogue in Capernaum he set a man free from a demon (4:31–36). Later he set another free in "the country of the Gerasenes" (8:26–39), and later still, he set a boy free (9:37–43).

In Capernaum, he also healed the sick. Upon leaving the synagogue, he went to Simon Peter's house where he found Simon's mother-in-law suffering from a high fever, from which Jesus set her free (4:38–39). Additional healings include the leper (5:12–16), a paralytic (17–26), a man with a withered hand (6:6–11), as well as other people from many parts of the country (17–19). He healed the centurion's servant (7:1–10), the woman suffering from hemorrhages (8:43–48), a crippled woman (13:10–17), a man with dropsy (14:1–6), ten lepers (17:11–19) and a blind beggar near Jericho (18:35–43). Linked with healings were compassionate deeds of raising the dead: the widow's son at Nain

(7:11–17), and Jairus' only daughter (8:40–42, 49–56).

Luke tells about not only liberations from demons, death, sorrow, destitution, illness, and handicaps but also about other sorts of liberations — the liberation from sin (7:36–50), from fear as when he calmed the sea by rebuking the winds and the raging water (8:22–25), from hunger as when he miraculously fed five thousand (9:10–17), from undue responsibilities as when he offered Martha the freedom to enjoy his friendship (10:38–42), from oppression as when he set Zacchaeus free from having his life ruled by the profit motive (19:1–10), and from injustice as when he cleansed the temple so that the Gentiles would have a place to pray (19:45–46). In the Christian view, liberation has to do with release from oppressive powers so that we can fulfill God's will. The Lord does not liberate so that we can pursue selfish assertiveness but so that we can experience divine fulfillment and the expansion of life in service to God. Earl Martin, my earliest teacher in theology, said it well:

> The Christian way is an enlargement of life. It is not suppression of life, limitation of life, restriction of life, or repression of life. It is expansion, release, liberation, enlistment, unfolding, completion; all of life's powers having been redeemed are released and energized, then engaged in living and serving.[12]

Jesus' liberating ministry was passed on to his disciples who, as Luke 9:6 says, "went through the villages, bringing the good news and curing diseases everywhere." Later the seventy whom he sent out in pairs to declare the gospel of the kingdom (10:1–12), "returned with joy, saying, 'Lord, in your name even the demons submit to us!' He said to them, 'I watched Satan fall from heaven like a flash of lightning.'" The Levitical jubilee had arrived; liberation from the bondage of Satan had been secured. The people of God could now go forth in that liberating power to minister to the nations. To his disciples after the resurrection, Jesus promised that they would receive power "when the Holy Spirit has come upon you and you will be my witnesses in Jerusalem, in all Judea and Samaria, and to the ends of the earth" (Acts 1:8). The Book of Acts tells about the ongoing ministry which the church had in that liberating power.

God intends for Christians to have a liberating relationship to all who are held in bondage to forces which keep them from being all that God wants them to be. We are sent forth as emissaries of Christ's liberating gospel "in Jerusalem, in all Judea and Samaria, and to the ends of the earth."

Notes

1. Winifred Gérin, *Branwell Brontë: A Biography* (London: Hutchinson, 1972), p. 282.

2. For a discussion on marital vocation, see William Johnson Everett, *Blessed Be the Bond* (Philadelphia: Fortress, 1985), pp. 111-127.

3. For a study of Paul's marriage rules, see O. Larry Yarbrough, *Not Like the Gentiles: Marriage Rules in the Letters of Paul* (Atlanta: Scholars, 1985).

4. Raymond C. Van Leeuwen, "Christ's Resurrection and the Creation's Vindication," *The Environment and the Christian,* ed. Calvin B. DeWitt (Grand Rapids: Baker, 1991), p. 62.

5. For a theology of creation, see Jürgen Moltmann, *God in Creation: A New Theology of Creation and the Spirit of God,* trans. Margaret Kohl (San Francisco: Harper and Row, 1985).

6. Millard J. Erickson, "Biblical Ethics of Ecology," *The Earth Is the Lord's: Christians and the Environment,* ed. Richard D. Land and Louis A. Moore (Nashville: Broadman, 1992), p. 89.

7. For a collection of essays by contemporary authors on this subject, see Mary Evelyn Jegen and Bruno Manno (eds.), *The Earth Is the Lord's: Essays on Stewardship* (New York: Paulist, 1978).

8. The argument for this interpretation is set forth by

G. B. Caird, *St. Luke* in the *Pelican Gospel Commentaries* (Harmondsworth, 1963), pp. 186f.

9. Milo Kauffman, *Stewards of God* (Scottdale: Herald, 1975), p. 21.

10. The *New International Version* is preferable in that it translates *charis* as grace and not merely as a "generous act" as does the *New Revised Standard Version*.

1.1 See Matt. 15:19–20; Mark 9:43–48; Luke 1:31,35,38; 11:27–28; John 15:1–2; Acts 5:1–11; Rom. 6:12, 13, 15; 1 Cor. 5 – 8, 10:23 – 11:1; 2 Cor. 6:14 – 7:1; 13:5; Gal. 5:16–26; Eph. 4:17 – 5:20; Phil. 2:5; Col. 3:5–17; 1 Thess. 4:1–8; 2 Thess. 3:6–13; 1 Tim. 4:1–5; 2 Tim. 2:21; Titus 2:11–14; Philem. 18; Heb. 12:1; James 1:19–27; 2:14–17; 3:1–12; 4:1–10; 1 Peter 1:13–16; 2:1; 4:1–5; 2 Peter 3:11, 14; 1 John 3:4–10; 2 John 6; 3 John 11; Jude 14–15; Rev. 21:27; 22:3, 11, 14–15.

12. Earl Martin, *This We Believe – This We Proclaim* (Anderson, Ind: Gospel Trumpet Company, 1952), p. 74.

For Further Consideration

Introductory Reading on "Christian Marriage"

For a contemporary study of divorce and remarriage see Kenneth Jones, *Divorce and Remarriage in the Bible* (Anderson, Ind: Warner, 1972).

On the history of Christian marriage, see David Mace and Vera Mace, *The Sacred Fire: Christian Marriage through the Ages* (Nashville: Abingdon, 1986).

For theologies of marriage, see Elizabeth Achtemeier, *The Committed Marriage* (Philadelphia: Westminster, 1976); James Tunstead Burtchaell, *For Better, For Worse: Sober Thoughts on Passionate Promises* (New York: Paulist, 1985); and Denise Lardner Carmody and John Tully Carmody, *Becoming One Flesh: Growth in Christian Marriage* (Nashville: Upper Room, 1984).

Subject Index

Scripture Index